D1109793

University of Birmingham
URBAN AND REGIONAL STUDIES NO 3

The Urban Future

University of Birmingham
URBAN AND REGIONAL STUDIES

The Urban Future
A Choice Between Alternatives

JOHN N. JACKSON

B.A., Ph.D., M.R.T.P.I.
Professor of Applied Geography, Brock University, Ontario

LONDON · GEORGE ALLEN & UNWIN LTD

ISBN 0 04 352034 0

Printed in Great Britain
in 10 point Times Roman type
by Alden & Mowbray Ltd
at the Alden Press, Oxford

There are many strange wonders, but nothing
More wonderful than man
....
Speech too, and wind-swift thought,
He has taught himself
And the spirit that governs cities.

Sophocles, from C. M. Bowra, *The Greek Experience*,
Weidenfeld and Nicolson (London), 1957, pp. 198–9.

Preface

This book is written for the student of urban affairs – for the university student who will debate the issues which are posed, for the individual and community groups who wish to be involved in the future of their urban environments, for the professional person who seeks to guide policy, and for the decision-maker who must decide between the respective merits of alternative feasible and practical strategies for urban growth. It is dedicated with humility, and an awareness of the greatness of the issues, to the survival of man in cities.

The content is concerned with some aspects of those very considerable changes which have taken place in the British planning process since the mid-1960s. The subject has matured to become altogether more sophisticated, scientific and complex than previously. It has changed from a primary concern with the preparation of precise development plans, to a concept of planning as a continuous process. The attitude of mind has become more comprehensive, in that transportation and land use have slowly been regarded as separate yet interwoven elements of the total urban process. Techniques have become more methodical and rigorous, the chain of reasoning more logical, and the computer has assisted with the development of urban models and other mathematical techniques as a contribution towards understanding the intricacies of the present urban situation. The delicate art of projecting from existing conditions has thus been refined, so that different possible solutions can now be tested for their relevance in meeting objectives against analytical criteria.

Long-term policy planning for the urban future has become less descriptive and more analytical. At the same time, it has appreciated the fact that citizen participation should play a vital role if strategies and plans are to be translated into action. It seeks to understand the urban system as a totality, and as a series of independent yet related parts. It is more often concerned with the processes of urban growth in the region and the sub-region, rather than with developments in the narrow confines of arbitrary local government boundaries. Ideas have been introduced from American and Western European experience and, at the international level, there has been a considerable discussion of techniques, the nature of scientific explanation, the role of value judgements, decision theory and the contribution of objectives to methodological studies. The traditional legal–architectural–engineering basis of the planning profession has been broadened, to include both an increasing proportion of social scientists and university trained personnel with undergraduate and postgraduate qualifications. Academic planners have moved into practice, and practical planners into higher education to blur the niceties of distinction between 'academic' and 'practical'.

The essential image of these important and significant changes is that the new style strategic planning reports now often present advice and interpretation on a series of viable alternative policies to the policy-maker. This in itself provides a commendable advance in techniques, in that planning can no longer be concerned with some mysterious sleight of hand manipulation of the urban environment. It must be open in its arguments, as the reasons for decisions are brought out for public discussion and professional scrutiny. As the creation and then the evaluation of alternative possibilities have become the central themes of this new planning methodology, the four essential and related questions about any planning strategy are: What issues are considered? What alternatives are envisaged? How are these alternatives chosen? How is the preferred solution selected from this range of competing alternatives?

The text will focus in particular on the alternative strategies for urban growth which have been developed in England at the sub-regional and regional levels of appreciation. It will examine the assumptions and beliefs which underlie the formulation of alternative strategies, the methods used in the evaluation procedures in order to obtain the 'best' strategy, and whether there are any other approaches, attitudes or conclusions which should have been considered. How planners think when deciding upon the form and location of *our* future urban and regional environments is, in essence, the theme of this book.

The principal Studies for examination are:

Coventry–Solihull–Warwickshire Sub-Regional Planning Study, 1971 (Warwickshire Study)
Humberside Feasibility Study, 1969 (Humberside Study)
North-Gloucestershire Sub-Regional Study, 1970 (North-Glos Study)
Nottinghamshire and Derbyshire Sub-Regional Study, 1969 (Notts–Derby Study)
Leicester and Leicestershire Sub-Regional Planning Study, 1969 (Leicestershire Study)

Teesside Survey and Plan, 1969 (Teesside Study)
South Hampshire Study, 1966 (Hampshire Study)
Strategic Plan for the South East, 1970 (South East Study).

Reference is also made to the Yorkshire Economic Planning
Council (Yorkshire EPC Studies) for Halifax, Doncaster and
Huddersfield in 1969–1970 and the Deeside Study, 1970. Certain
aspects of the West Midlands Study and the South Hampshire Plan
are also included, but these strategic policies had not been published
by mid-1971. Limited comparisons are also made with comparable
planning studies from abroad, especially the United States and
Canada with their greater awareness about the impact of the auto-
mobile on urban affairs.

Part 1 of the text is concerned with introducing the Studies in
Chapter 1, a background appreciation of urbanization and of
government intervention in the affairs of the environment in Chapter
2, and the terms of reference and administrative background of the
Studies in Chapter 3.

Part 2 dissects the content of the Studies and notes their salient
features item by item. Chapters 4 and 5 are concerned with the two
sets of basic investigations which underlie the planning approach in
all Studies, including the appraisal of the physical backcloth to
urban development and the assessment of the constraints and the
opportunities which exist in Chapter 4, and the projection and
anticipation of future population, employment, housing and other
socio-economic trends in Chapter 5. Chapter 6 compares the Studies
in their approach to urban form and spatial structure, and discusses
the range of feasible possibilities. It thus introduces Chapters 7 and
8, which are concerned with elements within this structure – industry,
housing, recreation, shopping centres, administrative boundaries,
the transportation network, movement and accessibility.

Part 3 is concerned more with the methodological approach. The
techniques of cost appraisal, the concept of the planning balance
sheet and the contribution of cost–benefit analysis are noted in
Chapter 9, the attitudes of the Studies to the formulation and interpretation of goals and objectives are considered in Chapter 10, and
the role of citizen involvement in the Studies is discussed in Chapter
11. Finally, Chapter 12 attempts an overview of the procedures for
generating and testing alternative strategies, notes two other statements about the nature of the urban future and indicates some areas
for future research.

The text therefore examines specific aspects of policy planning in

England for the urban future. It is concerned with those actions taken by government to influence the physical distribution of urban land uses and, specifically, with the way in which long-term planning strategies are formulated. It considers the factors that are taken into account and the assumptions that are made in order to reach the planning conclusion that a town should be expanded, that industry should be encouraged to locate in a selected locality, or that a shopping centre should be established or improved. It notes the alternative practical possibilities that are considered, and why the choice is made in favour of the preferred strategy. It quotes extensively from published material so that the arguments are phrased, as far as possible, in the terminology used by the planning team. Footnotes indicate further reading on selected subjects.

The content is concerned with urban land use planning. It also touches on many contributory themes in the social sciences including economic theory, locational behaviour, group dynamics, the incidence of migration, central place hierarchies, the conflicts and compromises of the socio-political framework, social values, and the spatial patterns of urban land use. Incorporation of the spatial dimensions involves an appreciation of the attributes, constraints and potential of the physical landscape, in so far as these elements can be modified by the technical competence of man. The temporal aspect of a dynamic urban environment weaves its relentless path through these social, economic and physical elements of man's urban situation, which is not and never has been static. The essential planning contribution is recognition of this changing situation, and a search to influence the direction, form, quality and location of new developments in conditions of uncertainty.

The subject is, and must be, inter-disciplinary. It involves several different professions, and is vast both in its range and its complexity. The Reports have each been written by highly competent inter-professional teams, and comments are made with respect for the knowledge and ability of the persons involved. The purpose, however, is to contribute towards an improvement of the situation as it now exists with constructive comment. The task is difficult, not only because of its size and complexity, but also because quite different views are possible about the significance of different factors and the relative importance of different concepts in the urban milieu. The whole subject also requires the sympathy and understanding of society. This means not just the support of the public but their true involvement because, the more soundly based the ideas which are propounded and developed, the more readily will they be accepted and receive support for action. The challenge of the future is tremendous and full of controversy, but it is of concern to everyone.

The author's contribution is that of an external witness to the British planning scene. His background is that he was born and educated in Britain; he practised planning first with a county planning authority and then with a county borough, before lecturing on the subject at an English University. More recently, he has spent the period from 1965 to 1970 establishing the Department of Geography in a new Ontario University, and has been introduced to the different urban approaches and regional attitudes of North America during this period. The opportunity of a year's sabbatical leave in a university research environment, with some time to travel and to talk with colleagues, permits the judgement of an external viewer – reliable in parts and biased elsewhere by this experience and background.

The author's own work on the themes under review began in the library of the Centre for Urban and Regional Studies at the University of Birmingham, where the Studies were examined and evaluated on the basis of the available published evidence. The next stage, when possible, was to discuss these findings and preliminary conclusions with a senior member of the team responsible for the preparation of each Study, with planning personnel engaged in comparable studies elsewhere and with academic colleagues. The first draft of the manuscript was then sent to the team leader of all the Studies for his comments, and many further useful points are included in the text as a result of this response.

It is relatively easy for an academic to comment upon a Study *after* its preparation and then, away from all the inevitable inter-office discussions and the pressures of day-to-day work which underlie every technical report, to comment on what should have been done. It should, therefore, be emphasized that all the study teams were breaking new ground. They were pioneering new attitudes to complex urban and environmental issues in their interdisciplinary approach, and were working in the difficult political terrain of a comprehensive study at the regional level of thought. The Study teams lacked the guiding framework of a national physical or societal plan, yet were required to prepare a regional strategy to cover the next thirty or so years of urban change and urban opportunity on the basis of certain national and regional assumptions. In such circumstances, all the Studies have much commendable content, and the author's first debt of gratitude is to the authors of these Studies. All were most helpful.

Acknowledgements are easy to record, but difficult to express in terms of real sincerity. The author is grateful to the President of Brock University, Dr James A. Gibson, for the privilege of a sabbatical leave, and to the Canada Council for its generous award of a Leave Fellowship.

In England very genuine thanks are due to Professor J. Barry Cullingworth, Director of the Centre for Urban and Regional Studies at the University of Birmingham, both for his initial encouragement and sponsorship of the author's work programme, and for a substantial number of comments on the early drafts from his own breadth of practical experience. Gordon E. Cherry, Deputy Director of the Centre, has likewise advised, assisted, and commented at length on the early manuscripts; he has provided encouragement at all stages of the work. Also, at the Centre, special thanks go to Tom L. C. Duncan and Brian Goodey who have provided advice on those sections of the manuscript which are within their own fields of special competence. The librarian, Anita Bough, and the author's secretary, Mary Grant, have provided the very best of assistance in their respective fields. Much of the typing has also been undertaken by Katherine Foster.

As for the Studies under review, many acknowledgements are made to source material in the text. In addition, the author would like to express his appreciation of discussions with the following, their welcome advice and kind assistance in interviews or by correspondence:

John F. Barrow, Manager of the South Hampshire Plan Advisory Committee

Julian C. Gyngell, Study Leader of the North-Gloucestershire Study and Member of the Gloucestershire County Planning Department

Nathaniel Lichfield of Nathaniel Lichfield and Associates

J. Brian McLoughlin, Director of the Leicester and Leicestershire Sub-Regional Planning Study

George E. Morran, Senior Planning Officer, West Midlands Transportation Study Group

Geoffrey C. Steeley, Assistant Director of the Notts–Derby Sub-Regional Planning Unit

John Stevenson, Director of the West Midlands Planning Study Group

Andrew Thorburn, Director of the Notts–Derby Sub-Regional Planning Unit

James W. Vernon, Chairman of the Humberside Feasibility Study
Urlon A. Wannop, Team Leader of the Coventry–Solihull–
  Warwickshire Sub-Regional Planning Study
Sir Hugh Wilson of Hugh Wilson and Lewis Womersley about the
  Teesside Study

And several other colleagues, who have been equally helpful, but
who would prefer to remain anonymous. But to them also, sincere
thanks.

At the stage of publication, the author greatly appreciates the
helpful advice and the points of editorial correction made by Charles
Furth.

It is for emphasis that the detail and interpretation in this review
represent the author's own assessment of the Studies, and cannot be
related back to any of the persons referred to above. They have assisted materially, but the content remains fully the author's responsibility.

May 1971

Contents

Tables

Tables

Part 1

INTRODUCTION

'The future is a field of uncertainty. What will be cannot be attested to and verified in the same way as an accomplished fact.'

B. de Jouvenel, *The Art of Conjecture*, 1967

Chapter 1
The Studies Under Review

This book is concerned with one aspect of current British planning practice. It reviews the selection and testing procedures of alternative strategies for the growth of cities and their regional environments, using recent case studies as a basis for comparative comment and interpretation. As Reade (1968) has commented, 'one is repeatedly surprised by the absence of any attempt in British planning to evaluate the results or assess the validity of policy. . . . When ultimately they are modified, this is often not because evidence has accumulated as to the probable consequences of either the original or the modified policy, but because new ideas have in the meantime become fashionable in influential circles. . . . It is undoubtedly the ideology of planning, far more than techniques of design and administration, which needs to be considered and developed.'[1] Or, in the words of an American commentary, 'while this decade has been described as the golden age of decision-making studies, there have been very few studies identifying the changing structures, the planning issues, the alternatives examined, the impact measures, and the evaluative methods. . . . Improved studies for systematically capturing the decision-making processes of planning are required.'[2] Steele (1970) has stated, 'there is scope for the definition of useful techniques and approaches which becomes more urgent as the number of sub-regional studies undertaken increases'.[3]

The present text seeks to redress this unfortunate lack of introspection. Its special importance is that, with the pending reorganization of local government into larger administrative units and as many urban issues overspill existing political boundaries, it seems likely that regional and sub-regional Studies will become much more frequent in the future. Also the Town and Country Planning Act 1968 makes dramatic changes to the form of development plans. Structure plans are now required, and these will be concerned with

[1] E. Reade, 'Some notes towards a sociology of planning', *Journal of the Town Planning Institute*, Vol. 54, 1968, p. 217.
[2] W. A. Steger and T. R. Lakshmanan, 'Plan Evaluation Methodologies: Some Aspects of Decision Requirements and Analytical Response' in Highway Research Board, *Urban Development Models* (Washington), 1968, p. 67.
[3] D. B. Steele in 'Book Reviews', *Urban Studies*, Vol. 7, 1970, p. 98.

broad policy considerations and general proposals, rather than with the allocation of land under major use categories as under the Town and Country Planning Act 1947. The Studies under review in this book thus provide a sort of precedent to the type of planning study which may be expected during the 1970s, and epitomize the more advanced techniques of investigation which have been developed during the 1960s for the formulation of urban strategies. Further, as Cooper (1970) notes, 'the interesting thing about regional planning is that the plans are still what we choose to make them. They do not have to conform to any statutory definition or regulations. This is in contrast to other levels of planning, notably the old development plans and the new structure plans, where the form and content are specified in some detail, even down to the colouring of maps.'[1] In these several circumstances, the Studies to be reviewed should repay careful scrutiny for their ideas and methods of approach to intricate urban and regional problems. The lessons to be learned can surely be applied with considerable future advantage.

THE STUDIES

The planning studies selected for examination are:

Teesside Survey and Plan.[2] A Report by two firms of Consultants, Hugh Wilson and Lewis Womersley and Scott Wilson Kirkpatrick and Partners to a Steering Committee of representatives from local authorities, public transport undertakings, the Ministry of Housing and Local Government and the Ministry of Transport. The Consultants were appointed in 1965, and the Report was published in 1969. Technical appendices had not been published by January 1971.

Leicester and Leicestershire Sub-Regional Planning Study.[3] A Report by a Study Team, Director J. B. McLoughlin, to the local planning authorities of Leicester City Council and Leicestershire County Council. Initiated in 1967 and published in 1969, Volume I contains

---

[1] C. Cooper, 'Regional Planning and Implementation', *Journal of the Town Planning Institute*, Vol. 56, 1960, p. 325.

[2] Hugh Wilson and Lewis Womersley, and Scott Wilson Kirkpatrick to Ministry of Housing and Local Government and Ministry of Transport, *Teesside Survey and Plan*, HMSO (London), 1969.

[3] Leicester City Council and Leicestershire County Council, *Leicester and Leicestershire Sub-Regional Planning Study*, Leicester City Council and Leicestershire County Council (Leicester), 1969.

the report and recommendations, and Volume II the technical appendices.

Nottinghamshire and Derbyshire Sub-Regional Study.[1] A Report by a Sub-Regional Planning Unit to a management committee of commissioning authorities, namely Nottinghamshire County Council, Derbyshire County Council, Nottingham City Council and Derby County Borough Council, under the directorship of A. Thorburn. The Study was begun in 1968 and was completed in late 1969. The Report includes technical appendices, and unedited but detailed technical reports are available.

North Gloucestershire Sub-Regional Study.[2] A collaborative study by Gloucestershire County Council, Gloucester City Council and Cheltenham Borough Council, initiated in 1966 and published in 1970, under the leadership of J. C. Gyngell. The steering group of officers included the above authorities, the Ministry of Housing and Local Government and the Ministry of Transport. The Report is written in general terms for public discussion of the issues raised. Technical papers are promised, but were not available by January 1971.

Coventry–Solihull–Warwickshire Sub-Regional Planning Study.[3] A Report by an independent Study Team, Team Leader U. A. Wannop, to Coventry City Council, Solihull County Borough Council and Warwickshire County Council. The Study was begun in 1969 and published in 1971. Seven supplementary reports record the technical processes employed in the Study, but were not available by May 1971.

South Hampshire Study.[4] A Report by Colin Buchanan and Partners commissioned by the Ministry of Housing and Local Government, Hampshire County Council and the County Borough Councils of

[1] Notts–Derby Sub-Regional Planning Unit, *Nottinghamshire and Derbyshire Sub-Regional Study*, Nottinghamshire County Council, Derbyshire County Council, Nottingham City Council and Derby County Borough Council (Derby), 1969.

[2] Gloucestershire County Council, Gloucester City Council and Cheltenham Borough Council, *North Gloucestershire Sub-Regional Study*, Gloucestershire County Council (Gloucester), 1970.

[3] Coventry City Council, Solihull County Borough Council and Warwickshire County Council, *Coventry–Solihull–Warwickshire: A Strategy for the Sub-Region*, Coventry City Council (Coventry), 1971.

[4] Colin Buchanan and Partners, *South Hampshire Study: Report on the Feasibility of Major Urban Growth*, HMSO (London), 1966.

27

Portsmouth and Southampton. The Consultants were appointed in 1964, and the Report with Supplementary Technical Volumes was published in 1966.

Humberside: A Feasibility Study.[1] A Report by the Central Unit for Environmental Planning for the Department of Economic Affairs. The Study, begun in 1966 and published in 1968, was under the chairmanship of J. W. Vernon. The Report contains Technical Appendices.

Strategic Plan for the South East.[2] A Report by the South East Joint Planning Team commissioned by the Government, the Standing Conference on London and South East Regional Planning representing the local planning authorities, and the South East Economic Planning Council. The Study, begun in 1968, was published in 1970, and was headed by W. Burns. No technical reports were available by January 1971.

For purposes of abbreviation, in the text and the footnotes, these Studies will to be referred to respectively as the:

Teesside Study	Warwickshire Study
Leicestershire Study	Hampshire Study[3]
Notts–Derby Study	Humberside Study
North-Glos Study	South East Study[4]

To facilitate comparisons, the Teesside, Leicestershire, Notts–Derby, North-Glos and Warwickshire Studies will be referred to as Sub-regional Studies, and the Hampshire, Humberside and South East Studies as Regional Studies. This distinction is somewhat arbitrary as the classification refers not only to scale and the size of the area, but also to differences in purpose, organization and terms of reference. The three latter studies are concerned more with the feasibility and the practicability of major urban growth, rather than with its disposition and specific form; they are also sponsored by Central

[1] A Report by the Central Unit for Environmental Planning for the Department of Economic Affairs, *Humberside: A Feasibility Study*, HMSO (London), 1969.

[2] Report by the South East Joint Planning Team, *Strategic Plan for the South East*, HMSO (London), 1970.

[3] *Not* to be confused with the South Hampshire Plan Advisory Committee which, where quoted, will be referred to under its full title. This is a joint committee set up by the Hampshire County Council, Portsmouth City Council and Southampton City Council after the above Hampshire Study had been published.

[4] *Not* to be confused with previous regional studies of the South East, e.g. Ministry of Housing and Local Government, *The South East Study, 1961–1981*, HMSO (London), 1964 or South East Economic Planning Council. *A Strategy for the South East*, HMSO (London), 1967.

Government whereas the five previous Studies are more the concern of local planning authorities. The words 'study' and 'report' are used interchangeably, and each is capitalized when reference is made to a particular study.

How these case studies were selected will be of interest. They are limited to Planning Studies undertaken in England between 1965 and 1970. Each is a pioneer report in one or other aspect of its contribution to planning thought, each includes the evaluation of alternative possible strategies in the formulation of its preferred solution, and each involves a joint approach by more than one authority; thus all transcend local administrative boundaries in their assessment of the urban condition within the regional matrix.

The sequence of the Sub-regional Studies begins with the Teesside appraisal, which has some considerable claim to being the first in England using the 'new' planning methodology of goals and evaluation between alternative strategies. Its technical methods are more advanced than previously and include the computer processing and analysis of survey data, sophisticated models, and the concept of structure planning and local planning as sequential parts of a continuous process. The study has indeed been described to us by a professional colleague as 'the pioneer report which brought together the planning techniques which were then known, and the foundation document from which all subsequent Sub-regional study reports have been derived'. The accolade of distinction is then transferred to the Leicestershire Study, where again new methods and techniques have been applied and a real attempt is made 'to avoid encroachment on local planning work by maintaining a strategic view of the sub-region'.[1] The experience gained in this Study, and its systems approach to urban and regional planning, are also discussed by the Study Director elsewhere.[2] The Notts–Derby Study extends this type of approach, and uses models and refined analytical procedures in order to select a preferred strategy to an even greater extent than in its predecessors.

Also of repute is the North-Glos Study which, unlike the others, did not have the advantage of a special team appointed for the task in hand but nevertheless, the outcome is a most commendable Report and a considerable improvement over the traditional local planning authority's development plan. The climax to this sequence is the Warwickshire Study, which learns substantially from the

---

[1] *Leicestershire Study*, p. 7.

[2] J. B. McLoughlin, *Urban and Regional Planning: A Systems Approach*, Faber and Faber (London), 1970.

previous lessons of procedure and is the most systematic in its methods of approach. 'We have had the great advantage of following these Studies, being able to borrow from the techniques which they introduced and having the benefit of the hindsight they allow as to the efficacy of certain recently introduced processes. Where we seemed able to repay our debt to these Studies was in improving the balance between the initial Survey and forecasting stage of the Study and the subsequent process of picking the best strategy based on analysis of existing and future economic and social conditions.'[1] This book is concerned with this ladder of cumulative achievement in understanding, projecting and interpreting the urban future.

At the level of appreciation described as regional, the Hampshire Study is of exceptional importance for its theoretical appraisal of idealized urban forms and structures and, like the Humberside Study, the prime concern is with a substantial influx of new population and its appropriate accommodation within the region under surveillance. The South East Study is the most recent of the Regional Studies reviewed in this book. As the team is headed by the Chief Planner of the Ministry of Housing and Local Government and backed with a formidable array of professional talent and supporting resources, the most competent of all Studies and a major contribution to regional planning thought may reasonably be expected in terms of its methodology. In the words of this Study, 'the role of regional planning is much less clearly defined [than local planning]. Its aims and methods are neither fully worked out nor generally agreed. . . . It is hoped that the outcome is a positive contribution to the further evolution of the role which regional planning can and should play in the planning system.'[2]

An essential feature of all the Studies is that planning is concerned with urban processes in the region and the sub-region, rather than being confined to the narrow and inhibiting boundaries of a single planning authority. The importance of this, in the words of the Leicestershire Study, is that 'serious difficulties can arise when large towns and their surroundings are divided administratively between two or more local government jurisdictions, but they are especially vexing in plans for land use and transport. . . . Although intelligent schemes of co-operation can and do exist, very often we find duplication of facilities with the consequent waste of scarce public resources. With the best will in the world, joint committees and the like are a poor substitute for truly integrated decisions based on area-wide studies of problems, comprehensive information on current trade

[1] *Warwickshire Study*, p. 23.   [2] *South East Study*, p. 4.

and estimates for the future, and a synoptic view of major policies.'[1]

In terms of methodology, the critical contribution is that the preferred strategy is presented for public discussion only after alternative possibilities and other feasible courses of action are considered. Some strategies are rejected, and a preferred strategy is examined and presented in greater detail as a basis for responsible decisions and public action. The creation and then the evaluation of alternative strategies is the central theme in each of the eight Studies under surveillance. There is not just one urban future but a whole variety and range of different possibilities. The physical environment may be used with discretion or usurped, the internal movement of population with England and Wales can be encouraged or discouraged, rates of housing clearance or road construction or the provision of public open space can each be high or low on the list of government priorities, many different policies can be pursued towards the location of industry or the directional growth of towns, and so on over the whole range of factors which affect man's life in urban communities. These are the topics which will be investigated in this book—the how's and the why's of planning including the range of issues which are (or should be) examined when formulating sub-regional and regional strategies of development, the nature of the alternative possibilities which are presented for consideration, how these alternatives are formulated and the means whereby the preferred solution is selected from the range of competing possibilities. These topics are each exceedingly complex but the answers given by planners and the interpreting of this advice by decision-makers are critical for the urban future of every citizen. As such the ideas and the thought processes which underlie the formulation of planning strategies merit considerable public discussion and professinal scrutiny. The eight significant English planning studies which have been introduced in this chapter provide the foundation for such a discussion over the ensuing pages.

SUMMARY

The Studies for review and evaluation over the subsequent chapters are introduced by their authorship and their sponsorship. They are each concerned with strategy formulation at the regional or the sub-regional level of planning responsibility, their conclusions for action are derived from an evaluation of alternative possibilities and each makes a meritorious contribution towards the development of new and improved planning techniques. Their content deserves careful study.

[1] *Leicestershire Study*, p. 1.

31

Chapter 2
Urbanization and the Planning Process

As background to the Studies under review, and before presenting and interpreting their detail, reference will be made to 'contextual' aspects of the urban situation. These include its world-wide significance, the continuum of change from past through present to the future, the characteristics of urbanization as a process of growth and change, the expansion of government intervention in the affairs of the environment, the emerging consideration of interrelations between land use and transportation at the regional level of appreciation, and the nature of the planning contribution as a disciplined approach to urban and regional conditions.

THE URBAN FUTURE IN ITS WORLD CONTEXT

The special importance of a world-wide awareness is that ideas spread. Urbanization has become a pervading characteristic of man's environment on earth.[1] Urban areas cover extensive tracts of land with their buildings, services, open space and transportation networks. The whole nature of society is deeply associated with and committed to life in cities. National prosperity depends to a considerable extent upon the adequate functioning, the economic accomplishments and the social achievements of its urban areas. There are critical issues for resolution, including the urgency of urban renewal, the accommodation of the motor vehicle in urban environments, the ravages of air and water pollution, the relationships

[1] Kingsley Davis, *World Urbanization, 1950–1970*, Institute of International Studies, University of California, 1969. In Western Europe the urban population increased from 77·9 to 109·7 million persons between 1950 and 1970, or from 63·2 to 73·0 per cent of the total population. By 1950, more than 50 per cent of the population living in Northern America, Temperate South America, Northern Europe, Western Europe and Australia–New Zealand were classified as urban. By 1970 South Africa, Middle America, Tropical South America, Japan, Eastern Europe and Southern Europe had also passed this half-way mark for the place of residence of their populations; Japan and Australia–New Zealand then exceeded the 80 per cent figure, and figures above 70 per cent are recorded for Northern America, Temperate South America, Northern Europe and Western Europe. See, for example, G. Breese, *The City in Newly Developing Countries*, Prentice-Hall (Englewood Cliffs, N.J.), 1969 and P. Hall, *The World Cities*, Weidenfeld and Nicolson (London), 1966.

between private enterprise and community responsibility, the pressures on a limited amount of available space for a whole range of economic and social requirements by expanding urban populations, and the sheer processes of physical growth over neighbouring terrain.

The issues posed in this book are not unique to England, but extend in varying form to all world regions. Despite many political, economic and geographic differences between nations, an international comparison of strategies for urban growth by Rodwin (1970) can conclude that,

> what is intriguing, however, is that even though these differences have affected opportunities for development, they have not otherwise changed the main outlines of the urban and regional strategies adopted or the more general definitions of the problems on which they are based. Each of these countries believes it suffers from overconcentration in congested cities in some areas, underconcentration in others, and from undesirable and unnecessarily large regional differences in levels of social and economic development. All believe that they need to change the way the metropolis grows and to promote urban growth centres in the less prosperous regions. . . . The adoption of variants of the same strategies in a wide range of different environments underscores the common problems and trends and conventional ways of thinking about these matters. Even more significant, perhaps, is the fact that in all of these countries, the common denominator is the conviction that the guidance of urban growth strategy cannot – or, rather, must not – remain only at the local level.[1]

Similarities may be more important than differences and Britain which has already contributed much to world thought about urbanization (e.g. through the New Towns movement and its legislative procedures for the control of development) has a substantial further role to play. It has absorbed into its planning methodologies advanced techniques from America and elsewhere, and these have been used with considerable advantage in the Studies under review. The discussion in this text will refer primarily to the situation as envisaged in parts of England by the Studies, but the real underlying concern is with how urban issues and problems are approached, the

---

[1] L. Rodwin, *Nations and Cities: A Comparison of Strategies for Urban Growth*, Houghton Mifflin (Boston), 1970, pp. 273 and 274–5. The comparisons are between experience in Venezuela, Turkey, Great Britain, France and the United States.

B

ideas that have been developed, and the lessons to be learned as a basis for future advantage. The local examples are almost incidental to this wider theme. The attitudes expressed have a greater relevance than to the particular localities under study, because urban modes of life and concern for the urban future have revolutionized world society.

THE DOMAIN OF THE URBAN FUTURE

Decisions about the emerging future are made by all members of the population and by all sections of society. But however made, and for whatever underlying motive or purpose, the consequences will leave their indelible stamp upon man's living and changing environment. It is an inexorable fact that the decisions which are now being made shape, form and achieve the urban future. The city of tomorrow is on the architect's drawing board and the planner's blue-print, in the politician's embrace and in the minds of men today. It is something which is being slowly and continuously created. It may contain new ideas and new thoughts, but it is not a new creation because of the processes of continuity and through the regular addition and frequent amendments to an existing urban fabric.

The past survives in the city of today. Its activities, structure and socio-economic characteristics, the distribution of buildings, open spaces, underground and surface networks, its people and their patterns of movement and association – these elements of the urban environment can be described in the conditions of today; they can be *explained* only in terms of their human and physical dimensions of past evolution to the present. And it is likewise with the future condition of man's urban and urbanizing environment. The only possible starting point for the appreciation of future possibilities is the city as it now exists. Healthy or decaying, efficient or wasteful, beautiful or ugly, it has become and will remain the prime environment of man on earth. The future exists in the city of today, and as the circumstances of today move forward inexorably into the city of tomorrow, society can if it so wishes bend, control, direct and lead the city as it now exists towards its horizon of doubt and uncertainty.

In this planning transition forward from the present into the future, the move is from the domain of facts which are knowable but over which there can be no power, to an area where the question of the truth or falsity of a statement of fact does not arise. In the words of de Jouvenel (1967),

34

for man in his role as an active agent the future is a field of liberty and power, but for man in his role as a cognizant being the future is a field of uncertainty. It is a field of liberty because I am free to conceive that something which does not now exist will exist in the future; it is a field of power because I have some power to validate my conception (though, naturally, not all conceptions indiscriminately!). And indeed the future is our only field of power, for we can act only on the future. Our awareness of this capacity to act suggests the notion of 'a domain in which one can act'. On the other hand, the future is a field of uncertainty. What will be cannot be attested to and verified in the same way as an accomplished fact.'[1]

Facts are the raw materials out of which the mind makes estimates of the future, but how we deem the future and our willingness to act to secure an envisaged future are the critical considerations. The city is man's creation, and it exists first in the imagination for later achievement on the ground.

THE NATURE OF URBANIZATION[2]

Each town is distinctive in its attributes. It has emerged through time as a product of the complex interplay of many forces. It has a physical site and there is a *raison d'être* for the first use of this location for purposes of settlement. From such slender beginnings, its evolution may have been continuous, spasmodic or regressive. Some of the operative forces include the attraction or repulsion of manufacturing activity, the strength of transportation routes, the operation of civic pride, the proximity of other settlements, the location of central place activities, the migration of population, the changing impact through time of technology and in the levels of living and demand, and the sheer skill, verve and opportunity which exist in different economic and social climates for its leaders and inhabitants. There is the importance of a head-start when two nearby centres are competing for urban domination. The interplay and cleavage of social, economic and physical forces is of long standing, and any

[1] B. de Jouvenel, *The Art of Conjecture*, Weidenfeld and Nicolson (London), 1967, p. 6.

[2] See, for example, L. Mumford, *The City in History*, Secker and Warburg (London), 1961; R. E. Dickinson, *City and Region: A Geographical Interpretation*, Routledge and Kegan Paul (London), 1964; P. M. Hauser and L. F. Schnore (eds.), *The Study of Urbanization*, Wiley (New York), 1965; A. B. Gallion and S. Eisner, *The Urban Pattern*, Van Nostrand (Princeton, N.J.), 2nd ed., 1964; H. Blumenfeld, *The Modern Metropolis: its origins, growth, characteristics and planning*, M.I.T. Press (Cambridge, Mass.), 1967.

THE URBAN FUTURE

explanation of patterns and forms as they now exist must extend over the whole array of human affairs. The commitment is to understand a spatial process in terms of time, and in terms of many interlocking events and circumstances.

The assessment must include an appreciation of economic and social conditions which promote the concentration of activities in cities; the physical and the locational aspects which result in a preference for a selected site; the spatial aspects which create an interplay between centres, and which encourage differences in the size and spacing of towns; the gradual achievement of existing features through time, and the changing significance of each factor in time; the whims, prejudices, beliefs, hopes and actions of man which have influenced this urban evolution; and his varying technological endowments, his abilities, his limitations and his changing attitudes to the use of resources, natural and human. Space, time and resources are inextricably mixed in the matrix of a city and its regional affinities and, at the very least, any study which seeks to explain or to understand emerging conditions must take into account these many factors, waxing and waning in their critical degree of importance to the chain of total events.

A characteristic of urban growth is that it does not proceed equally everywhere. It has been demonstrated by Christaller (1933)[1] and more recently by Berry and Pred (1961)[2] that, under the ideal circumstances of a uniform population distribution, the location of *central* services will produce a hexagonal pattern and a functional hierarchy of sizes rather than the even spread of activities over the landscape. Both concentration and dispersion are elements of growth. There are relationships between the size of the supporting population, the number of activities which are required and the transportation required to serve these distributions, so that the hierarchy changes substantially over time.[3] A second powerful force in shaping the locational patterns of urban areas is that of the *non-central* place activities such as manufacturing industry and the use of resources. Again, the concept must be of a changing use of space in time – a resource may become depleted through use, it will not be uniformly distributed, demands and technology change. The manufacturing

[1] The basic document is W. Christaller, *Die Zentralen Orte in Süd-Deutschland* (Jena), 1933. English translation by C. W. Baskin in 1966 by Prentice-Hall (Englewood Cliffs, N.J.), as *Central Places in Southern Germany*.

[2] B. J. L. Berry and A. Pred, *Central Place Studies: A Bibliography of Theory and Applications*, Regional Science Research Institute (Philadelphia), 1961.

[3] See, for example, R. D. P. Smith, 'The Changing Urban Hierarchy', *Regional Studies*, Vol. 2, 1968, pp. 1–19.

plant, even though once located in the most favourable situation, becomes redundant and a former waste product can achieve the market status of a profitable commodity. Nothing in the urban land-scape, neither people nor structures nor institutions nor resources, is either fixed or unalterable in the circumstances of time.

The human evaluation of space also changes in time. It changes as the needs, pressures and demands from people and society change. It changes in response to new circumstances such as the lift and public transportation which transformed the density possibilities of central areas. It changes in response to new purposes and attitudes, such as the greater need for recreational space as cities grow and as the hours available for leisure increase. Standards vary, habits change, people migrate, areas change in their demographic charac-teristics and socio-economic attributes. However, as the fixed assets of former investment decisions are immobile, they must adapt to the new circumstances perhaps through decline and oblivion, perhaps through accommodating new uses in old fabrics, and perhaps through the expansion in height, depth or intensity of use on the same site. Altered standards of living and altered activities have had to be imposed on spatial structures conceived for a different purpose in an earlier period. The city has adapted continually to changing circum-stances.

The extent of space is limited, not boundless. The boundaries may be natural as with oceans or rivers, or man-made as with political or administrative divisions. Events within and beyond these boundaries will exert their effect, so that no study of an urban region can exist in isolation. Controls, directions and imperatives are local, national and international. Take transport alone. Major railways, canals and highways will cross an area to serve important outside places but, once constructed, they then attract services, population and industry to the internal transportation network in its own right. Later trade embargoes, tariff agreements, transportation subsidies or the burden of additional costs, even if conceived for reasons external to the region, will exert their impact on the urban situation within the region. Almost every national decision, somehow or somewhere, exerts some impact on the characteristics of its associated urban areas – yet but few of these decisions are made with the welfare of the urban environment primarily in mind. The urban environment is the residual gainer or loser by such decisions.

Social determinants exert a powerful sway on urban form and urban characteristics. There is the desire of people to live close to people of similar socio-economic characteristics. There are various travel, interaction distances in modern society, such as from home to work-place or from home to cultural activities, and behavioural characteristics generally. There is the operation of market forces including competition, the market price of land and hard bargaining between site owners and potential users of this space. There is the location of community services and facilities such as schools, hospitals and clubs. The pattern of land ownership and its associated interests exerts a pervasive impact, as do institutional controls such as zoning, taxation, and other incentives or disincentives on the use of land. Changes in the standards of living create new demands, for example in terms of recreational facilities and the size and location of homes. There is always the difficult line of division between personal freedom and the necessary collective arrangements for urban living, and different views on such issues by the major political parties.

Migration, too, is a factor of special significance. It provides the spatial process which makes possible the redistribution of population and the concentration of people in a few selected localities. It permits selective industrial growth and change, so that urban populations both grow *in situ*, expand and contract. The motivations for personal movement, the distance of this movement, the number and the types of people who move, and the selective impact of these movements on the receiving and exporting localities provide highly important components of information towards urban understanding. They make possible the processes of location in a pattern of central places, and the selective preferment between scattered locations for industrial activities.

Urban locations result, therefore, from the continuing interaction through time and space and in a changing economic and social mould of innumerable public and private decisions. These decisions are not perfect; they are motivated by need and by greed, display errors of judgement and do not take into account all circumstances. The future itself is unknown, and the pattern and forces of the present, the known possibilities and the extent of possible divergence, the influence of pressure groups, the strength of historical inertia, and the goals of efficiency, profit or service to the community will each play their part in determining where, when and how to locate new developments. Rational decisions which are predictable in terms of location, and irrational decisions of uncertain location, are each reflected in the geographic landscape of urban settlements.

The urban environment of planning concern is thus exceedingly complex. An urban centre may consist of a highly developed nucleus, a less developed hinterland and exist as a part of a regional system of settlements. The nodal points of varying levels of performance are linked by a hierarchical system of communication, with the strongest links and attraction between the largest units. The importance of transportation in achieving this pattern is that until recently in the evolution of the urban pattern, the speed of transportation on horse, by foot or in a carriage was extremely limited. It was also the same outside settlements as within, so that growth was typically in concentric circles around the nucleus. When a new form of transportation is introduced, such as a railway or the motor vehicle and more recently the motorway, then the forces of growth are transformed. With the higher speed of travel, a greater distance can be travelled than previously in the same time and the traditional pattern becomes distorted. A new composite shape is created through transportation so that, if a city enjoys two such new highway connections, it may extend in these directions of its new accessibility. The previous feature of equal accessibility in all directions, as modified by relief and various other geographical features, will likewise be changed. The larger unit with the more favourable communications network extends its influence outwards along these favoured routes to capture the hinterland of lesser centres. There is a transfer of function from the small to the larger centre by such processes, new and more intense activities are required in the dynamic centre and its structure (geared to the requirements of an earlier age) will resist the changes which have become necessary – more traffic, more high intensity buildings for serving and servicing in various capacities the enlarged and enlarging population. The city, inflexible in its physical structure of roads and buildings, exists in a dynamic environment of changing social needs and new economic opportunities. This provides the essential yet difficult starting point for the emerging urban future.

INTERVENTION IN THE COURSE OF URBAN AFFAIRS

The gradual expansion of government intervention in the affairs of the environment may be considered under several distinct and sometimes parallel headings, which ultimately combine in the Studies under review. These events include a formative period culminating in the Town and Country Planning Act 1947, increasing criticisms of this mechanism for controlling the use and development of land, a growing awareness of the need to integrate land use planning with transportation planning and an increasing appreciation of the need to approach urban issues from a regional standpoint. These roots of origin for present planning procedures include:

1. Early Precedents

Man has always exerted some form of control over the location and civic design qualities of cities. The Greeks and the Romans built new towns; Edward I placed bastide towns at strategic locations; the spread of mediaeval cities across Europe was encouraged by decree; powerful Renaissance rulers dictated an urban form for their palaces and capital cities.[1] Even more significant is extended government intervention in the affairs of the city as its conditions become too dismal or too degraded to satisfy the mores of society. When ethical standards are disgraced, then public action to remove deficiencies becomes an acceptable proposition. The origins of the town planning or town improvement movement in the Victorian era had roots in just such conditions.[2] It was concerned with searching for a more pleasing, satisfying and aesthetic urban form; with removing the insanitary, inhuman and overcrowded conditions of nineteenth-century industrial cities; with achieving utopian interpretations of justice, equality and design in model communities; and with improving the quality of living in urban environments.

The sequence of government intervention is from public health legislation through housing reform to town planning. But towns also grow out into the countryside and consume adjacent land. New standards of houses with gardens, the pressures for green space within the expanding urban environments, and massive suburbanization of homes and work-places accelerated by the ubiquitous motor vehicle led to an initial awareness that town and country are not separate components. As each required some form of control and direction by government, legislation was broadened from Town Planning Acts to Town *and* Country Planning Acts from 1932 onwards. The incursion of urban and industrial growth onto unspoilt acres should be curbed, and the dominant tone was an attitude which emphasized that certain areas or places had to be 'preserved' against change. Thus town and country were seen as separate elements which pose their own distinct problems and which require their own

[1] See, for example, S. E. Rasmussen, *Towns and Buildings*, M.I.T. Press (Cambridge, Mass.), 1951.

[2] W. Ashworth, *The Genesis of Modern British Town Planning*, Routledge and Kegan Paul (London), 1954; G. E. Cherry, *Urban Change and Planning*, Foulis (Henley), 1971.

solution. The Barlow Report of 1940 was concerned with the concentration of the industrial population in large towns and in particular regional localities,[1] and the Scott Committee was set up in 1941 to consider the problems of land utilization in rural areas[2] – two subjects, two committees and two statements.

2. *Postwar Planning Legilsation*[3]

This traditional town-versus-country distinction is incorporated in the Town and Country Planning Act of 1947, which brought almost all development of land under control and awarded the basic mechanism for the exercise of this control to the administratively distinct and independent county boroughs and county councils. It was generally accepted in postwar Britain that the growth of large cities should be restricted, that the best quality agricultural land should be safeguarded against development, that sprawl as a decisive element in urban growth would be eliminated, and that large scale overspill movements of population and industry would be directed to new towns and expanded towns. The other side of the coin is provided by the National Parks and Access to the Countryside Act of 1949, the claims of amenity as a key concept, the frequent use of the phrase 'injurious to the interests of amenity' to prevent unwanted or harmful new developments, the establishment of national parks and of areas of outstanding natural beauty, a survey of public rights of way along rural footpaths, access orders to open country, the work of the Council for the Preservation of Rural England and by the establishment of the Nature Conservancy in 1949.[4]

The 1947 Town and Country Planning Act provided an important milestone for the intervention of government in the affairs of the environment. It required all local planning authorities to prepare and submit for the Minister's approval a 'development plan' showing the manner in which they proposed that land in their area should be used. This defined the sites of proposed roads, public buildings,

[1] *Report of the Royal Commission on the Geographical Distribution of the Industrial Population* (The Barlow Report), HMSO (London), Cmnd. 6153, 1940.

[2] *Report of the Committee on Land Utilisation in Rural Areas* (The Scott Report), HMSO (London), Cmnd. 6378, 1942.

[3] For a discussion on the functions of the relevant government department see Evelyn Sharp. *The Ministry of Housing and Local Government*, George Allen and Unwin (London), 1969.

[4] For a general view of the situation by about 1965 see J. B. Cullingworth, *Town and Country Planning in England and Wales*, George Allen and Unwin (London), 1st ed., 1964. For the rural dimension see H. E. Bracey, *People and the Countryside*, Routledge and Kegan Paul (London), 1969.

41

airfield and parks, allocated land for residential, industrial and other purposes, and designated land for compulsory acquisition. The emphasis was on land use and zoning for specific purposes, with the key concept being that of a Town or County Map making the necessary provision to meet future needs.[1]

3. *Criticisms of Government Control over Land Use and Development*

Certain deficiencies of the planning system under the 1947 Act soon became evident. The complex of inter-relations between land use, movement and environmental quality could not be dealt with by these one-dimensional maps. The powers to prevent development were much greater than for the initiation of positive and constructive development proposals. The administrative area of a single local planning authority was rarely suitable as a definitive planning area, because towns were divorced from their hinterlands and town maps were prepared separately from their regional context. Long administrative delays resulted as all detailed proposals had to be approved by the Ministry. It was increasingly recognized that land use decisions have economic and social consequences, and may be used to achieve social and economic objectives.[2] It was thus seen that planning had to become more comprehensive, and that a distinction was necessary between strategic and policy planning for extensive areas of the country and the detailed or local planning of specific localities.

In the words of one critic, McCulloch (1961) could state that,

we failed to realize that the range of land use planning is co-extensive with the scale and coincident with the purposes of capital investment. The guidance of land use in the public interest, nationally and regionally, requires the bringing together of the forces responsible for development of all kinds. . . . No attempt was made to relate directly the exercise of planning powers to geographical and social areas suited to the problems to be solved. The local powers divide naturally into control of development and policy making for development. The former . . . is a follow-up of development decisions independently taken. Adequate planning is more than this, and ideally is the determination of development policies and the preparation of projects that will help to carry out policies. . . . The

[1] See, for example, L. Keeble, *Principles and Practice of Town and Country Planning*, Estates Gazette (London), 1952 and Ministry of Town and Country Planning, Circular No. 40, *Survey of Development Plans*, HMSO, 1948.
[2] See, for example, R. E. Pahl, *Patterns of Urban Life*, Longmans (London), 1970.

42

restriction of planning powers within boundaries scarcely relevant to planning problems have made difficult the preparation of significant forward-looking Development Plans.[1]

A Planning Advisory Group was set up in 1964 to consider this prevailing type of criticism. Two of its main objectives were (1) to ensure that the planning system serves its purpose satisfactorily as an instrument of planning policy and (2) to improve the technical quality of development plans and to strengthen their policy content. Among the recommendations subsequently to be incorporated in the Town and Country Planning Act 1968 was that, 'each local planning authority should still be required to submit development plans for Ministerial approval. The content of these plans, however, will be limited to the major issues of policy affecting the area concerned and those matters in which the Minister has an interest. They will be primarily statements of policy . . . designed to clarify the basic physical structure of the area and its transport system. . . . The type of plans which we recommend cannot be produced by planning authorities acting in isolation. They require to form part of a regional pattern and also of what may be called a sub-regional pattern.'[2] The first of such plans provides the theme of this book.

4. *The Achievement of a more Comprehensive Approach*

It is important to emphasize that both the Ministry of Housing and Local Government *and* the Ministry of Transport were represented on this planning advisory group. Planning for transportation, so important in achieving the form, pattern and scale of the urban environment, had been undergoing changes in its attitudes and approaches which parallel the above changing circumstances in town and country planning.[3] Objectives have been extended and techniques have been improved in the fields of both land use and transportation

[1] F. J. McCulloch, 'The Background: The Social and Economic Determinants of Land Use', in Department of Civic Design, University of Liverpool, *Land Use in an Urban Environment: A General View of Town and Country Planning*, Liverpool University Press, 1961, pp. 9–10.

[2] Planning Advisory Group, *The Future of Development Plans*, HMSO (London), 1965, pp. 9–10.

[3] See, for example, R. Spence, *Transportation Studies: A Review of Results to Date from Typical Areas*, Ministry of Transport (London), 1964 and Colin Buchanan and Partners, *The Conurbations*, British Road Federation (London), 1969, for a review of progress. Method is discussed in P. Brenikov, 'Land use/transportation studies', *Town and Country Planning School, 1969: Report of Proceedings*, Town Planning Institute (London), 1969, pp. 24–30.

planning. Concern has broadened from a transportation study serving as a tool for highway planning, to the appreciation of transportation as an essential element in the process of urban structure planning. Thus the London Traffic Survey in 1962 had the limited objective of producing traffic forecasts for 1971 and 1981, and then of relating these to the envisaged highway network for these years. A later study of the Tyneside Conurbation had as its objectives in 1964 a five-year action programme, a fifteen-year transportation plan and an urban strategy plan to the end of the century. More recently, transportation studies for the Merseyside and the West Yorkshire Conurbations have considered substantial land use alternatives in a sub-regional situation, but with critics still emphasizing deficiencies in approach from the land use/environmental standpoint. Thus, 'hindsight is a great teacher and it is now clear that for land-use transport studies to be fully effective the sophisticated and expensive transport studies should be matched by equally sophisticated and expensive studies of the economic, social and environmental costs of alternative land-use plans'.[1]

Reference should also be made to the Buchanan Report,[2] in which traffic is regarded as a function of land use activities and traffic movements and demands are studied in their urban and environmental context. This study has exerted a significant impact on subsequent thought; it was published in 1963, and was followed in 1964 by a joint circular from the Ministers of Transport and Housing and Local Government.[3] The circular stressed the need for local authorities to adopt a coordinated approach to land use and transport, and advocated the use of combined land use and transportation studies to achieve this purpose. Later again the Sharp Report on the training of men for transport planning emphasizes that

strategic planning of land use and transport must be regarded as an integral and continuous key function. These two elements of the environmental planning job cannot be tackled in isolation, nor merely by liaison between two separate departments. . . . A single committee and a single chief officer, described as the head of land use and transport, should be responsible for the whole of land use planning and the whole of transport. This is a key recommendation.

[1] F. J. Amos, 'Alternative Plans for Sub-Regional Problems', *Regional Studies*, Vol. 1, 1967, p. 146.

[2] Ministry of Transport, *Traffic in Towns* (The Buchanan Report), HMSO (London), 1963.

[3] Ministry of Transport and Ministry of Housing and Local Government, Circular No. 1/64, *The Buchanan Report: Traffic in Towns*, HMSO (London), 1964.

It entails acceptance of interchangeability between those engaged in transport planning and those engaged in land use planning. . . . There is, indeed, no argument about the interdependence of land use and transport planning.[1]

In terms of either policy formulation or administrative responsibility, there has been the gradual appreciation that intervention in the affairs of the environment requires a unitary approach by government. Eventual recognition of this fact resulted in the amalgamation of the Ministry of Transport and the Ministry of Housing and Local Government into a single national government Department of the Environment in 1970. Land use planning, which had gradually accommodated the previously separate elements of town and country into the one concept of a continuous landscape, thus becomes more closely associated with transportation planning in order to achieve an integrated approach by government to the affairs of urban and regional environments.

THE REGIONAL DIMENSION

Advocates of regionalism have long been attracted to the idea of larger areas for land use planning, primarily to co-ordinate development across local government boundaries and to ensure a consistent approach to problems of mutual concern. That great futurist, H. G. Wells, predicted the large scale expansion of cities and the development of urban regions in 1902, Patrick Geddes discussed 'conurbations' or large urbanized areas in 1915, and the contributions by C. B. Fawcett and G. D. H. Cole are well known.[2] Commissions of inquiry have referred frequently to the need for organization on a regional basis by neighbouring local authorities, there were joint town planning schemes under the inter-war town planning legislation[3] and government departments have been concerned with the establishment of regional offices. The literature on regionalism is

[1] Ministry of Transport, *Transport Planning: The Men for the Job* (The Sharp Report), HMSO (London), 1970, pp. 15 and 26.

[2] H. G. Wells, *Anticipations*, 1902; Patrick Geddes, *Cities in Evolution*, Norgate and Norgate (London), 1949; C. B. Fawcett, *The Provinces of England*, Hutchinson (London), 1961 (Reprint); G. D. H. Cole, *Local and Regional Government*, Cassell (London), 1947.

[3] See, for example, R. J. Norton, *Joint Operations by Local Authorities*, Institute of Municipal Treasurers and Accountants (London), 1960; P. Abercrombie, *The Regional Planning Scheme for East Suffolk*, 1935; W. R. Davidge, *Cambridgeshire Region Planning Report, 1934, Hertfordshire Regional Planning Report, 1927*, and *West Kent Joint Regional Planning Report, 1934*.

45

extensive.[1] It emphasizes that considerations of land use, public services and utilities, transportation, the location of industry and service centres, pollution and urban housing *inter alia* cannot be confined to single administrative areas. There is a need for an 'in-between' body, which is linked to the local level of people who live in an area *and* to the national level of government with its funds, resources, centralized functions and overall responsibility. Regionalism implies a dual outlook, with its linkages and its directions of understanding to both higher and lower tiers of government.

Some of the more recent expressions of demand for a regional approach to urban problems include:

1. Concern for creating a better environment, expressed in regional reports prepared during the 1940s for extensive urbanized areas such as the Clyde Valley, Greater London, and the Birmingham–Black Country Conurbation,[2] and disappointment that the 1947 Town and Country Planning Act divided the administrative control of such areas between the county councils and the county boroughs and provided no superior mechanism to formulate either inter-urban or inter-regional land use strategies.

2. Concern for areas of high unemployment, with the regional problem being seen primarily in terms of economic growth as in the Barlow Commission Report, the 1945 Distribution of Industry Act, the 1960 Local Employment Act, and white papers concerned with industrial growth and development.[3] The growing unity between 'physical' planning and 'economic' planning is reflected by the requirement of the Town and Country Planning Act 1968 that local planning authorities in their structure planning have regard 'to current policies with respect to the economic planning and development of the region as a whole'.[4]

3. The 1946 New Towns Act to control the size and growth of great cities, especially London, by building new and expanded towns

[1] See, for example, R. E. Dickinson, *City Region and Regionalism*, Routledge and Kegan Paul (London), 1947; E. W. Gilbert, 'Geography and Regionalism' in E. G. Taylor, *Geography in the Twentieth Century*, Methuen (London), 1951 and 'The Idea of the Region', *Geography*, Vol. 45, 1960, pp. 157–75; B. Smith, *Regionalism in England*, Acton Society Trust (London), Vol. I, 1964, Vol. II, 1965, and Vol. III, 1965; R. Minshull, *Regional Geography: Theory and Practice*, Hutchinson University Library (London), 1967.

[2] P. Abercrombie and R. H. Matthew, *The Clyde Valley Regional Plan*, HMSO (Edinburgh), 1949; P. Abercrombie, *The Greater London Plan*, HMSO (London), 1944; West Midland Group, *Conurbation*, Faber and Faber (London), 1946.

[3] For an overview see G. McCrone, *Regional Policy in Britain*, George Allen and Unwin (London), 1969.

[4] Article 2(4), *Town and Country Planning Act 1968*.

and by dispersing population and industry to these new centres of activity, but not conceived in relation to achieving regional objectives.[1]

4. The nationalization of major industries and institutions such as railways, coal, gas, electricity and medical services, their subsequent regionalization, and the pressures to co-ordinate heavy government investment in capital investment programmes to the greatest regional advantage.

5. The effects of transportation on the form, growth opportunities and problems of the city. In America, where this impact is several years in advance of British circumstances, *metropolitan* transportation studies were undertaken and then metropolitan transportation–land use studies. Early landmarks include the Detroit study begun 1953, Washington begun 1955, Chicago begun 1956, and the Los Angeles and Penn–Jersey (Philadelphia) studies begun in 1959.[2] These ideas and methodology were soon discussed in England.

6. The increasing sophistication in techniques, including the construction of various land use and urban development models,[3] the mass handling of data by computers from 1960 onwards, operational research and management cybernetics,[4] and the general development of a systems approach to urban problems.[5]

7. An increasing awareness that local physical planning and national economic planning are mutually inter-related. In the words of Cullingworth and Orr (1969), regional planning provides 'a meeting place for the economic planner, previously engaged primarily at

[1] See, for example, L. Rodwin, *The British New Towns Policy*, Harvard University Press (Cambridge, Mass.), 1956.

[2] See, for example, R. M. Zettel and R. R. Carll, *Summary Review of Major Metropolitan Area Transportation Studies in the United States*, Institute of Transportation and Traffic Engineering, University of California (Berkeley), 1962.

[3] See, for example, R. J. Chorley and P. Haggett, *Models in Geography*, Methuen (London), 1967; B. Harris (ed.), 'Urban Development Models: New Tools for Planning', *Journal of the American Institute for Planners*, May 1965 and R. Drewett, 'Urban and Regional Models in British Planning Research', *Regional Studies*, 1969, Vol. 3, No. 3 (Special Issue).

[4] See, for example, S. Beer, *Decision and Control*, Wiley (London), 1966; R. A. Johnson, F. E. Kast and J. E. Rosenzweig, *The Theory and Management of Systems*, McGraw-Hill (New York), 1963 and R. N. McKean, *Efficiency in Government through Systems Analysis*, Wiley (New York), 1958.

[5] See, for example, B. J. L. Berry and F. E. Horton, *Geographic Perspectives on Urban Systems*, Prentice Hall (Englewood Cliffs, N.J.), 1970 and J. B. McLoughlin and J. N. Webster, 'Cybernetic and general-system approaches to urban and regional research: a review of the literature', *Environment and Planning*, 1970, Vol. 2, pp. 369–408.

the national level, and the physical planner, hitherto still largely concerned in urban problems. The inevitably fumbling attempts to fuse socio-economic and physical planning opened the way to consideration of planning issues within a much more comprehensive framework. The present process of re-thinking on planning strategy and policy, then, is an exercise in collaboration between the social scientist, in his various specialist roles, and the physical planner.'[1]

8. A growing appreciation that neither 'town' nor 'country' can be defined with precision, that each should be regarded as integral and related parts of the same continuous landscape, and that it is impossible to define in physical, economic or social terms where the one begins and the other ends. The only precise lines of demarcation are the necessary yet arbitrary boundaries for administrative purposes and statistical enumeration. The 'regional city' becomes a topic of growing concern and importance.[2]

There was therefore the gradual feeling by the mid-1960s that urban strategies *must* be concerned with the synthesis, the relationships and the mutual interplay between a range of urban functions over an extensive regional canvas. This entails a comprehensive and an integrative approach to many interlocking elements in the formulation of land use and transportation policies. Strategies, for example, must consider the impact of additional population on urban structure and translate these pressures into the terms of housing and employment demands, the effects of each of these demands on transportation, and hence the added pressures on traffic movement and therefore the need for road improvement schemes, which in their turn affect urban structure, and so on in a whole sequence of related events. It is certain in this type of situation that regional policy formulation for urban growth must provide a framework and an inspiration for the development of the region itself, it must take into account national objectives which relate to the region, and it must so devise the future policies and strategies that there is a valid basis for more detailed area plans and for the proposals of the many separate component systems. It is clear that regional planning has national–regional and regional–local connotations. It is concerned with both the 'advocacy' role of guiding national strategies for investment in the region, and with the 'implementation' role of

[1] J. B. Cullingworth and S. C. Orr, 'Participation of Social Scientists in planning', in S. C. Orr and J. B. Cullingworth (eds.), *Regional and Urban Studies: A Social Science Approach*, George Allen and Unwin (London), 1969, pp. 8 and 13.
[2] See, for example, D. Senior (ed.), *The Regional City: An Anglo-American Discussion of Metropolitan Planning*, Longmans (London), 1966.

achieving the physical disposition of national and local investment within the region.

Practical expression to these regional ideas was provided by the Rt Hon. Richard Crossman M.P. who, 'when Minister of Housing and Local Government (in 1965), promoted the idea of sub-regional planning: this would transcend administrative boundaries and involve adjoining Local Planning Authorities in active collaboration in the study of a Sub-Region and in preparing long-term plans on a broad basis'.[1] Or, and from the introduction to another Study, 'he believed that in advance of, and without prejudice to any subsequent reform of local government functions and boundaries, co-operative planning ventures could begin between the towns and their surrounding authorities. His initial aim was to persuade the authorities in a small number of selected areas to come together and set up *ad hoc* teams to prepare long term "broad-brush" plans for land uses and transportation. These were to be called "sub-regional planning studies".'[2]

LAND USE AND TRANSPORTATION ALTERNATIVES AT THE REGIONAL LEVEL

1. *The Transfer of Ideas from America to England*

One of the earliest attempts to produce a comprehensive statement of alternative possible urban forms at the regional scale is the Year 2000 Plan for Washington D.C.[3] Different alternative forms are structured including new independent cities, controlled outward growth, a ring of cities, radial corridor development and new towns. Considerable advances in the use of this technique follow in the American metropolitan transportation studies, where the approach becomes more sophisticated.[4]

In the Philadelphia programme, six alternative transportation policies were prepared whilst all other plans and policies were held constant. The Boston programme specified four transportation alternatives for 1990, made some variation in the areas served by water and sewer systems, and varied its population and employment forecasts to permit land use alternatives. Alternatives in the Baltimore

[1] *North-Glos Study*, p. 1.   [2] *Leicestershire Study*, p. 2.
[3] National Capital Planning Commission, *A Policies Plan for the Year 2000: The Nation's Capital*, Washington (D.C.), 1962.
[4] D. E. Boyce and N. D. Day, *Metropolitan Plan Evaluation Methodology*, Institute for Environmental Studies, University of Pennsylvania (Philadelphia), 1969, Chapter III. This report was published, with the addition of seven study summaries, as D. E. Boyce, N. D. Day and C. McDonald, *Metropolitan Plan Making*, Regional Science Research Institute (Philadelphia), 1970.

programme were based on various arrangements for the size and arrangement of commercial centres. In the Twin Cities programme, the levels of service on the highway system were modified in each of four alternatives to accord with the land use plan. Five land use alternatives were prepared for the Chicago programme, and three for the Milwaukee and Bay Area programmes.

A review of these metropolitan studies by Boyce and Day (1969) states that

> alternative plans should be used to explore and learn about the effects and implications of a wide range of diverse assumptions about objectives, attitudes, possible policies and programs. . . . The emphasis should be on (1) understanding a complex of inter-system relationships; (2) determining the compatibility and feasibility of selected sets of objectives, plans and policies; (3) identifying the proper geographic scale, level of detail and time horizon for a given problem or plan. In addition, more detailed aspects should be considered: (1) levels and allocation of public expenditures; (2) levels of service for public facility-service systems; (3) alternative staging programs for capital improvements; (4) differing assumptions about technological advances and socio-economic change; (5) variations in the distribution of development and control powers, within government.[1]

The role of alternatives is thus extensive; it is to test the practicality and the effectiveness of the numerous different types of decision and possibilities which exist as the urban environment of today changes from its present to its future dimension.

An early British example of the use of regional alternatives is provided by the study in 1964 of a potential new regional shopping centre at Haydock Park, between Manchester and Liverpool and on the M6 motorway.[2] The technique deployed to investigate this possibility examined different regional settlement possibilities. Subsequently there has been an increasing awareness that many different future possibilities exist for every facet of the urban condition. It may also be of interest to note that the faculty from the Department of Town and Country Planning at the University of Manchester provided the leadership for two of the Sub-regional

[1] Boyce and Day, *ibid.*, p. 74.
[2] R. H. Kantorowich, H. W. E. Davies, J. N. Jackson and D. G. Robinson, *Regional Shopping Centres: A Planning Report on North-West England*, Department of Town and Country Planning, University of Manchester (Manchester), 1964.

studies under review; D. F. Medhurst and H. W. E. Davies in the Teesside Study, and J. B. McLoughlin as Director of the Leicestershire Study.

2. *The Range of Choice*

A multitude of different planning possibilities exists at each of the national, regional, sub-regional and urban levels of appreciation. The form of urban growth can be by peripheral expansion, linear growth, or to new communities which are satellite to the parent city or independent. Urban structure can be of high, medium or low densities, and many different design possibilities exist within each category. The location of new development can be in one of several directions from the existing nucleus, and on or off high quality agricultural land, mineral resources, floodland or scenic sites. Service facilities can be arranged in some form of hierarchical distribution extending from the regional centre to the corner store: there can be a larger number of smaller centres or a smaller number of larger centres, and concentration or dispersal of facilities. In terms of transportation, many gradings are possible in the provision, frequency, convenience, accessibility and fare structure of public facilities. The degree to which private travel is encouraged can vary considerably through the road construction programme, pricing policies and traffic control devices. Investments which have cumulatively created the core areas can be safeguarded, or these costs can be 'written down' as new options become available with new transportation facilities. Settlement can be continuous and integrated into a single metropolitan system or it may consist of smaller scale diversified communities within the region. In the words of Doxiadis (1968), 'if we are aware that we should worry about the city of the future, and that this city depends on our decisions, then we must start thinking about what alternatives we have. The alternatives are as many as there are people who make decisions, as there are combinations of decisions that people can make.'[1]

In a situation where such a range of hypotheses exists for the future form and structure of the urban environment, effective planning must be concerned with a systematic understanding of the development processes, with projecting various alternatives within the range of feasibility, and with weighing the costs and benefits of different possible situations. One suggested method of approach, based on an appreciation of American experience, is that

[1] C. A. Doxiadis, 'How to Build the City of the Future' in R. Eells, *Man in the City of the Future*, Collier-Macmillan (Toronto), 1968, pp. 171–2.

alternatives should not be limited to the metropolitan scale, medium range (20–25 year), comprehensive, physical end-state plans that have dominated planning programs in the past decade. Alternatives should explore, to the maximum extent possible, both near and far time horizons, metropolitan and sub-metropolitan configurations, comprehensive and individual facility-service system schemes, as well as divergent assumptions and staging. Major resources should be allocated to the elaboration and evaluation of plans for social and economic growth and change, in addition to land development and facility-service patterns. . . . A series of generalized regional alternatives should be developed, projecting 20 to 50 years ahead in time. . . . The primary focus should be on the overall structure of urbanization and reconstruction, long term patterns of social, economic and technological change, and the impact of alternative development patterns on the natural environment with particular emphasis on pollution. Accordingly, there is a need to explore objectives and policies for resource management (water resources, areas of special amenity or unique natural features, agricultural lands and conservation areas) and the impact of possible radical changes in technology, the distribution and exercise of government powers, income levels, and patterns of leisure time.[1]

Having prepared this range of reasonable and practical options, then procedures must be devised to determine which of several alternative plans provides the 'best solution'. Lichfield (1970) has reviewed the nature of such plan tests, and suggests a sevenfold categorization:[2]

1. Internal consistency. The extent to which the varying quantitative elements in the plan relate to each other, either for the plan as a whole or to its separate parts.

2. Locational suitability. The suitability of the locations for activities and functions.

3. Conformity to standards and principles. The acceptability of the required levels of performance.

4. Problem solving. The degree to which problems revealed by analysis of the studies and forecasts are resolved.

5. Feasibility. The extent to which the planning proposals are feasible and practicable in relation to economic, financial, organizational and political constraints.

[1] Boyce and Day, *op. cit.*, pp. 77 and 82.
[2] N. Lichfield, 'Evaluation Methodology of Urban and Regional Plans: A Review', *Regional Studies*, Vol. 4, 1970, p. 153.

6. Design. The level of creativity which has been introduced into the problem-solving process.

7. Flexibility and open-endedness. The nature of the provision for changing course and the capability of the planning proposals for adjustment, if necessary by the direction of events.

It should by now be apparent that the development of alternatives at the regional level of appreciation does not simplify, but complicates greatly, the selection of the preferred solution. Great quantities of data have to be obtained, manipulated and examined for the relationships which exist. The availability of computers has assisted with this process. The task is to develop a system of knowledge about the city and then to use it, but more precision, knowledge and understanding also has its dangers. Caution is necessary because, against the advantage of modern management techniques,

> there may be serious losses in terms of seeing, feeling, hearing and absorbing the full situation, of being 'on the scene', or talking directly with the people involved in not using sufficiently the more 'normal' and traditional human organizational and information networks. Even if one does not actually degrade one's information by excessive reliance on the automated system but retains the more direct techniques, the enormously detailed and orderly information that one gets from the new system may lead to unjustified confidence that one understands what is happening, possibly resulting in overcontrol or miscontrol. In any case, the more impressive and 'scientific' system may out-compete the other sources of information and thus result in as much misinformed control as if the other systems did not exist.[1]

This important statement from the American Institute of Planners, where the consideration of such techniques is in advance of Britain, provides a necessary warning for those who must use such statistical exercises in the formulation of decisions.

Nor does better knowledge necessarily mean that conditions can or will be altered. They may be a conflict with certain established values, or the cost or consequences of remedial measures may be prohibitive. Knowledge about something does not lead automatically to intelligent action. Knowledge and objective information may be the first step in achieving planned change, but it does not necessarily procure that change. Planning must therefore establish a body of

---

[1] H. Kahn and A. J. Wrener, 'Faustian Powers and Human Choices' in W. R. Ewald, *Environment and Change: The Next Fifty Years*, Indiana University Press, 1968, p. 119.

knowledge concerning the principles of behaviour in urban settle-ments. This must be as objective as possible, and be free from subjec-tive interpretation. It is necessary to understand in exact and precise terms the nature of the problem. But this process must not be taken so far as to deny the personal, the intuitive or the creative achieve-ment of the urban future. A great danger of the present technocratic situation is that the demanding skills of greater understanding may take precedence over the achievement of an elegant and expressive solution.

PLANNING AS A PROFESSIONAL ACTIVITY

Urbanization involves, from the economic standpoint, complex judgements about the financial viability of proposals including the assessment by industrialists of whether the locale is suitable for a selected investment in order to achieve a given production, or the justification by an entrepreneur to invest in proposal 'A' rather than proposal 'B'. It includes innumerable decisions by the individual and by community groups, such as where to live, where to shop, where to work, where to go for leisure pursuits, and with whom to associate on a whole variety of personal, social, business, cultural and sportive pursuits. In physical terms there are innumerable conflicts in terms of a limited range of available space to accommodate all the expanding demands of society; recreational uses and the pressures for conservation are in conflict on the fringe of cities; housing and industry conflict in their claims on the use of land, and various com-mercial uses are in conflict for the most central and/or accessible locations. And, ultimately, a political decision is necessary to resolve between competing claims and interests on land. Urbanization is no longer the province of the economist, the sociologist, the geographer or the political scientist, but embraces all disciplines and all members of the community. It is, in all its aspects, the concern of society, with several professions seeking to advise and to lead society in those directions which *they* feel to be the most appropriate. Economic efficiency, social justice, physical quality and political expediency each refer to different aims and policies, and have differing degrees of support, in order to achieve the urban future.

Planning, in particular, seeks to direct and control the course of urban affairs and events in the interests of society as a whole. It has developed as a profession from several different roots. It has early antecedents in the founding of pre-industrial cities in the Greek, Roman and mediaeval periods of expansion and there is the

Renaissance concern with urban form, especially in capital cities and in the residential palaces of royalty, the nobility and religious leaders. It gained strength considerably and became more pervading in the Victorian period, when the dismal degradation of the urban environment sparked off a humanitarian and reforming crusade for the improvement of deplorable urban conditions. More recently government is concerned with how best to invest in the urban environment and how to order its priorities. Intellectually, there is increasing academic concern over the nature of policies, their immediate and long-term implications, and how best to cope with the demanding and burgeoning pressures on limited resources. In terms of government there are the often disparate loyalties between national, regional and local interests, and the new yet growing dimension of public participation. Planners are concerned with determining the location and form of future urban environments, but should they receive, accept and incorporate the views of the public on how this environment may best perform and function, or should the planner prepare his own best scheme of possibilities for its due implementation in the light of the political processes of adjustment, amendment and discretion?

In approaching the urban environment of the future, it is impossible for the planner to deal with all aspects and all dimensions of the urban condition. *He must be selective.* He has a limited range of tools at his command to influence the course of future events. Though not intended as an all-inclusive list, his means include at least the following items whereby urban and regional developments might be controlled and/or directed:

1. the availability and location of land;
2. the finances to permit development, including taxation, grant, subsidy and pricing policies;
3. the availability of labour supply, housing occupants and users generally of the land use developments;
4. the location of major utilities including water, sewage disposal facilities and power;
5. the reality of direct government investment to provide the infrastructure to permit development;
6. the extent of control over the means and the availability of communication, including the relative emphasis on private movement and public transportation facilities and their respective speed, costs, frequency, comfort and convenience;
7. the willingness to apply legal sanctions such as zoning procedures, town plans and various types of enactment at the local and national levels of government;

8. the degree of initiative afforded to private enterprise and private capital, relative to community attitudes;

9. the extent of physical constraints in terms of amenity and/or productivity on the use of land;

10. the degree to which control is exercised over the existing pattern of settlement, and its inertia for progress and change;

11. the degree of intervention over densities, the amount of clearance and redevelopment, and those uses to be conserved and retained for future generations;

12. the standards to be applied in terms of mobility, accessibility and for building construction;

13. the degree of acceptance for sociological determinants such as community groupings and social pressures, and the degree of public tolerance for traffic congestion, crime, slums, pollution and land acquisition procedures;

14. the technological abilities of the construction, engineering, architectural and other design professions;

15. the governmental and/or other legislative measures which might be established in order to achieve the best results.

The nature of the planning contribution is to identify needs and issues, to anticipate challenges, to identify goals and objectives, to formulate policies and to prepare strategies for the future which resolve problems, not separately, but with the means available and within their total urban and regional contexts. Planning must specify the spatial impact of alternative policies and strategies, evaluate the alternatives in relation to their several aspects and select the best alternative as a basis for action. Steger and Lakshmanan (1968) suggest that 'such a process by its nature calls into play a creative, subjective, and synthetic thought process on the one hand and an analytic and objective effort on the other. Thus in contextual (goal setting) and synthetic (development of plan alternatives) phases of planning, a great deal of imagination and subjectivity are called for in identifying what goal sets are desired and how existing or new structural and form elements can be combined to produce desired metropolitan futures. However, in the phase of "plan testing" or estimating the impacts of outcomes of alternative policy bundles, analytical techniques play a crucial part.'[1]

It is usual for planners to be optimistic about the future. It is

[1] W. A. Steger and T. R. Lakshmanan, 'Plan Evaluation Methodologies: Some Aspects of Decision Requirements and Analytical Response' in Highway Research Board, *Urban Development Models*, National Research Council (Washington), 1968, p. 47.

presumed that productivity will expand, that real incomes will improve and that industrial production will secure urban progress. The alternatives of decline and decay are not usually considered in planning reports. Large scale epidemics, the destruction of cities by mob violence, and the paralysis or decay of urban cultures are not presented as reasonable possibilities. Rather, the underlying assumptions are that man is capable of rational decisions. The future can be envisaged to some considerable extent, values can be assigned to conflicting issues and the preferences of society can be established. Given adequate information, then it *is* possible for the planner and the decision maker to choose rationally from among a series of competing alternatives. It *is* possible to have better cities in the future than exist today. It *is* possible to advance into the future in some form of orderly and acceptable manner, to relate the various components which exist in an urban environment and to state the consequences of different possible courses of action. The underlying concept is that, if man so desires, he can marshall for his own benefit the complex of forces which affect the form, pattern and quality of his urban environments.

The uncertainty of change provides the central focus of interest and attention. The target is moving. It is to shape the living and working environments of a dynamic society through the use of static components. Houses, roads, industrial buildings and all physical elements of the urban infrastructure are immobile. They are produced at a point of time, but influence the future course of events for decade after decade. The force of historical inertia is great indeed, because of the investment involved and because of people's traditional loyalties and allegiances, but the power of new technological developments increases exponentially, with each exerting an inexorable and accelerating impact on human life focussed in towns and cities. The volume, speed and quality of this change all pose severe problems, and there is as yet no evidence of a decelerating process. The Luddite response (no Concorde aircraft, no lead in petrol) is unlikely to proceed as far as no aircraft and no motor vehicles. This will occur only if we achieve Rachel Carson's prognosis of ecological disaster. All urban functions and activities, their land use and transportation framework, are changing. There are also new organizational factors, new behavioural patterns, new motivations for the investment of capital, new demands for public intervention, new patterns of consumption and new materials, new machines and new ideologies. Each must be appreciated in its emerging form by the planner.

There are also the social and economic revolutions of rising

57

expectations. As average per capita incomes increase, as lower income groups move into the middle income groups of today and as this sharp upward movement will occur over the short period of a few decades, so too will there be burgeoning demands for all types of urban space. Planning, as envisaged by the Victorian middle classes to avoid some of the industrial degradation on the working classes, now extends to all sections of society as population characteristics and attitudes have changed and therefore a wider range of abilities are required from the practitioner.

Planning as a discipline is descended from architecture, engineering and law.[1] Each produces a finite object – a building, a bridge, a statute. The inclusion first of the geographer and then of other social scientists introduced a new dimension. Planning now is conceived as a process of continual development and evolution, in which there can be no ultimate achievement or time-date. But old loyalties also die hard. The City Beautiful, the aesthetics of urban form and the quality of the urban environment are great tenets of urban belief. They remain extremely important as objectives, within the context of the social forces and economic pressures which are operating to change the urban environment. The geographer, nurtured on the physical and spatial dimensions of the urban environment, must extend his vision so that he becomes aware of social, economic, political and technological horizons – and likewise for every other profession concerned with an aspect of the urban problem. Humility rather than arrogance has become the supreme professional requirement of all concerned with urban affairs.

But practice must also be supported by a growing body of theoretical knowledge. The totality of a structure and the working of its many parts must each be envisaged. The motor car or aeroplane, the orchestra and the human body each provide examples of where there are both specialists who probe further and further into particular problems and issues, and generalists who maintain the necessary comprehensive overview of the whole functioning entity as series of mutually inter-related parts. Discussion about the respective merits of each is arid, because neither can function without the other. In the words of the Chairman of an International Planning Forum, 'integration cannot be brought about by magic. It depends on a patient and trustful multi-disciplinary approach by people who are willing to come out of their specialist holes and to work together for a common

[1] For one discussion see A. Faludi, 'The Planning Environment and the Meaning of Planning', *Regional Studies*, Vol. 4, 1970, pp. 1–9 and many volumes of the *Journal of the Town Planning Institute*.

purpose. There is also a matter of education and training. It is of the utmost importance that future leading people, doing their Study at university, are brought into contact with other disciplines, are made to understand the other fellow's language and most of all to get the notion impressed on their mind that a whole is more than the sum total of its parts.'[1]

Thus, in addition to being at the research frontier, the modern planner is at the forefront of contentious inter-disciplinary exercises. The more general academic and professional approach is to study the many separate components in relative isolation, though some geographers, architects, social scientists and utopian writers have attempted a wider synthesis. Thus housing, traffic, employment, ecology, recreation, social conditions, industry and other aspects of the city each have their own body of literature. Central place theory developed in geography, industrial location theory in economics, and urban theory must now combine both with social and behavioural studies in a political context.

The planner must know the objectives for which he is planning and have the analytical ability to translate these into an operational form. This means that he must know about the system being planned, including its existing characteristics and its potential attributes, so that he can appreciate the parameters in which he will be working. He must know about or assume the materials and the resources which are available, in terms of technological possibilities, social acceptance, institutional competence, financial feasibility and physical practicability. He must be able to synthesize, to compose and, intuitively and rationally, to perceive the future. The output from these thought processes will be a series of alternative plans or possibilities for the chosen time-period. The optimal design, the preferred solution is that proposal which best satisfies the goals which have been advocated, and the best course of action then becomes a policy-making problem. The choice between options can be clarified by the use of indices and by devising various comparative measures such as monetary return, effectiveness, efficiency or feasibility for the the community and its various sub-groups. Ingenious mathematical skills may be used to assist with these judgements.

Imagination and systematic abilities, a broad awareness and detailed analysis, are each required by the planning team but, in the

[1] J. Vink, Ministry of Housing and Physical Planning of the Netherlands in Economic Commission for Europe, *The Future Pattern and Forms of Urban Settlements*, Vol. 1, United Nations (New York), 1968, p. 15. Several points in this section have been adopted from this source.

59

final analysis between options, there may be a conflict in values. Different social groups may be affected and conflicts between values may require something different from a planner's view of what is desirable. Public interest, pressure groups and political decisions have their role to play in the dynamics of urban growth. In the words of Teilhard de Chardin, 'however far science pushes its discovery of the Essential Fire, however capable it may one day become of re-shaping and perfecting the human element, it will find itself in the end confronting the same problem: how to give their final value to all and to each of these elements in grouping them within the unity of an Organized Whole'.[1] Planning as an operational procedure involves judgement and choice; it is not a coldly scientific and dispassionate subject, but is rooted in implicit social assumptions.

SUMMARY

Urbanization is an exceedingly complex phenomenon of world-wide importance. It results from, and is being achieved by, a multitude of personal and group decisions so that urban areas, everywhere, are aggrandizing. The starting point for future under-standing must be an evaluation of the present with all its strengths and its weaknesses, and a willingness to act because the future is a 'field of power'. Urban growth is unequal in response to an extensive range of physical, economic, social, political and technological pressures, change is an endemic characteristic of the urban environ-ment and man's intervention in the affairs of the urban environment, though of long standing, has gathered increasing momentum over recent decades. The appreciation has now extended from towns to the wider regional environment of town and country, and earlier considerations of land use have been broadened to encompass the interlocking aspects of transportation and land use within the frame-work of a total urban and regional situation. The planning exercise focusses on the uncertainty of change, and seeks to shape the future environment of a dynamic society by selective means. It undertakes this process both systematically and intuitively, and requires objective knowledge and imaginative judgement in the formulation of policy proposals for action by society.

[1] Quoted from S. Beer, *op. cit.*, p. 370.

Chapter 3
The Terms of Reference and Administrative Background

The main task of this book is to review, on a comparative basis, the technical content of the Regional and Sub-regional Studies which have been introduced in Chapter 1. This assessment may however depend upon or be influenced by how the Study was conducted as an administrative exercise. It may be important to know whether the advice of consultants is 'better' or 'more independent than' that provided by the interested agencies of government, or if some Studies are more 'cautious' or 'politically unreliable' than others. The more desirable means of co-operation between adjacent local planning authorities, how joint units may best be established and staffed, and the operational difficulties involved in establishing inter-departmental and inter-disciplinary teams are important matters of prior concern.[1] These topics are examined after noting the similarities and the contrasts which exist between the Studies in their terms of reference, the particular problems for resolution, and the form and quality of presentation of the final Report.

TERMS OF REFERENCE AND THE PROBLEMS FOR RESOLUTION
The terms of reference for the Teesside Study are

> to take into account the growth envisaged for Teesside both in population and employment and to work out on this basis a unitary plan covering both the disposition of the main land uses and the transport requirements. ... To consider the industrial and commercial functions of the area, the extent to which existing industries may vary and new industries may be attracted, the likely rate of growth of population and employment, and the extent of obsolescence in the physical environment. To produce broad planning proposals for future land uses and relate these to an improved communications system including considering in some detail the question of central area functions ... and the size and distribution of new shopping areas. ... To estimate the cost and feasibility of implementing such a plan.[2]

[1] Relationships between central government departments and local authorities are discussed in J. A. G. Griffith, *Central Departments and Local Authorities*, George Allen and Unwin (London), 1966. [2] *Teesside Study*, p. 4.

The approach in the Study against this background is first to determine urban structure policy, and then to prepare detailed local plans.

The terms of reference for the Leicestershire, Notts–Derby, Warwickshire and North-Glos Studies are similar to a model brief provided for Sub-regional Studies by the then Ministry of Housing and Local Government.

> The object of the study is to prepare proposals for the major land uses in the sub-region, having regard particularly to the development of population, employment, recreation and shopping in relation to each other and to transport. The purpose of the study is to serve as a bridge between regional considerations and the development plans of local planning authorities and to provide the authorities concerned with a common framework within which they can co-ordinate their plans and programmes.[1]

The emphasis on land use, including transportation, should be noted and also the relatively open nature of the terms of reference. The Study directors are not unduly restricted by these directives.

Of the Regional Studies, those for Hampshire and Humberside, by contrast, are 'feasibility' studies for the large-scale accommodation of new populations.[2] Humberside's task 'has been to make a detailed economic and physical study of Humberside and an assessment of the prospects for the planned movement of people into the area on a large scale. . . . [The task was to investigate] the problems, costs and benefits of a large-scale build-up of population.'[3] The Hampshire Study examines 'the physical suitability and potential for development of the Southampton/Portsmouth region; the feasibility of accommodating within that region an intake of population, in addition to natural growth . . . the form and phasing of, and suitable locations for this expansion and for the natural growth of the existing population, with comparisons of the broad costs of any alternative solutions; the impact of such an intake of population upon areas of high amenity value . . . and the steps which should be taken to preserve them and to enhance their value for recreation; the effect of such an intake on the existing major centres of employment within the region, and the steps to be taken to meet it; the provision of an

---

[1] *Leicestershire Study*, p. 5 and *Warwickshire Study*, p. 184.

[2] Analogous in its terms of reference is also the Severnside Study. Central Unit for Environmental Planning, *Severnside – A Feasibility Study*, HMSO (London), 1971. This report was not available in time for consideration in this text.

[3] *Humberside Study*, pp. 1 and 6.

62

adequate system of transport and communications'.[1] The attitude of these Studies is expressed in the Hampshire statement that 'our work has convinced us that testing of feasibility is a vitally important stage in planning. The range of alternatives can be explored, the limits examined and established before time and money are spent on the details of a physical "master plan".'[2]

Different again are the terms of reference for the South East Study. These are, 'to report on patterns of development for the South East . . . with the object of providing a regional framework for the local planning authorities to carry out their planning responsibilities . . . and for government decisions on investment, and economic and social policies relating to the region's future development'.[3]

The problems stated for resolution are thus those which centre upon transportation and land use development including industrial provision, housing location, service centres, recreation amenities, travel facilities and the quality of the environment in order to meet the existing and anticipated demands from a primarily urban population. The various physical, social and economic circumstances of a defined Sub-region or Region must be studied and policies for action recommended. Within this overall context, the specific dimension of the problem varies from locality to locality.

The Teesside Study is concerned with a self-contained industrial region and the other Sub-regional Studies, to a varying extent, with a dominant urban issue, areas of industrial decline, and substantial rural localities with their associated market towns and dependent populations. The challenge of Teesside 'lies in the legacy of nineteenth-century obsolescence; the opportunity is to make it one of the most productive, efficient and beautiful regions in Britain; a region in which future generations will be able to work in clean and healthy conditions, live in dignity and content, and enjoy their leisure in invigorating surroundings'.[4] Leicestershire, more prosaically, is 'East Midland par excellence. . . . A moderately prosperous area. . . . A moderately diversified economy. . . . Renowned for its pasture land. . . . For over 100 years the city and the county together have been growing at a faster rate than the nation. . . . All the signs augur well for the future.'[5] The problems are quite different; rejuvenation and reinvigoration in the first instance, and the positive direction of new developments to retain existing attributes in the second case.

For the Notts–Derby Team, the primary issues are two prosperous and expanding cities adjacent to a declining coalfield area and close

[1] *Hampshire Study*, p. 5.   [2] *Ibid.*, p. 8.   [3] *South East Study*, p. 1.
[4] *Teesside Study*, p. 3.   [5] *Leicestershire Study*, pp. 11 and 15.

to areas of high landscape value, with an intervening county boundary which now prejudices a joint approach to common problems;
Greater Sheffield also sits beyond the northern administrative
boundaries, and exerts its impact into the Sub-region of study. The
North-Glos Study, with comparable terms of reference, does not
have the problems of an intervening County boundary. The Study
was initiated because of concern with an area of rapid and complex
urban growth in and around Gloucester and Cheltenham, but the
area for study was broadened for analytical reasons to cover the
County area west of the Cotswolds' escarpment.[1] The Warwickshire
Study is concerned with a national growth area on the fringe of the
Birmingham Conurbation and acute problems of land supply to meet
expanding urban demands after the mid-1970s.[2]

The Regional Studies all have the common background of an
escalating urban population to be housed somewhere and somehow.
Humberside followed a national review of population trends and
settlement patterns in 1966, which then anticipated a national
growth of fifteen million persons by the end of the century. It
assumed that 'the extra population in Humberside by the end of the
century should for study purpose be 300,000–750,000'.[3]

South Hampshire, in a like vein, was deemed to be suitable for 'a
planned intake of population of the order of 250,000 of which
150,000 should be provided for by 1981. . . . This represents a total
growth of the order of 300,000 by 1981, with provision for a further
intake after that date of the order of 100,000 as well as further natural
growth'.[4] The South East Study is concerned with the most populous
region in Britain. 'There are now over 17 million people living in the
South East. By the end of the century there will be four or five
millions more and the pressures on the environment, already formidable, are bound to increase. The Report seeks to deal with this
prospect.'[5]

In terms of the extent of the Study Area, this is confined to the
dimensions as prescribed or the administrative coverage of the
Commissioning Authorities for physical and land use surveys, and
for all strategic decisions. It normally extends beyond the boundaries
for socio-economic studies, in order to determine the external repercussions into the sub-region and the out-going factors such as

[1] *North-Glos Study*, p. 4.   [2] *Warwickshire Study*, pp. 6–7.

[3] *Humberside Study*, p. 1. Parallel Studies are for Severnside (not available at
January 1971) and for Tayside – *Tayside: Potential for Development*, HMSO (Edinburgh), 1970.

[4] *Hampshire Study*, p. 4.   [5] *South East Study*, p. ix.

journey-to-work or journey-to-shopping from the area under review. This coverage later raises the question of the relationship between the findings of the Study, and the reform of local government structure and the boundaries of the envisaged larger authorities.

THE PRESENTATION OF THE STUDIES

The Leicestershire, Humberside, Hampshire and Warwickshire Studies are written as complete and inclusive reports. The technical appendices are published at the same time as the major Report, and are included either in the main text or in companion volumes. This supplementary material is published at a later date for the Teesside, South East and North-Glos Studies. In the Notts–Derby instance, the forty Technical Record Reports are unedited; they have been written as internal office reports by members of the planning team and have not been approved by the Management Committee for publication. In some Studies (e.g. Leicestershire) detailed papers were prepared for the Officers of the Local Planning Authorities, but these have not been published.

Certain of the Studies may be criticized in this respect. A volume of technical appendices in a revised and corrected form should always be published to accompany the principal Report, in order both to provide the necessary documentation for interested lay and professional persons and to demonstrate with clarity the nature of the techniques which have been adopted. This thought is given additional weight by the fact that all Studies pioneer new ways of understanding and projecting the regional and sub-regional environment. Incidentally, the only report thoughtfully to provide an index in order to assist the reader is the Humberside Study. The cost of all Reports should be low to encourage their purchase and as a contribution towards citizen participation.

Ideally, every Report should be presented in three parts, though no Study yet meets the exacting requirements of:

a. A Summary Booklet, identifying the main arguments and the principal conclusions for free distribution to all organizations, schools, libraries, institutions, public bodies, elected representatives and members of the public in the study area.

b. The Major Report, with a full range of summary statistics and diagrams, and with the text presenting the evidence from several surveys to describe their interrelationships, and to suggest how and why alternative strategies are selected and evaluated. The details of

C

the preferred strategy would then be presented, with clarity and conviction.

c. The Technical Appendices, presenting in detail the methods of approach which were used throughout the planning investigations and describing, in particular, the sequence of assumptions which are necessarily made at each stage of the analysis.

The difficulty in achieving this desirable range of publication is that the Sub-regional Studies have been commissioned by local planning authorities, and their purpose is to resolve planning issues by suggesting and achieving solutions. The costs involved in their preparation, in terms of staff time and the pressure of other work commitments, must normally preclude introspective and analytical reports on work procedures. The need however exists. The Ministry of Environment, as the government department responsible for planning matters, might well initiate a methodological series to introduce new techniques of investigation and analytical procedures to a wider audience. As one Study Director has written, 'the report we published was written for the purposes of Sub-regional discussion. Nobody would pay us to write up our methods for the benefit of the profession.'[1] Conferences and professional symposia[2] also have an important role to play in the dissemination of new techniques, as do the pages of the professional journals, but the regular publication of papers on research methodology (or summary evaluations of recent techniques) would also assist materially on this matter.

The purpose of publication varies. The Warwickshire Report 'is being published immediately upon being received, because before taking any decisions the authorities wish to discuss it with the public, with County District Councils in Warwickshire, with other authorities and organizations, and with government departments. The Councils are embarking on Consultations . . . so that the implications of the Report can be fully discussed before the Council decide.'[3] The North-Glos Report 'is intentionally written in general terms so as to enable a broad section of the public to consider the issues raised, and to take part in the processes which will eventually establish the basis for planning the future development of North Gloucestershire'.[4] By contrast with this request for public discernment, the Notts–Derby, Leicestershire and Teesside Studies are more in the nature of advice to the elected members of the local planning authorities

[1] Personal communication to the author.
[2] See, for example, Centre for Environmental Studies, *Papers from the Seminar on the Process of the Notts–Derby Sub-Regional Study*, CES 1 P 11 (London), 1970.
[3] *Warwickshire Study*, p. 2.   [4] *North-Glos Study*, Preface.

commissioning the study. The Notts–Derby Study is 'confined to conclusions, explanations and recommendations'.[1] It also notes that there may be conflict between the aims of the policies; 'it will then be necessary for the people of the sub-region to decide, through their elected representatives, the extent to which one shall have priority over another'.[2] This difference between the purpose of the Sub-regional Reports is interesting – two referring the issues to a broad section on the public, and three emphasizing more the role of elected representatives. It is relevant to ask, whom should strategic planning reports be written for – the public, or elected representatives? The Teesside Study refers to 'urban structure policy', the Leicestershire, South East, Warwickshire and Notts–Derby Studies each present a 'recommended' strategy, whereas the North-Glos and South Hampshire Studies refer to a 'preferred' strategy or structure. Do these phrases imply subtle differences in outlook?

In terms of readability and the quality of presentation, all Reports attain a very high standard of competence. They may be used, for example, by adult discussion groups concerned with examining community problems. Public discussion is possible on the issues which are raised, and information is made available in a clear and concise form on the complex and difficult subject of policy formulation. They make a valid contribution within the context that, as Hender (1970) notes, 'the greatest political change of the present time is the growth in public awareness of the needs of a community and an increasing regard for the social and environmental conditions in which people live. This is shown by a greater degree of sensitivity to the actions of public bodies and a move toward more public participation in their decisions. This is something to welcome.'[3] The publication of original technical material and the basic evidence which underlies planning policy provides one critical stage in this process of public enlightenment. All the Studies deserve credit in this respect.

ORGANIZATIONAL AND ADMINISTRATIVE BACKGROUND[4]

Some preliminary differences between the Studies may be noted

[1] *Notts–Derby Study*, p. 1.   [2] *Ibid.*, p. 1.

[3] J. D. Hender, 'The urban political process and the role of the planner', *Town and Country Planning Summer School 1970, Report of Proceedings*, Town Planning Institute, p. 7.

[4] Some of the ideas in this section are based on R. M. Zettel and R. Carll, *Summary Review of Major Metropolitan Area Transportation Studies in the United States*, Institute of Transportation and Traffic Engineering, University of

immediately. The Humberside and South East Studies are directed by Senior Officers of the Central Government, the Teesside and Hampshire Studies by Consultants, the Leicestershire, Warwickshire and Notts–Derby Studies by independent Study Teams appointed by the Commissioning Authorities, and the North-Glos Study is achieved through a collaborative effort by the responsible Local Planning Authorities. Of the Sub-regional Studies, Teesside and North-Glos include the two most vitally involved Government Departments on their Steering Committee. Publication is by the Local Planning Authorities for the North-Glos, Leicestershire, Notts–Derby and Warwickshire Studies, and by H.M. Stationery Office for Teesside and for all Regional Studies.

1. *The Role of the Study Leader*

The organization of the Study raises many interesting administrative and management questions, including the contribution of the 'team leader'. He has to manage the Study, and should be appointed at an early stage of the proceedings. His preliminary task must be to define the nature of the methodological inquiries, to indicate the range of relevant data to be collected and the degree of analysis and interpretation, to formulate a work schedule and to devise an organizational structure for his team so that the work to be undertaken can proceed as a systematic exercise. Towards the end of the programme the writing of the final report will usually be his responsibility. Technical reports may be in the same style, but are more likely to be written by members of the planning team. How was the Director selected and could he personally recruit staff, or were they seconded from existing planning and highway authorities? If on loan to the Study, was he freed of other assignments and all immediate problems, so that he could focus his whole attention on long-term strategies? Were outside specialists or consultants appointed, or had reliance to be placed on his own staff and the resources (staff, computer facilities) of the commissioning authorities? Was legal, financial, administrative and clerical assistance made available? Did his powers include publication, or had he to report through a management committee?

To a considerable extent, the whole nature of the study and the

California (Berkeley), 1962, pp. 8–18. For a recent study of decision making in local government see J. K. Friend and W. N. Jessop, *Local Government and Strategic Choice: An Operational Research Approach to the Process of Public Planning*, Tavistock Publications (London), 1969.

quality of its final recommendations will depend upon the prowess and professional attitude of the Director. For example, the Director of the Notts–Derby Study has written that, 'from the outset the study was conditioned by a number of decisions made by myself which, for tactical reasons, have never been made public. The most important decision was that the principal study recommendations must be agreed with the chief planning officers and other relevant chief officers of the four authorities sponsoring our work before they were presented to elected members and the public. Without such agreement there would be no hope of the plan's being accepted by all four authorities.'[1] But also, with such an agreement innovatory ideas may be resisted and the nature of the advice provided has to be 'acceptable' to a larger degree than might otherwise be considered desirable. However, in this instance, 'the study recommendations have been adopted in principle and in some detail by the four local planning authorities who commissioned the work',[2] so this type of agreement presumably facilitated the achievement of the recommended strategy. There are complex and subtle distinctions between the 'best professional advice', and 'the most acceptable recommendation likely to be achieved in practice'. It should also be noted that the planning strategy as a technical formulation of the problem is not prepared in isolation or independent from the political and social processes of decision making.

2. *The Policy, Advisory, Steering and Technical Committees*

A Steering or Management Committee is often indicated in the Preface to the Reports. Full details would be welcome about Committee structure, their respective functions, the nature of the guidance provided, and the working relationships between the Committee members and the Study Director and/or the planning team. How were the Committee members appointed? Did participation include only elected representatives, or were agencies, the lower tier district authorities and/or the public represented? Were discussions open to the press? What degree of financial control was exercised? Were 'liaison functions' with government departments undertaken by Committee members? Was their role constructive, or defensive? Did a committee have to 'approve' the possible alternatives, or the

---

[1] A. Thorburn, 'Preparing a regional plan: how we set about the task in Nottinghamshire/Derbyshire', *Journal of the Town Planning Institute*, Vol. 57, 1971, p. 216.

[2] *Ibid.*, p. 216.

methods of evaluation, or the preferred strategy? Were voting procedures used in Committee and, if so, were all agencies and representatives entitled to equal votes? Do financial contributions to the cost of the Study imply control over its work programme or conclusions?

Such points are of both administrative and professional interest, because most Studies have one or two dominant urban localities, and also many smaller divisions by either population or area. These localities may be the recipients of urban development in certain of the envisaged strategies. The future may broadly be as now, or major changes might be proposed. Sharp political differences may thus exist between the urban, suburban and rural parts of the region under review because of their different social and economic circumstances. Are such differences, either as they now exist or as they may exist, recognized in the organizational structure and control of the Study?

3. *The Cost of the Study*

How was the Study financed, and how much did it cost? Were funds sufficient to conduct the necessary surveys, or to buy computer time? Could funds be augmented to meet additional or unexpected needs, or was the cost fixed in advance? What assistance was provided by the supporting agencies? How were the central office costs apportioned? Were funds available for research to innovate new techniques? What special investigations are included under the costs? On such points Masser (1970) has stated that 'most of the models used in these studies are crude in the extreme. . . . This is due partly to the poor quality of the data base . . . and also to deficiencies in the technical facilities available. Apart from Teesside, a major obstacle to the development of models was the shortage of money, and the results have been obtained on budgets which many American studies would find laughable. One lesson to be learnt from these studies is that, if real progress is to be made, there should be much better provision in future for both work data collection and technical assistance for this purpose'.[1] It would be interesting to know for each Study, not only its total cost, but its breakdown as between salaries, computer time and special surveys, such as air photographic work and social studies. The only known data are that the Teesside Study

[1] I. Masser, 'Methods of Sub-regional Analysis: A Review of Four Recent Studies' (Leicestershire, Teesside, Humberside and Notts–Derby), *Town Planning Review*, Vol. 41, 1970, p. 158.

is reputed to have cost £400,000 or ten times the Leicestershire amount of £40,000,[1] the Notts–Derby Study £100,000 and the Warwickshire Study £75,000.[2] Secretarial and other assistance is usually available from the Local Planning Authorities, in addition.

4. *The Length of the Study*

The period of time from commissioning date to the publication of the report has been indicated in Chapter 1 and, though normally about two years, may extend up to four. If a period of one year is then added for consultation and public involvement, and in most cases the translation of sub-regional strategies into the official content of structure plans must also be taken into account, at least four to five years are likely between commissioning date and the approval for action of the recommended strategy. Are the Studies too ambitious, and can this period be shortened without destroying the effectiveness of the planning process? Would additional funds permit a speedier production, or would greater speed jeopardize the efficiency of the work schedule? Does any significance attach to the fact that the political complexion of government (which often initiates the Study) can change between the initiation and completion of the Study? Can the 'quality' of the study, its 'research-inventiveness' and its contribution to the 'advancement of thought' be related to the time-factor or cost of production? Can later studies benefit from regular reviews of the available material, as in this text? Can intermediate results from the Studies be used in the formulation of planning proposals? How may data banks be used to decrease the length of time spent on Studies? Would more time on planning the Study reduce the overall time commitment?

It is important also to note the tyranny of a time schedule, especially when innovatory work is involved. This point is well made for the Leicestershire Study. Its director notes that young recently qualified personnel were appointed, the low budget limits had to be respected and manual procedures of handling data were used. 'The absolute time limit of 2 years had to be upheld. Authorities on fully computerized mathematical models have maintained that two years is a reasonable minimum period for research, development and testing before any operational runs can be attempted. Clearly we had to

---

[1] *Ibid.*, p. 151 and J. B. McLoughlin, 'Simulation for Beginners, The Planting of a Sub-regional Model System,' *Regional Studies*, Vol. 3, 1969, p. 314.

[2] *Warwickshire Study*, p. 24. Extra grant assistance from the Department of the Environment is also referred to.

borrow and adapt methods which could reasonably be expected to give useful results within a short time. The prime objective was a sub-regional plan rather than model research and development.'[1] It is not easy to conduct advanced research under such rigid conditions.

Research in an operational setting invariably presents special problems both for the team and the commissioning authorities. The latter require advice on situations of uncertainty where an explicit choice is being considered between two or more alternative courses of action. The former can always justify the need for more research, in the sense of further investigations to improve the technical basis of the decision-making process. There must be some form of balance between the extremes. On this point the Director of the Notts–Derby Study has commented, 'when the Study was started the Authorities indicated that the advice was wanted within one year. . . . I think that was a reasonable attitude to take. In fact, the time taken was fifteen months from the date of assembly of the full staff to the beginning of printing the report. . . . It seemed that if we took too little time, our advice would be poor; too much time and it would be too late, unnecessarily detailed, or have diminished in usefulness due to the interval between information collection and decisions. In practice it was necessary to draw up a firm timetable with working deadlines every few weeks, and to cut information collection or processing whenever it looked as if we were getting behind.'[2]

The sheer fact that the Studies were completed within time schedules approximating to their deadline periods represents a considerable compliment to the teams involved. A salutary reminder in the opposite direction is provided from the comparable American metropolitan studies, where some have not fulfilled their objectives after several years of endeavour. Boyce and Day (1969) observe that 'considerable difficulties and delays were experienced in operationalizing the theoretical models, and these were compounded by appreciable data management problems. Consequently, the number of alternatives prepared and the differences among them were severely limited, and work schedules were drastically revised, often resulting in a loss of credibility for the planning effort. Alternatively, agencies resorted to crude short cuts, interim plans, or dropped the use of mathematical models altogether to stay somewhat close to schedule.'[3]

[1] J. B. McLoughlin, *op. cit.*, p. 315.

[2] A. Thorburn, 'The decision orientated framework for the Study', in Centre for Environmental Studies, *op. cit.*, p. 15.

[3] D. E. Boyce and N. D. Day, *Metropolitan Plan Evaluation Methodology*, Institute for Environmental Studies, University of Pennsylvania (Philadelphia), 1969, p. 14.

Such strictures cannot be applied to the British Studies; they have been completed *and* provide a marked advance in techniques.

The reason for this more favourable outcome may indeed be budget stringency. In the words of the Warwickshire Study, 'the budget made it necessary to clearly define the priorities in our work. It made it clear that surveys, forecasting and computing had to be aimed primarily at the needs of the Study. . . . The computer data file and its accompanying programs could not be extended to the authorities' wider needs for structure planning. . . . The budget and the relatively limited period of two years available to complete the Study precluded attempts to construct and calibrate any comprehensive or computer models.'[1]

5. *The Staff Involved*

The Studies have generally employed their own professional staff, but against the difficulty that the appointment of Staff and Director are for a relatively short term duration compared with the prospects of more permanent employment in the civil service and local government. In addition, there has usually been some secondment of senior personnel from the commissioning authorities, which assists materially both with the provision of information and with subsequent monitoring and implementation procedures. In other instances independent staffing is the preferred solution, often with a commitment to full-time employment in one or other of the constituent authorities upon completion of the Study. A range of inter-disciplinary professional talent has been engaged in each Study rather than just planners *per se* and, towards the end of a Study, there are frequently staffing difficulties as some of the professional talent may disperse to new employment opportunities. The commissioning authorities have assisted with clerical, draughting and other non-technical staff and, upon completion of the exercise, a proportion of the senior personnel may be employed by the permanent monitoring body to ensure continuity in the planning process as in the Notts–Derby situation.

In terms of staffing the Sub-regional studies it would seem that the North-Glos Study is the exception in that, of the Staff involved in the Study, 'none of these persons was appointed specifically for this work or was engaged on it full-time'.[2] The work of the Study was on a part-time basis, 'subject to the manpower requirements of a previously committed work programme';[3] it involved for varying

[1] *Warwickshire Study*, p. 24.   [2] *North-Glos Study*, p. ix.   [3] *Ibid.*, p. 4.

periods twelve members of the technical staff in the County Planning Department including the Study Leader, four in the County Surveyors Department, and three in the City of Gloucester's Engineering and Planning Department. The Leicestershire Study lists a technical staff of eleven, including the secondment of an assistant director from each sponsoring authority.[1] The Notts–Derby Study had a technical staff of ten, a transportation project leader, an assistant director and a director;[2] the Warwickshire team eleven technical staff plus four who are described as part-time.[3] These staff resources are extremely limited for the task in hand, and do not exceed ten to twenty persons to design the living conditions of several hundred thousand persons over a thirty year period.

'Think-tank' resources are also used by each Sub-regional Study. Notts–Derby acknowledge external assistance in developing their three models on transportation, population and employment, and shopping centres. The Director of the Leicestershire Study provided guidance on technical matters to the North-Glos Study, the Teesside consultants refer to three sources of external advice and the Warwickshire Study to external advice on operations research and transportation. In addition, county resources such as computer facilities are used extensively and all Studies acknowledge the advice received on technical matters from government departments. An important aspect of each Study is that techniques, ideas and methods are exchanged frequently between members of the different study teams by informal discussion and to some extent by using the same consultants for certain phases of the work.

THE CONDUCT OF THE STUDIES

As a supplement to the above details and as a contribution towards the several questions that have been posed, a brief questionnaire was sent to team leaders against the promise of strict anonymity. Six questions were asked:

1 As Study Leader to what extent were you free to choose your own team within a given budget?

2. As Study Leader, what degree of freedom had you in the preparation of the final report? Had this to be approved by any group and if so which, or does it depend *solely* on your own professional judgement?

---

[1] *Leicestershire Study*, p. 105.   [2] *Notts–Derby Study*, Preface.
[3] *Warwickshire Study*, p. ix.

3. What was the contribution of your various guiding committees to the generation and testing of alternative strategies?

4. With the hindsight of experience, what changes would you advocate in terms of (a) your internal administrative arrangements and (b) your working relationships with the commissioning authorities and other external groups?

5. Were there any particular difficulties in staffing the Study, given that it was a commitment over a relatively short period of time?

6. Who determined the budget, and how adequate was it; i.e. did financial stringency jeopardize any particular aspect of your study?

The response was most gratifying.[1] The impressions gathered from discussions and correspondence are that the team leaders had a considerable degree of genuine independence. The first stage is the appointment of staff. This was normally at either so many posts and their grades, or within the context of a total salary budget. The team leader could usually interview applicants, and had the power both of appointment and to select the range of required skills, but salaries paid to individuals had generally to be comparable with appointments elsewhere so that special inducements could not be offered. In some instances it was not possible to obtain the desired range of talent, and a team may have been deficient in a particular skill. Advice in this professional area could usually be obtained from one or other of the commissioning authorities or consultants. Staffing is not generally seen as a problem despite the short-term nature of the work programme, but commitments to subsequent employment by one of the commissioning authorities or in government is essential.

Some special consideration should be given to the appointment of the team leader. It is easier to appoint junior staff than to invite the more senior personnel and mature professionals to posts of only two or three years' duration. More secondment arrangements from Universities and from government might here be made against grant assistance from central government (e.g. payment of existing superannuation contributions, housing provision). The major problem in making appointments is therefore the length of the contract and the associated personal and domestic arrangements for senior staff. Short-term contracts at the junior end, with the additional opportunity of advanced and pioneer work in an operational research

[1] It is acknowledged with special thanks by the author. The comments which follow represent generalized statements, and my own interpretation from this response and interview. As the coverage by questionnaire is broader than the eight Studies under review and is not inclusive of these Studies, the comments which follow cannot be related back to any Study (which may not have been included). Nor can they be attributed to any individual.

75

setting, are regarded as a positive virtue by some junior appointees. Secondment of staff from existing authorities may also sometimes pose difficulties because, again, senior personnel are involved, there are only a limited number of mature professional planners available anyway and the established authorities have existing commitments to work which may need the same talents as required by the Study.

The team leader either wrote or edited the first draft of the final report, and normally had full discretion within the dictates of professional conscience and judgement about its content. Often the whole staff would participate in this exercise and it may therefore at this stage, and often in its final form, be described as 'an agreed co-operative effort'. Variations then exist between the Studies in the procedures which follow. The draft report rarely had to be approved, but it may have been scrutinized by chief officers, or put formally to a steering committee to obtain useful comment on points of detail, or be circulated to a limited group for their observations. Deletions, improvements, and occasionally 'alterations against my advice', 'modifications by the committee', 'political amendments' or 'tactical changes' are incorporated in parts of the published version. These changes may be substantial at particular points in the presentation in a small number of instances. The controlling power of the Committee, if any, was over publication and the degree of freedom given to the team leader at this stage.

The teams generally worked away from the political process and/or usual government procedures, and were independent of external control. The internal office atmosphere was informal and more akin to an 'atelier' than to a formal organization. The Studies were set up to perform a given task within a given budget, and were generally given sufficient freedom to proceed with the preparation of a report divorced from routine office work. Committees did not determine the form of the work in the sense of providing direction, but their guidance was appreciated. Ideas could be tested for a considered reaction, objectives tested for their validity, and methodology discussed. There could be reports on the programme of work, the range of alternatives and on intended evaluation techniques, and a check that the evidence to be provided would be wide and deep enough for the authorities. Some team leaders have reported that it was sometimes difficult to get sufficient comment on techniques. In one instance 'a criticism of our intended evaluation procedure was made. I was glad of this, because we were able to turn it back to ask for further advice on improved methods. When a month later the critic reported that he now agreed with our procedure, it was another step in the right direction of obtaining the authorities' acceptance of the recommended strategy'! The role of committees was generally that of assistance, rather than control or guidance, and the team were free to absorb or reject comments as they saw fit.

The question about hindsight resulted in several suggestions. Changes in the team during the course of the study should be avoided if possible. 'Extra clerical help', 'more secretarial assistance', 'the presence of a high level administrator with the team', 'more meetings to discuss and explain the language and significance of techniques', 'the happiest experience of my professional life', 'more understanding by the Commissioning Authorities about the purpose of the Study and its functions', and either more or less integration with other comparable work and government departments are among the points made. Some team leaders felt rather too remote and isolated; others too close to involvement in day by day affairs. More *formal* contacts with government and various operative agencies would sometimes have been welcomed, and continuity in all staff appointments throughout the whole period of study until the final report is in the hands of the publisher are recommended. The final run-down period in staff also often poses exceptionally severe demands on the senior personnel.

About the availability of resources generally, one team leader after making various comments, could state that 'on reflection I could not say that any aspect was thereby jeopardized'. Another, 'we fitted the programme of work to the budget available, and having adopted those limitations, I cannot now say that we went seriously short of money', or 'I don't regret not doing anything which we would have been tempted to if the money had been available'. Or, 'it would, of course, have been possible, with more resources, to have analysed certain aspects in greater depth; one would always "do more with more", but I am by no means sure that any extra would have been significant to the recommendations of the team or justifiable in terms of the other use to which such resources are put'. In a similar vein, 'strict economy in professional time on certain projects was exercised which, at the time, was thought to be detrimental, but now I do not believe this to be so'. These answers are extremely honest. They must not be read as implying the need for financial stringency but, compared with the North American experience of both larger budgets and many uncompleted planning studies, the experience in England has been fruitful of results which may reasonably be described as independent and free from political control and direction. The Reports present a valid professional appreciation of the urban future.

77

The break-up of their Study teams upon completion of the planning exercise is a matter for regret by many of the team leaders. As the sub-regional planning process is frequently described in the Reports as a 'learning procedure', there is a fear that the cumulative wisdom and experience gained will be lost. As one team leader has stated about his Study, 'we were entering an almost unknown field of activity. One of the problems with such projects is that there tends to be no continuity of the teams or even of personnel and any study which can draw the necessary lessons is of great value. Certainly we could have carried out another sub-regional study derived from the benefits of our work on this sub-region but, of course, things never happen in that way.'

Despite this waste through the lack of continuity and the dissipation of staff resources, substantial organizational and educational achievements have been derived from each Study. Technical officers from a number of local authorities have been brought into contact with novel ideas and interesting possibilities about long-term strategic planning, and also with certain of the new techniques which are now available for resolving complex urban issues. There has been a close inter-association and working arrangements between adjacent local authorities, and with and between departments of central government, on issues of mutual concern. The barriers to inter-professional communication have been lowered slightly by the employment of inter-disciplinary teams. Through presentations to steering and management committees and with the publication of the Reports, some elected officers and members of the public have received a greater understanding of the decision-making process for future urban and regional environments. At the personal and professional levels of involvement, further insights have been obtained about the requirements and the difficulties of public policy formulation. It may be that these aspects will provide the basis for considerable further advances over the next decade as structure planning and policy formulation come more to the forefront of the planning process.

SUMMARY

The terms of reference for the Studies emphasize a physical approach to issues of land use and urban development but, as the problems for resolution differ from locality to locality, each Report is a distinctive document. Many points of administrative and organizational detail are introduced, and the information available from the Studies is supplemented by the response to a questionnaire. A field of fruitful research in urban politics is here available for examination. The results should be of particular interest, as all the Sub-regional and Regional Studies by definition involve some form of co-operation between more than one local planning authority and cross the boundaries between government departments to resolve problems of mutal concern. They involve many functional departments, and both different units and different levels of government. It could be that embarrassing difficulties would sometimes be described, because neither professional nor inter-government co-operation is necessarily an easy venture, but planning as a professional discipline should be as much concerned with these topics as with the technical content to be discussed over the ensuing pages.

Part 2

THE CONTENT OF THE STUDIES

'Regional planning is, in the deepest sense, a policy that should result in a reorganization of space and man's habitat which will give him an optimum environment in which he and the community to which he belongs will find the best possible conditions, both material and spiritual. Hence, the term implies an intention to provide the country – and accordingly also society – with a certain structure deliberately selected by the community for reasons which are only partially economic ones.'

Regional Planning: A European Problem, Council of Europe, 1968, p. 28

Chapter 4
The Physical Environment

A prior planning task is to state the physical constraints which exist on major urban developments, and then to specify the effects of each constraint so that the optimal solution may be envisaged. If the constraints are changed, this will alter the position and change the opportunities for development. Intricate problems of choice, definition and significance are involved for each variable, and no one constraint can be absolute and inviolate under all circumstances. Each is more an expression of reluctance to develop for some social, economic or technical reason than a complete and irrevocable embargo. The attitudes of the Studies to such issues will be examined in this chapter.

PHYSICAL CONSTRAINTS AND THE FORMULATION OF ALTERNATIVE SUB-REGIONAL STRATEGIES

One avowed purpose of Town and Country Planning is to protect the rural scene through its planning and development control procedures. To some people, this provides its greatest *raison d'être* and its most marked successes. As Bracey (1970) notes, 'in its modern form, planning has been operating in Great Britain for some twenty years and it has made many enemies, but one shudders when one considers what the condition of the countryside would have been today had the slender planning controls which existed before World War II been carried over into the postwar period. In moments of gloom, one has to admit, however, that the greatest successes of planners have been negative ones, in preventing undesirable development.'[1]

Planners are the custodians for those virtues which exist in the landscape. The phrase, England's green and pleasant land, is no misnomer. Every county has its historic landmarks, its scenic attractions, its architectural glories and its staunch protectors of the established scene. Every town has its more dignified localities, its settings which are pleasing to the eye, and its buildings of local association and community pride. The rivers, hills, moorland, the coastline and the countryside generally are extolled for their beauty.

[1] H. E. Bracey, *People and the Countryside*, Routledge and Kegan Paul (London), 1970, p. 123.

There is a pride in the past, a love of the present, and a trust that our present glories will be handed down to oncoming generations to embellish their lives. A strong depth of sentiment exists in Britain for the countryside. Much of our traditional literature, poetry, music, painting, songs and hymns praise the charm and pleasantness of the rural scene. It has become an ingrained part of the British way of life which should be protected and safeguarded for the advantage of present and future generations.

All Studies accept this very considerable challenge, and make firm recommendations on these issues in their preferred strategies. Thus all the Sub-regional Studies refer to those physical limitations which place constraints on land for major urban development. Such areas are therefore excluded from consideration whenever possible in the final selection of the preferred strategy. Although the intent is the same, the details however vary from Study to Study. In the first place, the several localities have different environmental backgrounds in terms of their resource endowment, natural features and physical landscape. Second, there are the considerable problems of precise definition and demarcation of boundaries, for example, various interpretations are possible of 'floodlands', a 'scenic resource' or 'high quality agricultural land'. It is easy enough to state that such localities should not be developed, but at what precise position on the ground is there a transition from an unacceptable to an acceptable site for development? Third, having identified the localities to be constrained, at what stage in the processes of thought should the weight of urban pressures be accepted in order to justify the use of a resource for urban purposes? Can social and economic values be placed on a resource so that the relative importance of two different resources can be measured? These questions suggest that substantial value judgements are involved in each strategic decision about physical constraints on land development, and the nature of these assumptions at the sub-regional level will now be demonstrated. Individual references and source material will not generally be cited.[1]

Constraints are sub-divided into categories based on their degree of severity in the Leicestershire and Notts–Derby Studies, but are presented under one heading only in the North-Glos and Teesside Studies. Leicestershire distinguishes between 'land upon which we would try not to allocate any development in any strategy', 'land

[1] Unless otherwise stated, references are to *North-Glos Study*, pp. 57–60; *Notts–Derby Study*, Record Reports 24 and 34; *Leicestershire Study*, Vol. I, pp. 32–3 and Vol. II, pp. 125–32, 143–5; *Teesside Study*, Vol. I, pp. 28–32; *Warwickshire Study*, pp. 121–55.

upon which only modest growth would be allowed', and 'land constraints applicable in only certain strategies'. Notts–Derby distinguishes between major constraints which are 'absolutely inviolable except under extreme duress', and minor constraints which 'would be left free of development where possible'. North-Glos identifies 'the decisive physical factor which would almost completely inhibit development on a large scale'. Teesside examines 'the suitability of different parts of the area for different types of activity purely from the points of view of landscape resources and the natural environment to establish the main geographical constraints on future urban development.' Warwickshire's priorities in the rural areas are 'based on four criteria representing the merits of an area and three factors denoting the extent to which it is threatened and how far it is vulnerable to these threats.' The merit criteria are landscape value, wild-life potential, agricultural land quality and townscape quality. 'These measures were sufficient to establish the inherent quality of an area, but to determine absolute priorities it was essential to consider to what extent each area was threatened by urban or population pressures and how far it was vulnerable to these.' The vulnerability factors are the degree of accessibility by road access, footpath access and proximity to population.

The interpretation of the physical environment as expressed in the Sub-regional Studies is as follows:[1]

1. *Areas of no development.* Areas which should *not* receive large-scale development invariably include those sites and areas already subject to strong protection and controls such as national parks, national trust properties, conservation areas, reservoirs, protected water catchment areas, forestry commission holdings, ancient monuments, sites of special scientific and historic interest, areas of outstanding natural beauty, and localities with tree preservation orders.[2] In addition all Studies identify their areas of special landscape, scenic or amenity value, generally admitting that these surveys of landscape quality depend on subjective judgements and that the precise boundaries are indeterminate; in the words of Leicestershire, 'the boundaries between zones represented transitions between one sort of landscape and another rather than firm lines

[1] For a general discussion of physical and other background studies in planning see J. N. Jackson, *Surveys for Town and Country Planning*, Hutchinson University Library (London), 1961.
[2] See F. H. B. Layfield, 'Powers for Conservation', *Journal of the Town Planning Institute*, Vol. 57, 1971, pp. 142–51.

across which marked differences could be observed'. Few people will quarrel with the above designations, though many would seek for some extension of these inviolate zones. The remaining items are subject to greater degrees of controversy and variance between the Reports.

2. *Floodland.*[1] Floodland is certainly a constraint, but interpretations vary. Thus North-Glos consider as generally unsuitable for development 'areas defined as washlands, within and adjoining the Severn flood-plain, or where the land lies within 8 feet of previously known floods.' Their argument is that 'the risk of inundation by flood water from the River Severn is the most important and decisive of natural restraints to the location of new development'. Notts–Derby in the different circumstances of the Trent Valley consider that 'essential washland is that land which floods more frequently than once in 25 years to a depth greater than 6 inches;' non-essential washland can be flooded, but less frequently than once every 25 years, and development is possible with precautions. Development in the flood plain is regarded as feasible but with additional costs being involved to raise land above flood level; the recommended floor level is two feet above the highest known flood level. Likewise, in Leicestershire, floodland would be 'relaxed if necessary to permit development' in the Soar Valley.

Apart from the possibilities of raising land or placing buildings on stilts or flood control measures, the strategic planning problem is to balance the advantages of urban use against the disadvantageous extra costs which are incurred by this development. Also the location of certain urban uses in flood plains is permissible, as periodic inundations do not necessarily provide a problem and can be beneficial for playing fields, seasonal car parking or agricultural activities. Further, the régime of a river can be changed by forestry practice, the drainage of peat, reservoirs for the storage of water, or water abstraction schemes in the upper river catchment areas. Flooding is not a fixed, but a variable element, and various assumptions are possible about development in its limits.

A related topic is drainage, including the capacity of local surface-drainage systems to cater for additional run-off, but this item is more generally included as an adverse factor in the assessment of costs than as a physical constraint. As the Leicestershire Study observes, 'it seemed clear to us that in the long term no land should be

[1] This information is generally made available by the River and Drainage Authorities.

incapable of being developed on drainage grounds, but the work and expenditure involved was obviously a retarding factor.'

3. Agricultural land. The general planning policy in all Sub-regional Studies is that high-grade agricultural land shall not be diverted to other uses, where land of lower potential is available. This is interpreted against a national system of land classification, which grades all land to one of five categories.[1] Grades I and II are of the highest quality with deep, well-drained soils on gently sloping sites to produce high yields of a wide range of crops; these sites are normally excluded from development.

Grade III land is of average quality, provides much of the general purpose farm land in the country, but lacks the versatility and flexibility of cropping which is the hallmark of the best land. Teesside, Leicestershire and Notts–Derby argue that it should 'preferably' remain in agriculture use, or that it is 'a minor constraint which would be left free of development where possible'. Leicestershire, to assist their evaluation procedures, obtained from the Ministry of Agriculture a further breakdown to identify a Grade III category of 'land which just failed to achieve Grade II standard'. In Warwickshire, where most of the land is Grade III and where about 6 per cent of the Sub-region's total will go out of use between 1976 and 1991, 'special consideration was given to the conservation of agricultural land. . . . The recommended strategy has the conservation of agricultural land as a major policy.'

All studies accept that Grade IV and V, of below average quality and limited in both the range and quantity of crops which can be grown, *may* be used for urban development purposes without disadvantage. This policy is not, however, always practicable for other reasons. As Warwickshire note, 'a strategy which put the preservation of good farmland far above all other considerations would direct urban growth to the poorer farmland. . . . But neither these factors nor any others are so important on their own that they over-ride all other considerations', such as the economic and social suitability of the land for development.

The classification of agricultural land is concerned with the inherent physical quality of the land. It takes into account climate (particularly rainfall, transpiration, temperature and exposure), relief (particularly slope) and soil (particularly wetness, depth,

[1] Ministry of Agriculture, Fisheries and Food, *Agricultural Land Classification Map of England and Wales*, Provisional Maps at the scale of 1:63,360 and *Explanatory Note*, 1968.

texture, structure, stoniness and available water capacity). It is concerned with the long-term potential of land 'on the basis of physical quality alone. Other less permanent factors such as the standard and adequacy of fixed equipment, the level of management, farm structure and accessibility have not been taken into account.'[1] In these circumstances, when the possibilities for development have been narrowed down to a few preferred localities, a desirable refinement should be for the Study team to assess the *human* condition of the land. This would include the structure of farming, the quality of management, productivity levels, the degree of specialization, the amount of capital invested in fixed equipment, the detrimental effects of adjacent land uses and the size of agricultural holdings in order to suggest the 'survival potential' of different agricultural areas. The social response of land owners and of land holders to development is also a relevant consideration.

4. Minerals. Mineral deposits receive varied treatment, in part because the occurrence and working of each mineral presents different problems but also because knowledge about the depth, extent and quality of deposits is not generally available. However, the prevailing planning intention is that constraints should be imposed on development where known workable deposits of proven value exist, so that these resources are not sterilized by new developments. A typical objective, as in the Warwickshire Study, is 'to locate new development so that the loss of workable mineral resources is kept to a minimum.' The difficulty is that geological details, the value of deposits and the costs of extraction are not known with precision and also change with marketing conditions.

The problem is also compounded by the possible after-use of worked out deposits. Thus, the North-Glos Study notes a wide distribution of superficial sand and gravel deposits, 'no precise information on the productive capacity of individual areas', and the possibility of using exhausted wet workings for recreational and amenity purposes as envisaged in the Cotswold Water Park. In Leicestershire, potential opencast sites and sand and gravel workings are considered as areas where constraints may be lifted where a strategy favours an area; this argument is applied to the concentration of basic employment in greater Leicester where potential sand and gravel-bearing land close to the city is included in the recommended strategy. The Notts–Derby situation is comparable, as

---

[1] *Ibid.*, Explanatory Note, p. 2.

open-cast reserves and sand and gravel fields are regarded as 'minor constraints' on urban development.

Mining subsidence, though a separate factor, may be associated with mineral development. It is a hazard regarded as a minor or removable constraint in the Notts–Derby and Leicestershire circumstances. As with floodland, development can take place provided precautions are taken and these, in the Notts–Derby Sub-region, are estimated at about 10 per cent of house structural costs.

5. *Ecological areas.* In the North-Glos Study woodlands 'should be preserved from future development as they contribute invaluably to the natural heritage'. The Notts–Derby Study has the advantage over the other Reports in that the Nature Conservancy classified by ecological criteria all areas likely to be developed. 'The method of classification consists of sub-dividing the area under consideration into homogeneous units or "ecological zones" to each of which is assigned a value ranging from one to five in order of declining importance. The peculiarities which will distinguish any one ecological zone will represent the sum of its geology, soils, topography, climate and past land use and will usually be reflected in its current land use.'[1] Grade I includes areas of semi-natural or unseeded vegetation including non-commercial woodland, which are of the highest value as wildlife reservoirs; Grade II includes areas of unsown vegetation and commercial or non-commercial woodland (particularly mixed deciduous woodland) of slightly lower value for wildlife; Grade III includes the remaining area of woodland including most coniferous woodland and parkland; Grade IV is agricultural land of habitat diversity and Grade V is agricultural land with little in the way of suitable plant and animal habitats. The view of the Nature Conservancy is that land in Grades I and II should not be developed and it therefore becomes a major constraint in the Study. The loss of Grade III would represent a reduction in diversity and is regarded as a minor constraint, whereas Grades IV and V have no valid wild-life arguments and may be used without restrictions.

A wild-life survey is also undertaken in the Warwickshire Study. The results, against inadequate available information, are to suggest that 'although broad-leaved woodland holds the greatest variety of species, water is so scarce in this sub-region that it emerged as the most important wild-life habitat. . . . Both are well worth

[1] *Notts–Derby Study*, Record Report 24, p. 6. See also *East Hampshire: Area of Outstanding Natural Beauty – A Study in Countryside Conservation*, Hampshire County Council, 1968, Appendix II.

conserving.' As with agricultural land, there are many conflicts involved; recreational use can conflict with wild-life habitats, and woodland may be converted to coniferous plantations or agriculture. To safeguard such sites against urban development is not the only factor which is involved.[1]

6. *Atmospheric pollution.* The main belt of atmospheric pollution is regarded as 'unsuitable for urban development' in the Teesside Study. In Notts–Derby, 'air pollution and above average fog' is considered to be an important aspect of 'environmental welfare', but adequate data were not available for use in a stringent planning context. In the Warwickshire Study, 'all new growth has been located whenever possible outside areas of existing atmospheric pollution. Naturally this caused conflict with other objectives, especially those which relied for their fulfilment on population growth being kept near to jobs.'

7. *Steep slopes.* Gradients of $1:7\frac{1}{2}$ or steeper are avoided in choosing sites in both the Notts–Derby and North-Glos Studies because of the high cost of construction, their prominence as landscape features, layout difficulties and access conditions. This strategic provision is made despite the fact that in each Sub-region, e.g. Matlock Bath and overlooking the Wye Valley, attractive residential areas now occur in such localities. The gradient unsuitable for development is lowered to $1:10$ in the Yorkshire EPC Studies.[2]

8. *Height.* Land over the 800 foot contour is considered a 'major constraint' in the Notts–Derby Study because of 'severe micro-climatic conditions'. This height bar upon development varies with regional location. In the Humberside Study, because of 'bleakness, exposure in winter, snowcover and amenity', land over 300 feet in height on the Southern Yorkshire Wolds and over 200 feet elsewhere, 'could be left untouched by building'.[3] Land below 10 feet, because of susceptibility to fogs, exceptional flood conditions and as 'their unrelieved flatness renders them uninteresting areas in which to live',[4] should also be avoided on Humberside.

9. *Areas of featureless or tree-less environment.* These are avoided initially in the Teesside Study, as 'such areas were not likely to be

[1] See, for example, *The Countryside in 1970: Proceedings*, Royal Society of Arts (London), 1970.

[2] Yorkshire and Humberside Economic Planning Council, *Doncaster: An Area Study*, HMSO, 1969, p. 91.

[3] *Humberside Study*, p. 19.   [4] *Ibid.*, p. 20.

capable of transformation into an attractive urban environment without substantial investment in landscaping'. At a later stage in analysis, one such site was regarded as 'suitable for urban development; the means of achieving this would be by a tree planting and woodland management programme'.

10. Airfield and other noise zones. The boundaries of airfield noise and safety zones can be established from aircraft flight characteristics, and such operational areas with a noise nuisance are regarded as major constraints in the Notts–Derby and Leicestershire Studies. In the Warwickshire Study, where noise pollution from aircraft, road and rail traffic are each considered, 'the future looks noisy because it is impossible to foresee other than a rapid increase in the number of noise sources . . . Care was taken to keep future growth away from noise pollution in the alternative strategies.'

11. Constraints in the Regional Studies. The above physical constraints are normally included with comparable comment and variations in emphasis in the Regional Studies.[1] However, the additional or contrary attitudes in these Reports include:

1. The need to safeguard fishing interests, e.g. trout fisheries (Hampshire).
2. That certain villages have considerable environmental merit and, in some instances, their immediate vicinity may require protection (Hampshire).
3. A cordon of open country 'should be established next to chemical complexes and other heavy industrial areas because of smell, dust, noise and over-powering scale' (Humberside; also Yorkshire EPC). Nuclear power stations and other potential sources of hazard might also be included under this type of heading as 'a dangerous neighbour'.
4. Networks of overhead electricity lines radiating out from switching and power stations, 'ought to be accepted as constraints' (Humberside).
5. 'Areas which suffer from very poor access and which could not be developed without expensive new investment in bridges and substantial new lengths of road' (Yorkshire EPC).
6. A safety zone around an explosives magazine (Yorkshire EPC).
7. The South East Study emphasizes productivity, land particularly suitable for certain crops, existing and prospective farm

[1] *South Hampshire Study*, Vol. I, pp. 15–19 and 113; *Humberside Study*, pp. 19–22; *South East Study*, pp. 32–6; and *Yorkshire EPC, Doncaster*, pp. 90–8.

structure, and immunity from present and foreseeable urban intrusion. Distance from existing urban areas is thus an important factor when considering alternative possibilities.

SURVEYS OF LANDSCAPE QUALITY[1]

It has been noted that all Studies have classified their localities by some form of qualitative or landscape survey. Some elaboration is desirable, however, because of the differences in approach and attitude. Teesside discusses nature conservation, divides its area in a series of generalized ecological areas, and distinguishes between educational nature reserves and landscape resource zones 'where, unless there was some overriding consideration, urban development would not be allowed and special arrangements would be made for access, management and control of use'. The North-Glos Study maps its areas of high landscape value and of intermediate landscape value, and regards this as 'one of the more important aspects of evaluation, but it is also the most prone to subjective opinions'.

To remove this element of subjectivity Leicestershire's survey of environmental quality is more extensive. It takes into account morphology, surface cover, the visual effects of resource activity (agriculture, forestry and mineral working) on the landscape, the extent to which the landscape is already occupied by urban development and the quality of such developments, and a subjective assessment of visual quality generally. The Sub-region is divided into zones against one of five categories. These are 'areas in which urban growth would be beneficial (i.e. growth would improve the visual quality of the environment); highly acceptable; acceptable with some qualifications and restrictions; acceptable with stringent qualifications and restrictions; and unacceptable'.

Notts–Derby, by contrast, undertake a landscape survey which classifies all land in the Sub-region to establish tracts of similar landscape type. The description integrates slope, vegetation, hedgerow and farming characteristics. However, within this context, 'no attempt has been made to classify the sub-region's landscape according to its quality as individuals vary greatly in the value they attach to different landscapes, and this is subject to changes of fashion. However, it may be necessary to seek a consensus of opinion on the matter if it becomes critical to a choice of future policy.'[2] This

[1] See, for example, R. A. Waller, 'Environmental Quality: Its Measurement and Control', *Regional Studies*, Vol. 4, 1970, pp. 177–91.

[2] *Notts–Derby Study*, p. xxxvi.

consensus would have been easier to achieve had the landscape been classified into its possible qualitative character by the Study team, and had this detail then been subject to public evaluation.

Notts–Derby also make the significant point that the quality of a landscape is not something which is fixed. It can be manipulated and changed, for better or worse, by planning policies. Their approach is to seek to improve upon the quality of the environment in the more harassed areas. The advocacy is especially for an improvement plan in the Erewash Valley.

Substantial improvement of the environment is necessary and this can best be achieved if it is co-ordinated, and related to new development, by means of an Improvement Plan for the whole area. . . . The Improvement Plan should include land use proposals, and programmes for tree-planting and clearing up derelict land, reducing air and water pollution, renewing obsolete housing, constructing or improving educational, health and welfare facilities, new roads and road improvements, redeveloping town centres, providing 'facelifts' for groups of buildings, releasing land for development, providing recreational facilities and laying out greenways.[1]

The importance of such proposals needs to be emphasized on social and moral grounds, especially as it can be argued on economic criteria that these types of investment are not productive of the highest return. Regional planning seeks, amongst other things, to redress some of the imbalance which exists between regions; it is equally as important that it be seen by people living within a region to correct those differences which exist now within regions.

Warwickshire's appraisal is also extensive. It relies on two indices.

The first index, which was derived from land form, land use and land features, expressed the Landscape Value of each unit as a piece of isolated land, disregarding anything related to adjacent units. The second index reflected intervisibility or the extent to which one unit could be seen from others. An indication of the total landscape significance of any unit could then be obtained by multiplying both indices together. Conversely the value of a view could be found by adding together the Landscape Values of all its component units. In practice, though, it was usually better to keep both measures separate.[2]

Factors included are slope and shape for land form; land use

[1] *Ibid.*, p. 41.   [2] *Warwickshire Study*, p. 135.

93

includes farmland, woodland, parkland, heathland, water, residential, industrial and other developed and unused land; land features include the natural elements of watercourses, hedgerows and hedgerow trees as well as man-made ones like roads, power lines, railways, farmsteads and other buildings and significant features; and the inter-visibility index was developed from a series of cross sections designed to show views across the Sub-region.[1]

The attempt, by these means, is to remove the element of subjective interpretation and thus to provide a rational basis for selection and determination between alternative strategies. Varying degrees of sophistication are involved but the endeavour, in each instance, is to define those tracts of country where the urban incursion should be restricted for the greater advantage of both urban and rural localities. The outcome is expressed on diagrams which indicate priority grades in the quality of the landscape.

THE USE OF PHYSICAL CRITERIA IN EVALUATING ALTERNATIVE STRATEGIES[2]

Alternative strategies have been developed in each Sub-regional Study, relying in part on the physical constraints which have been presented above and in part on other objectives of the planning process. Ideally all development would have been allocated to constraint-free localities but other pressures, such as employment–home relationships or the new accessibility of a locale because of access to a motorway, may have intervened. Also, when the scale of operations is changed down from a coarse to a finer mesh, the availability of more detailed information may indicate that some of the proposals are located in areas where constraints exist. For a variety of reasons, it is therefore desirable to test the performance of alternative strategies against physical criteria.

Simple manual procedures and sieve map techniques indicate the extent to which each strategy transgresses the various constraints. This procedure was undertaken in the Notts–Derby Study, with the amount of land in acres of each strategy being charted against each of their major and minor constraints. It provides a significant aspect of the North-Glos evaluation and is there applied to the proportion of new development affecting Grade I plus Grade II agricultural land, potential sand and gravel deposits, and in areas of high plus

[1] *Ibid.*, pp. 135–6.
[2] *North-Glos Study*, pp. 82–4; *Notts–Derby Study*, Record Report 34; *Leicestershire Study*, Vol. I, pp. 61–2, and Vol. II, pp. 125–30 and 144–5.

intermediate landscape value. In the Leicestershire Study, the proportional loss against each strategy is measured for agricultural land, separately for each mineral (but 'we found that the limited extent of land taken in any strategy did not justify the retention of this factor in evaluation'), to some extent for the land taken in flood areas, and for the land in each class of environmental quality.

Two refinements are attempted to these procedures, neither very successfully. The problem is to assist the value judgement as between 'X' acres of constraint A and 'Y' acres of constraint B. Notts–Derby attempted to assess the notional cost to the community of using constrained land for new purposes, including both the costs of sterilizing natural resources based on the current market value of the resource in question and the additional structural costs required to overcome obstacles to development (e.g. floodland). But 'the figures thus produced had a number of deficiencies which prohibited a direct comparison between the costs of overcoming different types of constraint. . . . For these reasons its was decided to proceed no further with the measurement of constraints in financial terms.' In Leicestershire, 'as it is extremely difficult to put a monetary value on the respective classes of land, production loss was calculated in the form of a weighted index number'. Grade II land was awarded 3 penalty points per acre, Grade IIIA 2 points and other Grade III land 1 point. This Study also uses a variety of different weights for the amount of land allocated to development against each category of environmental quality; 'this represented the relative merit of each strategy from the visual environmental point of view'.

The weighting of physical criteria, and the relative balance to be ascribed to different landscapes and features of the rural environment, remains a vexed problem to which there is as yet no real answer. Some resources can be given a monetary expression, whereas natural history sites, a scenic view or the charm of a landscape cannot now be valued. Agricultural land is an everlasting asset which should be valued in perpetuity, whereas the value of mineral resources relates to exploitation on a once-and-for-all basis. Market values neither reflect future changes in public opinion, nor take into account the increasing demands for a whole range of outdoor recreational and visual experiences. As weighting and notional values each have their limitations, in those instances where planners *have* to ascribe relative values to quite different physical components, or *must* identify zones of landscape quality, then surely here lies a rich field for public participation and real involvement in the planning process. The technician can only go so far. He can plot and evaluate factual data such as mineral distributions, ecological areas and the distribution of high quality agricultural land. He is on less certain ground when he refers to amenity, aesthetics and landscape quality and how these features are valued by the public. A citizen response might here reasonably be obtained, to assist with the delicate and suspect process of ascribing value-judgements on subjective and debatable features of the natural landscape, and their areal extent.

Comment has verged onto three subjects, each of which will be discussed below: cost–benefit analysis, public participation, and the inherent conflicts which exist between the use of a resource (including urban development) and the conservation or retention of existing attributes. Illustrative of such conflicts are the acceptance of proposals for heavy industrial development at Spurn Bight in the Humberside Study, and at Seal Sands in the Teesside Study. As each locality is a recognized site of scientific interest, it would seem that no physical resource or element of the landscape can ever be regarded as completely inviolate by development. There are varying degrees of possible or acceptable use which must be assessed, and compared with costs and opportunities elsewhere. The task is delicate, but the landscape for present and future generations is in the balance at every decision.

The developing subject matter of environmental perception may have fruits to yield in this context. Learning, educational background and social habits each influence the individual's view of the world, their response to different types of scene and their bias. Thus Shafer and others (1969), basing their arguments on preference scores for landscape photographs, have developed 'a method of quantifying variables in landscapes which are significantly related to public preference for those landscapes'.[1] Fines (1968) has suggested a method of ascertaining landscape values to guide planning decisions.[2] By such means, the present subjective opinions which are expressed in the Sub-regional Studies may be improved. A model for predicting human response to landscape environments in relation to socio-economic variables is not without possibilities of achievement. Various attempts are also being made to place some sort of value on non-tangible benefits. Thus, Burton and Wibberley (1965) have

[1] See B. Goodey, *Perceptions of the Environment: An Introduction to the Literature*, Occasional Paper No. 17, Centre for Urban and Regional Studies, University of Birmingham, 1971. The reference to E. L. Shafer is quoted from this monograph.

[2] K. D. Fines, 'Landscape Evaluation: A Research Project in East Sussex', *Regional Studies*, Vol. 2, 1968, pp. 41–55 and Vol. 3, 1969, p. 219.

looked at the recreational value of open access land;[1] Helliwell (1967 and 1969) has referred to the amenity value of trees, woodlands and other wildlife resources.[2] The latter takes into account the diversity of the habitat in its number of species, the scarcity of similar areas, its educational value in terms of the accessibility of the area to students, its usefulness for research and its local character.

The selection of physical criteria and the determination of their qualities is an extremely important aspect of the regional planning process. It influences substantially the planner's appreciation of suitable locations for future development, because localities with physical constraints are excluded as far as is possible from further consideration. Thus in the North-Glos Study, 'an analysis of the various restraints indicated four major areas within the Sub-region which were not subject to major limitations and which would there-fore be suitable for new urban development on a substantial scale'. In the Teesside circumstances, 'certain areas should remain in agri-cultural use, or are suitable for conservation policies . . . other areas appear to be suitable for general urban development'. In Leicester-shire, Warwickshire and Notts–Derby, localities not constrained provide one basis for the strategic allocation of land.

The reader should pause at this point. Against the sum total of the physical constraints and interpretative comment that have been presented, he is invited to prepare his own comprehensive statement of *all* physical constraints which *should* preclude or limit major urban developments on land in his sub-region, then indicate the boundaries of each on a large-scale map, and finally suggest the degree of urban pressure at which each embargo might be relaxed. The task is not easy, and differences of opinion are certain. A contribution which is outwardly physical and non-controversial in its external dimensions soon demands quite complex value-judgements to justify the inclu-sion or exclusion of a particular item. Further, in planning, no one factor can be considered in isolation but in its wider interplay, and the justification must be in terms of the future and not by today's standards of appreciation.

Other physical factors which might be significant and which so far have been excluded from consideration include:

1. inadequate support capacity of the ground. This has in part

[1] T. L. Burton and G. P. Wibberley, *Outdoor Recreation in the British Country-side*, Wye College, University of London, 1965.

[2] D. R. Helliwell, 'The Amenity Value of Trees and Woodlands', *J. Arb. Assoc.*, Vol. 1, 1967, pp. 128–31 and 'Valuation of Wildlife Resources', *Regional Studies*, Vol. 3, 1969, pp. 41–7. See also the critique by M. D. Hooper, *Regional Studies*, Vol. 4, 1971, pp. 127–8.

been included under mining subsidence but is capable of some extension in other geological circumstances;

2. areas particularly subject to strong winds;

3. high ground-water levels;

4. areas susceptible to disease, which would include the high incidence of atmospheric pollution and its severe impact on health;

5. coastal inundation, which might reinforce the incidence of river flooding or be a separate factor;

6. saline or other soils unsuitable for planting;

7. the directions of working, the present and presumed future extent, of underground mineral workings;

8. areas of ground movement, including the stability of slopes.

GREEN BELTS

Rather surprisingly, green belts do not appear in the above list of constraints on urban development. This omission is despite the fact that such areas have been established by local planning authorities to place physical constraint on exuberant urban growth, and now exercise considerable effects on the shape, direction and rates of urban growth. They were conceived as barriers to urban expansion in order to exclude the urban monster, to protect the seclusion of the nearby rural environments, and to prevent the coalescence over intervening agricultural land of adjacent urban communities. But very little prior consideration was given to the use of land inside a green belt, and how it would in reality serve its dual function as a barrier to urban growth and provide a recreational lung for the urban populations living inside its limits.[1] Despite these issues and conflicts, green belts are not mentioned in the formulation of sub-regional strategies in either the Teesside, Leicestershire or the Notts–Derby Studies, their retention is not an objective in the Warwickshire Study, and the green belt is regarded as a variable constraint in the North-Glos Study.

The Gloucester–Cheltenham green belt now exists so that these two cities shall not coalesce. The Study argues that no change should be countenanced until 1891 and, after that date, the preferred strategy then envisages that about one-fifth of the total area will be developed. The argument is that 'the total estimated land requirements in this "core" area were of such magnitude as to make the

[1] See D. Thomas, *London's Green Belt*, Faber and Faber (London), 1970 and D. G. Gregory, *Green Belts and Development Control: A Case Study in the West Midlands*, Occasional Paper No. 12, Centre for Urban and Regional Studies, University of Birmingham, 1970.

retention of the Green Belt a strategic issue. . . . The two alternatives (which retained the Green Belt) were anticipated to have considerable inherent disadvantages, thus compelling the serious consideration of the remaining locational option in the Gloucester–Cheltenham area – namely parts of the Green Belt.'[1] As the preferred strategy suggests that additional areas of Green Belt should be defined 'in order that substantial breaks in development should be maintained'[2] the concept is what might be described as a 'creeping green belt'. It serves the purpose of setting bounds to the growing city for a period, and the boundaries are then relaxed and moved outwards to permit the next stage in urban growth.

The Notts–Derby situation is different. A green belt notation does not appear on the strategy map, because other mechanisms are proposed for controlling the out-growth of towns, protecting the countryside and providing opportunities for outdoor recreation. The argument is that

> . . . alternative ways of securing these objectives are set out in the strategy, not just for the areas immediately around the large towns, but for the whole of the sub-region. The countryside policy will protect and enhance all the resources and assets of the rural areas, the regional parks and greenways will provide opportunities for outdoor recreation, and the locations and scale of development intended will be determined in principle by the adopted strategy, and worked out in detail in individual development plans. It is therefore open to the authorities concerned to choose whether to continue with the Green Belts or to rely on these new policies to achieve the same objectives.[3]

The Warwickshire situation is comparable. A countryside management policy is recommended and the idea of a green belt is replaced by 'a permanent countryside buffer between the Conurbation and the corridor of towns from Nuneaton, through Coventry, to Leamington and Warwick';[4] elsewhere this is referred to as 'a permanent, effective and viable wedge of countryside'.[5] The expression green belt is avoided in the policy recommendation which is 'that a permanent boundary be defined to a permanent buffer of countryside'.[6]

At the regional level, the Humberside and Hampshire Studies are concerned with major urban growth and the distribution of new populations. Again there is no mention of a green belt, either as a

[1] *North-Glos Study*, p. 65. [2] *Ibid.*, p. 100.
[3] *Notts–Derby Study*, p. 107. [4] *Warwickshire Study*, p. 85.
[5] *Ibid.*, p. 5. [6] *Ibid.*, p. 90.

natural resource or as a planning policy to achieve some desired urban form; nor does it appear as a notation on the strategy maps. In Hampshire there is the fluid concept of open space in and about the built-up area, and emphasis on a total approach to the design and management of all land. Humberside does not consider green belts in its hypothetical plans. The Metropolitan Green Belt is mentioned *en passant* in the South East Study, but does not enter the discussion of alternative hypotheses.

Thus, in each instance, other constructive policies for urban growth and rural land management would seem to provide the preferable alternative, rather than reliance on green belts, where landscape conditions may be poor or usurped by urban characteristics. Thus, in the North-Glos Study, 'the landscape quality of much of the Green Belt is indifferent and is affected by such conspicuous intrusions as power lines, major communications, sporadic development and a commercial airfield'.[1] From the evidence of the Studies under review, it would appear that inviolable green belts are no longer an essential element in the formulation of planning policy for urban growth. Constructive land policies over the whole of the Region or Sub-region serve to take their place.

RESIDENTIAL DEVELOPMENT IN RURAL AREAS

The Studies generally emphasize the concentration and focus of new developments in a few selected localities, whereas the increasing dispersal of population is significant in North America with greater affluence and improved mobility. The typical reaction of the Studies to this type of possibility may be illustrated from comments made in the Warwickshire and Notts–Derby Studies.

In the Warwickshire Study,

the other solution which had to be considered was a wide spread of people and jobs over the countryside at a very low density.... In this part of England it would bring the town into the country to the disadvantage of both. It would almost certainly intensify the operating difficulties of public transport and isolate poorer families in the sub-region to their further disadvantage.... If the extra houses of the next twenty to thirty years were spread throughout rural Warwickshire, the whole County would become latticed with villages, touching one another at two or three points on their outskirts. This pattern would destroy the countryside setting which is

[1] *North-Glos Study*, pp. 61–2.

inherent in our present regard for villages, and it would destroy the rural landscape.[1]

Rural development policies restrict the amount of house building in country areas and 'substantiated our conclusion that the strategy for the sub-region must be based upon disciplined and compact growth of towns, not of villages or dispersed population'.[2]

In the Notts–Derby Study, several of the earlier strategies included increased opportunities for dispersal but these were discarded in the outcome of the final analysis.

The principal arguments against such a dispersed pattern are that it would be inconvenient for the people ... who will have been brought up in the more urbanized areas and cannot easily move away from kinship groups and familiar surroundings some distance away. ... It is unlikely to lead to the conditions favourable for the economic growth urgently needed. ... It would be more harmful to agriculture, forestry, natural history and landscape than the strategy proposed. It would probably be more expensive in terms of roads and services.[3]

These arguments may each be correct but they exclude consideration of the increasing proportion of the population who are expected to move into the present higher income brackets over the next thirty years, the reasonable expectation of increased demands for larger homes on more spacious sites, increased personal mobility, the growing demands for second homes and the attraction of physically-favoured sites for retirement homes. As stated in a professional review of the North-Glos Study, 'can we be so confident that nucleated settlement will be so strongly favoured in 2001 as this study assumes, and that a swing to dispersal will not have taken over?'[4]

Sub-regional strategies could have examined the implications of locating 'x' and 'y' per cent of the population increase in other than concentrated urban locations, and new possibilities now exist for the creation of 'retirement villages', the modernization of old cottages and the construction of new dwellings in a rural setting through the expected further decline in the number of agricultural workers. Instead of rejecting such developments, the Studies might preferably have considered the more suitable localities and have suggested how a limited amount of dispersed and isolated developments might best

[1] *Warwickshire Study*, p. 19.   [2] *Ibid.*, p. 88.
[3] *Notts–Derby Study*, p. 96.
[4] 'Current Practice and Research', *Journal of the Town Planning Institute*, Vol. 56, 1970, p. 315.

be accommodated in the environment through careful location and landscape design. For example in the North-Glos Sub-region there already exists, in the Forest of Dean and in the Lower Wye Valley areas, an extensive existing commitment to these types of settlement through the historical processes of land development, the Welsh upland influence, the former establishment of hill settlements and ridge roads, in association with previous iron-pit and coal-mining activities, and through the ongoing basic activities of agriculture and forestry. It is not suggested that specific areas should necessarily be indicated, but it would seem that the possibilities which exist for dispersal could have been considered to a greater extent in this and the other Studies.

A related point is the extent to which residential development may, or should, be considered in areas of scenic importance. The areas of highest quality landscape are regarded as a physical constraint in all the Sub-regional Studies, yet these same localities are often in substantial demand for residential purposes. Thus, in the North-Glos Study, new development on any scale is not envisaged in such areas but is 'confined to areas of intermediate and lower landscape value'.[1] Likewise, to the south of Nottingham and Derby, 'it is necessary to restrain population growth in the small towns and villages. . . . There are other places where restraint is necessary . . . and where building should be restricted to land already commited in view of the harmful effect which further development here will have on the countryside.'[2]

As strong pressures of demand also exist for quality housing in attractive rural settings, this type of policy decision provides a severe test of strength for planning policies. It presumes that areas with steep slopes, commanding views and the more attractive areas of the English countryside cannot and should not be developed. Although the wealth of grandeur which exists is accepted to the full as a major asset for both citizens and visitors from abroad, the qualitative judgement of severe restrictions on development presents a land use decision which conflicts with likely possible trends. Such sites can be especially attractive because of the views which they afford and the setting of excellence which they provide for residential development, tourist centres, retirement homes, holiday cottages, hotels and restaurants, and other demands in association with recreation. They offer considerable architectural and landscape potential for new developments, and a university, hospital or other public building can embellish a favoured site. The danger is that a dilapidated miner's cottage of the eighteenth century, or the now unwanted home of a

[1] *North-Glos Study*, p. 83.   [2] *Notts–Derby Study*, p. 44.

former agricultural labourer, can be modernized with taste and discretion, but that the adjacent field of bracken has an embargo upon its useful development on grounds of amenity.

The Notts–Derby Study makes a useful contribution to this issue, as the recommended strategy seeks to transfer this demand elsewhere by providing comparable opportunities in alternative situations. The concept is that 'the demand for higher quality housing might be met by putting new housing in the more attractive areas and accepting commuting. . . . The alternative is to improve the environment of the areas with good economic prospects, mainly the central urbanized belt so that it is sufficiently attractive to meet all housing needs.'[1] The Warwickshire Study likewise envisages this possibility. 'The insurance against these risks must be to improve the environment of the less attractive parts. . . . Landscape planning and environmental design should be central to Urban Structure and Local Planning. . . . It is a matter of diverting pressures from the better landscapes of the south to where they can be used to social and economic advantage in the north.'[2]

This transfer of development to other sites will not be easy to achieve. It clearly depends upon the successful improvement in practice of the alternative localities, and both the time factor and the quality of this alternative environment must be critical. It is only when a suitable range of valid alternatives are provided that there can be a substantial transfer of development pressures to relieve the scenically attractive hill and village localities. The need is urgent for additional government assistance, not just to improve the less attractive environments, but to safeguard and to reduce pressures on the more favoured localities.

ECOLOGICAL AND QUALITATIVE ASPECTS OF THE ENVIRONMENT

All Studies are concerned with the quality of their living environments, and considerable distress is expressed at certain features. Atmospheric pollution has been mentioned previously. The Notts–Derby Study notes that 'most of the major rivers within the Subregion are seriously polluted to the extent that they cannot be used for water supply'.[3] The Warwickshire Study states that 'from a subregional standpoint the river position is serious. Unpolluted rivers must be protected at all costs as possible sources of water supply, as

[1] *Ibid.*, p. 64. [2] *Warwickshire Study*, p. 88.
[3] *Notts–Derby Study*, p. 17 and Map 4.

vital sources of living water supporting a balanced environment, and as vital sources of dilution to alleviate conditions in polluted rivers. . . . The Study took great care to ensure that the future growth areas in alternative strategies could be drained without threatening any of the unpolluted rivers.'[1]

Even so, not all Studies have taken sufficiently into account that a new ecological dimension has been bestowed on planning, by a woman writing one book in *her* dying years. Rachel Carson's *Silent Spring* was published in the United States in 1962, and appeared in Britain the following year.[2] The subsequent furore over the quality of the environment, the destruction of air and water resources, and the possibilities of ecological suicide can no longer be avoided in the regional approach to environmental issues. There are now at least two legitimate areas for concern; the one comprises the location of those multitudinous demands which stem from our primarily urban mode of life; the other is the quality of land, water, air and scenic resources within and beyond the urban limits. Neither can be studied without taking into account the demands of the other. It is a matter for regret that some Studies emphasize the former to the detriment of the latter. Maps concerned with the quality of water, and the means for remedying such deficiencies, require much consideration.

The message is now well known. Chemicals and technology are defiling the total involvement. The world is becoming uninhabitable. As chemical residues accumulate in flesh, bone, water and soil, life is endangered. Air, water and land can no longer be used indiscriminately for the disposal of effluvia. The resources of a region are both limited, and subject to thoughtless destruction. The savage dilemma is that urban man has become trapped in an environment of his own making. On the one hand, the control of a river can provide water supplies and hydro-electric power – but it may prejudice scenery, solitude and fish life. Round every airport there is the struggle between progress and the quality of life, as residents contend with noise and fumes and yet depend upon air services for modern means of rapid communication. Vehicle fumes in the street spell mobility for thousands, but aggravate pollution, cause annoyance and the possible asphyxiation of large urban environments. Recreational opportunity

---

[1] *Warwickshire Study*, p. 132.

[2] Rachel Carson, *Silent Spring*, Houghton Mifflin (Boston), 1962, became a book of the month selection. It is not the first statement on this problem, and itself relies on a thirty page bibliography. Its forceful impact on public opinion is the point of this comment.

and conservation practice are in severe conflict in many rural localities. One cannot now reverse the clock and manage the urban life
without electricity, aircraft, motor vehicles and leisure time. Science
has made possible expanding food supplies, the control of sickness,
the extension of life and an improved standard of living, which are
reflected in the heavy and concentrated growth of urbanization and
expanding urban frontiers throughout the world – and yet the underlying technology is now attacked because it endangers life on earth
itself.

These points suggest most strongly that *all* physical land use plans
and strategies which are evolved from social and economic criteria
must always be extended to assess the *ecological* significance of
proposed developments on the quality of the inherited environment
Concern for land use and land development must now incorporate the
multiple of relationships which exist between land, water and air.
Strategies should indicate how environmental abuses are to be reme-
died, the extent of improvement or deterioration over time, and those
deplorable or extreme conditions which deserve special attention.
Cleaning up the rivers has become as important an objective for
public policy as clearing out the slums, and clean air as important as
housing or employment policies.

THE URBAN INVASION OF THE COUNTRYSIDE

The Studies, by definition, cover an extensive area which ripples outwards from the central city or cities to include smaller towns and
rural environments. The intention is to formulate major strategies for
land development over a period of about thirty years for urban and
rural localities. A point of critical importance is that the townsman
has come to be regarded as the 'invader' of the countryside, and the
'destroyer of its amenities'. Hoskins (1955) in his vital essay on the
making of the English landscape, states that 'since that time (the
latter years of the nineteenth century) and especially since the year
1914, every single change in the English landscape has either uglified it
or destroyed its meaning, or both. Of all the changes in the last two
generations, only the great reservoirs of water for the industrial cities
of the North and Midlands have added anything to the scene that
one can contemplate without pain. It is a distasteful subject but it
must be faced.'[1] This may be an over-harsh judgement, but it nevertheless represents a severe indictment against the ravages of modern

[1] W. G. Hoskins, *The Making of the English Landscape*, Penguin Books
(Harmondsworth, Middlesex), 1970, p. 298 (first published by Hodder and
Stoughton, 1955).

urban man. If this is to be the quality of the developments proposed in the regional and sub-regional strategies, then it is obvious that further inroads of 'town' into 'country' will (and should) be resisted to the hilt. An important aspect of every Study must be to offset this antagonism and mutual mistrust. The safeguards to retain, or enhance, the quality of existing environments must be clearly stated, and affirmed in each development control decision.

Examples of the fundamental and essential divergence of opinion between opposing rural and urban interests are easy to find. The antithesis between town and country and between urban and rural is deep-seated. The emotive outcome is an immediate and foreseeable reaction against all new urban developments in the countryside. These will spoil the environment, which must be protected. Almost every edition of the daily and weekly newspapers contains the evidence for some new enraged outcry, and the annual reports of the Council for the Preservation of Rural England provide a regular résumé of the more strident causes for alarm. The dilemma is clear and easy to state, but exceedingly complex to resolve. The Studies in their discussion of such issues will, hopefully, have contributed to the relief of tension.

There is conflict between farming/rural/country/amenity/conservationist/protectionist interests and urban/commercial/financial spoliation, because two contrary interpretations of the planning process exist. In the words of Bracey (1970), 'in general, the countryman sees planning as a body of legislation which can be invoked ... to keep cities within bounds, for example to prevent townsmen building bungalows along the sea coast and dormitory suburbs to swamp the village (and the countryside). Townsmen and many politicians regard planning as the instrument which will secure a supply of land, wherever it may be found, adequate to provide for schools, houses and recreation for an ever-increasing, mainly urban population.'[1] Although both these views are narrow and unfair, both attitudes exist. The dialogue between town and country is often one of acrimony and mutual distrust.

From the urban standpoint, the land, water, air and other resources of the country are limited, population has increased to about fifty-five million persons in England, Wales and Scotland or about one acre per head to accommodate *all* the increasing demands on land from virtually every aspect of an expanding technological civilization. Land is required somewhere for recreation, to

[1] H. E. Bracey, *op. cit.*, p. 109. Many further internal conflicts also exist within the context of this wider divergence of opinion.

manufacture goods, to house people, to provide water, to dispose sewage and to provide power – but from the rural or conservationist stand-point practically everything should go somewhere else than to this threatened valley, hillside, beauty spot, green belt location or fine rural setting. The comforts of good living are often seen to be at variance with how to make best use of a proud national inheritance. The city may have options as to *where* it gets its water, power, recreational land, housing areas, industrial sites, and its other comforts and needs, but to cut back or to deny its legitimate demands is both regressive and impossible. Existing antipathy between urban and rural will not be resolved until regional studies are concerned with urban *and* rural environments as one inseparable entity. The strategies, to gain public acceptance, must be considered for their contribution towards the continuous and total environment of a region in its physical *and* its qualitative aspects.

The most critical question about physical criteria, for society as a whole as well as for those concerned with planning each regional environment, is at what stage should technology be halted, or economic growth be denied, in the interests of conserving an existing environment? In the words of H.R.H. The Duke of Edinburgh at the *Countryside in 1970* conference, 'the gross national product which is rapidly assuming the religious significance of a graven image, can be worked out by any competent accountant, but exactly how do you arrive at a comparable figure for the quality of life? The subject of conservation has become a large and extremely awkward spanner in our well-oiled, materialist economic system.'[1] Such issues must remain at the forefront of all regional strategies.

SUMMARY

The physical dimension provides an important facet of each Study, emphasizing in particular the resources which are available and seeking to accommodate new development in the landscape without detriment to these resources. Although definitions may vary, the localities normally excluded from development are the protected sites of scenic and conservation value, floodland, high quality agricultural land, mineral deposits, impressive ecological sites, steep areas, high land and featureless environments. Constraints may be relaxed under varying degrees of urban pressure. The Study areas are frequently divided into landscape zones, and strategies are tested against the

[1] H.R.H. The Duke of Edinburgh, 'Opening Address', *The Countryside in 1970: Proceedings*, Royal Society of Arts (London), 1970, p. 34.

THE URBAN FUTURE

degree to which they might prejudice the quality of the landscape or
sterilize its resources. The future of green belts, the possibilities of
more dispersal, the encouragement of development in attractive
localities, the significance of ecological factors and the means whereby tension between urban and rural residents might be reduced are
each discussed. A continuing dialogue on such issues is extremely
probable over the next decade, given the magnitude of the forecasts
about future rates of urban growth.

Chapter 5
Forecasts and Projections

Many socio-economic forecasts must underpin the preparation of alternative strategies. Social scientists are wary about even general predictions, but the planner *has* to make assumptions about the future and also has the additional arduous and contentious task of applying these generalities as specific predictions in terms of time and space. It is reasonable to expect that there will be changes in family structure as real incomes and social opportunities increase, age of marriage decreases and mobility increases for each of its members. Employment in the service sector may be expected to expand as traditional manufacturing industries decline. The standard working week may become shorter and productivity higher, to result in longer hours of leisure but also greater difficulties for the worker with poor education or no formal training. With rising affluence there will be increased demands on the physical environment, and for public services such as water, electricity and an improved road network. As incomes rise, higher standards of housing may be expected and shopping habits will change by location, distance travelled and the type of goods purchased. A larger population and larger expectations underlie all the Studies. Not one envisages any decline in the gross national product, or the curtailment of activities. Growth, and change, provide the basis for future urban life. A policy of no additional services and no further allocations of land to permit urban expansion has not been followed in any instance.

POPULATION AND ASSOCIATED FORECASTS

As a basis for the development of their alternative strategies, all Studies rely on the intensive forecasting of selected variables as an indication of future socio-economic possibilities. These provide 'a general indication of the total scale of new development which it was thought reasonable to expect up to the end of the century'.[1] Such forecasts parallel the appraisal of physical potential, and together with this environmental assessment provide the twin bases for the

[1] *North-Glos Study*, p. 35. See, for example, R. H. Best and A. G. Champion, 'Regional Conversions of Agricultural Land to Urban Use in England and Wales, 1945–1967', *Institute of British Geographers, Transactions* No. 49, 1970, pp. 15–32.

formulation of future strategic policies. The forecasts interpret the present situation in relation to presumed changes in the future. The topics generally considered include:

1. the composition and size of the migrant population by age and sex; fertility rates;
2. survival rates at birth, and survival rates by five year age groups;
3. the proportion of children in each age group attending state primary and secondary schools;
4. the male and female population of working age in employment, which includes the effects of raising the school leaving age, a continued growth in further education and assumptions about the proportion of married women who go out to work;
5. car ownership and expenditure patterns;
6. the extent of travel to work;
7. employment projections for the major industrial sectors of the sub-regional economy;
8. the breakdown of employment projections by industry, and into socio-economic groups;
9. the appreciation of expected employment change by location;
10. the rate of household formation and the number of future households, through change in population size, household composition, headship rates and the proportion who are married, single, widowed and divorced;
11. the relationship of households to dwellings, including the clearance, rehabilitation, and sub-division of existing stock, new constructions, vacancy rates and temporary dwellings;
12. the institutional population, not requiring housing accomodation;
13. the division of housing demand, by local authority and private building;
14. the demand for shopping floor space, emphasizing durable goods in the principal centres rather than local service shops;
15. the attractiveness of each shopping centre by the extent of its catchment area and the size of its sales area in square feet;
16. retail sales per square foot, allowing for improvements in efficiency;
17. real per capita earning power of the population, based on national income levels, the growth of the national economy and adjusted to sub-regional levels in relation to the distribution of socio-economic groups;

110

18. expenditure on retail durable goods, based on Family Expenditure Surveys in relation to income groups;

19. the number of daily trips produced by and attracted to each zone, classified by purpose and by length of trip for each purpose, and by the mode of travel. Journeys and travel patterns are thus related to land use and its associated socio-economic variables, including car ownership patterns, population densities, employment opportunities, distances and accessibility.

These many details provide the factual basis of the alternative strategies and are generally projected from a base date of 1966 to approximately 'the end of the century'. This time scale is often given in the written terms of reference. It involves a twenty-five year period from 1966 to 1991 by the Leicestershire, Warwickshire and Teesside Studies, and a thirty-five year period from 1966 to 2001 by the Gloucestershire and Notts–Derby Studies. Intervening estimates are generally at five-yearly periods. Extensive reliance is placed on the 1966 Census of Population, the 1961 Census especially for journey to work and retailing information, and the range of further statistical information available through government departments (e.g. traffic studies and employment data). It may be supplemented by field surveys including interviews with employers and household surveys. The details of forecasting methods are presented fully in the various record reports (Derbyshire), the supplementary reports (Warwickshire) and the technical appendices (Teesside, Leicestershire), with summary statements in the main text.[1] Projection is generally by a series of incremental stages to the final forecast.

The total population changes envisaged in each Sub-regional Study are:

	1966	1976	1981	1986	1991	2001
Teesside	479,000	558,000	—	—	704,000	—
Leicestershire	682,920	—	833,900	—	927,030	—
Notts–Derby	1,725,000	—	—	1,981,000	—	—
North-Glos	453,410	—	560,920	—	—	752,400
Warwickshire	991,500	1,169,300	1,238,700	—	1,410,400	—

[1] Many of the methods employed are discussed in J. B. Cullingworth and S. C. Orr (eds.), *Regional and Urban Studies: A Social Science Approach*, George Allen and Unwin (London), 1961. Procedures used in the Notts–Derby Study are discussed in *Journal of the Town Planning Institute*, Vol. 57, 1971, pp. 203–18, and by the South Hampshire Plan Advisory Committee, in 'Research techniques in structure planning: South Hampshire Plan', *Journal of the Town Planning Institute*, Vol. 56, 1970, pp. 211–33. Some problems are discussed in R. V. Arnfield (ed.), *Technological Forecasting*, Edinburgh University Press (Edinburgh), 1969 and J. N. Jackson, *Surveys for Town and Country Planning*, Hutchinson University Library (London), 1961.

These population figures provide the outward evidence for rapid if not rabid urbanization. Their significance is at the sub-regional level and they underline the need to formulate policies to accommodate this growth. They raise many national implications, because these five (typical) Sub-regions are but a part of the wider spectrum for England and Wales. Further, they represent only an iota in the world-wide prospects of aggrandization through urbanization. Who in 1870 could look forward and visualize conditions one hundred years later? In 1970 one Study has had the courage to make this daring venture into the future. It does not wish to be alarmist but 'a general continuation of past relationships could lead to pressure to build over the whole of Warwickshire as soon as 170 years hence, or 145 years if a buffer of countryside is retained between the West Midland and the Coventry Conurbations, as will then exist. That is a long time away in terms of detailed land use planning, but the direction and pressure of long term growth are powerful.'[1] Events from 1870 to 1970 provide but an introductory foretaste of the forthcoming century, but man can now take action to guide the direction and course of urban affairs. He has received sufficient warning about the consequences of inaction over the past hundred years.

INTERACTION BETWEEN FORECASTS

The previous forecasts are derived from different sets of statistics, and various methods are used. The population projections are based on the age–sex structure of the population, include assumptions about birth and death rates and more speculative forecasts of migration. The anticipations about future employment and labour supply are based on anticipations of the national and regional economic potential; projected national rates of change are applied to the subregional distribution of employment. In addition, studies may be undertaken of trends and prospects in the main industrial groups. The projections therefore stem from different bases, and for any one projection (e.g. of future employment) different methods and different assumptions may be used as a guide to the veracity of the figures. The outcome may be a high and a low figure, so that a midpoint or 'most likely' forecast is frequently used.

The point of particular importance is however not each individual projection and the nature of the underlying assumptions, but that the forecasts are interconnected and interrelated to each other in order to understand the potentiality for change of the total environment as

[1] *Warwickshire Study*, p. 89.

a series of interlocking relationships. The totals and their breakdown are internally consistent within each Sub-regional Study, given certain assumptions, and therefore provide *one* set of 'policy bundles' for subsequent locational decisions. Thus employment forecasts are linked with the population forecasts by activity rates, i.e. the proportion of the population that are gainfully employed. Income projections are derived from both the population and the employment projections, in order to provide the basis for further calculations on retail durable goods expenditure, car ownership and travel patterns. Traffic forecasting and housing demand rely on both demographic considerations, and the quality of existing facilities. The concern is with measuring the capacity for growth and change of the urban system and its several sub-systems. Accuracy and confidence must diminish both with greater detail (e.g. when distributed to sub-areas), and as the length of the time projection is extended.

This degree of interconnectedness is identified in each Study. In the North-Glos Study, 'projections of both total population and its age structure formed, in effect, the keystone of statistical forecasts of basic and service employment, housing and other future needs'.[1] In Leicestershire,

the key to exploring the possible future size of the sub-region lay in closely linked processes of forecasting population and employment. The link we decided to use was the relationship between the supply of and demand for workers of all kinds to serve all of the sub-region's economic activities. . . . On the one hand, a given population will provide a number of men and women who comprise the workforce and this can be estimated by making assumptions about the activity rate of each age group of males and females. . . . On the other hand, all the economic activities of the sub-region taken together require a labour force to sustain them and this in turn requires a population to provide it.[2]

Or, more succinctly from Teesside, 'to some extent these population forecasts are capable of manipulation by policy to achieve a desired result'.[3] In the Warwickshire growth situation, separate forecasts are made of expected increases in population and the work force, but resulted in 'so near a balance struck between jobs and workers that no adjustment to either forecast was necessary'.[4]

Against this background of interrelated forecasts, the Studies then proceed to develop a sequence of further interactions in terms of

[1] *North-Glos Study*, p. 35.   [2] *Leicestershire Study*, Vol. II, p. 27.
[3] *Teesside Study*, p. 17.   [4] *Warwickshire Study*, p. 116.

113

spatial relationships. The approach generally adopted is to determine the location of basic employment opportunities which in turn provides the rationale, in relation to trip time or trip distance for the daily journey to work, of residential distributions. Local services, and especially the journey to shopping and other centralized functions, are then computed in relation to the residential patterns. The strategies emerge as a form of cumulative accretion, determined by previous assumptions and decisions, and relying upon the selection of certain key variables for their simulation.

The socio-economic forecasts have therefore focussed on the measurable and tangible components such as population, housing, industry, employment, shopping and traffic – with recreation and tourism receiving less statistical attention – and their interaction. The impact has then been translated into generalized terms of land demand for housing and industrial sites, often as both a total figure for the Sub-region under review and in terms of the expectations within the various sub-districts. Sometimes alternative possibilities, e.g. in the rate of household formation or in the extent of migration or in employment expectations, have been considered, but these are less important than the total package of interrelated assumptions.

This package of interrelated assumptions is prepared both for the Sub-region under surveillance, and for its separate sub-districts and smaller areas. This disaggregation of regional totals is a complex and often suspect (though necessary) statistical procedure. To forecast Sub-regional populations, employment or income statistics twenty and thirty years ahead is a delicate task. The necessary breakdown of these global figures to sub-units, and then the necessity of placing reliance on the results for residential locations, trip generation and shopping habits, is no easy task. This divison of the Sub-region for analytical purposes varies both as between the Studies, but also within each Study for different purposes. The distinction between the rigid and regular division of the region by grid-squares, and the use of census areas or other informal units, will be noted. Each offers advantages and disadvantages. The former assists computer analysis but is alien to the geographical concept of environmental change and variation as a continuum. The latter may be easier for the handling of existing data, but the boundaries between units change in time.

The 360 square miles of Teesside are divided into a basic system of 350 zones, based on the enumeration districts in the 1961 Census of Population.[1] Leicestershire uses the 2 km × 2 km grid square as the minimum size of zone for simulation purposes, a procedure which

[1] *Teesside Study*, p. 6.

provides 187 zones for shopping expenditure, and 79 internal zones
and 17 external zones for trip production and attraction in the traffic
model.[1] Notts–Derby use traffic zones in both the traffic and shopping models. These are based generally on enumeration districts and
include 132 zones with an average population of 12,800 persons.
This compares with an average of 3,700 persons in the 187 Leicestershire zones.[2] In Notts–Derby also, because 'there was a computer
program restraint on the number of zones that could be handled, 62
zones were used in the Garin–Lowry model'[3] and 48 zones averaging
40 square miles in the Potential Surface model.[4] North-Glos divide
their 1,000 square miles into 'five divisions of local authority areas to
enable socio-economic characteristics and trends to be compared in
some detail'; 116 zones of parishes, groups of parishes or urban
wards are used for estimating the future distributions of population,
housing and employment, and the simulation of traffic movements
and shopping potential.[5] In the Warwickshire Study, 'the level of
generalization for most surveys, forecasts and for evaluation was the
1 km grid square, of which there are 2,300 in the sub-region',[6] and
the traffic model used 78 zones.[7]

The nature of the daunting computational problem involved is
quite apparent from the Teesside statement about their preparation
of a final land use policy and probable road system; 'the work
included the preparation of a detailed set of predictions for a system
of 211 "fine" zones about the likely distribution of population,
employment, housing, personal income and retail sales within the
selected land use proposals'.[8]

HOUSING PROJECTIONS

Donnison (1970) makes the point that 'research cannot tell us the
"right" or optimum output of houses. . . . The answers to such
questions call for judgements about the priorities to be given to
different sectors of the economy and different groups of people –
political judgements, in fact, about the kind of society we want to
create.'[9] The assessment of housing need to clarify this judgement

[1] *Leicestershire Study*, Vol. II, pp. 80 and 109.
[2] *Notts–Derby Study*, Record Report 40, p. 7 and Record Report 37, p. 3.
[3] *Ibid.*, Record Report 39, p. 3.
[4] *Ibid.*, Record Report 38, p. 3. and Record Report 32, p. 2.
[5] *North-Glos Study*, pp. 13–14.   [6] *Warwickshire Study*, p. 24.
[7] *Ibid.*, p. 158.   [8] *Teesside Study*, p. 7.
[9] D. Donnison, 'Estimating Housing Needs', *Town and Country Planning
Summer School 1970: Report of Proceedings*, Town Planning Institute, 1970, p.
23. See also P. A. Stone, *Urban Development in Britain: Standards, Costs and Re-*

involves both demographic and physical considerations. Demographic factors include the future projection of population by age, sex and marital status, the estimate of future households formed by that population and the number of households requiring their own dwellings (i.e. excluding the institional population, and those wishing voluntarily to share dwellings). Headship rates and household formation, in relation to the envisaged total population, are the critical factors. Physical considerations involve criteria for the demolition, rehabilitation and conversion of the existing housing stock. Allowances must be made for temporary dwellings and vacant premises. Each calculation, separately, has its difficulties with the situation (both in total and in the sub-districts) being dependent upon employment opportunities, the migration of population, attitudes towards investment in public and private housing, and the availability of land to secure the desired rates of construction. In addition, and especially when substantial increases or a redistribution of population are involved, the capacity of the building industry will provide a further relevant consideration.

Data sources generally used in all Studies include:

1. Local authority housing returns. This source provides the traditional source of information on housing quality, with data provided by public health inspectors. This may be taken to indicate the minimum numbers for clearance and the worst slum properties, but uniform standards are not applied. The legal criteria of unfitness in the Housing Act 1957 do not lend themselves to uniform interpretation, and estimates of unfit houses for clearance or for rehabilitation made by local authorities are sometimes based on the numbers which can be dealt with in the foreseeable future in the light of its resources. Also, housing standards and acceptable minimum standards of accommodation may be expected to rise over long-term strategy periods. No data are available either about the 'degree of unfitness', the criteria which are used, or the extent to which environmental factors and the condition of the dwelling unit are involved.

2. Housing surveys. Planning authorities have undertaken extensive surveys of the use, age and condition of buildings in their administrative area, and these details are used in the Studies. Comparability may sometimes be difficult because of different dates of survey and definitions but, in conjunction with the above local

sources, Cambridge University Press (Cambridge), 1970; L. Needleman, 'The Comparative Economics of Improvement and New Building', *Urban Studies*, Vol. 6, 1969, pp. 196–209; and D. F. Medhurst and J. P. Lewis, *Urban Decay: An Analysis and Policy*, Macmillan (London), 1969.

authority returns, the areal incidence of the problem can be studied.

3. Census data. The use of the Census of Population avoids dependence on local knowledge and personal judgement, and provides objective information by enumeration districts for certain physical criteria. Census households without access to a hot water supply, with no fixed bath and lacking an internal water closet may indicate a greater problem than suggested by the lists of statutorily unfit houses.

4. Rateable values. The rating list indicates not only the size of each dwelling, but its ownership, condition and situation. However, rateable comparisons within towns may be easier than between towns because of different economic and social circumstances.

The Notts–Derby and North-Glos Studies each examine this range of data.[1] In addition, Notts–Derby note that 'it will be necessary to carry out a comprehensive sample survey of the sub-region's property, and to devise a method of using this to help make the choice between improvement and replacement of buildings in each case',[2] and Teesside and Leicestershire include additional material from sample surveys in their Studies. Their evaluation procedures cover the condition of the dwelling, its internal facilities, age, house type, means of access, outdoor space, environment and location under several sub-headings. Thus, 'Teesside was divided into 75 environmental areas. The survey showed for each area its priority for treatment; the number of dwellings likely to be affected by clearance, rehabilitation, development and redevelopment, making due allowance for changes of use . . . and a first indication of the likely cost of treatment.'[3] Four priority groups are identified and these, in sequence, are areas where nearly complete clearance would be required, areas which will need either comprehensive clearance or intensive area rehabilitation, other areas with houses built before 1914 and which are described as 'the heart of the rehabilitation problem',[4] and areas built during the last thirty or forty years where deficiencies are likely to be of nominal character. Great importance is attached to this survey and analysis of housing stock as a basis for the housing programme; the evaluation is of environmental conditions as well as the individual buildings.

In Leicestershire the field survey of dwellings resulted in the award of penalty points against the estimated cost of remedying the deficiencies and this led through to the use of a mathematical model. 'The rate at which the existing housing stock will deteriorate to the

[1] *North-Glos Study*, pp. 41–2 and *Notts–Derby Study*, p. 15.
[2] *Notts–Derby Study*, p. 15. [3] *Teesside Study*, p. 34. [4] *Ibid.*, p. 34.

point of needing replacement is difficult to assess with any degree of certainty. . . . As an approximate measure of the problem, we have developed a simple model for determining which dwellings should be replaced and which could be improved and given an extended life. The basis of the model is the cost of remedying faults in the structure, content and environment of the dwelling.'[1] The survey was a 1 per cent sample in kilometre squares and the penalty points were 3,065, including 635 for structure, 2,200 for environment and 230 for facilities. Duncan (1971) suggests that this distribution provides for an undue weighting towards environment. 'The whole system is an economic-based one and this would appear to be acceptable in relation to the dwelling exterior items. . . . When transposed to remedying environmental defects, however, the same technique involves too many assumptions to be credible. . . . The methodological defect here is surely in weighting environmental items independently of dwelling items, rather than in first balancing up the overall case between the two groups.'[2]

Warwickshire also made use of an environmental survey but, instead of a cost-based assessment with points related directly to the costs of improving the environment, the preference is for 'an assessment based on socially-desirable weightings defining a level of environment, but not immediately related to costs on a points basis'.[3] It included a variety of visual elements (e.g. a noxious category is directly affected by dominating large scale industrial/commercial use/derelict land/with/without intensive street parking; closeness of other dwellings and badly maintained aspect); traffic danger and noise; the presence of amenities including car parking space, the proximity of public transport, shops, schools, public open space and play space; and additional penalty points for exceptional factors such as excessive noise, smell, dust, smoke and serious visual problems.[4] There is in addition a structural assessment in terms of the condition of the walls and the roof, but not internal fittings, services and the size of rooms.

The great unknown in all such assessments is not so much the systematic survey analysis of the housing stock, but the sheer factor of estimating the future response to these conditions. Standards and attitudes are likely to change from the standpoint of the occupants.

[1] *Leicestershire Study*, p. 52.

[2] T. L. C. Duncan, *Measuring Housing Quality: A Study of Methods*, Occasional Paper No. 20, Centre for Urban and Regional Studies, University of Birmingham, 1971, p. 105.

[3] *Warwickshire Study*, p. 174.   [4] *Ibid.*, p. 175.

The costs of rehabilitation, vacancy rates, the attitudes of the housing authorities to clearance, the role of the national government, the level of grants and subsidies, and the interplay between public and private enterprise are each factors of considerable importance which can radically affect the future position. The plea in all Studies is for substantial volumes of action against these uncertainties and in the light of known existing conditions. The Studies themselves help to formulate policy whereas, for example, when assessing the changes in employment or population, the basic policy decisions are more generally formulated elsewhere.

A variant to the above Sub-regional approaches is provided by the Halifax Area Study. In this instance alternative investment possibilities in housing demonstrate the effects of the shortage of land and the poor quality of the housing stock on population projections. Four population trends are 'based on the assumption that the number of existing houses which should be cleared by 1981 is equivalent to all those with a rateable value of less than £30';[1] other population trends are based on a reduced standard of acceptability, and the clearance of only half of such houses. Further combinations result by varying the replacement rate, from the recent rate of 1,000 houses a year upwards to 1,500 houses a year. Eight alternative projections thus result from varying these alternative assumptions, to emphasize the importance of housing decisions for the future size and well-being of urban populations. In the Teesside Study, the same type of issue presented itself, and three alternative policies for housing rehabilitation and new house construction are examined. An increased rate of clearance is needed over existing policies; 'if the clearance and replacement of slum dwellings continued at its present rate, then serious consequences would follow'.[2]

Against these several contingencies (population increase, improved space standards, clearance of existing sub-standard dwellings, rate of household formation, the deterioration of existing housing stock, the possibilities of rehabilitation), the Studies each make substantial demands for new housing provision as follows:

Teesside. Against an existing construction rate of 3,000 to 3,800 new dwellings each year, the recommended policy requires 4,200 dwellings per year in 1966–1971, rising to 5,100 by 1968–1991.

[1] Yorkshire and Humberside Economic Planning Council and Board, *Halifax and the Calder Valley*, Department of Economic Affairs, HMSO (London), 1969, pp. 107–8.
[2] *Teesside Study*, p. 36.

North-Glos. The housing stock at 1966 is 149,200 units. A replacement of 50,000 houses is envisaged between 1966–2001; 57,300 houses are required between 1966–1981 and 73,900 from 1981–2001.

Leicestershire. Against 238,590 dwellings at 1966, the replacement of 31,000 units between 1971–1991 is recommended. The rate for new constructions will increase from 10,000 over each five-year period between 1966–1981, to 12,200 between 1981–1986, and 15,000+ from 1986–1996.

Notts–Derby. Comparable figures are not included in this Study. 'The Sub-region as a whole has an above average proportion of lower quality housing, but needs far more housing of the standard sought by the more highly skilled workers and up-and-coming executives.'

Warwickshire. The stock of all dwellings at 1966 is 321,000. The clearance of obsolete and unfit dwellings should increase from 3,250 (1966–1971) to 6,600 (1976–1981) to 15,700 (1986–1991). Total household spaces should increase to 392,160 by 1976, 448,020 by 1986 and to 477,290 by 1991.

The housing situation is quite obviously severe, and urgent needs are apparent not only for higher rates of construction but for higher standards of space within and around dwellings. As incomes and real standards of living rise, a growing social dissatisfaction with the poor standards of housing in certain areas may be expected. It is figures such as these which must be borne in mind when considering the physical and other constraints on development discussed in Chapter 4. The magnitude of the housing problem should be apparent from these statistics. It underlies the continuing prospects of urban growth which have been demonstrated in each Study. The Warwickshire figure of 'homes for nearly three million people (1·1 million at 1971) to live in the sub-region around the middle of the next century',[1] is not an astounding invention. It is founded on the bedrock of reality, and may be echoed and re-echoed from other localities in Britain for its implications on land use and urban development.

RECREATIONAL PROJECTIONS

Even more difficult and imprecise than for population, employment or housing, are the future forecasts of recreation needs. The Notts–Derby Study notes that 'quantifying the expected demand is an

[1] *Warwickshire Study*, p. 27.

extremely complex problem in view of the large number of variable factors which affect it. . . . There is no information which is adequate for refinining the global estimate into demands for particular types of recreation. There is no body of information on a consistent basis for the sub-region which allows present level of activity to be assessed.'[1] The conclusion is that 'a substantial shift in preferences, influenced by the charges levied for facilities, may mean that the rise is much greater in some types of recreation than others. . . . The only way to meet this uncertain situation will be to provide further facilities whenever those existing become overcrowded.'[2] The South East Study make a comparable comment. 'A recreational supply and demand balance sheet would be helpful in identifying present and future problems and in establishing priorities for investment, but adequate information in many fields is lacking and techniques for using such information as is available are not in an advanced stage of development.'[3] Against this backcloth of uncertainty, to use the words of the North-Glos Study, 'it is now generally accepted that the demand for outdoor recreational facilities is likely to increase rapidly during the next few decades as a result of growth of population, car ownership and leisure time available'.[4] The statistical basis is slender, but an awareness of the need exists in all the Studies.

The Warwickshire Study, as befits the latest contribution, makes more extensive but nevertheless still uncertain projections. 'A model was constructed of available leisure time at 1966 and 1991, taking into account various demographic and socio-economic factors. This time allocation was then broken down into broad recreational groupings. . . . Little or no evidence is available about changing patterns of leisure and therefore many important assumptions have to be made. This is inevitable in any forecasting but the problems associated with recreation are particularly difficult. . . . Another limitation was the shortage of available data on leisure in the sub-region.'[5] The results, as with housing or population itself, are quite astounding. 'The demand for all kinds of recreational facility is certain to increase by 1991 and probably at a much faster rate than due to the sub-region's population growth alone.'[6] In addition, there are the pressures onto the area from the Birmingham Conurbation and the growing incidence of international tourism. The previous need for a countryside management strategy is seen in perspective against such data.

---

[1] *Notts–Derby Study*, p. xliv.   [2] *Ibid.*, p. 27.
[3] *South East Study*, p. 37.   [4] *North-Glos Study*, p.100.
[5] *Warwickshire Study*, p. 149.   [6] *Ibid.*, p. 152.

SHOPPING PROJECTIONS

The Sub-regional Studies assess future shopping needs, emphasizing the retail trade in durable goods and with local service (mainly food) shops not being regarded as a subject for concern at the sub-regional level of planning. In the North-Glos Study the conclusion is that, 'whilst spending in real terms on durable goods will increase as the standard of living rises, the effects of this in terms of space requirements in town centres will be largely offset by the effects of increased efficiency in the use of shop floor space. . . . It was assumed, therefore, that the size of centres in terms of total floor space could be expected to increase proportionally with increases of their population catchments.'[1] The analysis in the Leicestershire Study indicates an existing and committed floorspace of 2·9 million square feet in 51 centres at 1967. 'The additional increase beyond this yet to be provided either in new planned centres or by extensions of existing ones in the sub-region by 1981 was between 276,200 and 293,200 square feet and by 1991 between 754,500 and 771,400 according to strategy selected.'[2]

The Notts–Derby Study states that,

the amount of selling space required in each shopping centre in the future will depend upon a number of factors which cannot be determined by a sub-regional study. These include the ability of shops to increase their turnover within their existing premises, the rate at which retailing spending increases as a result of the rising standard of living, the ability of the centre to compete with its rivals of similar size, the local access and car parking arrangements and the ease with which sites can be obtained for expansion. Assuming the effect of all these factors is uniform, there will be some additional changes in turnover in certain centres arising from the proposed strategy.[3]

Six centres have an increase of between 29 to 38 per cent between 1961 and 1986; three others have an increase, and twelve diminish in their durable goods turnover.[4] On Teesside, 'the increase in sales per square foot is likely to be of the order of 70 per cent during the next twenty-five years. But total retail expenditure is likely to increase by about 160 per cent because of the compound effects of the increase in population and the increase in per capita expenditure. At present Teesside has about 5·1 million square feet of shopping

[1] *North-Glos Study*, p. 98.   [2] *Leicestershire Study*, Vol. II, p. 101.
[3] *Notts–Derby Study*, p. 45.   [4] *Ibid.*, p. 49.

floor space and an additional 3·5 million square feet are likely to be required during the next twenty-five years.'[1]

The Studies thus envisage increasing demands, though a formidable array of assumptions underlie this assessment. The future is based on prediction techniques of socio-economic variables such as population, income and travel, rather than entrepreneurial behaviour and the reorganization of retailing (e.g. the large outlet replacing many individual stores). The models used are derived from Reilly's law of retail gravitation, which was used to examine the prospects for a new out-of-town regional centre at Haydock in 1964.[2] The basis of the model used in the Studies extends the concept from the gravity relationships between population size and accessibility to incorporate something of consumer behaviour, and the probability of travel to more than one centre for the purchase of different types of goods. It relies, in particular, on a model developed by Lakshmanan and Hansen (1965) to evaluate alternative strategies for the location of retailing centres in the Baltimore Region.[3]

The Warwickshire Study provides the exception to the above comments. It does not undertake these investigations, and defers their consideration to the later stage of structure planning by the local planning authorities. The argument is that 'it was not useful to calculate demand for shopping floor space in the centres in 1991, nor would any short term calculations have helped in evaluating the alternatives. The authorities will wish to make calculations of this kind during Structure Planning within an agreed sub-regional strategy.'[4] With so much importance attached to these calculations elsewhere this approach is surprising, but the location and internal structure of the settlement pattern takes precedence over an uncertain assessment of future journeys to shops and the translation of retail expenditure into floor-space requirements in each shopping centre. These details will be discussed below under urban models.

THE SIGNIFICANCE OF INTERRELATED FORECASTS

It is important to note that all strategies in each Study are based on

[1] *Teesside Study*, p. 54.

[2] R. H. Kantorowich, H. W. E. Davies, J. N. Jackson and D. G. Robinson, *Regional Shopping Centres: Planning Report on North-West England*, and *Part 2: A Retail Shopping Model*, Department of Town and Country Planning, University of Manchester (Manchester), 1964 and 1966.

[3] T. R. Lakshmanan and W. G. Hansen, 'A Retail Market Potential Model', *Journal of the American Institute of Planners*, Vol. 31, 1965, pp. 134–43.

[4] *Warwickshire Study*, p. 87.

123

one series of interrelated forecasts. There is the *one* expectation of growth to an assumed regional figure or range of expectancy, which is then distributed in the area under review. Thus, if the assessment is that the Sub-region should expand by 500,000 persons over the next thirty years, the discussion then focusses on the alternative possibilities for the distribution of this increase in terms of its location, density and urban form. Should there, for example, be one new independent centre, four smaller satellite cities or peripheral expansion, and which areas of land should be used for these developments? In the transportation studies, the number of trips are calculated from socio-economic forecasts and remain constant in all the alternative strategies. Even though different networks and different land use patterns are proposed, as these depend on the same total population and the same total employment, variants are made only in the distribution of trips to the network and in their division between modes of transport. The total number of trips remains a fixed ingredient, because there is the same basis of population, employment and their related projections in each Study for all strategies. As the alternative strategies always depend upon this one set of interrelated statistical assumptions, a likely weakness of all Studies is that the situation will almost certainly be falsified by the outcome of events. An unexpected change in any one factor can invalidate by chain reaction several other assumptions.

The reasons for this 'unified package' are that, if population growth is distributed within the Sub-region against varying hypotheses, then evaluation procedures are possible by various means *within* the context of the Study. Comparative tests by cost, transportation, accessibility and physical criteria can be applied. This approach no longer becomes possible if '*x*' per cent of the new industry or population is exported to other localities in one strategy and if all growth is retained in another strategy. Measurement of the differences is not then possible at the *sub-regional* level; the differences, in costs and benefits, now become a national responsibility. The same argument would apply for immigration. Thus, whether 100,000 additional population from Greater Birmingham can best be accommodated in the Leicestershire, Notts–Derby, Warwickshire or North-Glos Study areas cannot be examined on a comparative base at the sub-regional level, but involves a national evaluation of the relative differences. An important feature of all Studies is that they are concerned with variations within a given framework, rather than with varying the framework itself.

In the absence of a national land use plan and with no directives about the future national distribution of population, population forecasts have necessarily been derived from the best available information and in the light of local circumstances and envisaged trends. Reasoned assumptions about migration have been made, but population totals (except in the two Regional Feasibility Studies) are *not* a given factor in the terms of reference in order to ensure some predetermined distribution of a national total. It thus cannot be expected that the sum of all regional expectations would be the same as the national forecast. The same argument must apply to the provision of job opportunities and dwellings, *inter alia*. There will be deficiencies or excesses at the sub-regional level in relation to national expectations. Also, it is not necessarily true that the proposals which are best, separately, for each sector of the community are the best for the country as a whole envisaged as a totality of interlocking relationships. The preparation of Regional and Sub-regional studies does not obviate the need for the guiding framework of a national plan and, in fact, reinforces this need.

These arguments are not invalidated by the fact that in several forecasts, the projected figure is based on ratio-apportionment from the presumed national data. For example, the population statistics in the North–Glos Study assume the same trend in its share of population in England and Wales as exhibited between 1939 and 1966;[1] in the Notts–Derby Study the estimates of future employment are based in part on national forecasts of changes in individual industries,[2] and in the Leicestershire and Warwickshire Studies ratio-apportionment techniques are used for the forecasts of the working population.[3] 'These techniques rest on the observation that the share (whether of production or employment in a particular sector of industry) which any area possesses of the respective total for a larger "parent" area exhibits regularity and stability over time.'[4] This assumption diminishes in validity as the length of the projection extends, and regional relationships to the national situation cannot be expected to remain fixed as at a given point or over a given period in time. Regional preferment and regional advantage is certain to result in varying degrees of divergence from an established or existing situation in the future. Again the requirement is for a national plan to provide guidance on such matters. In the meantime the only possibility at the sub-regional level is to proceed on the basis of logical deductions from present circumstances.

[1] *North-Glos Study*, p. 36.   [2] *Notts–Derby Study*, p. xii.
[3] *Warwickshire Study*, pp. 93–110 and *Leicestershire Study*, Vol. II, pp. 28–46.
[4] *Leicestershire Study*, Vol. II, p. 29.

The forecasts are therefore internally consistent with each other, and are based on certain assumptions derived from existing relationships. Rather than toss a coin, draw straws or rely on conjecture, a systematic process of thought has been developed with one event being related to another as part of a progressive sequence. There is recognition of the geographical concept of the urban community as 'a complex web of diverse and functionally interdependent interacting parts, with the parts evolving over time as they attempt to adapt to constantly changing contexts around them'.[1] But if *all* the key variables have not been identified, then the chain of argument and the processes of thought must be incomplete or inexact. The need is not necessarily for more analysis, but for better analysis and for a greater appreciation of the subtle inter-dependencies between sets of statistics, of the relationships as they now exist and how they may be expected to change in the future. Otherwise, inaccuracies must result. In the words of Alonso (1968), 'long chains of argument are the delight of theorists and the source of their mistrust by practical men. There is some merit in this distrust. Imagine that we argue that if A then B, if B then C, etc. If we are 80 percent certain of each step in the chain, from the joint probability of the steps it follows that we are less than 50 percent certain of where we stand after four steps. Thus the brilliant deductive chains of Sherlock Holmes or the young Ellery Queen, while dazzling, leave us with the feeling that they will not secure a conviction.'[2]

Flow diagrams are often incorporated in the Studies in order to indicate this chain of reasoning and the nature of the data required or the assumptions to be made at each sequential stage of the argument. Ten, twenty or more blocks of information or procedural assumptions may be involved to assess, for example, the required amount of additional retailing space in a central area or the anticipated flow of traffic between two points on the road network. Data are included from a variety of different sources, and are subject to different sets of qualifications because of the accuracy of sample studies, problems associated with precise definition and other statistical points of interpretation. Any progression through the series of steps which are necessary in virtually all projections must involve a compounding of different types of uncertainty. The final estimates, inevitably,

[1] W. A. Steger and T. R. Lakshmanan, 'Plan Evaluation Methodologise: Some aspects of Decision Requirements and Analytical Response', in Highway Research Board, *Urban Development Models*, National Academy of Sciences (Washington), 1968.

[2] W. Alonso, 'The Quality of Data and the Choice and Design of Predictive Models' in Highway Research Board, *ibid.*, p. 178.

are less certain than the previous material on which they are based. This problem is offset to some extent by deriving a range of high and low estimates, by using mid-point figures and by using different methods of analysis to arrive at the most acceptable figure, but much more information is required in all Studies about the probability of error in the major forecasts. 'Accuracy' cannot be expected in the uncertain conditions of the future, but the 'degree of uncertainty' which might be attached to various estimates, assumptions and projections of the future could be identified more clearly.[1]

The Studies are aware of this problem. Leicestershire record that 'it is widely recognized that forecasting economic activity is one of the most hazardous jobs in applied social science. The number of factors to be considered is large'.[2] Warwickshire aver that 'our employment forecasts will not be realized exactly, for they effectively predict the consequences of a multitude of public and private policies and decisions on investment, and can reasonably be expected to foresee only a range of possibilities'.[3] Or in the North-Glos terms, 'the predictions embodied certain assumptions which are supported by current evidence. However, because of the rapidly changing socio-economic characteristics of modern society these will need to be checked against fact at regular intervals in the future'.[4] The purpose of all forecasts is to establish the scale of the problem, to furnish a reasonable basis for future decision and to anticipate pressures on scarce land resources. A spurious accuracy is not pretended. They provide a 'guide to possibilities' and, as conditions alter, the forecasts will have to be amended.

To compound the statistical problem, a great planning difficulty in the development of an 'accurate' and consecutive argument is that the sequence must also rely on evidence of human behaviour, which is not fully known for the present and which cannot be predicted with certainty over periods of thirty and thirty-five years into the future. No planning interpretation of the future has yet pretended to infallibility, and the great danger is that uncertain assumptions are faithfully accepted as certain eventualities. The important task, both professionally in academic institutions and practically in planning offices, is to ensure that the underlying socio-economic assumptions are reviewed continually for their improvement. The public have an especially important watch-dog function in this respect because

[1] See, for example, J. Parry Lewis, *Mis-used Techniques in Planning: Cost Benefit Analysis*, Occasional Paper No. 2, Centre for Urban and Regional Research, University of Manchester, Undated (1970?), pp. 9–10.
[2] *Leicestershire Study*, Vol. II, p. 27.　　　[3] *Warwickshire Study*, p. 92.
[4] *North-Glos Study*, p. 35.

ultimately, and through their elected representatives, it is their function to approve or reject the strategic proposals for action.

URBAN MODELS

Models, as generalized representations of relationships, have their own special appetite for quantities of data. They illustrate the interconnectedness between data, a chain of reasoning and the use of sub-zones in statistical analysis. For example, building a gravity shopping model requires information or assumptions on the following socio-economic detail:[1]

1. the area of the study, its division into sub-areas and the criteria for drawing these boundaries;
2. population resident in each zone;
3. retail spending rates, reflecting income differences;
4. a subtraction figure from income to allow for holiday and other non-regional expenditures;
5. a further subtraction figure to be spent on local service goods;
6. future rates of income growth and its distribution to zones in relation to the envisaged population, ten, twenty and thirty years hence;
7. the effects of income change on items 3, 4 and 5 above;
8. the selection and grading of the shopping centres to be used both within and beyond the study area (i.e. distinguishing between central area trade and total trade);
9. car ownership rates, now and tomorrow, and itself derived in part from the income projections; current and future allowance for public transport routes;
10. travel speeds, and calculation of distances, between each zone;
11. the accessibility of differing retail centres, with each centre classified by its size and position in the shopping hierarchy;
12. the relative attraction of each shopping centre to each grouping of the population, perhaps distinguishing between different types of goods.
13. expenditure by external residents, including visitors and tourists in each shopping centre.
14. allowances for the growth or decline in the existing areas of central area retailing space, and the introduction of new centres with their degree of attraction.

[1] This listing is based, in part, on A. S. Pope, 'Gravity Models in Town Planning: Use in Retailing Exercises', in *Gravity Models in Town Planning*, Department of Town Planning, Lanchester Polytechnic, Coventry, 1969, pp. 65–6.

15. the translation of anticipated sales into retail floor space, including an allowance for changes in productivity over the planning period.

There will always be debate on the most suitable means of analysis, in relation to the available resources, the time schedule and the purposes for which data are required. Models provide considerable assistance; there are also considerable doubts about their use, the accuracy of the data which are used and the nature of the assumptions which have to be made. As Alonso (1968) states,

> what is lacking is a dispassionate report on findings and failures from which scholars in this field, including those in the project, can test and evolve new understanding of the phenomena with which we are dealing and techniques to deal with them. Researchers are being put in the very difficult position of being both practitioners and innovators. As practitioners, they are called upon to use techniques that have a high probability of success. . . . The institutional context of these studies . . . [is] the pressing need to decide how to spend vast quantitites of money in urban infrastructure, and thus hampers the openness of method, the candidness of reportage, and the freedom of discussion of these important studies. This represents a dreadful waste, as errors are repeated and successes are not followed up.[1]

Professional publications and commentaries in learned journals do not offset this need.[2] Papers on the subject are written primarily for technical audiences, and a gulf of misunderstanding exists in the profession (and between the profession and the public) over those who are numerate and those who lack this mathematical ability. Some writers are also highly critical of recent attempts at developing new techniques. Lewis (1970) states that, 'if knowledge or techniques are so mis-applied, or publicized in terms that so exaggerate their merits, that the whole course of teaching, researching and practising in the invaded subject is in danger of being wrongly redirected, he who sees it must say so plainly. In my view this is happening in planning. . . . I feel, not simply that there is a danger that planning and urban studies will be mis-directed, but rather that the mis-direction has already occurred.'[3]

[1] Alonso, *op. cit.*, p. 191.

[2] A rudimentary conceptual framework is discussed in A. G. Wilson, 'Models in Urban Planning: A Synoptic Review of Recent Literature', *Urban Studies*, Vol. 5, 1968, pp. 249–76.

[3] J. Parry Lewis, 'The invasion of planning', *Journal of the Town Planning Institute*, Vol. 56, 1970, p. 100.

E

As the Studies under review and much of strategic planning for the urban future must stand or fall by the validity of such comment, there would seem to be the immediate and urgent need for a detailed, unrestricted, dispassionate and critical appraisal of the role of models and advanced statistical analysis in the planning process. Such an inquiry should be instituted by the Department of the Environment and by the Royal Town Planning Institute, and should have on its membership both 'doubting Thomases' and 'adherents to the cause'. Its purpose would be to describe the construction, the strengths and the weaknesses of the models which have been developed over the past few years, and to present a discerning and accurate assessment of their practical significance. The report would be written for a wide professional and public audience, rather than as an abstruse technical document. In the words of Harris (1968) summarizing the proceedings of an American conference on urban development models, 'another major area of concern in the exercise of model-building has to do with the confidence of the general public, the decision-makers, and the model-builders themselves in the accuracy and reliability of their work. A whole area of this problem has to do with decision-making under uncertainty, including uncertainty as to tastes and technology.'[1]

It is essential that the planning profession be able to assure this confidence. Work which is avowedly pioneer and exploratory in its method deserves this follow-up appraisal of its real merit and an impartial evaluation of its meaningful contribution to the planning process. Should the outcome be favourable, then an official manual for practitioners might also usefully be prepared, with regular up-dating as new techniques are explored and proved to be trustworthy.

THE TIME PERIOD OF THE FORECASTS

The earlier town and county development plans, prepared from 1951 onwards under the aegis of the Town and Country Planning Act 1947, are based on a twenty-year planning period, with the first five years being presented in greater detail than for the subsequent period of fifteen years. Sites required for later developments could also be reserved if deemed necessary. The Studies under review have extended this time period of twenty years to about thirty-five years, and have been tested against various models at ten- or fifteen-year periods into the future for their essential validity. They are not 'leaps into the

[1] Britton Harris, 'Conference Summary and Recommendations', in Highway Research Board, *op. cit.*, p. 11.

future', but progress by reasoned stages. It is generally considered that the overall time span cannot be extended further with any degree of statistical accuracy, because the distant future must be unknown in precise terms. Many social scientists would in fact doubt whether thirty-year projections on points of detail are valid and would not consider that reasonable estimates of possible conditions can be made beyond a fifteen- or twenty-year period. Certainly, beyond thirty years there can be no reasonable limits of confidence about precise future conditions.

An alternative argument is however that the length of the planning period should be extended, because it is shorter than the life expectancy of many existing structures and of all the major works to be constructed. Communications, housing, the various utility systems, and other development above and below ground will certainly outlive the strategy period, and will continue thereafter to influence the form and direction of subsequent urban growth. An average life expectancy of from seventy-five to a hundred years would thus not be unreasonable, but a century ahead is far beyond the capacity of economic, social and technological prediction.

The answer is to avoid being hypnotized by the grandeur of 2000 or the magic of 2001 and end-of-the-century predictions. The strategy period should always be regarded as just one phase in the continuous evolution and change of man's environment on earth over time. Geographic and historic perspective are necessary, and some thought should be given to the longer term and emerging prospects of urbanization. The need for *two* periods of strategic planning may indeed be suggested. The first, as identified in the Studies, would be based on various statistical forecasts for about thirty years. The second would be for a longer period unsupported by statistics, but assuming a continuation of urban development trends which have been initiated over the first period. The latter would be schematic in terms of major transportation arteries and land use only, and would be concerned with expressing the directions and significance of urban growth patterns. The idea is as developed in the Hampshire Study in that, in an area of growth, 'a fundamental requirement . . . [is] a physical form of development which is adaptable and grows as circumstances dictate'.[1] The second stage might, for example, consider the situation when the Sub-region or Region of study accommodated a population 25 and 50 per cent over the envisaged end-of-the-century population.

The need for this longer-term consideration may be illustrated

[1] *Hampshire Study*, p. 37.

from the Humberside Study which envisages, but does not include in its hypothetical development forms by 2001, two important proposals. The first is the possibility of large-scale reclamation and industrial development at Spurn Bight on the north shore of the Estuary and, second, another Humber Crossing after the first bridge reaches its saturation point about 1991. A further important consideration is that one major city centre at Hull would upgrade the provision of urban services to those of a provincial centre, whereas the outcome of the Study as conceived with one bridge is that, 'unless a crossing could be provided which would lead from the south bank into the Hull city centre, major population growth in South Humberside would have its own major city centre, eventually almost rivalling Hull in size'.[1] A second bridge is excluded from the proposals because the emphasis is on the feasibility of development over a relatively short period of time but, had the time span been extended, then the significance of a second bridge on the form of development would have been appreciated. If would for example permit the elevation of Hull's status to the higher order of a Provincial Capital, offset the duplicate provision of two lower-category centres and strengthen the possibilities for a linear form of development in horseshoe shape around the Humber Estuary, including the Spurn Bight possibilities.

In a like vein, the longer the period of forecast, the greater the extent of urbanization which might reasonably be anticipated, and the higher therefore the pressures for existing cities such as Birmingham/Coventry, Gloucester/Cheltenham or Nottingham/Derby to coalesce. An extended perspective should therefore provide some additional weight for policies of great long-term importance such as improvements to landscape quality, the safeguarding of productive farmland, the provision of additional recreation facilities, and generally when management or conservation measures are required to protect dwindling environmental assets. The problems of conflict are likely to aggravate rather than lessen in the future, and the longer-term perspective permits a 'grander vision' on where urbanization is likely to take us. The precision required in urban systems analysis can inhibit this long-term perspective, so that an important ingredient at the generalized level of consideration may be omitted from the desirable processes of planning thought. In the words of the Teesside Study, 'urban structure policy for the next twenty-five years should be flexible at least to the extent that it does not actively impede (or prejudice) long term growth beyond 1991. . . . There are several key

---

[1] *Humberside Study*, p. 121.

locations in which the opportunities for long-term development must be preserved as part of the current urban structure policy.'[1] In such circumstances, the situation beyond 1991 must at least be glimpsed.

The South East Study provides another illustration. This incorporates population data up to 1969, anticipates the situation in the region by 1981, and then examines two alternative hypotheses for the 1981 to 1991 period. As the situation by 1981 is largely predetermined by existing commitments, the only effective planning period over which the direction of future development can be influenced is that of ten years from 1981 to 1991. To examine thoroughly the feasibility of alternative propositions, to examine the effectiveness of alternative hypotheses, and to guide future urban dispositions in a meaningful and positive direction, requires a longer time period. As it is, the major issues as the South East continues to grow are being deferred for later examination. The requirement is for a longer-term perspective indicating the major form and directions of growth on a continuing basis in addition to and beyond the envisaged time span. For example, in the Warwickshire Study, there is some anticipation of the long-range pressures for homes until about the middle of the next century. This gave 'perspective to the Study by emphasizing that the alternatives being considered were not absolute, and that the preferred strategy and 1991 are stages in the long-term development of the sub-region'.[2]

An important aspect about the time period for strategic urban policies is that the implementation of a strategy requires a regular and co-ordinated flow of resources from a variety of public and private sources to achieve integrated development within the Sub-region. Resources from various sectors of the economy (housing, industry, education, public utilities, communications) must be ensured in sequence and in harmony over several years, if not decades. But planners do not have absolute authority, reliance must be placed on the continuity of government and public support in order to achieve envisaged policies. A useful reminder in this context is that planning forecasts are for longer periods than the usual extent of political control, at either the local or the national levels of government. Councillors and members of parliament seek re-election and may well prefer to support short-term measures to remedy some apparent deficiency, than a series of long-term undertakings that cannot be financed on the basis of annual or quinquennial budgets. Strong public support and backing, including the sympathetic encouragement of the public media, have important roles

[1] *Teesside Study*, p. 111.   [2] *Warwickshire Study*, p. 27.

133

THE URBAN FUTURE

to play in this respect because the planning need is to ensure continuity in decision-making over an extensive period of time.

One difficulty at this stage of the argument is that, in the early
stages of the planning period, the availability of resources to achieve
development is a (relatively) known factor. The possibilities of
significant divergence from the present state of affairs, because of
existing commitments, does not occur until perhaps five or sometimes
ten years after the period of plan preparation. The time period when
alternatives can first be realistically considered therefore occurs
when there is increasing uncertainty about the availability of financial
and other resources to achieve development. The optimistic viewpoint is that resources will increase and that the gross national
product will rise – but there can be no certainty about either this or
any other conclusion.

The period referred to, i.e. when strategies can effectively be bent
towards some predetermined future, may be described as the 'effective time period'. It results from existing commitments to development, and has been identified above to be from 1981 to 1991 in the
South East Study. In the North-Glos Study, with its division into the
two phases of 1966 to 1981 and 1981 to 2001, the greater scope of the
second phase for change and modification is recognized. Thus, 'it
was considered realistic to assume that Green Belt policy would not
be modified at least until after 1981, except in relation to small
areas'.[1] With regard to the distribution of housing, for the first
phase this 'broadly followed current development trends . . . and
tended towards the major locational options particular to the
strategy'.[2] The phrase 'tended towards' becomes 'taking full account
of' the major locational options particular to the strategy in the
second phase.

The Teesside Study indicates that existing commitments are
strong. They include 780 acres of committed industrial land on
various industrial estates which, if developed, would strongly influence future employment distributions. These sites are assumed to
provide for 31,000 additional jobs by 1991, leaving 'a deficiency of
nearly 22,000 jobs for which new industrial estates will have to be
selected and laid out with services.'[3] Only the latter can be used to
exert an influence on alternative possible strategies. A comparable
situation exists with regard to housing sites. There are existing
residential land commitments to 50,700 houses, and 'land will be
required in the next twenty-five years for about 103,800 dwellings.'[4]

[1] *North-Glos Study*, p. 67.   [2] *Ibid.*, p. 67.
[3] *Teesside Study*, p. 60.   [4] *Ibid.*, p. 38.

134

In Warwickshire, 'the scope to channel new employment to the advantage of alternative strategies . . . is much less than the total increase in employment might suggest. Of the extra 90,000 jobs which might arise between 1976 and 1991, perhaps 52,000 will settle in existing town centres and industrial and commercial centres. 14,000 new manufacturing jobs may be sited adjoining existing urban areas because of ties with existing factories. . . . As few as 24,000 jobs may be so footloose that the sub-regional strategy can completely influence where they will locate.'[1] The scope for amendment is limited, the inertia from the existing situation is strong, and the scope to change the situation is long-term rather than immediate.

Given this situation, in the Leicestershire Study, 'the period 1966–71 was uniquely treated because we believed that up to the end of that quinquennium at least, no major change of direction could be introduced – that the decisions which would shape the Leicester and Leicestershire of 1971 had already been taken and nothing we could say or do would alter the course of change before then. . . . In the period 1971–76 commitments began to play a less important role in guiding the steps in simulation (but they still exist). . . . Beyond 1976 we felt free to introduce our own suggestions for road construction and improvement.'[2]

A necessary part of each Study is to identify commitments in terms of land already allocated for specific purposes, and new utilities, roads, buildings and structures which are already under construction. The future, to a considerable extent, is largely determined by the existing situation and by commitments. If a strategy is prepared in 1966 for an end-date of 1991, developments in the pipeline carry the momentum of the existing urban situation onwards, and little can be done to achieve redirection until 1976. These arguments are expressed in physical terms. They are less applicable in terms of social policy, budget controls or legislation where more immediate changes are possible. They are summarized by the statement in the Warwickshire Study which identifies a series of six significant dates for analysis, projection and evaluation, and a context period of one hundred and fifty years, as follows:[3]

1961 Projections based upon returns of 1961 Census of Population.

1966 Projections calibrated or based upon returns of 1966 Census of Population.

1971 Year of publication and consultation on the Study.

[1] *Warwickshire Study*, p. 15.   [2] *Leicestershire Study*, pp. 38–9.
[3] *Warwickshire Study*, p. 27.

135

1976   The earliest date at which the strategy could start to have a visible effect on the sub-region, and effectively the base year from which alternative strategies for subsequent years were developed.

1981   The date by which most districts will run out of building land as allocated within present plans, and the earliest date by which sufficient development could be envisaged to justify any examination of alternative land use and transportation strategies.

1991   The major stage in forecasting and evaluating alternative strategies.

1801–
2051   The Study period in perspective.

VARIABLES EXCLUDED FROM THE FORECASTING PROCEDURES

The discussion has focussed on the forecasts and anticipations which precede the preparation of planning strategies. It is not a simple task even to understand the present situation, and the complexities increase and the assumptions expand as the attempt is made to predict future conditions. The chosen degree of emphasis in the Studies relies on certain selected and measurable variables. The emphasis is on accessibility, population, housing demand and employment and the use of these variables to determine the location and spatial distribution of industrial areas, residential districts and service facilities. However, it is also important to know *what is left out* because, if the omitted items are considered to be important, or if a different weight of emphasis becomes attached to an included variable, then a different set of relationships and a different strategy will result. The models and projections used are an operational simplification of the real world of human affairs in relation to the physical environment; they depend on theory, which may or may not be supported by empirical investigation and the excluded non-policy variables may exercise a greater impact than now anticipated. New behavioural patterns and technological change deserve special consideration in this respect.

1. *Behavioural patterns.* Behavioural patterns, generally, require far more understanding of the range of factors which are involved, the key variables, their relationships to each other and, when the existing situation is understood comprehensively, those changes in

136

policy which should be advocated in order to achieve different patterns. Thus, how is population mobility within and between cities influenced by the housing market, and what is the relative importance of availability of private-rental, owner-occupier and public-rental accommodation? How do spatial location within the urban area, occupation and employment, length of time at present address, the quality of the urban environment, socio-economic status, income, stage in the family cycle, rapport with neighbours, family size, the distances of daily movement, type of job, type of housing and social opportunities influence mobility? What are the true aspirations for suburban living, given the *qualitative* redevelopment of inner city areas? Which components of the population remain in one residence or one urban area over extensive periods, and how do they vary from out-migrants and internal-migrants? Is the generalized picture of a prevailing outward movement to the periphery correct for all social groups and, if not, what should be the significance for postulated urban residential densities? How are the benefits of expansion and the disadvantages of stability measured, in terms of social response and the behavioural patterns of different groups in the community? Is emigration abroad promoted by frustrations to family life and personal achievement by over-rigid planning policies in the allocation and availability of land for urban purposes? These massive research questions are hardly considered in the Studies.[1]

The suggestion is that many professions have to interpret the needs of man as an individual, and the needs of man in society, to the practising planner. The sociologist, the psychologist and the philosopher must identify the wants, needs and aspirations of man and provide some form of accepted system of values by which plans and achievements can be measured. Without this there is only the inadequate measure of the cost yardstick, with all its admitted imperfections and bias towards a materialistic society.

In the South East Study there is some evidence that a different approach has, in fact, been followed. The discussion about housing needs is pitched in a stronger sociological vein than in the other Studies, where economic and physical conditions tend to predominate. For example, the South East Study discusses the distinct demand for housing against occupational rather than income groups and describes, separately, the needs of the senior salariat, the middle mass and the less privileged.[2] The housing of the low income groups, as

[1] See, for example, *Urban Studies*, Vol. 6, 1969, where certain of these issues are discussed.
[2] *South East Study*, pp. 21–9.

with the other groups, is not just a physical issue in terms of location, accessibility and the quality of environment. It is tied in with the cycle of deprivation for Inner London's children, it involves problems associated with immigration and poverty (which are not necessarily the same), and mobility in the occupational structure. A resultant objective refers to the need 'to give to semi-skilled and unskilled workers remaining in Inner London, an appropriate measure of priority (a) in housing, and (b) in additional provision of educational and occupational training facilities of all kinds'.[1]

2. *Social and economic unknowns.* Certain factors which affect future urban characteristics cannot reasonably be included within any planning analysis, even though they are certain to exert an impact. For example, the skill, verve, ability and pressures for action which can be exerted by elected representatives and appointed officials in order to achieve some particular policy must be discreetly omitted, as are the different attitudes towards development, investment, public responsibility and private initiative by the major political parties. Conservationists are no longer ploughing a lonely furrow but, with strong public backing, can expect increasing support from government and an increasing allocation of funds to meet their passionate pleas which may be at the expense of housing or transportation. No planning team can reasonably be expected to assess the urban impact generally, or specifically in terms of a selected environment, of the Channel Tunnel, the Concorde aircraft, oil discoveries under the North Sea, or joining the European Common Market. At the end of 1970 the outcome of each of these topics is unknown, yet each must inevitably have some form of urban significance over future years. Racial or religious tension may become a disruptive element as in North America, Montreal or Belfast, and the growing numbers of resident non-whites in British cities can affect their future. The prospects of international peace, a major epidemic through chemical pollution or some uncontrollable disease affecting grass as in John Christopher's *The Death of Grass*[2] are further unknowns. Can Britain improve its balance of payments position and achieve a higher rate of economic growth? Will industrial relations deteriorate to the detriment of normal urban life? The point is that these factors, which have influenced urban form and growth rates in the past, cannot be incorporated in future assessments of the urban environ-

[1] *Ibid.*, p. 29.
[2] John Christopher, *The Death of Grass*, Penguin Books (Harmondsworth), 1958.

ment. They are not predictable in terms of the appropriate strategies for regional development, though perhaps the South East Study might have considered the future of its region in terms of with or without the Channel Tunnel, and with the third London airport at either Foulness or Cublington.

3. *Technological change.* Advances in technological performance and the development of new scientific achievements must also be predicted with a fair degree of accuracy for their impact on the regional environment during the period of the plan. They provide elements which must be allowed for in the 'flexibility' of planning, even though no one can have a clear picture of future conditions after an intervening time span of thirty-five years. The first industrial revolution is now history; it brought about the factory complex and the railway and concentrated urban populations in or near the coalfield areas, at ports and in other critical locations in relation to the new resources. Automation, electric and atomic power, the explosion of communication techniques, data processing and the storage and retrieval of information, individual mobility, new construction techniques and greater speeds of travel over all distances are new forces which have aggrandized the urban situation at phenomenal rates over the past few decades.

But what of the future? It would seem that the incidence of likely change has received insufficient recognition in the Studies and that they have perhaps been rather too cautious on this unknown and contentious ground. New technologies can, as in the past, transform the output of the building and construction industries; develop new forms of transportation which change inter-urban relationships; create new potentials in land use and reclamation; pose new demands on limited land, air and water resources; provide basic manufacturing and service industry with a new range of choices for site location; and raise the standards of living and the expectations of society. The obverse side of the coin is that technology also creates new opportunities for the destruction, erosion or change of existing assets. As during the first industrial revolution, and it is easy now to look back with alarm and to cry 'Shame', there is the ever-present danger that technological advance will outpace man's willingness to control himself and place depredations on the physical landscape.

The thought which underlies this argument is that the future must be couched in the terms of the technical operations now known to be possible, but it is highly unlikely that a technological plateau has been reached by modern society. To quote from the Economic

139

Commission for Europe (1968), 'we are at present on the threshold of a period of technological development which would appear to be *more significant* for the future way of living than *any* previous development during the last 150 years or so of the industrialization of Europe'.[1] In such circumstances it might reasonably be expected that each Study should list its own expectations of technological change, and describe how these events might be expected to influence their Sub-region.[2] Guidance from the central government and academic research might also reasonably be expected on such matters.

PLANNING FOR UNCERTAINTY

'The growth of the sub-region will inevitably vary from the most likely course plotted by the Study's forecasts'.[3] The same comment applies to all the Studies but, because there are social, economic and technological unknowns, this does not mean that doubts about the future should be translated into inaction. Honest doubt can be the beginnings of urban wisdom, as research workers seek to improve upon their knowledge and predictive abilities. Uncertainty about an unknown future must not be extended into the syndrome of no action, more research, and then still more information required to justify a decision. There are many known certainties which require action now, including continuing urban growth, more demanding pressures on all resources, population expansion with all its attendant demands, and the changing factors of greater personal mobility. The conceptual basis for understanding the urban situation, and knowledge about the relative strengths of the different forces in the process of urbanization, is incomplete, but it is not insufficient to make decisions. Planners cannot proceed on any other basis than the best available intelligence at any point in time, plus intuition, assumption and sheer guess-work to fill in the gaps of understanding. New methods, new ideas and new thoughts are a part of the daily practice of the planner, and should be built into his forecasts as a basis for strategic actions. Monitoring and the flexibility of strategies are important in this context. Planning can never be for a certain future condition.

The common factor underlying all forecasts is that human decisions are made on a rational basis and can be predicted with some fair degree of accuracy. Hence planning policies can be formulated

[1] Economic Commission for Europe, *The Future Pattern and Forms of Urban Settlement*, United Nations (New York), 1968, p. 42. Author's emphasis.

[2] See, for example, South Hampshire Plan Advisory Committee, *Technological Change*, Study Report G1, 1969.

[3] *Warwickshire Study*, p. 13.

against this reasoning to guide future developments into some more acceptable form than would otherwise occur. Knowledge can be brought to bear in order to resolve problems which can now be envisaged. Fundamental to each set of guidelines is that systematic explanation is possible of complex urban and transportation phenomena. Characteristics can be understood and trends projected, causative factors and interactions between the separate component elements discerned, behavioural patterns observed, and social and technological change can be understood with sufficient exactitude to determine future policies. The exercise must therefore in part be imaginative, in part rely on assumption, and in part depend upon scientific analysis. The most difficult aspect of forecasting is the achievement of balance between these three aspects of planning judgement. It is possible to know about *existing* environmental problems, but there can never be certainty about unknown *future* conditions.

THE ROLE OF MONITORING

It has been established that unknowns provide a point of miscalculation, and it is this type of change which upsets the extrapolation of past trends and the use of current experience to solve future problems. However, as forecasts must by their very nature always be uncertain, one planning answer expressed in the Studies is the suggestion that future trends must be monitored. A continuing review of trends is advocated of the individual statistics, their inter-connections and policy so that planning becomes a continuous process, examining performance against action and with a feedback from achievement or failure to a review of policy. But if the growth in population is twice or half that expected, two quite different possibilities may be envisaged. The policies can be strengthened to achieve the desired strategy, or the strategy may be amended to accommodate the new trends.

The Leicestershire Study states that 'the key measure of the success with which the plan is being implemented is the correspondence between the *actual* states of the sub-region at those times (five-year progressions from 1971 to 1991) as compared with those *intended* in the plan. It is therefore necessary for the authorities to keep watch on certain indicators of the sub-region's condition and e.g. to make regular checks to see if the area is on course. . . . An information and intelligence service is therefore the vital element in successful implementation'.[1] Forecasts are thus tested continually

[1] *Leicestershire Study*, p. 102.

141

against performance. The statistics to be maintained include, for the sub-region and for its various parts, the details of total population, households, persons of school age, total employment in various sectors, private motor cars, average per capita income, expenditure, the size of main shopping centres, the transport networks and traffic volumes. Comparable statements are made in the North-Glos, Warwickshire and Teesside Studies,[1] Notts–Derby have established a permanent Sub-Regional Monitoring and Advisory Unit and, at the regional level, this process is recommended in the South East Study.[2] Regional planning does not end with the preparation of a Report, but begins.

It is therefore argued that policies should remain under continual review in the light of achievement. As Teesside remark, 'a regular review should be made, probably every year, on the progress of urban structure policy; the validity of the planning objectives bringing up to date the recommended policies; and reviewing the priorities for work on planning and implementation'.[3] Planning, as envisaged in the Studies, has no end-product. It is part of a continuous and continuing process, rather than a master plan of envisaged conditions by a particular date.

THE FLEXIBILITY OF STRATEGIES

Because of the unknown quantities, it is generally stated that strategies must be flexible. All Studies evaluate qualitatively the performance of their alternative strategies against this criterion. To North-Glos, 'the essence of flexibility was considered to lie in the extent to which a strategy, evolving through time, would leave options open to the variety of interests involved, both personal and corporate, and thereby enable that strategy to respond to changes in circumstances'.[4] Leicestershire used the three elements of scale, rates of land development, and movement demand and locational preferences.[5] Humberside interprets flexibility to mean 'the ease with which development could be staged'.[6] Hampshire included, *inter alia*, that 'as the structure grows, it should be possible for each phase to function efficiently and not to be dependent upon further growth taking place. . . . The versatility of the structure should not be limited by rigid standards in such matters as transport modes or

[1] *North-Glos Study*, pp. 104–5; *Warwickshire Study*, p. 90; *Teesside Study*, pp. 110–11.
[2] *South East Study*, p. 87. [3] *Teesside Study*, p. 112.
[4] *North-Glos Study*, p. 84. [5] *Leicestershire Study*, Vol. II, p. 148.
[6] *Humberside Study*, pp. 119 and 125.

housing groupings.[1] Warwickshire developed four tests on flexibility. 'The first test was to gauge the vulnerability of the strategies to growth at a rate higher or lower than the most likely rate, and the second to examine the effect of major happenings which might deflect the sub-region from its expected course of development. The third test looked at the strategies' ability to cope with unexpected changes in social attitudes towards the objectives of the strategy. . . . The fourth test was concerned with the ability of each strategy to change its direction of growth to that of other strategies.'[2] Quite obviously this notion, though generally accepted in principle, causes considerable confusion and difficulties in its interpretation and application. The meaning attached to 'flexibility' varies considerably.

The qualitative assessments of flexibility generally rely on verbal reasoning, and only the Warwickshire Study attempts a quantitative evaluation. This, though not easy, enforces some greater clarification of what is now a nebulous concept. For example, when decisions are made, these have to be firm and definite with regard to specific policies, locations and the commitment of finance and other resources. Is it possible to specify the additional costs or land requirements necessary to provide for flexibility in given circumstances? Are there not situations where the provision of unnecessary flexibility is as much to be regretted as its absence, in that both involve the risk of misuse or the waste of resources? Some flexibility must also exist through the possibilities of converting existing buildings, structures and land uses to different purposes or more intensive occupation.

An aspect of flexibility is also incorporated in the various projections, which indicate future possibilities against uncertain magnitudes. Thus the North-Glos Study notes that a variation in the levels of migration of ±50 per cent from the assumed level for 2001 and in the birth rate of 10 per cent, would result in a combined effect of ±66,000 persons (or 9 per cent) on their 2001 population projection. In other words this change would 'advance or retard by about 7 years the date at which the projected population of 752,000 persons would be reached'.[3] Leicestershire, in their population projections, examine (1) a wide range of *possibilities* determined by varied assumptions about birth and migration rates, (2) narrow the field to a more *probable* range by reference to employment and economic activity, and (3) take an average from the extremes of probability.[4] 'The birth-rate

[1] *Hampshire Study*, p. 96.

[2] *Warwickshire Study*, p. 75. The examination was in co-operation with the Local Government Operational Research Unit and was supported by a grant from the Ministry of Housing and Local Government.

[3] *North-Glos Study*, p. 36.   [4] *Leicestershire Study*, Vol. II, p. 2.

may fall below, or rise further above, the national average; Board of Trade policy may restrict more severely the growth of industry within the sub-region and inhibit migration, or the position may be eased so that the area's economy moves ahead at a quicker pace. These two contingencies taken to reasonable extremes of probability would produce a low projection of 866,000 people at 1991 and a high projection of 980,000. The overall range of likely population for the sub-region is therefore 927,000 plus or minus about 6 %'.[1] In Warwickshire the speculative extremes in population 'can be expressed in terms of a high rate of growth producing a population of 1·4 million about 1984, or a slow rate of growth delaying a 1·4 million population until about 1997'.[2]

The population forecast is thus fluid, but it is tied in with other projections and is related to a variety of different needs. The important point is not so much the date of achieving a population target but that the expected population (with its various associated relationships) will be achieved at plus or minus a few years from the target date. It is therefore preferable that the Studies should be concerned with accommodating 'x' hundred thousand persons within the Sub-region, rather than with a given number by a particular date. The scale and scope of the urban operations are more important than their specific date of accomplishment. On this argument, an aspect of flexibility is thus that the end-period of the plan is not fixed but represents more the culmination of a series of successive phases in development. Migration can be higher or lower than envisaged, and jobs more or less plentiful, but these changes are more likely to affect the rate and date of achievement than the strategy which has been advocated.

SUMMARY

Forecasts may be made separately, but are then interrelated with each other for critical future elements such as population, housing, movement, employment and shopping facilities, with recreation receiving rather less attention. A range of selected variables is used to indicate the urban future. The demands for new housing, to replace existing structures and to accommodate the envisaged growth of population, results in substantial demands on land, and underlines the previous arguments for greater concern about the ecological and qualitative aspects of all new developments. There is much scope for inaccuracy in the forecasts, because of the lengthy chain of reasoning, the various

[1] *Ibid.*, Vol. I, p. 45.   [2] *Warwickshire Study*, p. 118.

sources of data which are used and their several degrees of statistical reliability. More data should be presented about the probability of error, an independent inquiry should be undertaken into the role of models in the plan-making process, and more research is required into the likelihood of social and/or technological change over the planning period. The length of this planning period has now been extended to about thirty years, but it is arguable that a longer time perspective is necessary for the consideration of emerging urban patterns. The effective time period, i.e. the period during which the urban situation can be veered in a particular direction, begins some ten years after the date of plan preparation because of developments which are in the pipeline. Uncertainty about the urban future has three important implications: the inevitable lack of precision is not an argument for no action, the regular monitoring of events is thought to be essential, and a degree of flexibility (though a some-what indistinct concept) should be incorporated in the strategies.

Chapter 6

The Overall Form and Structure of Urban Growth

The planning process used in every Study both examines the physical constraints which inhibit the extensive use of land for urban development purposes, and develops a consistent series of forecasts to indicate the demands from the population for industry, housing, recreation and other land use provisions, and their associated transportation needs. The next stage involves the design of feasible and possible strategies. The expected demands on land are distributed in a spatial context safeguarding, where possible, those important sites for agricultural, recreational and other rural pursuits. In each instance, a variety of different urban forms and structures are considered.

THE JUSTIFICATION FOR CONSIDERING ALTERNATIVE STRATEGIES

Boyce and Day (1969) note six reasons for developing alternative possibilities in the American planning situation. These are (1) to challenge or confirm a plan that had been recommended; (2) to discover or verify some expected advantage inherent in one particular pattern of development; (3) to discover and document the deep-seated societal values about urban development and life style that residents of an area hold; (4) to provoke public discussion on critical issues; (5) to educate the general public and their representatives as to the values of planning; and (6) to identify needed changes in government, structure, powers or financing to accomplish specific objectives.[1]

The justifications in Britain are comparable, with perhaps items 1, 2 and 4 providing the prime motivating forces in the Studies under review. They are concerned with assessing whether or not there is any *one* possibility which offers any inherent advantage over other formulations. The development of alternatives is described frequently as 'part of the learning process'. Notts–Derby state that 'the Unit's approach to strategy formulation was dominated by the desire to avoid giving weight to the personal predilections of the planners

[1] D. E. Boyce and N. D. Day, *Metropolitan Plan Evaluation Methodology*, Institute for Environmental Studies, University of Pennsylvania (Philadelphia), 1969, pp. 17–18.

concerned. . . . We took the view that by looking at the area with which we are concerned, postulating various forms of future development for it, and testing these forms against objectives, constraints and activity patterns, we should come to a better understanding of its needs and opportunities.'[1] Hampshire notes that alternative possibilities exist and may be studied in the present environment; 'we were able to observe a variety of more or less inefficient structures in the towns of this country and abroad'.[2]

The process of producing alternative strategies is generally thought to be desirable. North-Glos explore the possible alternative ways in which these needs [the distribuion of population, employment facilities and a related transportation system] could be met in the form of development variously distributed in the Sub-Region'.[3] Valid but competing claims on land exist, and various feasible solutions are possible. By this line of argument the preparation and study of reasonable alternatives becomes the normal or accepted procedure. It replaces 'inspired guesswork', and implies a rigorous and systematic methodology. As Leicestershire observe, 'although we were required to produce only one plan for the growth of the sub-region, we believe that we should first examine a number of distinct, but credible, alternatives in terms of spatial form and sequence of change.'[4] In Warwickshire's phraseology, 'we took the purpose of the study as being to demonstrate how alternative strategies might perform'.[5]

THE APPROACH TO THE FORMULATION OF ALTERNATIVE
URBAN FORMS

The discussion in the Sub-regional Studies is primarily in terms of socio-economic performance, and location, rather than the specific evaluation of different types of urban form. This results both from the terms of reference and from the methodology adopted. In the North-Glos Study the analysis of physical constraints indicates the major areas suitable for development and land is then allocated in these areas against certain criteria. 'Over the period 1966 to 1981 the appropriate number of housing development modules were, in the main, located adjacent to, or near, existing development in locations with good accessibility to existing employment opportunities.'[6] After 1981 industrial areas are allocated to accord with new situations such as motorway access points and housing is distributed, 'taking

[1] *Notts–Derby Study*, Record Report 31, p. 1. [2] *Hampshire Study*, p. 95.
[3] *North-Glos Study*, p. 63. [4] *Leicestershire Study*, p. 9.
[5] *Warwickshire Study*, p. 24. [6] *North-Glos Study*, p. 67.

full account of the major locational options particular to the strategy and also . . . accessibility to both existing and postulated centres of employment'.[1] Within this context, five urban forms are considered including peripheral growth, a linear pattern of development, a new town situation and urban concentration in the Gloucester–Cheltenham complex.

In Notts–Derby forty-seven separate possibilities are considered initially, including several ideal spatial forms such as corridors of growth, commuter towns, new towns, grid-based developments, 'non-plan' and scatteration.[2] They are examined for spatial similarities and reduced to twelve groups for Stage I testing. Six new integrated strategies on the basis of physical constraints, employment opportunities and residential location in relation to employment opportunities are considered for Stage II testing. 'These strategic ideas were intended to examine the merits of alternative quantities of development and alternative directions of growth for each of the major centres, together with the advantages of more or less concentrated forms of development and greater or lesser amounts of rural dispersal.'[3] Three further strategies are examined at Stage III. 'These strategies were devised to represent the realistic extremes of concentrated and dispersed development; more or less favourable economic growth prospects; and varying amounts of individual and industrial mobility.'[4]

Leicestershire 'did not attempt to set up different urban forms at the outset and then go on to interpret these in terms of population and employment distribution. Rather we based our alternatives on varying the rates of basic employment growth among the constituent parts of the sub-region and simulating the consequences for all other main land use changes. By evaluating these sub-regional growth patterns we could discover the best direction of change in the urban structure of the sub-region.'[5] In addition, account is taken of a possible flood control scheme, a 'tickover' rate of basic employment so that no locality is allowed to decline, and variations in housing replacement and redevelopment to accord with the economic characteristics of each locality. The outcome is six alternative strategies for simulation. These emphasize concentration, dispersal and combinations of accessibility-trend, accessibility-rejuvenation and trend-rejuvenation with and without the flood control scheme. Strategic assumptions about employment strategy, land development and housing are included in each strategic policy bundle;

[1] *Ibid.*, p. 67. [2] *Notts–Derby Study*, p. lxix. [3] *Ibid.*, p. lxxii.
[4] *Ibid.*, p. lxxvi. [5] *Leicestershire Study*, p. 33.

recreation, shopping, journey to work, and public transport are left completely to the evaluation stage. In Leicestershire, the essential approach is thus not with the urban form *per se*; urban form results from the methodology of the approach.

On Teesside, the emphasis is again on location. 'Seven alternative strategies are put forward . . . by suggesting locations for the additional population and employment for which land has not yet been committed. . . . They illustrate alternative forms and directions for future development. Formal considerations included peripheral development, linear extensions to the built-up area, a new town and dispersed settlement.'[1] There are then variations by direction so that the seven possibilities include three linear extensions – westwards, southwards and southeastwards; two forms of dispersed settlement – southwards and northwest; one satellite development to the south; and one compact development as close to the built-up area as possible.

In Warwickshire, 'the method we employed to crystallize the alternatives relied on identifying the relative attractiveness of different parts of the sub-region for new development. . . . We use our Development Potential analysis as a tool for generating the alternative strategies and for their subsequent detailing. The approach evolved from the data collection stage of the study and the construction of a computer data file which enabled all factors influencing an area's suitability for development to be expressed quantitatively and incorporated into a single composite factor diagram, or "surface", of Combined Development Potential. . . . This approach to shaping the alternatives provided a systematic means of progressing from objectives and survey material to a recommended plan.'[2] The possibility of testing an infinite number of shapes and locations for growth had been considered, 'but it would have been both an impracticable and a grossly inefficient approach.'[3] As with the Leicestershire and Notts–Derby Studies, and in terms of a more systematic methodology, the concern was with location and the complex pattern of social and economic organization, with the shape of the urban area resulting from these other previous decisions.

By contrast, in the Regional Studies, a difference in attitude may be observed. The emphasis here is more on urban form and the advantages and disadvantages of varying possibilities. In the Humberside Study, the four hypothetical sketch plans comprise two major cities, the radiating form, the dispersed form and the linear form. The outcome is however inconclusive for a particular urban

[1] *Teesside Study*, p. 69.   [2] *Warwickshire Study*, p. 31.   [3] *Ibid.*, p. 31.

149

form as 'the analysis has been more concerned with alternative locations than with differences between possible alternative structures
for the proposed urban areas.'[1] Within this context, a linear form of
development received some cautious support. 'More than any of the
others examined, [it] would give the advantage of enabling centres
and sub-centres to develop at nodes in the road system as growth
proceeded without unnecessary disturbance to the existing major
centres.'[2] The costs of transportation 'also appeared to be on the
high side on both banks with the Linear Form, but it is possible
that these could be offset by the better opportunities which this
form of development might offer for a system of rapid mass transit.'[3]
The linear and the radiating forms 'would permit considerable
flexibility in planning and timing and could be more readily curtailed
than schemes involving the creation of large free-standing new
towns and cities'.[4]

In the South East Study two strategic concepts for 1991 are considered. 1991 A identifies counter-magnets forty to eighty miles away
from London, and 1991 B places much greater emphasis on development closer to London. The Report states that 'it was recognized
that in the time available it would be impossible to undertake thorough
tests of more than two hypothetical patterns of development at
1991. A number of theoretical patterns were therefore considered,
ranging from large-scale peripheral expansion of London to a
general scatter of development throughout the region, with the
intention of finding a logical and feasible distribution of the development for the period to 1991 which could be contrasted with 1991 A
and which should therefore be markedly different from it.'[5] The
reason for this marked difference, the degree of detail in the other
theoretical patterns and the grounds for their exclusion are not
included in the Report. This lack of justification for the selected
alternative pattern of development is a matter for regret. It would be
of interest to know (a) the full details of the ten alternatives which
were considered and (b) the reasons for their exclusion, including
the standards and the objectives which were applied in reaching this
decision.[6]

In the Hampshire Study, the search was for 'a physical form of
development which is adaptable and can grow as circumstances
dictate. . . . The task was to discover the principles upon which it

[1] *Humberside Study*, p. 126.   [2] *Ibid.*, p. 121.   [3] *Ibid.*, p. 125.
[4] *Ibid.*, p. 125.   [5] *South East Study*, p. 60.
[6] Though not available at the time of writing, it is understood that this detail
will become available in Studies Volume IV.

could best be developed as one coherent, integrated urban system.'[1] Three basic forms of idealized structure are considered. These, with the outcome favouring the directional grid, are:

1. Centripetal Structure, where each small part of the area focusses on a minor centre, the minor centres are satellite to a major centre, and so on into the one primary centre for a whole region.

2. Directional Grid, evolved from a linear form of growth and depending on a basic communication spine along which dominant elements are located.

3. The Grid, with nodes of urban facilities related in category to the scales of the network, and dispersed evenly over the network.[2]

The Sub-regional Strategies should also have been concerned with this type of analytical exercise. Their content could have included a *theoretical* evaluation of alternative possible urban forms, and the respective advantages and disadvantages of various possibilities could have been assessed in the light of Sub-regional characteristics and objectives.[3] The Hampshire Study is unique for this approach in its thought processes. It is not necessarily clear from the other studies how the alternative strategies evolved, what processes of thought led to the preferment for a certain range of choices, and what explicit relationships existed between the strategies and the planning objectives. As it is their conclusions are practical, but tend to be traditional rather than inspired relative to possible technological change and possible modes of life thirty, forty and fifty years hence. They are over-concerned with trends, rather than indicative of new possibilities in shaping the form and structure of urban environments. Theoretical formulations in relation to regional objectives have their role to play in this respect Alternative policies should be seen to emerge from the planning process of imaginative thought about future possibilities.

THE BASIS FOR THE GENERATION OF ALTERNATIVE
STRATEGIES

When the degree of emphasis in the formulation of the various stages by each Study is compared, it may be noted that several different methods have been employed at this crucial stage of the plan-making process. As these overlap in each Study, and as no one Study is

---

[1] *Hampshire Study*, p. 90.   [2] *Ibid.*, pp. 96–8.
[3] See, for example, G. B. Jamieson, W. K. Mackay and J. C. R. Latchford, 'Transportation and Land Use Structures', *Urban Studies*, Vol. 4, 1967, pp. 201–17.

confined to a single method of approach, it is difficult to identify the key or dominant concept. All Studies take into account a range of aspects including housing demand, the location of employment opportunities, home-work and other accessibility relationships, and physical constraints. Urban form, the pull of nodal points on the transportation system, and various locations and directions of growth are each considered. Even so, a generalized classification may be attempted of the key concepts which underlie the selection of alternative strategies. It would seem that the interpretation of urban form is most significant in the Hampshire Study, an important secondary consideration in the Humberside and Teesside (and perhaps the North-Glos) Studies, and more of a resultant product in the other Studies. Transportation, and especially the motorway network, is an important locational element in all Studies, but is used as the primary motivation to structure urban form only in the Hampshire Study. In the Leicestershire and Notts–Derby Studies the distribution of basic employment is regarded as a very important central consideration, whereas in the North-Glos, Teesside, Humberside and the South East Studies the strategies tend more to emphasize locational factors. The Warwickshire Study is related most closely to its range of planning objectives.

There are differences here from American precedents and American practice, where the most common method of selecting general concepts as a point of beginning is 'to identify a series of "plan forms", each exhibiting a singular organizing principle for the structure of the region. Concepts such as "linear city", "satellite towns", "compact city", and "spread city", are typical of the plan form approach.'[1] Another method is to vary the key structural characteristics, centralization versus decentralization or high-density residential versus low, or to induce change in the transportation system by varying the modal emphasis or changing the balance between different types of road network. The latter procedures are for example incorporated in the Teesside Study, and represent a desirable approach to the preparation of integrated land use and transportation strategies. Densities are more often fixed than subject to discretion, and decentralization receives less discussion as an issue than in America.

With regard to the number of strategies, Notts–Derby are the most prolific. They begin with forty-seven different conceptual plans, which are co-ordinated and combined for testing purposes. Varying numbers of newly-devised strategies are tested at each sequential

[1] Boyce and Day, *op. cit.*, p. 21.

stage of their testing processes, including twelve strategies at Stage I, six at Stage II and three at Stage III. Teesside, Leicestershire and North-Glos examined seven, six and five strategies respectively. Warwickshire tested four final alternatives, but also considered trend, new town and dispersal possibilities. The Regional Studies are more restricted; Humberside considers four strategies, Hampshire five and the South East two. Two strategies is too slender a number of alternatives for testing. Four to six reasonable and feasible alternatives, fully worked out in their interrelated statistical detail, land use locations and transportation details would seem a more appropriate number for initial study, and might later be blended into composite strategies during the testing process. Combined with its limited time period, the South East Study has been over-restrictive in examining different possibilities.

Within the context of the preferred strategy, sub-variants are considered in two Studies. Teesside examines three public transport systems and three road systems. Leicestershire devises three variants, which heavily concentrate development in greater Leicester or allow for a dispersed form of growth either northwards or northwestwards.

A distinction should also be noted between linear and cyclic processes. The linear process involves 'gradually refining a set of land use and transportation alternatives, followed by the selection of one alternative as the final plan. The other approach focusses more on specific plan elements and policies in a cyclic process, each cycle of which consists of the generation, elaboration, and evaluation of alternatives, followed by a decision and reformulation stage as the basis for a new cycle.'[1] The latter approach is most developed in the Notts–Derby Study, though some recombination and recognition of common elements exists in the Leicestershire and South East Studies. The North-Glos, Teesside, Warwickshire, Hampshire and Humberside Studies are more concerned with evaluating the distinctive merits of alternatives which are mutually exclusive, though each has some limited elements of interchange. The choice between these processes will depend on the nature of the alternatives, the stage at which they are chosen, the criteria for testing, and the degree of detail both in the testing procedures and the strategies. Either a cyclic or a linear approach may thus have its strengths and its weaknesses, depending upon the merit of the generation and testing procedures. Combination is only possible when the different parts are interchangeable, and is not feasible when the strategies differ radically in

[1] *Ibid.*, p. 18.

location or form or fulfil different objectives. More important is to devise a series of different tests of performance against stated objectives.

THE LOCATION OF NEW URBAN DEVELOPMENTS

Given the urban situation of today as the starting point, the location of urban growth beyond existing urban limits can take place in three different spatial contexts. It may be (1) attached to the existing urban areas, (2) separated from the existing pattern in either nearby satellite communities, or (3) independently located.

Of these three alternatives, peripheral expansion on the fringe of existing urban areas implies the gradual and orderly outward expansion of the built-up area at appropriate locations on the perimeter. Suitable sites are serviced, and land is developed in the best community interests for residential, industrial and public open space purposes. The intrusion into areas which should be used for agriculture or mineral workings, or remain under an attractive landscape, is minimized. Planning becomes primarily the guidance of existing pressures, and regional strategies concentrate upon the desirable location of key elements including the main highway routes and their access points, the location of shopping and other central community facilities such as schools, areas of landscape value requiring special protection, and the broad zoning of the areas to be developed into their principal use categories. Green belts, green wedges or green areas generally can be retained if required, with their width and location related to the local conditions of terrain. The burdens of urban expansion can be reduced by ensuring the full use of all unused, under-used and vacant sites within the urbanized area, and by giving a maximum emphasis to redevelopment activity at higher population densities. This traditional process of growth is the likely future for most of the smaller urban localities across the country, but with increasing size other possibilities are likely to be envisaged.

Satellite towns, garden cities, town expansion schemes and new towns each have a long history.[1] Their essential idea is that the maximum proportion of outward growth shall be encouraged to

[1] See, for example, F. J. Osborn and A. Whittick, *The New Towns – The Answer to Megalopolis*, Leonard Hill (London), 1963; I. H. Seeley, *Planned Expansion of Country Towns*, Goodwin (London), 1968; F. Schaffer, *The New Town Story*, MacGibbon and Kee, 1970; and R. Thomas, *London's New Towns* and *Aycliffe to Cumbernauld*, P.E.P. (London), 1969.

occur in self-contained areas away from the parent community, and separated from its urbanized area by a distinct and continuous zone. Further lateral spread of the existing urban environment is discouraged by these means, though the intermediate zone could contain a mixture of urban and rural land uses including agriculture, horticultural pursuits, golf courses, reservoirs, institutional buildings such as hospitals in their own large and landscaped grounds, and recreational space. This land may have to be purchased to retain in perpetuity this degree of control, as ministerial decision may not necessarily be sufficient to safeguard such land against the constant economic pressures for urban expansion.

The assumption is that growth beyond the present urban limits will be directed to more distant localities, which may contain existing developments or be on substantially new sites, and that the infra-structure of the receiving locality will be so designed as to achieve the successful transfer of urban developments to the new locale. The new and expanding localities can have serviced industrial estates and commercial areas, a variety of housing types, be well designed and be under private or public sponsorship. The former category would include Reston and Columbia in the Greater Washington and Baltimore areas of the United States; the latter the new towns located twenty-five to thirty miles from Central London and their later variants at higher densities and with higher degrees of pedes-trian and vehicular segregation (e.g. Cumbernauld or Redditch). However, if location is too close to the metropolitan core, then the new urban unit (despite the provision of buffer areas) becomes in essence an integral part of the continuous urbanized area. The infilling of land by development between the new or expanding urban unit and the metropolitan complex may destroy those very advantages of being a distinct entity which motivated their founding.

One prevalent criticism of satellite communities is that their number and population size are insufficient to cope with the sheer magnitude of the urban growth problem which exists. Though successful in many design features and in their cost performance characteristics, they have received only a small portion of the urban increment since their inception. Also, often situated too close to the major urban core, they may be regarded as leap-frogging in the urban expansion race. When the green belt is thin in its width, it becomes susceptible to pressures from two directions – the city growing outwards and the new town itself which, after establish-ment, may seek to expand to beyond its predetermined size. Thought about the size of such units has gradually increased upwards, from

155

30,000 by Ebenezer Howard and the early Garden City movement, to 50,000–60,000 in the early British New Towns, to 100,000–120,000 in the early 1960s, and with Dawley, Milton Keynes, Northampton and Warrington being planned for ultimate population of 200,000–250,000 persons in 1969.[1] With larger figures, a greater measure of functional independence from the initiating locality or localities may be expected, and the spatial concept merges gradually into that of a more substantial and independent urban grouping.

In this instance the idea is of large progressive community in its own right. The critical factors are the location of the site, and the regional associations which may be developed with existing communities. This type of proposal is neither as extreme nor as radical as would appear at first glance, because in one sense all industrial cities are newly emerged over the past one hundred and fifty years. A city has to be initiated somehow and somewhere, and major investments are anyway necessary to permit expansion on the urban fringe. Given the substantial expectation of high urban growth rates, then new communities with several hundred thousand or even with a million and over population are not impossible. Space exists in the British landscape for such stimulating ventures, and one important consequence could be the relief of the hard-pressed existing conurbation or metropolitan centres from certain of their prophesied contraints.

The prime distinction between satellite communities and large-scale independent centres also relates to functions and service activity, as well as to population size. Satellite towns may become local centres of attraction with their own range of functions and activities, but this expansion also requires new services and professional contacts of a higher order in the existing central towns of higher status. Satellites close by a metropolitan centre may thus relieve some of its physical pressures of growth and provide creative opportunities for the achievement of a designed community but, as with outward suburban growth, they will still require additional services of a higher order in the central city (major hospitals, higher education and cultural services, range of large departmental stores, specialized retailing and commercial facilities). Dispersal within the ambit of the same organizational structure does not reduce, but may increase, these pressures of centralization. The large-scale units would be more independent, and their nurture requires the provision of higher order

[1] Central Office of Information, *The New Towns of Britain*, HMSO (London), 1969.

156

services as a deliberate act of faith in the credence of planning policies.

LINEARITY AND URBAN GROWTH

The above spatial aspects of urban growth are concerned with physical expansion as the city covers a larger area of space, the more intensive occupance of this space through changes in density on the ground and in terms of height, and the change in regional form and status which accompanies growth. The whole is changing as the parts change and many variables are involved such as the relationships between new growth and existing centres, different interactions between land use and the transportation network, the legislative means of achieving new growth, and its internal characteristics in economic, social and design terms. The outcome from the Studies is generally for some form of linear growth. Hampshire's directional grid is a linear growth form, and the preferred option in the South East Study takes advantages of a finger plan, using the main radial communications from London for further urbanization. In the Humberside Study, the linear possibility receives some commendation in that 'this system, more than any of the others examined, would give the advantage of enabling centres and subcentres to develop at nodes in the road system as growth proceeded without necessary disturbance to the existing major centres'.[1]

At the sub-regional level linear policies did not receive preference in the Teesside and Notts–Derby Studies, though in each instance new developments are related closely to the major highway network. In the North-Glos Study the M5 forms in effect the growth axis for the preferred strategy and considerable elongation of the Gloucester–Cheltenham complex takes place along this motorway. In the recommended strategy of the Leicester Study, 'the growth of the Greater Leicester area should be achieved largely by the development of two growth corridors'. The larger of these leads northwestwards along the axis of A50. . . . Whilst the smaller corridor uses A46 and a proposed Coventry to Leicester motorway as its twin backbones. . . . Development of these corridors will be achieved in a variety of ways.[2] One justification for this linear growth is the need for flexibility. 'Being based generally upon a programme of progressive linear extension the whole area will continue to function effectively even if economic growth is very much slower or faster than we have

---

[1] *Humberside Study*, p. 121.   [2] *Leicestershire Study*, p. i.

forecast.'[1] In the Warwickshire Study, 'the strategy being recommended is to consolidate the long established axis of growth between Nuneaton and Warwick'.[2]

A linear method of urban growth uses the transportation system as an axis of development to structure the location and form of the urban growth potential. The concept is one whereby most outward growth will be encouraged in specific corridors focussed on motorway routes and public transit systems. Development may be discontinuous or continuous, depending upon the frequency and location of access points to the transportation systems. Either a bead-like structure or an elongated wedge-like structure may be achieved with the nodes, in either instance, being located in relation to the transport routes. Industrial, retail, commercial and other functions would be established in these service centres, and residential accommodation would be located nearby. A whole range of design possibilities, including different densities and varying economic-base structures, may be envisaged. The possibilities are legion. Intervening areas, penetrating towards the central cities, can be retained under an open, green belt or agricultural usage where physical constraints upon development occur.

The linear form should provide rapid access to the central city and its range of service activities, through the integration of public rapid transit systems with access to the stations by the private motor car. However, the overburdening of all transport media at peak hours is probable. The full provision of space, equipment and services to meet all expected peak loads, though still prohibitively expensive, may have to be borne by the public in exchange for other advantages. The preservation of the green wedges, unless they occur in the landscape as strongly marked finger or divisive features such as a wide river or lake, will require firm planning policies on a continuing basis or land purchase by Government. Homes generally will be closer to the country than through controlled outward growth. The initiation of linear growth requires substantial investment in the transportation network, the promotion of development activity to create the regional, community, service and other centres, and the cultivation of strong and consistent government policies to offset the normal tendencies towards peripheral growth on the urban fringe.

The plan for Copenhagen provides an illustrative example. Its famous finger plan, with the city being encouraged to grow outwards from its core along five main transportation lines, was published in 1947 (when Britain was concerned with resisting urban growth by

---

[1] *Ibid.*, p. 3.   [2] *Warwickshire Study*, p. 80.

green belts and with transferring pressures to new towns as the urban solution). By 1961 (with Britain still thinking in terms of plans prepared for County Boroughs and separately for their surrounding Counties, and with motorway construction and fast inter-urban railway services still being regarded as something to do with transportation), the five-finger plan was replaced by a one-finger southerly extension of the city along a rapid mass-transit system. Industrial zones and high density residential areas would be related to this corridor of movement; open space would be retained as might be vital within the internal detail of development, to separate units of development and to retain the more significant features of the landscape. The city would grow spatially; its central area would remain, as befits the capital city, at the heart of the new development and would continue to expand in its selective array of functions. Washington D.C. in 1962 also broke with tradition in its plan for the year 2000. A star-shaped plan, rather than concentric growth, was envisaged by the National Capital Planning Commission.

Also of interest is that these linear solutions each resulted after the study of alternative possibilities. Copenhagen considered satellite centres at a distance from the central city; Washington's thought included peripheral growth, a ring of cities, independent cities and satellite towns. It is likewise with the range of proposals which have been mooted for Metropolitan Toronto in a recent transportation–land use exercise by the Ontario Provincial Government.[1] The background situation is of an anticipated regional growth of from 2·8 million persons in 1964 to 4·0 million by 1980 and 6·4 million persons by the year 2000. Population and employment are projected to the end of the century, and residential and industrial land requirements are assessed from these projections. One approach is to depict the approximate form which the region would take if past trends and present policies are continued into the future (The Trends Plan). Four alternatives are then presented, based on different concepts as to where the region is headed. Goals Plan I is for a regional lakeshore city, with accommodation for 20 to 25 per cent of the population in high density areas in corridor cities, with the proportion increasing towards the central city. Goals Plan II takes the pressure off the existing lakeshore transportation corridor by developing a second tier of cities along a northern transportation corridor. Goals Plan III shifts the concept of a northern transportation corridor further north, and accommodates the 500,000 persons shifted to this

[1] Metropolitan Toronto and Region Transportation Study, *Choices for a Growing Region*, Government of Ontario, Queen's Printer (Toronto), 1968.

tier in seven principal areas (population 50,000–100,000), and to five smaller communities of 20,000. Goals Plan IV assumes the characteristics of a large central city linked radially by road and rail to an arc of four cities, each with a population of 250,000 and large enough to generate a measure of local employment and to act as strong sub-regional centres. The next stage, the Design for Development, presents a regional development concept based on five principles. The first of these is 'the principle of linearity, which seeks as far as possible to align urban places along a series of more or less straight paths to take maximum advantage of parallel routes for transportation and Services'.[1]

Nor, of course, are linear strategies a new idea. La Ciudad Lineal was proposed for Madrid by Soria Y Mata in 1882, Tony Garnier's 'La Cité Industrielle' of 1917 was a linear industrial city, as was N. A. Milyutin's plan for Stalingrad and many of Le Corbusier's plans. The M.A.R.S. Group Plan for London in 1942 was linear in concept. More recently the West Midland Study has suggested a north–south axis of growth through the Welsh Marches northwards towards the Dee and southwards towards the Severn estuary.[2] The Northampton, Bedford and North Bucks Study considers dispersed developments with new and expanded towns, clusters of development, and corridors of development; the latter was the form selected because of its flexibility for expansion, and its important role in the provision of public transport facilities for large urban settlements.[3] In Paris, 'the basis of the new plan is to canalize the major anticipated growth of the Paris region into certain defined channels. ... The main principle is to extend Paris outwards in certain selected directions . . . related to major new transport routes, both road and rail.'[4]

THE FORM OF URBAN GROWTH PATTERNS

It would be fair to suggest from this evidence that the linear concept of development is the prevailing form of planning belief, both at home and abroad, in the future form of urban settlements. A review of metropolitan area plans by Hall (1967) notes that 'every plan

[1] The Government of Ontario, *Design for Development: The Toronto Central Region*, Queen's Printer (Toronto), 1970, p. 10.

[2] Department of Economic Affairs, *The West Midlands: A Regional Study*, HMSO (London), 1965, pp. 68–9 and 76.

[3] H. Wilson and L. Womersley, *Northampton, Bedford and North Bucks. Study*, 1965.

[4] E. Sibert, 'Regional Plan for Greater Paris', *Town and Country Planning*, January 1966.

rejects the hypothesis of the green belt and self-contained centres, either explicitly or by implication. All rely on a form of corridor or axial development in which a variety of urban centres are strung out along high-speed radial communication lines'.[1] Linear development would seem, for many of its advantages, to offer the most desirable of suitable growth forms in conjunction with some degree of urban peripheral expansion. The most pervading problem of all is, however, how to connect this emerging linear form of future urban environments with the radial and concentric cities of today. The critical point here is that different urban patterns can be achieved through different locations of the transportation system, and vice versa. It is not a matter of devising a land use structure and then fitting transportation to this, or devising a system for movement and then adding the land use component. The Studies recognize that both sets of interacting elements must be approached as a comprehensive and integrated whole. It is on this point that ideas in the Hampshire Study make a particular contribution to more effective planning practice. To quote from this Report, 'to assume . . . a fixed pattern of new development, and to treat it as though it existed, and to calculate the movement demands in the conventional way, would be to miss altogether the opportunities which exist in new development to exploit the interplay between land use and movement. By this we mean the manner in which land uses give rise to movement patterns, and conversely the influence which movement systems can exert on land use patterns. More precisely we have in mind the manipulation of land uses, densities, etc. in order to encourage economical movement systems; and, vice versa, the design and phasing of transport systems in order to foster desirable patterns and phases of growth.'[2]

But whatever the approach and the outcome in physical terms, the rapid rates of expected urban growth provide the pervading factor which must be accommodated somewhere. The urban–rural fringe and the rural landscapes beyond the urban limits are not a no-man's land, but the critical area which is *now* most subject to rapid and irreparable change through the speed of the urbanization processes. These processes are extensive and far-reaching, and can be understood in their external impact only in the matrix of their broader regional context. The often dismal and wasteful features of existing fringe areas can be substantially improved by a guiding framework

[1] P. Hall, 'Planning for Urban Growth: Metropolitan Area Plans and their Implications for South-East England', *Regional Studies*, Vol. 1, 1967, p. 128.
[2] *Hampshire Study*, p. 104.

161

F

of comprehensive urban policies. Various alternative approaches are possible, and the student of urban affairs should examine these several options critically. The urban fringe of today lies within the city of tomorrow, and the ultimate selection from the many alternatives must be made by informed citizens. The city may sprawl indiscriminately over the landscape, or it may be planned by private and public agencies as a decisive expression of urban living.

An important reminder is however that it is the purpose, function and effectiveness of these urban forms for social and economic life which is important in the Studies, and not the form *per se* or in isolation from other circumstances. In the words of Webber (1963),

> one pattern of settlement and its internal land use form is superior to another only as it better serves to accommodate ongoing social processes and to further the nonspatial ends of the political community. I am flatly rejecting the contention that there is an overriding universal spatial or physical aesthetic of urban forms. . . . The task is to seek that spatial distribution of urban populations and urban activities that will permit greater freedom for human interaction while, simultaneously, providing free access to natural amenities and effective management of the landscape and of mineral resources. . . . Part of the task will be to disabuse ourselves of some deep-seated doctrine that seeks order in simple mappable patterns, when it is really hiding in extremely complex social organizations, instead.[1]

Urban form cannot be discussed as if it is a distinct entity. In all the Studies under review it is embedded in a series of physical, social and economic considerations which combine to create a specific form or pattern of regional and urban settlements. The concern is with the total urban–regional future in which form *per se* plays a role of limited significance.

This approach is made quite explicit in the Warwickshire Study. 'We sought to build up alternatives from individual components and our understanding of economic, social and physical relationships, rather than to force these into a pre-determined conceptual envelope. . . . The shape of this urban envelope is essentially of less significance than its location and the complex pattern of economic and social organization which must operate within it.'[2] There is, however,

---

[1] M. M. Webber, 'Order in Diversity: Community without Propinquity', in L. Wingo (ed.), *Cities and Space: The Future Use of Urban Land*, Resources for the Future, Johns Hopkins (Baltimore), 1963, pp. 52 and 54.

[2] *Warwickshire Study*, p. 31.

inadequate knowledge about the varying costs and benefits of different urban forms in financial, social and technological terms. There is an urgent need to know the sum of costs and benefits for different types of urban forms, in both theoretical circumstances and in various practical situations. As Stone (1967) has stated, 'some forms will provide more value in relation to costs than others, both absolutely and in relation to their locality. Far too little is known of the way people value the qualities of a settlement. Information is needed on the relative preferences for such qualities as the accessibility of different types of facility, freedom from noise, privacy and urbanity. If such information were available, in the form of demand prices, the design of optimum settlements could be approached directly'.[1] In the absence of this detail, planners have no alternative but to proceed cautiously against stated assumptions, which can be tested for their relevance by continuing research. Urban forms are created by the decisions which are made.

SUMMARY

Alternative strategies are examined as a desirable feature of the planning process for several different reasons, but especially so that the best solution can be seen to emerge from a consideration of competing possibilities. Although many variants are examined in the Studies, the justification and the range of argument which selects these alternatives are not always clear. Linear and cyclic processes of plan selection are each used, and in one instance the options between various urban structures are considered from theoretical foundations. It is suggested that, in spatial terms, urban growth can take place by peripheral expansion and/or satellite communities and/or in large-scale independent centres. In terms of urban form, linear possibilities tend to be favoured both at home and abroad, and may be expected to become the prevailing future experience in Britain. A linear concept of development would seem best suited to meet the social and economic circumstances of society, and can be adapted to meet varying conditions of physical terrain and different patterns of existing settlement. Research, however, is necessary to determine the social, economic and technological costs and benefits of various urban forms in the city region.

[1] P. A. Stone, 'Urban Form and Resources', *Regional Studies*, Vol. 1, 1967, p. 95.

Chapter 7
The Major Land Use Components

PART A: HOUSING AND INDUSTRY

Industry, housing, service activity, recreational provision and rural life, in association with transportation and accessibility, provide an interwoven and interconnected set of land use elements which together create the main components of the regional and sub-regional landscape. Their location and form, and how they interact with each other, lies at the root of much decision-making about the urban future. Together with the interwoven threads of transportation and inter-accessibility between spatially separate activities, they provide the essential fabric for urban life. The policies considered for these essential land uses will now be considered, with those for industry and housing being the most critical as so much else depends on how employment and population are distributed.

THE ROLE OF INDUSTRY

The importance of major job opportunities in determining the location and form of alternative strategies varies, in part, through the different economic circumstances of each sub-region and in part, through the different degrees of emphasis which are attached to industrial location factors. Does one determine a desirable location for new urban development and then locate industrial areas, or does one locate industrial areas and then derive residential distributions from these locations of basic employment? Teesside, Warwickshire and North-Glos are more within the former category, whereas Leicestershire and Notts–Derby tend more to the latter viewpoint.

It would seem preferable for industrial location and transportation to be used, as far as is practicable, to structure the required long-term urban forms. Pressures from existing concentrations of population, though strong, need not necessarily be regarded as all-pervasive in an era of increasing mobility, technological and social change. Within this context, it should however be borne in mind that existing commitments are strong, which again emphasizes the need for long-term planning strategies so that the directions of new developments

164

can be 'bent' towards achieving the most desirable future urban forms through controls over the location of employment.

On Teesside, where the present economic strength relies upon heavy industry, the Study argues that the limited extent of the available estuarial sites should be reserved for these basic activities. 'The development should be restricted to heavy, site-oriented industry including chemicals, oil, steel or non-ferrous metals. . . . The purpose of this restriction is that it is the only land suitable for this type of industry and such land is in relatively short supply.'[1] For light industrial development, the existing industrial estates have an employment capacity for about 1,600 additional jobs, and 780 acres of committed industrial land on Board of Trade, local authority and private industrial estates can be expected to provide an additional 53,000 jobs by 1991. This leaves a deficiency of only about 22,000 jobs for development in order to influence the direction of development for the alternative strategies. It is suggested that 'policy will be more easily implemented if due recognition were given to the business interests of prospective employers',[2] including convenience of road access from the Midlands, Yorkshire and Lancashire for raw materials and markets. The preference is also for industrial estates of about 75 to 125 acres within one mile of an access point to the primary road system.

In the Leicestershire study, basic job locations provide the means for generating all six alternative strategies. 'The main generator of varied growth patterns is the way in which public stimuli and controls might be used to affect the distribution of basic employment among the several zones of the sub-region.'[3] Five elements of policy for the location of basic employment are recognized. 'The first, concentration, is concerned with protracted efforts to concentrate as much basic employment as possible into Greater Leicester. The second (dispersal), with an attempt to direct growth to the main county towns. The third element, "trend", involves the continuation of the pattern of basic employment growth since the war. Rejuvenation assumes a policy of reviving the industrial base of declining areas by introduction of basic employment in quantity. Finally accessibility is concerned with the growth of new industrial sites near the main national road network (present and future) and Castle Donington airport.'[4] These five elements are amalgamated to form six alternative strategies – concentration, dispersal, accessibility and trend, accessibility and rejuvenation, trend and rejuvenation, trend and dispersal.

[1] *Teesside Study*, p. 59.   [2] *Ibid.*, p. 60.
[3] *Leicestershire Study*, Vol. II, p. 79.   [4] *Ibid.*, Vol. I, p. 30.

165

Notts–Derby use a potential surface model for the distribution of employment. The indices of industrial potential are derived from the planning objectives. These 'factors of attraction' focus around clusters of economic opportunity in association with the expansion of employment opportunities and the size of the labour force, and around clusters of social opportunity through natural population growth and the size of the job pool available to the population of each zone. Given this emphasis on large job inputs, and large population inputs, and their interdependence, then the resultant conclusion is that 'the very large economic benefits are to be obtained if population and employment growth are encouraged to aggregate, and to be located where they can interact with existing towns . . . the large concentrations of population and employment have more of the conditions favourable to growth than do smaller concentrations. . . . Conversely, it is difficult and expensive to stimulate growth in areas which have few people and jobs at present. . . . It is normally easier to attract and sustain development in towns within commuting distance of existing towns than in free-standing towns.'[1] The self-reinforcing nature of urban growth, and the perpetuation of existing points of attraction, is emphasized by this form of argument. Completely new possibilities of industrial location are not envisaged, and physical factors are excluded from the model.

North-Glos considers spatial modules of 25 hectares, and assesses five circumstances for the distribution of this industrial development. These are 'established industrial areas with which new industry or relocated industry might require to maintain linkages; the network of communications in which motorway access points provided convenient industrial locations; accessibility to population; the major locational option(s) particular to the strategy being evolved; and suitable level areas'.[2]

The development potential surface in the Warwickshire Study, with the weighting in parenthesis, is access to principal roads and access to labour supply (each weighted at 6), the availability of flat land (weighted at 3), minimum costs for new utility services (weighted at 2) and located so as to conserve areas of high landscape value (weighted at 1). By these measures access to principal roads is given a greater significance than in the Notts–Derby Study and 'the potentials so produced were used to identify sites suitable for industry within the main strategy areas suggested by the Residential Development Potentials.'[3] This sequence is already reflected in the above

[1] *Notts–Derby Study*, p. 58.   [2] *North-Glos Study*, p. 67.
[3] *Warwickshire Study*, p. 53.

classification; the allocation of industrial land follows that of land for residential purposes.

At the Regional level Hampshire 'envisage the steady build-up of industrial land in conjunction with the major housing phases. Reservations for the former are located principally along the spine, where the South Coast Trunk Route and railway offer good accessibility.'[1] This reflects the theoretical evaluation, in which industry is located at inter-sections where routes cross; 'industry needs accessibility to its employees, but also to a regional freight route'.[2]

Humberside offers many similarities to Teesside. 4,500 acres were in industrial use in 1966, a further 750 acres are being developed and, in addition, almost 8,000 acres are subject to some form of planning commitment. Deep water estuarial sites should be reserved for heavy industrial expansion. 'However neither the distribution of employment nor its rate of build-up would be closely predictable on these estuarial sites, nor would it be sufficient to support a very large population. If a rapid, and therefore necessarily continuous, population intake is to be secured, general manufacturing industry not tied to an estuarial location would be needed.'[3] Sites are suggested for this latter purpose, whereas 'site selection for small industrial and commercial estates would hinge mainly on consideration of detailed urban layout and local amenity'.[4] A threefold classification of industrial sites is thus envisaged.

Discussion in the South East Study focusses on employment centres, and the possibilities of moving employment to selected new locations, rather than on industrial sites. These details will be referred to below. At this point the relative importance of manufacturing industry in the Region's economy should be noted. 'The manufacturing industries employed about 30 per cent of the region's labour force in 1966, 5 per cent less than the national average, and the proportion has been declining more swiftly than nationally.'[5]

The conclusion is that all Studies envisage industrial growth, and sites have been indicated to permit this expansion of employment in heavy and light manufacturing industry and service activities. Residential developments are related to these industrial groupings. The Leicestershire, Warwickshire and North-Glos strategies can be achieved through the internal rearrangement of their expected growth in employment opportunities, whereas Teesside and Notts–Derby each rely upon some external contributions to the Sub-regional

[1] *Hampshire Study*, p. 39.   [2] *Ibid.*, p. 99.
[3] *Humberside Study*, p. 121.   [4] *Ibid.*, p. 121.
[5] *South East Study*, p. 9.

167

economy. The amount required is less in Notts–Derby but 'nevertheless, the strategy put forward assumes some inward movement because without this there would be a shortfall of jobs in parts of the Sub-region likely to lead to pressures for outside assistance.'[1] Teesside estimates that 'about 61,000 jobs are likely to be needed. . . . The scale of this deficiency is a crucial figure for the preparation of an urban structure policy for Teesside as it makes possible an estimate of the maximum amount of additional land to be provided for future growth in employment and the necessary investment in a communications system and infrastructure to serve these activities.'[2]

At the Regional level, of the two Studies concerned with the feasibility of major urban growth, this would be self-supporting from the major internal trends in the case of Hampshire, but would rely upon external assistance in the Humberside situation. The South East Study is also self-sufficient, but relies upon some internal rearrangement of employment opportunities. The Humberside strategies therefore involve the most complex administrative situation. 'To be sure of success these efforts would have to be supplemented by financial inducements to industry. . . . It seems very probable that to initiate the large and rapid expansion which would be necessary for the large schemes we have examined, there would have to be financial inducements for general manufacturing industry to move into the Area for at least the first five or ten years of growth.'[3]

THE INTERNAL RELOCATION OF INDUSTRY

Against the previous evidence of an ebullient overall growth, not all sub-localities of a Region or Sub-region are necessarily either prosperous or expanding. All Studies express concern at the disparities which exist within their localities. Typical are the contrasts between areas of opportunity around the edges of major cities, and areas where the geography of need predominates.[4] The latter may include unattractive or run-down environments, isolation from the main centres of population, areas dependent upon old industries with declining demands for manpower, and where new growth is scarce. Such localities often grew to urban importance during the late eighteenth and nineteenth centuries with basic industry depending upon the local availability of raw materials, the proximity initially

---

[1] *Notts–Derby Study*, p. 31.   [2] *Teesside Study*, p. 25.
[3] *Humberside Study*, p. 40.

[4] Report of a Committee under the Chairmanship of Sir Joseph Hunt, *The Intermediate Areas*, HMSO (London), Cmnd. 3998, 1969, pp. 108–9.

of water and later of coal for power, and transportation of the product by rail. As market demand changed, as electric power freed industry from a coalfield location and as the motor vehicle diminished dependence upon a railway-oriented transportation system, new industries tended to develop in different localities. There was a shift in economic gravity to leave, as it were, high and dry in inaccessible or otherwise undesirable locations the urban patterns and landmarks of a previous technological age.

Nor are the conditions in these old by-passed urban areas necessarily in accord with the higher living standards and the greater social aspirations of the twentieth century. There are the substantial physical handicaps of industrial dereliction, visual eyesores, subsidence, abandoned buildings, derelict land, tip heaps of mineral waste, excavated pits and old mine shafts. As a place in which to live there are higher proportions of sub-standard, poor quality, small size and low cost housing units, the sins of air pollution, rivers and streams contaminated with industrial waste, hospitals and schools and other public services having to make do with older buildings and equipment, and low relative municipal or district rates per head of the population to remedy these deficiencies of environment. Add to these dimensions a considerable degree of local pride, a powerful community spirit, the contrasts between the 'haves' and the 'have nots', disparities in the measures of opportunity for human dignity such as unemployment or the level of personal incomes, and restricted work opportunities for women and juveniles. When hard times and the slump of the great depression are remembered with cold discomfort, then a net outward migration of population to more favoured areas at home or abroad expresses the inevitable reaction of individuals, families and deprived social groups. How do the Studies approach such problem areas within their Sub-regions?

The recommended Notts–Derby strategy focusses attention on the Mansfield/Alfreton growth zone, an area of existing and predicted unemployment as coal mining declines. An inward movement of jobs is to be encouraged. 'This inward movement of jobs will be encouraged by the Intermediate Area assistance which the government is making available, but a government training centre to provide the skilled labour required should be set up within the zone without delay. It is also necessary to encourage the concentration of public and private investment in the area, particularly during the next few years.'[1] These few words reflect at the microscale the national dilemma of expanding and prosperous localities existing close by declining and

[1] *Notts–Derby Study*, p. 37.

less virulent localities. Government assistance and planning measures will be used to attract into the growth zone employment opportunities which might otherwise locate in or close to the main urbanized areas of Nottingham and Derby. Can the pressures on the latter be diminished, to the advantage of less fortunate zones?

In both the Leicestershire, North-Glos and Warwickshire Studies, and away from their respective areas of planned growth, a special concern is also expressed for those localities where employment opportunities in basic manufacturing and extractive industry have either declined or are expected to diminish further over the period covered by the strategy. Leicestershire recommends the creation of new forms of employment in the northwestern parts of the Sub-region to rejuvenate the local economies. Referring particularly to this coalfield area, 'the first aim of the strategy is to build up new employment to offset these declines and at the same time to create centres of industrial and commercial activity which have the prospect of long-term growth within the framework of the strategy as a whole. ... Such growth can best be assured by industrial sites which are near to existing centres and have good accessibility to high-quality roads (or the prospect of it).'[1] In the North-Glos Study a policy 'of diverting new industrial development to less favourable industrial localities in order to achieve some other non-industrial objective' is considered, but is rejected as 'unlikely to be acceptable or realistic'.[2] The argument is that 'employment growth prospects might well be prejudiced due to firms preferring more favourable sites outside the Sub-Region as compared with available sites within it: general economic disadvantages might also ensue'.[3] Growth is however advocated especially at Lydney, but also at Coleford and Cinderford. These centres are accessible to extensive hinterland areas in the Forest of Dean, with its former mining settlements. In the Warwickshire Study, one policy recommendation is that 'because there will be continuing employment difficulties in North Warwickshire and in the more remote rural districts, special measures to help areas of declining industry and North Warwickshire in particular should be continued for a long period'.[4] A previous argument for landscape improvement will also be recalled.

The triple package suggested for the relief of urban decline in the Sub-regional planning strategies is thus (1) the simulation of new employment growth, (2) environmental improvement and (3) an emphasis on selected points of growth. The alternative possibilities of

[1] *Leicestershire Study*, p. 87. [2] *North-Glos Study*, p. 64.
[3] *Ibid.*, p. 64. [4] *Warwickshire Study*, p. 90.

encouraging the run-down of such localities, their environmental reclamation, the resettlement of families, and the re-use of the localities for recreation, agriculture or forestry have apparently not been considered, yet constructive policies in this direction may reasonably be considered. Given a much stronger national contribution towards the removal of blighting influences from the landscape, the encouragement of afforestation and perhaps the creation of reservoirs as appropriate within the physical and ecological circumstances of each locality, then the derelict areas of today *can* become the Country Parks of tomorrow. The steep-sided valleys can become major recreational localities, areas for retirement, and *attractive* for urban development. Should this sound a far-fetched utopian dream, then the transformation of the Tennessee Valley and parts of the Appalachian Range may be used to illustrate the potential.

A programme of environmental reclamation will not have immediate effects, and a period of a century may be necessary to accommodate the desirable changes in landscape, but regional landscape design and tree-planting schemes for amenity must inevitably be long term to achieve their expected visual impact and to provide their true reward for future generations. The important point is to assess the best contribution which each sub-district can, in the future, make to the sub-regional and national economy and then to use its human endowments and physical resources to achieve these objectives, rather than to begin with the concept that declining localities *must* receive industrial support. The poorer localities do not wish to receive only crumbs of comfort from the rich man's table, but to be self-sustaining in their own right. Industrial transfer is not necessarily either the correct or the best answer. In the words of Cullingworth and Orr (1969), 'little attempt was made to assess the economic cost to the country as a whole of limiting development in prosperous areas and subsidizing it in less prosperous ones. If the issue was raised at all, the implicit assumption made was that some economic cost was incurred but that it was justified by the social benefit gained.'[1] This statement of the national condition remains valid at the sub-regional level of analysis.

THE DISTANCE OF INDUSTRIAL MOVEMENT

The distance of willing transfer is most critical in the Notts–Derby Study where 'it seems reasonable to expect that about a quarter of the

[1] J. B. Cullingworth and S. C. Orr, 'Participation of Social Scientists in Planning' in S. C. Orr and J. B. Cullingworth (eds.), *Regional and Urban Studies*, George Allen and Unwin (London), 1969, p. 6.

total number of manufacturing jobs in the Sub-region (including new jobs) will be located or re-located elsewhere than on their original site within the next twenty years. In the past, such relocations have been relatively local moves, but in view of improvements to roads and other services a more optimistic view can be taken, and it can be assumed that a larger proportion will move up to twenty miles.'[1] Their recommended Mansfield–Alfreton growth zone, and their transfer of industrial activity from Derby and Nottingham, depends upon the validity of this assumption. The significance of this distance of movement is that 'mobility of jobs emerged as the key factor in producing a strategy that most nearly satisfied the objectives adopted. ... In the second round of tests three alternative strategies were produced for 1986, all following the theme of the preferred strategy that was emerging but each based on a different assumption of job mobility'.[2] These three assumptions were (1) a high level of job mobility and a medium amount of economic benefit resulting from Intermediate Area status, (2) a low level of industrial mobility and no economic assistance from Intermediate Area status, and (3) a high level of job mobility and a large measure of Government economic aid.[3] Subsequently a mobility study has been commissioned by the monitoring and advisory unit but, even should these conclusions be satisfactory, difficulties remain over the nature of government financial assistance, to the possible detriment of the recommended strategy.

Comparable difficulties, though at a different scale of appreciation, underlie the South East Study. The team 'assumed that it will remain Government policy, for the immediately foreseeable future, to steer, where possible, new employment opportunities from the South East'.[4] Internally, their advocacy is for 'the creation of employment centres of sufficient size to ease problems of labour supply for employees and to offer workers a wide range of employment opportunities, and to allow for operational economies, without posing substantial journey-to-work or congestion problems'.[5] A labour survey of units which had moved was undertaken. Unfortunately, it is restricted both to manufacturing industry and to plants employing more than a hundred workers, but within these limitations it indicates that a diminishing percentage of all staff transfer with a firm as the distance moved increases, and that a greater proportion of

[1] *Notts–Derby Study*, p. 51.

[2] Notts–Derby Sub-Regional Planning Unit, *Nottinghamshire and Derbyshire: Sub-Regional Road Network*, 1970, p. 44.

[3] *Ibid.*, Record Report 31, p. 8.   [4] *South East Study*, p. 6.   [5] *Ibid.*, p. 6.

managerial and skilled staff transfer than clerical, office, semi-skilled and unskilled production workers.[1] The conclusion is that 'there would seem to be little difficulty in attracting firms to most parts of the South East'.[2] The magnitude of the need is that 'the requirement for mobile manufacturing and office jobs might be of the order of 15–20,000 a year in each category',[3] and the strategy envisages a number of growth areas to assist with this redistribution.

OFFICES AND SERVICE EMPLOYMENT

The service sector of employment is projected separately in all Studies and, in terms of location, the Teesside Study anticipates that employment distributed throughout the residential areas will increase from 18 to 22 per cent of all employment; 'there is likely to be a tendency for bigger centres within and close to housing areas: district centres giving shopping, commercial and administrative services with employment of the order of 2,000 jobs; district hospitals, employing between 1,000 and 2,000; and secondary school campus sites. A wide range of employment would be in local shops, primary schools and so on. In total, it is likely that a large new residential area might offer a stable employment of the order of 100 jobs for 1,000 population though it could rise to higher levels.'[4] In the Leicestershire strategy, 'an essential element should be the development of a nucleus of service employment – offices and shops – in addition to manufacturing and other kinds of industry. . . . Suburban locations for employment are more likely to succeed if employment can find a range of shopping and other services near at hand and grouping of employment should assist in their provision.'[5]

In the Warwickshire Study, service employment is expected to increase at 2 per cent per annum, compared with 1 per cent for all employment and manufacturing at about +0·5 per cent. Of the increase in service employment, approximately half will be located in the existing central areas and about half will be located wholly within the new residential areas.[6] The North-Glos argument is that 'commercial and service development, including shops, offices and storage facilities other than large scale warehousing, is expected to continue to be concentrated in the town centres. Apart from shops, there would be scope also for new office development, not requiring central locations, in the major surburban centres proposed.'[7]

[1] *Ibid.*, p. 17.   [2] *Ibid.*, p. 17.   [3] *Ibid.*, p. 81.   [4] *Teesside Study*, p. 61.
[5] *Leicestershire Study*, p. 89.   [6] *Warwickshire Study*, pp. 103 and 111.
[7] *North-Glos Study*, p. 92.

This viewpoint is repeated at the regional level in the Hampshire Study where 'the tendency for offices to cluster in city centres is, at least on present evidence, well-founded and not likely to be abandoned in favour of wide dispersal. The reasons for concentration are the greater accessibility from a wide area, the importance of "linkages" between offices, the proximity of a wide range of specialist services, and the presence of shops, restaurants, etc.'[1] In the South East Region, where the proportion of office workers increased by 42 per cent against 11 per cent for all occupations between 1951 and 1961, and then by a further 14 per cent between 1961 and 1966 (7 per cent for all occupations), concentration is again envisaged in the above-mentioned employment centres. The Humberside Study presents a different picture and argues that, quite apart from additional service employment in relation to population growth, 'Humberside has sites that could be developed on a large scale as research and commercial office centres. . . . Its promotion for these purposes would however call for a new national policy involving the deliberate encouragement of a limited number of major office centres away from London, since otherwise the natural tendency would be for office dispersion to take place within or near the South East.'[2]

Inadequate attention has probably been paid to the role of service employment in the formulation of strategies. The general approach has certainly been to diminish the proportion of manufacturing and other basic employment, and to expand the proportions in service employment, but it may be doubted whether either the extent or the significance of this revolution has yet been fully appreciated. Traditionally, the Victorian City and manufacturing industry, urbanization and industrialization, have been associated as the twin pillars of new development. The increasing role of service employment, the significant urban interrelationships which continue to aggrandize certain major central areas on a *selective* basis, and the extent to which service activities are redistributed in association with the residential population have received less research understanding in the Studies than basic manufacturing activity[3] – yet the former is expanding and the latter is declining. The service proportion of total employment in Great Britain at 1966 was 57 per cent, with 38 per cent in heavy industry and other manufactures, and the national expectation (quoted in the Humberside Study) is for an increase to about 70 per cent of total employment in service activities by the year 2000. How

---

[1] *Hampshire Study*, p. 47. [2] *Humberside Study*, p. 36.
[3] See, for example, M. Wright, 'Provincial Office Development' and other papers in *Urban Studies*, Vol. 4, 1967, pp. 218–85.

should strategic policies be adapted to this growing importance of non-industrial employment? Will the growing concentration in larger centres be to the further detriment of smaller towns? How does office employment as a 'growth industry' differ in terms of social attitudes, income, housing, shopping and recreational demands from manufacturing distributions? Such questions, and the critical role of locations for service industry to achieve desirable strategies of urban development, have not been examined with the same degree of critical attention as employment in manufacturing, and yet service employment is likely to play the greater future role as its relative increase in employment is expected to be greater than for manufacturing industry.

HOUSING DENSITIES AND LAND NEEDS

Definitions may vary and hence comparisons are difficult but, using the phraseology of each Study, Teesside and Leicestershire each distinguish between local authority and private sites, and adopt varying densities. Teesside suggests relatively low density standards at 40 persons per acre over local authority sites and 30 persons per acre over private sites,[1] whereas Leicestershire varies its density assumptions by location – from 8 dwellings per acre in rural locations to 10 dwellings on the city fringe and in county towns, to 24 in the inner city and 36 in the central city.[2] North-Glos refers to gross densities of 8 dwellings per acre on new sites.[3] Notts–Derby assumes a net density of 10 dwellings per acre for calculation purposes, and observes that ± 20 per cent will not substantially affect the strategy.[4] Warwickshire indicate gross and net residential densities of 20 and 24 persons per acre.[5] Humberside uses an overall urban density of 22 persons per acre.[6] Hampshire develop six residential models to meet varying types of socio-economic demand; their net residential densities range from 130 persons per acre (3 models), 45 persons per acre (2 models) to 15 persons per acre in the high income, low density, dispersed patterns.[7]

The outcome from each Study, as a sum total of the many population and housing variables which are involved, is for very considerable land commitments to meet urban growth. There is therefore the need either to relax physical constraints on the use of land/or to use

[1] *Teesside Study*, p. 37.　　[2] *Leicestershire Study*, Vol. II, p. 135.
[3] *North-Glos Study*, p. 44.　　[4] *Notts–Derby Study*, p. 56.
[5] *Warwickshire Study*, p. 55.　　[6] *Humberside Study*, p. 42.
[7] *Hampshire Study*, pp. 56–7.

substantial areas of lower grade agricultural land. Indicative of this incessant growth and the cumulative pressures of outward urban expansion are that in North-Glos, 'additional land required for dwellings and ancillary uses in the Sub-region was assessed at approximately 12,100 acres or 19 square miles for the 35 year period between 1966 and 2001.'[1] Teesside requires a total construction of about 19,200 dwellings on new sites between 1966 and 1991.[2] In Leicestershire, 'it will be necessary to build about 94,500 new dwellings between 1966 and 1991 to meet the various kinds of demand. . . . There will be heavy demands for more primary and secondary schools, and all of this will involve the development of over 12,000 acres of land.'[3] Notts–Derby require 24,000 acres for their recommended strategy by 1986.[4] In Warwickshire the maximum increase in urban land (i.e. more extensive than residential) between 1976 and 1991 might reach as high as 25,000 acres.[5]

At the regional levels, where demands are much greater because of the greater magnitudes which are involved, the South East Study requires an additional 42,000 houses a year over the present rate of housing completions at 87,000 dwellings a year. The problem is seen not in terms of house construction, but 'concentration of building activity in a limited number of major growth areas would pose administrative and logistical problems and achievement would depend on strong organization in each'.[6] Humberside would require about 43,000 acres of housing land;[7] the current output from the building industry is about 6,000 houses a year, and 'would have to rise to about 10,000 a year in the first ten years and probably 12,000 in the second to meet the needs of newcomers alone. In addition existing housing will have to be replaced as it grows older and homes will be needed for the growing local population, requiring altogether a further 5,000 houses during the 1980s and the 1990s'.[8] Hampshire's construction targets are based on high and low assessment rates; the increase is from about 70,000 dwellings per decade (1961–1971) to 185,400 per decade by 1991–2001 at the high rate, or 121,500 dwellings at the low rate per decade by 1991–2001. Land acquisition rates would involve a gross average of 20,700 acres per decade at the high rate and 13,500 acres at the low rate, compared to about 10,300 acres over the 1961–1971 period.[9]

[1] *North-Glos Study*, p. 44.   [2] *Teesside Study*, p. 38.
[3] *Leicestershire Study*, pp. i and 94.   [4] *Notts–Derby Study*, p. 107.
[5] *Warwickshire Study*, p. 55.   [6] *South East Study*, p. 59.
[7] *Humberside Study*, p. 42.   [8] *Ibid.*, p. 46.
[9] *Hampshire Study*, Vol. II, pp. 94–5.

It is clear from this resumé that a remarkable expansion in the extent of the present urbanized areas is envisaged in all Studies. These substantial demands on land provide ample justification for the physical constraints and land management policies which have been discussed, and underline the impact of the population and employment forecasts. They emphasize, above all else, that the size and extent of urban developments are as yet in their infancy. The regional city has burgeoning and as yet insatiable demands on land and these pressures, on the forecasts thus far available, tend to be on the increase over future decades. More people require not only more land, but more land per capita for almost every urban purpose. Of total land needs, a higher proportion (almost 50 per cent in the Warwickshire Study between 1976 and 1991) is required for residential purposes.

THE DISTRIBUTION OF HOUSING TO SUB-AREAS

The total demand for housing is distributed to sub-areas in each Study based on the accessibility to employment, the proximity of existing concentrations of population, and locational considerations. Although the nature of the argument varies both from Study to Study and in accord with their various strategic possibilities, the impetus from existing conditions emerges as the single most powerful formative element on future locations.

On Teesside, the position is largely predetermined. 'The pattern of distribution in 1966 was such that nearly 80 per cent of the dwellings and the population . . . was located in urban Teesside. Much of the future pattern of distribution of dwellings is already known in a sense.'[1] This includes a 1:5 replacement on cleared sites, and sites already committed either by planning permission or by allocation on a town map. Of the total stock of 221,600 dwellings estimated to be needed by 1991, the probable location of 173,100 is known. This leaves only about 5,000 acres to achieve one or other of the alternative strategies for development which have been identified. The sequence of factors in allocation is then, first, 'the actual character of the site and its capacity to form the basis of a high quality of environment after development. . . . The second factor will be the location of the new housing areas so as to provide a variety of types of environment.'[2] Physical conditions thus prevail in the Teesside approach.

The North-Glos approach is similar in that, 'over the period

[1] *Teesside Study*, p. 39.   [2] *Ibid.*, p. 79.

1966 to 1981 the appropriate number of housing development modules (at 25 hectares each) were, in the main, located adjacent to, or near existing development in locations with good accessibility to existing employment opportunities. This broadly followed current development trends but observed physical and landscape restraints.'[1] The next phase, from 1981 to 2001, is distributed in the same manner, including accessibility to the new postulated centres of employment and the major locational options particular to each strategy. During the first period, residential locations could only 'tend towards' these major locational options.[2]

By contrast, both Leicestershire and Notts–Derby use mathematical models to simulate the future position. The Leicestershire approach is based on the strength of home–work relationships and, in particular, on their conclusion that 'a zone's share of [total sub-regional] change in employment and its share of population change in any five-year period in a certain combination could enable us to predict with reasonable accuracy the share of total population change which that zone would receive in the subsequent period of five years. In other words, population change in a zone is strongly related to its past experience of employment and population change, and this response is lagged by about five years.'[3] A two phase sequence then follows. First, the mathematical model is used to distribute population change between a small number of broad zones by a gravity formula with basic employment priming the distribution of population and this in turn calling forth service employment. Second, the broad zonal totals are broken down to smaller cells by manual procedures to allow for localized constraints and opportunities; 'manual procedures allow judgement and discretion to be exercised in estimating the local effects of such factors as access to work, the road network, utility developments, environmental quality and land development policies'.[4]

The Notts–Derby approach is comparable, using the same roots but a different model. Thus, capacity constraints are introduced to reduce intensive pressures on urban areas, to decentralize such pressures in relation to the housing market, and calibration procedures avoid bogus parameters. Input also includes the basic/non-basic split in employment. The model 'assumes that the quantity and distribution of residential development is directly related to the quality and distribution of employment, and to the characteristics of the road network in the area. Changes in basic employment patterns and in the

[1] North-Glos Study, p. 67.   [2] Ibid., p. 67.
[3] Leicestershire Study, p. 37.   [4] Ibid., Vol. II, p. 80.

road network will therefore produce consequential changes in the pattern of residential development and service job location.'[1] The main variable in the Garin–Lowry model is thus the availability of basic jobs. The nature of this dependence is emphasized by the fact that, on the very day when these words are first written, Rolls-Royce has been declared bankrupt and many employees in its Derby plant are expected to become redundant. One should also note that this model excludes households where the household is not gainfully occupied (e.g. of pensionable age), the institutional population, and the many social, cost and amenity factors which might be involved in the selection of a home. The model predicts the residential location of workers, and relies on the economic base method to generate successive increments of population and then of service employment from a given distribution of basic employment. Population is allocated by the gravity law of human interaction.[2]

The residential model relies on an observed correlation that the number of persons who journey from home to work declines in relative frequency with increasing distance, but it may be queried whether this correlation is necessarily a cause and effect relationship. Could it be that the low density areas are further from the centres of employment and have smaller populations than the nearer high density areas, and therefore smaller numbers will travel the longer distances? As incomes rise then the preference may increase for good housing conditions and a pleasant living environment. In such circumstances the journey to work becomes a consequence of the residential decision and, within reason, the costs and time of travel are borne willingly for compensating advantages in the home location. Given motorways providing fast access and rapid commuter train services, then very extensive areas exist within thirty minutes' travel time of nodal situations. With higher incomes and greater personal mobility, the ties between home and place of work become less important than for lower income groups and conditions may change quite radically in the future.

Humberside offers similarities with Teesside, in that physical considerations are paramount. 'There are certain physical factors which, though rarely sufficiently weighty to stop development entirely, when taken together influence the selection of the sites that would provide the best living conditions and be cheapest to develop.'[3]

[1] *Notts–Derby Study*, p. lxxi.
[2] See M. Batty, 'Models and Projections of the Space Economy', *Town Planning Review*, Vol. 41, 1970, pp. 121–47.
[3] *Humberside Study*, p. 19.

These include the various topographic, amenity and drainage factors which we have already identified and, of the 93,000 acres suitable for major residential development, 6,000 acres are Grade I agricultural land, 62,000 acres are Grade II and 23,000 acres are Grade III land.

In Hampshire the major residential areas are located within the network grid and take on either a dispersed, concentrated linear or concentrated non-linear pattern. The typical relationship between facilities and the residential areas envisages 'the centre adjacent to a transport inter-section with residential areas linked by the route of lower category and industrial areas located alongside the higher category routes; the centre being accessible to both'.[1] The South East Study does not explain the sub-allocation of its housing demand, except that the details emphasize certain sociological aspects. Housing demand is discussed against occupational groups with their differing requirements, and some allocations would seem to be made on this basis. Thus, in one planning district, 'it would be in the regional interest for sites to be made available for some upper occupation group housing'.[2] A rather unusual example of a social factor influencing the locational decision is provided by the Deeside Study. In this instance a disadvantage of one area with the capacity for development is stated to be 'English immigration into Welsh-speaking areas. . . . The other site by contrast would be in an area already largely English-speaking.'[3]

The Warwickshire procedures, as the climax to the previous accounts, are made within the context of the policy recommendation that 'the sub-region's growth be concentrated around urban areas, not dispersed in villages or through the countryside. The pressures on the countryside from towns and the farming industry justify further restraint on house-building in rural areas.'[4] The analysis then involves three stages:

1. the selection of objectives 'likely to be useful in producing different spatial patterns.'[5] These include: the conservation of areas with a high landscape value, the avoidance of good quality farmland, the minimum costs for new utility services and land development, development in areas of high environmental potential, development in areas which will not be adversely affected by atmospheric and noise pollution, the greatest possible choice of jobs available to all workers, the greatest possible choice of labour supply for all firms, the greatest

[1] *Hampshire Study*, Vol. II, p. 37.   [2] *South East Study*, p. 103.
[3] Consultants' Report to the Secretary of State for Wales, *Deeside Planning Study*, Shankland Cox and Associates (London), 1970, p. 61.
[4] *Warwickshire Study*, p. 90.   [5] *Ibid.*, p. 34.

potential accessibility to the potential range of shopping facilities, and locations in relation to principal roads and in order to provide the greatest possible potential for public transport services.[1]

2. The preparation of 'factor surfaces' for each of the above ten objectives in order to generate the alternative strategies of residential development. 'Since most objectives were expressed in terms of maximizing or minimizing opportunities the scores for each surface were put in the range 1–100, whatever their original units of measurement – whether hectares lost to agriculture or levels of job opportunity. The worst conditions prevalent in the sub-region for each factor were always measured as 1 and the best always scored 100.'[2] Factors could be compared with each other on the basis of their range and are mapped for each factor.

3. The derivation of 'different weighting systems for the ten factor surfaces, so that varying emphasis could be imposed before the scores were added to produce combined potentials'.[3] These weights are derived (a) from members of the planning team and liaison officers in the three planning authorities, and (b) by exaggerating or depressing weights as the general policy demanded. 'By varying the weights given, it enabled the emphasis to be shifted between the factors to measure how the potential for development changed when policy assumptions were varied.'[4]

The approach, therefore, in the Warwickshire assessment is closely related to goals and objectives. It follows systematic procedures to a greater degree than any previous Study. It depends to a considerable extent upon professional judgement over a series of sequential decisions such as the selection of relevant objectives, their translation into meaningful levels of performance, the determination of these for each unit of measurement (the 1×1 km or 5×5 km grid square) at 1969 and for the forecast position in 1991, and in the use of weights to distinguish between the relative importance of the various factors. The Study Team do not pretend that the techniques are perfect, and certain limitations are mentioned in the Report. Their purpose, against these assumptions, is to express the relative attraction of the different parts of the Sub-region for new residential areas.

THE ALLOCATION OF LAND TO URBAN DEVELOPMENT

The reader is again invited to pause, and to consider the nature of the urban growth problem and the implications of the above

[1] *Ibid.*, p. 29 and Table 4.1. [2] *Ibid.*, p. 35.
[3] *Ibid.*, p. 40. [4] *Ibid.*, p. 31.

commentary. He has previously considered that land which *should* be subject to some form of constraint and has indicated those areas which *could* be suitable for urban development. He will accept the considerable pressures for urban growth and the needs which demand the new provision of land for a variety of purposes, as expressed through the previous forecasts and projections. He may, indeed, wish to reinterpret these projections and to assess the likely future trends in his own sub-region. He may at this stage consider the possibilities which exist for peripheral growth, new communities, town expansion and linear developments, together with the pros and the cons, the 'ifs' and the 'buts' of each possibility. His concern now is with the actual allocation of land in order to accommodate the envisaged growth pressures and within the context of the constraints which have been identified. How would he proceed? Which factors are relevant? How do they compare and relate to each other?

Two extreme situations may be considered, against the common background of two large expanding cities separated by an intervening green belt of pleasant rolling English countryside, and linked by a connecting motorway and a railway line with fast inter-city services. One possibility might be to develop a compact urban community intermediate between the two cities. The design would be related closely to both a motorway junction and an existing railway station, the frequency of trains to the two cities would be up-graded in performance and the quality of its services and local functions would be developed in a town centre, which would have direct access from the motorway and be situated over the railway station. Residential densities would diminish outwards from high blocks in and close to the town centre, to external sites for private housing in the less accessible situations. There would be an extensive provision for landscaping schemes within the urban community, and a green wedge would be retained between this community and the existing cities.

The second possibility is quite different. Planning controls, directives and policies would be reduced considerably by a government which believes strongly in the virtues of private enterprise, a free market in land and that entrepreneurial abilities will best resolve the conflicts of the existing imposed situation. The outcome in these circumstances of greater freedom might include peripheral expansion of the two large cities, ribbons of development along road routes accessible to the cities, a large regional shopping centre at a convenient motorway junction between the two cities, a considerable amount of dispersed development especially in the more favoured physical localities, some co-ordinated estate developments in the vicinity of the shopping centre and/or the railway station, and many isolated buildings or groups of buildings. More land would be used than under the previous possibility.

Neither of these extreme situations is intended to be either a caricature or impracticable. Both possibilities now exist, and each could be achieved in the circumstances of tomorrow. The point is that different sets of values are possible, and a range of options exist in the forecast and anticipation of future urban environments. The degree of management and direction on the one hand, and the degree of personal freedom and initiative on the other hand, raise extremely awkward social, moral and political issues which must be resolved by each successive generation in the light of the conditions then prevailing. The dilemma faced by every planner in a democratic situation is how to reconcile the conflicts which exist between the need for a rational managerial approach to urban systems and land resources with the equally important need to encourage initiative, freedom, private responsibility and personal discretion.

It can be argued that the planning situation in Britain is inflexible, inelastic, excessively precise and overwhelming and that, in the long run, the sum total of its restrictive policies is reflected in the poor performance of the national economy and the low rate of increase in the gross national product. It can equally be argued that the greater degree of private freedom on the other side of the Atlantic Ocean has resulted in the wanton destruction of important natural resources, the gross pollution of existing environmental assets, indiscriminate and costly urban sprawl, and a grievous *laissez-faire* situation which now requires immediate redress and responsible action by government.

Wherein lies the sensible middle path between the excessive extremes of frustration by government or private licence? One thought is offered for discussion. Just as a vacancy rate is assumed in the provision of housing accommodation,[1] so too should there be a vacancy rate in the provision of land for urban development. The planning strategy might recommend that a thousand acres of residential land are required to permit the expansion of a given urban environment over each five-year period from 1976 to 1996. At the beginning of the first period a thousand acres plus a vacancy rate to

[1] The South East Study (p. 23) assumes that this is 4·5 per cent of households at any one time. Warwickshire (p. 170) increase their rates from 2 per cent of the housing stock in 1966 to 3 per cent in 1976 and 4 per cent in 1981. Leicestershire (Vol. II, p. 55) state 'a 2% vacancy rate is both reasonable and desirable' and Teesside (p. 33) argue that the existing proportion of vacant dwellings should increase from less than 2 to about 4 per cent. Can such differences be explained?

achieve freedom of action (say 30 per cent) are released for residential and urban development purposes. If the planning forecasts are correct, then only a thousand acres will be developed but the process of land development by private developers and government agencies is given some room to manœuvre and to select preferred sites; the balance is carried forward into the next five-year period. If the planning forecasts are incorrect and more land than the thousand acres is developed, this excess amount is in effect borrowed from the next five-year period; the strategy, as argued in Chapter 5, has been advanced in time from its previous end-of-the-century position to perhaps 1995. If the thousand acres are under-used, then the period of the planning forecast is extended to beyond the end of the century. This procedure of a 'reserve land capacity' would allow the economic and social forces of the market to play a more constructive role than at present, it provides a land bank against contingencies and in order to encourage the development process, and the location of the land and its spatial organization would still be as determined in the planning strategies.

A further and more obvious point is the need for substantial discussions with land-owning and land-development interests, in order to appreciate the degree of reliability which may be attached to the planning assessment of the situation. For example, when weighting is involved in order to determine the degree of preference for certain factors, these weights could be tested for their validity with members of the estates and land management professions. The thought here is that planners, because of the legislative controls which exist over development, seek to understand demands and latent pressures in order to make the best provision of land in the most suitable locations. In this function, planning studies replace the market reports which would be made of the financial prospects for development by private enterprise. A set of values and judgements are being made, which act as substitutes for or supplement the economic mechanism to reach decisions about land development. The methods of assessment are often the same in many respects, though the underlying purpose is markedly different.

PART B: OTHER LAND USE AND RELATED COMPONENTS

Against this background of extensive urban provision for exacting industrial and housing demands, several further land use and other spatial considerations receive their considered attention in the Studies. Each, in its own right, can be extremely important in terms of location and form for the future characteristics and well-being of the sub-regional environment.

SHOPPING CENTRES[1]

Planning variables include both the location and size of new shopping centres, and the degree of change to be encouraged in existing centres. An important difference may be noted between the Studies with Notts–Derby, Leicestershire and North-Glos each using a 'prediction' approach, whereas in the Teesside and Humberside Studies a 'regional design' concept is tested for its potential achievement. Prediction (*a posteriori*) means that the distribution and hierarchy of shopping centres results from the distribution of the residential population whereas, in the regional design (*a priori*) approach, some desired hierarchy of service centres is one of the planning objectives. Warwickshire even defer the discussion of shopping provision and the hierarchy of shopping centres to the later stages of structure planning, but retain accessibility to the principal shopping centres as a factor in generating and testing the alternative strategies; 'it was not useful to calculate demand for shopping floor space in the centres in 1991, nor would any short-term calculations have helped in evaluating the alternatives. The authorities will wish to make calculations of this kind during Structure Planning within an agreed sub-regional strategy.'[2]

The Teesside argument is that, if it is 'possible to demonstrate that the provision is likely to be commercially viable', then there is the need 'to foster the growth of one or other of these two centres into a dominant regional shopping centre for Teesside'.[3] A resultant test, in evaluating between the strength of alternative strategies is 'sustaining the development of a regional centre at Middlesbrough'.[4] Similar arguments for upgrading the regional capital are used in the Humberside Study, where one measure for the assessment of the alternative strategies is its contribution towards upgrading the facilities of Hull's central area. 'We have, for example, assumed in the employment projections . . . that Hull's development as a higher

---

[1] See for example P. Scott, *Geography and Retailing*, Hutchinson University Library (London), 1970. Shopping models are discussed in *Urban Models in Shopping Studies*, National Economic Development Office (London), 1970.

[2] *Warwickshire Study*, p. 87.   [3] *Teesside Study*, pp. 52 and 54.

[4] *Ibid.*, p. 77.

order centre would materially increase total service employment in the Area as a whole. The role of Hull is crucial, particularly as its centre has space for considerable expansion.'[1] Previously, in advocating a Humber Bridge, its important unifying element had been emphasized; 'the longer a bridge is deferred the greater the likelihood that central area facilities will become set in a pattern which duplicates "lower order" facilities on each bank, while the creation of "higher order" facilities is inhibited by lack of a sufficiently wide catchment area'.[2]

Nor is this structuring of urban form in the Teesside and Humberside Studies by changing the urban hierarchy untypical. For example, in the Deeside Study an operational objective is 'to establish a third order (sub-regional) shopping and service centre that would (1) raise the level of services in Flintshire; (2) add to the number and variety of jobs; (3) help to attract industry and peoples; (4) provide a suitable location for offices; and (5) create a focus for the enlarged community'.[3] In the Hampshire Study, in the opposite direction but again emphasizing the effects of new development and changing patterns of activity on the distribution and status of service centres, a new dominant regional centre is envisaged, and the expectation is that Southampton will decline over the long term to one of several district centres.[4]

The *a priori* approach is preferred. In the Notts–Derby and North-Glos situations, where there are nearby competing centres (Nottingham, Derby and Gloucester, Cheltenham) and the possibilities of major residential growth in the vicinity, the desirability or otherwise of a bi-focal situation should have been considered in the Studies. Does the existing situation offer any advantages, or should one selected centre be encouraged to rise to dominance? The present pattern of service centres is not fixed and predetermined; it has changed historically and is amenable to alteration, if so required, by the planning strategies for urban development.

With the exception of Humberside and Warwickshire, all Studies take advantage of retail gravity models in order to distribute expenditure to shops and to assess the implications for shopping of their several alternative strategies. The statistical input has been noted in Chapter 5. This mathematical technique examines the relationship between the residential distribution of population, their per capita expenditure on durable goods in service centres of varying size, and accessibility or ease of travel along the interconnecting transportation

[1] *Humberside Study*, p. 121.   [2] *Ibid.*, p. 31.
[3] Deeside Planning Study, *op. cit.*, p. 55.   [4] *Hampshire Study*, p. 77.

network. The essential basis of the model is again the gravity interpretation of behaviour, which states that the retail expenditure by a
population is influenced by both the size and the distance of competing centres. As the attraction of centres is directly proportional to the
size of the centre and inversely proportional to the cost of overcoming the intervening distance, the larger centre attracts some
custom from the catchment area of a smaller competing centre; the
smaller the centre the less will be the interaction between it and the
population within its hinterland area.

Humberside does not use a mathematical model. Their argument is
that 'in this field there can be an infinite grading of possibilities
between a concentration and a dispersal of facilities. There are some
mathematical techniques, at present rather crude, for evaluating such
factors as the competitive strength of developing centres, but we were
unable to devise a satisfactory way of applying them to major new
developments because of a lack at present of suitable data.'[1] Whilst
accepting the uncertainty of the models which could have been used,
the use of this method would at least have provided certain objective
criteria for measuring the relative impact and desirability of different
hypothetical urban distributions against certain prior assumptions.
It may also be argued that one function of a government-sponsored
Study is to explore critically the use of potential new techniques, so
that the quality of planning analysis may continually be improved.

The task undertaken by the model is, in fact, to distribute the cash
flow from each residential zone to each shopping centre, based on the
relative attraction of each centre in terms of its time (or cost) distance
and the size of its mass value. The performance of each strategy in
minimizing the length of the average shopping journey can now be
measured on a comparative basis. The evaluation procedures in
the North-Glos, Warwickshire, Leicestershire and Notts–Derby
Studies each assess the least amount of travel and the greatest relative
accessibility to durable goods shops, as one determinant in the
selection of their preferred strategy. Considerable doubts may be
expressed about the importance of this particular index. The length
of the average journey will automatically be less for concentrated
groupings than for dispersed patterns of settlement, and will favour
high-density developments over low densities. It also presumes that
the length of the shopping journey by the end of the century will be
important, which may be doubted with increasing car ownership, a
possible trend to one-stop weekly family shopping as in North
America, rising real incomes, and the many other factors which

[1] *Humberside Study*, p. 119.

187

influence residential locations and which have precedence over accessibility to shops in a society of increasing mobility. For many socioeconomic groups it may be irrelevant whether the time-distance to a shopping centre is 10, 15 or 20 minutes away by car.

THE FUTURE OF TOWN CENTRES

Shopping facilities are now concentrated in town centres, and their difficulties of access, vehicle congestion and parking difficulties have in most cases worsened over recent years. There is an existing tendency for the dispersal of services. Schiller (1971) can, for example, observe that 'there seems to be a growing tendency for specialist services to locate in non-central sites'.[1] The Studies have a choice – to foster concentration or to encourage dispersal – and varying attitudes are followed.

The major growth of city centres is envisaged in neither the Leicestershire nor the Notts–Derby Studies. Thus for Leicestershire, 'an important part of our recommendation is that there should be no growth in the numbers of people working in Central Leicester. . . . Every effort should be made to encourage reductions.'[2] And for Nottingham in the Notts–Derby Study

much of the expansion of shopping space needed in the city centre by 1986 is already taking place, but as [traffic] congestion increases it will be necessary to consider whether additional shops should be located there or decentralized to suburban centres. Similarly, it may be necessary to decentralize other uses which can be located outside the city centre in order to minimize the cost, disturbance and effect on environment of the very substantial road and car-parking schemes needed to provide adequate access to the centre. . . . It may be more economical not to develop land to the extent indicated by its market value in order to avoid the cost of providing for further traffic within and approaching the centre.[3]

Decentralization in these two instances is thus expected to give rise to a more extensive regional city than at present, combining within its structure both substantial central area shopping facilities and outlying shopping centres with regional dimensions for its clientele. The planning problem is not so much that of an either/or situation, but the extent to which each type of retailing-cum-office

[1] R. K. Schiller, 'Location Trends of Specialist Services', *Regional Studies*, Vol. 5, 1971, p. 1.
[2] *Leicestershire Study*, p. 89. [3] *Notts–Derby Study*, p. 40.

complex should be encouraged, the space provision under different uses within each centre, and their spatial distribution over the regional landscape. The new motorway patterns, and the changes in mobility and accessibility which result, become imperative ingredients in achieving the emerging pattern, which like recreation (and unlike many other aspects of the development process) is likely to remain primarily the responsibility of private enterprise.

Gloucester, Middlesbrough and Coventry, by contrast, are each expected to expand substantially in the preferred strategies of their respective Studies. Gloucester has a potential need for durable goods shopping floor space which by 2001 would 'be about twice that which existed in 1961'[1] and 'floor space at Middlesbrough should rise from about 1·2 to 2·6 million square feet if it is to attain the status of a specialized shopping centre'.[2] Contributory elements towards this latter achievement would also include the administrative offices of the new Teesside County Borough, a Teesside University, and a special-ized hospital. In the Warwickshire Study, a policy recommendation is that 'Coventry should be fostered as the main sub-regional commer-cial and shopping centre.'[3]

An important consideration for the future of established town centres is that the new regional style out-of-town shopping centre has become a familiar aspect of the North American scene over recent decades. Is it to become a British characteristic? One of the strategies in the North-Glos Study 'postulated a large concentration of new development, and a new main shopping centre to serve it, between Gloucester and Cheltenham. . . . However the forecasts of shopping potential indicated that anticipated development of the new centre at Staverton would be likely to affect the viability of existing centres of Gloucester and Cheltenham, particularly the latter.'[4] In the recommended strategy for Leicester, 'new centres are proposed at suitable locations (to be determined by local planning studies) in the two growth corridors; these should be close enough to the margins of the present Greater Leicester area to gain initial sales potential and to avoid any undue competition with e.g. Hinckley and Coalville. They will be needed early in the period 1976–81 or conceivably a little sooner.'[5] And in the Notts–Derby Study, 'most facilities serving more than their immediate locality will be attracted to one of the four larger towns, all of which are within half an hour's travelling time. . . . There is little chance of establishing a large out-of-town

---

[1] *North-Glos Study*, p. 98.   [2] *Teesside Study*, p. 55.
[3] *Warwickshire Study*, p. 90.   [4] *North-Glos Study*, p. 78.
[5] *Leicestershire Study*, p. 95.

189

shopping centre anywhere in the Sub-region, particularly bearing in mind that for at least the next twenty years there will be reasonably easy access to the existing major centres.'[1]

The approach in the Studies is thus basically to consider the possibilities of major new shopping centres in relation to the strategic prospects for new residential developments. New retailing opportunities which jeopardize existing investments in established central localities will not be encouraged, but they might nevertheless provide both an improved retailing service in more efficient and safer surroundings than now exist in town centres *and* also reflect greater degrees of accessibility by a population of increasing mobility. Planning tends to preserve the existing pattern of town centres and to safeguard the status quo of retailing distributions, whereas retailing demands may be for the establishment of new large regional centres at key nodal points on the network of major highways. Radical changes in accessibility induced by motorways transform existing space relationships; rising real incomes and increased personal mobility change the significance and pattern of shopping journeys, traditional habits of retailing are not sacrosanct and the sheer growth of population each exercise pressures which may not have been fully appreciated in the Studies.[2]

RECREATION

The countryside is seen to provide an important recreational resource for the inhabitants of urban areas in all Studies. Thus Notts–Derby notes that 'hills, woods, rivers and quiet countryside are within convenient reach of almost all the population and where a shortage of outdoor recreation facilities occurs it arises not from any fundamental reason but because the rapidly rising demand has outstripped the arrangements for provision by either public action or private enterprise.'[3] They introduce the concept of 'greenways'. 'Certain areas of open country of indeterminate length and varying in width from a few yards to several miles have been given the name "greenways". These are intended to facilitate movement between recreational areas and living areas in pleasant surroundings, and to provide

---

[1] *Notts–Derby Study*, p. 85.

[2] For a discussion of this type of issue see R. H. Kantorowich, H. W. E. Davies, J. N. Jackson and D. G. Robinson, *Regional Shopping Centres: Planning Report on North-West England*, Department of Town and Country Planning, University of Manchester (Manchester), 1964.

[3] *Notts–Derby Study*, p. 27. See, for example, J. A. Patmore, *Land and Leisure*, David and Charles (Newton Abbott), 1970.

sites for outdoor recreational facilities . . . as and when the demand arises. Parts of the greenways will remain in use for agriculture or forestry, and parts which now comprise derelict land will need to be restored. The outdoor recreational facilities may include picnic spots, country parks, riding schools, nature trails, fishing and boating clubs, golf courses and sports fields. Footpaths, bridlepaths and water-ways are also appropriately sited here, together with places of refreshment.'[1]

New recreational localities are included in each Study within the overall context of the countryside as a recreational resource. North-Glos adds the Cotswold Water Park from reclaimed wet-gravel workings, two country parks, and scenic tourist routes in the Forest of Dean and along the Cotswold Escarpment.[2] Teesside propose an internal open space system with parks, playing fields and golf courses linked by pedestrian greenways, four country parks, and a coastal marina; 'by this policy most people would be attracted to a few places where special provision would have been made for their reception. The converse is that other areas (i.e. the National Park, moors, several villages and the centres of some small towns) would be subject to conservation policies. That is, the aim of planning policy would be to preserve as much as possible of their existing quality.'[3]

Leicestershire refers particularly to the Charnwood Forest area and to sections of the Grand Union Canal, as potential Country Parks and as major sub-regional recreational areas.[4] The Notts–Derby strategy recommends three regional park areas in Sherwood Forest, the Trent Valley and the Matlock Hills. These 'are intended to be rural areas within which recreation is a major activity, although existing uses will normally be allowed to continue. New recreational development will be encouraged provided that it is appropriate to a rural area, but it may sometimes be necessary to divert this away from land of particular significance for agriculture or natural history, or places where it would harm the landscape.'[5] Warwickshire recommend that 'a strategic policy framework for conservation and recreation should be formed to meet the growing pressures which leisure activities are placing on the countryside'.[6] and indicates extensive zones on its strategic map as first priority rural conservation areas.

In the South East Study, 'an objective of the regional strategy should be to provide more scope for outdoor recreation requiring extensive areas of land. This would mean giving priority to those parts

[1] *Ibid.*, p. 46.
[2] *North-Glos Study*, p. 101.
[3] *Teesside Study*, p. 58.
[4] *Leicestershire Study*, pp. 96–7.
[5] *Notts–Derby Study*, p. 46.
[6] *Warwickshire Study*, p. 91.

of the region where such opportunities are at present limited and to the development of intensive recreation facilities particularly where these will divert pressures from parts of the countryside more sensitive to intrusion. One means would be the creation . . . of a network of large regional country parks, related to major growth areas, to satisfy a variety of recreational needs.'[1] At the stage of evaluating between alternatives, one criterion adopted was that of accessibility between the population growth centres and different environmental resources.[2] The Hampshire Study also takes recreation seriously, and includes an intensive appraisal of the New Forest to suggest how increasing pressures might reasonably be accommodated within the existing landscape.[3] The argument is that each area must be designed to its own unique standard. By contrast, in the Humberside Study, recreation receives minimum discussion over a few paragraphs and no recommendations are made.

These several proposals are each attractive in their own right, and are warmly to be encouraged. The emphasis on focussing activities in selected localities will be noted. It may however be suggested that neither the magnitude and the burgeoning dimensions of the problem, nor the substantial opportunities for new attitudes and new approaches, have been fully grasped. The provision for new facilities needs to be set against the thought that 'the British hotel industry will have to provide a further 100,000 bedrooms by 1975 to cope with the expected increase of tourists. . . . Projected figures indicate an increase from the present 6m. a year to 10m. a year halfway through the decade. . . . The regions themselves had to make efforts to attract this growing market, promoting their own amenities and facilities.'[4]

More consideration could have been given to the creation of *new* recreational resources. For example the construction of motorway spurs can be used to promote recreational developments in selected localities, or an expansion of recreational facilities in association with changing patterns of agriculture and forestry management could have provided an additional approach to the formulation of strategies. Thus the Forestry Commission, 'as the largest landowner in Britain, with holdings in the uplands and in traditional recreational areas . . . are able to do a great deal to meet the demand for countryside recreation'.[5] The important point is that the bulk of the forestry revenue is

[1] *South East Study*, p. 37.   [2] *Ibid.*, p. 70.
[3] *Hampshire Study*, Vol. II, pp. 127–73.
[4] Report by Sir Mark Henig, Chairman of the English Tourist Board, *The Times*, September 17, 1970.
[5] Countryside Commission, *The Countryside in 1970*, Report No. 13: 'Leisure', 1970, p. 13.

192

harvested at the time of timber felling, and the rate of return is low if not negative. Returns from recreation include camping and car parking receipts, rentals for cafés and service facilities, and the intangible personal returns to individuals in health and recreation. These returns are generally higher than from forestry operations and need not diminish to any great extent the income from timber as a primary resource. Hence, more thought could be given to the planned development of forestry and woodland areas for intensive recreational purposes. The Hampshire Study considered such possibilities in the New Forest but, with this exception, the opportunities for such major new developments are not examined critically in the Sub-regional Reports. The opportunities for creative new developments may be immense, but remain largely an unknown quantity. Not one Report evaluates recreational possibilities, against the costs of woodland maintenance, a warden service, and the slight loss of timber if stores, information areas, picnic tables, recreation facilities, game areas, camping sites and nature trails are provided to encourage intensive usage zones of forest parks. In addition, the use of reservoirs for recreational purposes need not affect the purity of the water, and marginal farming areas on sloping land may also prove admirable for recreational purposes.

Would it not have been possible to indicate on the strategic maps those areas where recreational developments on a large scale would receive positive encouragement? There are many locations where recreational villages, areas for second homes (vacation cottages in American parlance), guest houses and service facilities could be dovetailed into the existing landscape. Perhaps the focus of attraction could be a reservoir, and the buildings could be located in a woodland or park-like setting. With earlier retirement and shorter working weeks as a future possibility, the average family may be expected to devote more time and to require more space for recreation. Add to this the burgeoning incidence of massive international tourism and that many existing facilities are already overcrowded, then the demands are both urgent and unsatisfied. Erosion of the landscape by excessive pressures can be relieved if new developments are created as a deliberate act of policy in order to attract the crowds. Concentration of recreation developments (the so-called 'honey-pot' approach) can produce the minimum of environemtal blight, the accommodation of large numbers of people will reduce the pressures elsewhere, and intensive recreational developments at selected points provides the best means of protecting the more vital and delicate localities.

G

Large-scale focal points for recreational activities also exert substantial outgoing consequences from this new investment in terms of its multiplier effects on the sub-regional economy, and these should also have been assessed. Only the North-Glos Study, and then almost *en passant*, refers to this subject. 'When the motorway system is completed, the Sub-region's affinities with South Worcestershire and Herefordshire will be reinforced; especially in cultural, touristic and economic terms.'[1] No evaluation follows about the detail of this expected impact, presumably in terms both of the above greater tourist potential for the lower Wye Valley and the Forest of Dean areas, and the inputs which these additional expenditures might contribute towards Gloucester and Cheltenham as the established centres of attraction. Shopping habits will change, quite apart from those changes already considered through the various locational possibilities for new residential development, and tourism in relation to road proposals provides one element in these emerging new circumstances. The Studies can be criticized for their *relative* lack of attention to this new *basic* activity of recreation, and its potential for regional development. The ideas which are available have not been considered to their full extent.[2]

THE RURAL SCENE

Areas of high agricultural productivity are preserved in all the Studies, but issues which are barely discussed, if at all, include rural depopulation, rural poverty, the economics of transportation in rural areas, the rural economy as its own system, and the impact of further decline in basic rural employment opportunities. The North-Glos Study argues that the detail of rural development prospects would not affect the design of strategies at the Sub-regional level, and such changes can therefore be deferred for later consideration. A two phase planning sequence is envisaged. There is first the strategic solution to the major urban problems and generalized proposals for the Sub-region as a whole, and then the second stage preparation of more detailed studies of the rural components. A concluding statement is that 'the search for strategic solutions ... revolved principally around alternatives in the Gloucester/Cheltenham area.

[1] *North-Glos Study*, p. 8.

[2] See R. J. S. Hookway and Joan Davidson, *Leisure: Problems and Prospects for the Environment*, Countryside Commission (London) 1970 and T. L. Burton, *Recreation Research and Planning*, George Allen and Unwin (London), 1970 for the type of appreciation which could have been applied at the sub-regional level of analysis.

. . . Rural settlement studies are now required to define in greater detail the policies for the proper distribution of future development in rural areas.'[1]

As the terms of reference in this and the other Studies are not restricted to urban elements but imply rural, recreational and agricultural options in so far as these influence or may be influenced by planning policies, the concern should be with all aspects of environment in its interlocking relationships. This wider and more intensive approach to rural issues in sub-regional studies is appreciated by the County Planning Officers' Society when it states that 'the myth of a clear social and economic distinction between townsmen and countrymen is now disappearing. Planners today consider problems within a sub-regional context. . . . These plans must detect all that is needed for full community growth in the sub-region ranging from refuse disposal to air travel and be able to integrate these requirements to a plan which will give an optimum return on investment compatible with civilized environment. . . . Planning policies for the countryside must begin to approach the depth of consideration of those which apply to built-up areas.'[2] The Studies tend to be urban-oriented.

CONTAINMENT OF THE LARGE CITY

Many comments over the previous pages have referred to the problems of containing the large city. Several strategies have limited the growth of employment, or reduced the expected population of central cities, or diverted some of its economic potential to other localities. Debate has centred on how far development should be pushed out and to which locations. Satellite communities have been considered, and the expansion of selected small towns encouraged. Is there an anti-urban bias in the Studies because, as Cherry (1969) notes, 'there has always been an anti-urban tradition in British town planning, and the conventional policies of recent decades which support containment of the large city in favour of satellite development beyond a Green Belt stem directly from attitudes, especially of the late Victorians, towards the big city?'[3] And in the words of Pahl (1965), 'it is important that those concerned with an understanding, at a more theoretical level, of the develop-

[1] *North-Glos Study*, pp. 103–4.

[2] The County Planning Officers' Society, 'Urbanisation', Report No. 2, *The Countryside in 1970*, The Countryside Commission, 1970.

[3] G. E. Cherry, 'Influences on the Development of Town Planning in Britain', *Journal of Contemporary History*, Vol. 4, 1969, p. 52.

ment of a metropolitan region escape from the mental strait-jackets of nineteenth-century anti-urbanists, and their twentieth-century counterparts who abhor bigness'.[1] How do the Studies respond to this type of criticism?

At the Regional level the two feasibility Studies each accept the possibility of substantial urban expansion. However, Humberside distributes this growth evenly on either side of the estuary, and does not consider either the creation of one major metropolitan area or substantial peripheral expansion in its alternative possibilities. Hampshire cannot be regarded as anti-urban; the team, *ab initio*, 'realized it was not a matter of searching for a site for a conventional, if large, "new town" (i.e. the Humberside approach). The area is so complex already and the potential increase of population and activities is so great, that we obviously had to regard the area as a single unit. The task was to discover the principles upon which it could best be developed as one coherent, integrated urban system.'[2] The South East Study may also be accused of some anti-urban bias, even though it deals with one of the most urbanized regions in the world. Large growth areas external to Greater London are considered, in preference to examining major alternatives within the inner city area. The nature of the overall problem is also minimized, both by the regrettably short time span from 1981 to 1991 and by the nature of the projections, 'which assume a slight but increasing net outflow of population from the South East'.[3] With 17·0 million persons at 1966 and 18·6 millions at 1981, a preferable approach might have been to envisage regional growth to say 20, 25 and 30 million persons over successive periods of urban evolution, at varying densities, with different patterns of communication, and with and without the constraints of a Metropolitan Green Belt.

At the Sub-regional level, the Leicestershire, North-Glos, Notts–Derby and Warwickshire Studies offer an interesting comparison in that new motorways pass through or close by the main urban areas. M5 passes between Gloucester and Cheltenham, M1 between Nottingham and Derby and to the west of Leicester, and a complex of motorways pass through Warwickshire. Ideally, the impact of a motorway on urban structure within a region should have been determined *before* its construction, so that the route and its critical access points could have been designed to fulfil both regional/urban *and* movement/transportation objectives. As it is, the Studies are

[1] R. E. Pahl, *Urbs in Rure*, London School of Economics, Geographical Papers No. 2, 1965, p. 12.
[2] *Hampshire Study*, p. 90.   [3] *South East Study*, p. 18.

faced with a *fait accompli*, and must consider whether nearby urban areas should now be encouraged to aggrandize towards the motorway as might reasonably be expected. Should one larger comprehensive unit now be envisaged rather than distinct localities as at present in the Nottingham–Derby, Cheltenham–Gloucester and Birmingham–Solihull–Coventry situations, or would coalescence along and/or round the motorways provide cause for apprehension?

In the North-Glos Study, one strategy envisages peripheral growth of the urban areas, and another the pull of urban development towards the motorway and the gradual establishment of one major urban physical unit. However, neither possibility is accepted. The preferred strategy restricts development to the west of the motorway and, although it makes Gloucester the clearly dominant centre, substantial breaks in development are retained between Gloucester and Cheltenham.

The idea of one larger urban unit is likewsise eschewed in the Notts–Derby Study. In this instance there is preference for the transfer of job opportunities to a growth zone. 'Many of the jobs will arise from industrial growth which would otherwise take place in Nottingham or Derby.'[1] It is also stated that 'there is one possibility which has not been fully explored. This is the possibility that the economic benefits of large urban concentrations are so great that every attempt should be made to encourage unlimited development at Nottingham. . . . The techniques of economic analysis which are needed to test this hypothesis have not been developed and it has therefore been ruled out as involving too great a sacrifice of non-economic objectives.'[2] The growth of the large city and existing trends towards coalescence are not to be encouraged. In fact 'the proposals set out in the [recommended] strategy depart substantially from what can be described as the existing trend, the ever increasing concentrations of development around the largest centres. It is neither feasible nor desirable for this trend to continue.'[3]

In the Warwickshire Study a policy of containment for the Birmingham Conurbation has been noted previously. This includes the 'first Priority Rural Conservation Area' and 'the permanent boundary to a permanent buffer of countryside'. These localities also include a substantial number of new motorways. They are crossed from east to west by the Midland Motorway Link (M6) and the Oxford–Birmingham Motorway (M40), and from north to south by the Nottingham–Birmingham and Strensham–Solihull Motorways. The tussle for containment will be interesting especially as, in the

[1] *Notts–Derby Study*, p. 34.   [2] *Ibid.*, p. 59.   [3] *Ibid.*, p. 99.

197

re-organization of local government, the proposed West Midlands metropolitan county includes both Birmingham and Coventry and may thus be taken to imply an east–west axis of development in contrast with the Study's north–south axis of growth. The evidence and conclusions of the later West Midlands Study on this point will be of interest.

In these three Studies, the outcome from the planning deliberations is therefore to curb to some extent the 'excessive' growth of the dominant and expanding urban environments, not to accept all the envisaged trends, and then to transfer a portion of their expected growth potential to alternative situations. The Leicestershire and Teesside Studies express quite contrary attitudes, with each appreciating the benefits of further urban concentration. The Leicestershire conclusion is that 'a policy which would deliberately seek to accelerate the growth of the main centres of the county as opposed to Greater Leicester has no particular advantages and, indeed, several disadvantages.... On the other hand, a policy which would emphasize and foster the growth of the Greater Leicester area has a great deal to commend it.'[1] The Teesside Study likewise prefers compact development adjacent to the existing built-up area. 'The most important conclusion is that the future development must be located close to the existing and committed built-up area.'[2] The argument in these circumstances is that the concentration of growth 'will result in a wider range of choice from many points of view. People will find a greater variety of job opportunities, of entertainment and cultural activities whilst employers have a large number of potential workers within reach of their factories, offices and shops. A larger urbanized area will also mean a wider choice of housing, shopping centres, transport services and most elements of a full life.'[3]

The contrasts between these two different types of policy are quite interesting. For example, a large volume of population is encouraged on Teesside, +225,000 persons by 1991 on a 1966 figure of 479,000 because 'the fundamental assumption is that it will be regional policy for the population of Teesside to grow by an inward migration attracted by its high level of employment'.[4] The opposite situation occurs in the prosperous Nottingham and Derby divisions, where growth is restricted to only +38,000 on 528,000 and +34,000 on 278,000 between 1966 and 1986 for these two cities, and 30,000 population and 23,000 jobs are *exported* in order to meet other Sub-regional needs. Gloucester and Cheltenham, with a combined population

[1] *Leicestershire Study*, p. 79.   [2] *Teesside Study*, p. 81.
[3] *Leicestershire Study*, p. 86.   [4] *Teesside Study*, p. 25.

in their divisions of 265,900 at 1966, are not to be united physically, whereas in Leicester with 454,900 in its three zones at 1966 there is to be further suburban expansion. In the Warwickshire Study the expansion of Coventry is encouraged and its possible change in population is from 343,000 in 1970 to 410,300 in 1991; Solihull, which is physically attached to Greater Birmingham, increases from 114,600 to 185,000.

When the policy is to curb growth and to transfer the excess of population and jobs to alternative situations, the approach is in accord with traditional thought since the 1930s, when the Barlow Commission[1] recognized the twin problems of urban congestion and regional areas of substantial unemployment. Their suggestion for the dispersal of economic opportunity apparently provided a solution which was mutually advantageous to both the exporting and the receiving localities. Green belts, too, have been conceived to restrict the excessive growth of the large city. Yet the cities under surveillance in North Gloucestershire and in Notts–Derby are much smaller than other major cities in the British Isles, and would remain so even if their physical consolidation was to be the strategy for fulfilment. The question that nobody can yet answer is, at what stage in its growth and by what criteria does a city become over-large? It has not yet been conclusively demonstrated that the large city is necessarily an unsuitable environment in economic, social, political and physical terms and the factor of continuing pressures for growth suggests that there are persuasive social and economic advantages in large-scale groupings. It is also a world-wide characteristic that urban populations are concentrating in a few large and rapidly expanding urban localities. Given these trends it is surprising that planning is sometimes afraid of formulating strategies to accommodate this bigness. As Barbara Ward (1967) has stated, 'however desirable decentralization might seem, it has to take place against some of the strongest unplanned forces in modern society – the sucking, pulling attractions of the megalopolis'.[2]

ADMINISTRATIVE BOUNDARIES

The presence of administrative boundaries exerts a powerful influence on the location and form of the land uses which have been

[1] *Report of the Royal Commission on the Distribution of the Industrial Population*, Cmnd. 6153, HMSO (London), 1940, p. 223.

[2] Barbara Ward, 'The Process of World Urbanization' in Department of Economic and Social Affairs, *Planning of Metropolitan Areas and New Towns*, United Nations (New York), 1967, p. 14.

199

discussed in this Chapter. There are different political persuasions, attitudes, power groups, vested interests, officials and elected representatives involved on the two sides of a boundary, so that planning decisions and patterns of land use development may change radically as one passes over a boundary from one jurisdiction into another. These varied constraints on urban growth could have been examined with the same alacrity and degree of confidence as the (more discernible) economic and physical forces which have been portrayed. Administrative boundaries can provide a substantial impediment to urban growth and be more inflexible than a physical feature. In fact it may be easier to dam and divert a river, or to relocate an industry than to change a local authority boundary. Theoretically such boundaries can be changed at will; in practice such units are most resistant to change because of established loyalties, traditional power structure, historical inertia, financial commitments, administrative arrangements, legal bonds, procedural difficulties and the inherited and cherished quality of independence. Resistance can be strong from elected officials, professional employees and the public, and is likely to receive endorsement from Members of Parliament (who are elected to serve local constituencies) and from local newspaper and communication media which rely greatly on local support.

It is therefore not surprising that no Study examines either the full effects of administrative boundaries or the disparate attitudes of elected authorities on the processes of urban development. This reluctance will be enforced by the fact that the Studies are not independent, but are sponsored by local government agencies. The subject admittedly is one of thorny internal debate – but so are development prospects in relationship to patterns of land ownership, the effects of different strategies on land values, and the sheer incidence of development in certain locations. Who gains and who pays will, inevitably, occasion political debate.

The nearest approach to a discussion of such issues is contained in the Notts–Derby Study, where part of the testing routine was concerned with administrative feasibility and where the Report contains some comments about the relationships between development and local government. It is noted that 'it would have been possible to put forward a strategy which assumed that development will be implemented by the normal processes [of organizational structure] which are in operation in the sub-region at present. However, this assumption would have ruled out any proposals for major growth points, and would have reduced the possibility of finding a satisfactory solution to the improvement problems of much of the area. . . . To a large extent development would have had to have been located on the peripheries of existing towns and villages.'[1] The recommended strategy thus requires the removal of existing internal administrative constraints for its successful implementation, depends on outside assistance and external national support for its achievement and, 'of the organizational problems, development across administrative boundaries seemed to be the most serious'.[2]

Referring to the need for continuing planning co-operation across local government boundaries Teesside states that 'arrangements must be made for joint planning operations by the three authorities at the urban structure and sub-regional levels';[3] Leicestershire that 'the measures we outline above for co-operative effort would be advantageous and indeed highly necessary';[4] and North-Glos, 'the scale and timing of developments will call for a continued and intensified collaboration of the Local Authorities and other public bodies represented in the Sub-Region'.[5] Notts–Derby takes this subject the farthest; they refer to 'agencies to carry out the major development proposals' and describe their tasks, and also to co-ordinating committees with advisory or limited executive powers.[6] Warwickshire simply recommends that, 'the Planning Authorities continue the co-operation shown in the Sub-regional Study during the period of Structure Planning'.[7]

In the Regional Studies, administrative issues will undoubtedly arise if their recommended strategies are implemented but implementation procedures are not within their terms of reference. In the few paragraphs devoted to this theme the concern is not with the structure of local and regional government, but more with the scale and intricacy of the operation, the control of costs through the latest management techniques and cost–benefit analysis, and the co-ordination of physical, economic and social components. The Humberside Study observes that 'greater powers than are usually given to a new town corporation would almost certainly be needed. . . . The project is likely to be successful only if all the main tasks of planning, physical construction and encouragement of employment growth are given to a single well-staffed authority or agency.'[8] The Hampshire Study notes that 'these priorities postulate the rapid build up of a design team and a construction programming organization, which, ideally,

[1] *Notts–Derby Study*, p. 93.
[2] *Ibid., Record Report 36*, p. 4.
[3] *Teesside Study*, p. 112.
[4] *Leicestershire Study*, p. 104.
[5] *North-Glos Study*, p. 106.
[6] *Notts–Derby Study*, pp. 93–4.
[7] *Warwickshire Study*, p. 91.
[8] *Humberside Study*, p. 48.

would involve the manufacturers and the contractors themselves. . . . It would doubtless be considered to what extent the personnel already in post with the Local Authorities and statutory bodies could be re-deployed. The scale of the operation would be so large . . . that we think some quite drastic re-orientation of attitudes and loyalties might be needed.'[1]

LOCAL GOVERNMENT REFORM

A major initiating justification for the Sub-regional Studies is that the sheer pressure of urban problems can no longer be confined to one administrative area. A combined approach by adjacent local planning authorities, or by some form of joint study group established for the occasion, has become a prerequisite through the changing needs, emphases and opportunities of modern urban society. The Studies have also been prepared during a period when local government reform was under serious consideration by government,[2] and it is possible that locally conceived patterns of revised local authority structure could emerge and produce more acceptable proposals than might otherwise be selected by the Central Government. Thus 'a fierce battle . . . is yet to be fought between local and central government for control of the regions. Most of the parties have declared their positions on this, but public debate has not yet been joined. The regional issue, however, is vital to the reorganization of local government and could be the decisive factor in shaping the new local government structure.'[3] Subsequently, in 1971, the government proposals for reorganizaton have been published.[4]

As the Sub-regional Studies are the only available documents which consider corporate policy over several local authority areas, and are commissioned by the local planning authorities through their awareness of common problems, it would seem that the study teams must be in a good position to comment on certain aspects concerned with the future form of local government and, in particular, the identification of areas with common problems and on those elements of management where control should be exercised at the sub-regional rather than at the local levels of government, the extent

[1] *Hampshire Study*, p. 148.

[2] *Royal Commission on Local Government in England, 1966–1969* (Chairman: The Rt. Hon. Lord Redcliffe-Maud), HMSO (London), Vols. I-II, 1969.

[3] J. Ardill, 'Battle opens for control of the regions', *The Guardian*, September 3, 1970.

[4] *Local Government in England: Government Proposals for Reorganisation*, HMSO (London), Cmnd. 4584, 1971.

of suitable areas and the tasks and the objectives that the new structures should perform. This type of challenge is not accepted, presumably because of its delicate character and the nature of what can be written in a public document by public employees when commissioned either by government and/or the local authorities concerned with reorganization.[1]

Only the Leicestershire Study refers to the future administrative structure of the area under surveillance. 'Matters would be simplified greatly if the whole of the sub-region fell within the area of *one* local planning authority.'[2] In fact, in the later publication of the Redcliffe–Maud Commission, both the Majority Report and its Memorandum of Dissent recommend Leicester and Leicestershire as one authority, plus parts of Northamptonshire and Rutland. The Study itself had also included parts of Brixworth R.D. in Northamptonshire in its survey area because 'it had fairly strong links with Leicestershire and particularly with the Market Harborough area. . . . Precisely where to draw the line was a matter of conjecture.'[3]

The North-Glos, Notts–Derby and Warwickshire Studies were published after the Redcliffe–Maud Commission. The North-Glos Study notes that its area of coverage, which extends over nineteen local authority areas, 'was virtually self-contained in terms of population and employment and it broadly conformed with the areas served by the major centres of Gloucester and Cheltenham. It was also convenient both administratively and from the point of view of assembly of statistical information. It is pertinent to note that it coincided with the area recommended later for a proposed unitary authority in the Maud Report.'[4] This comment, however, ignores the Memorandum of Dissent, which would associate most of North Gloucestershire with Herefordshire, and no preference is argued for one or other alternative. The Warwickshire Study, where the possibility of conflict and of divergent attitudes to development has been noted above, was published after both the Commission's Report and the government proposals for reorganization but administrative aspects are apparently not considered in the formulation of strategies.

The Notts–Derby situation is one of particular interest. The Report of the Royal Commission is mentioned, but no discussion follows on their proposition that Derby and Derbyshire, and Nottingham and Nottinghamshire, should continue to function as

[1] It is understood from discussion with team leaders that these attempts were, in fact, made in a few instances; in other instances, the possibility has been described as 'quite untenable'.
[2] *Leicestershire Study*, p. 104.
[3] *Ibid.*, p. 6.
[4] *North-Glos Study*, p. 3.

distinct local government units in their proposed reorganization. Their observations would have been appreciated, especially as in this instance both the Memorandum of Dissent by Mr D. Senior and the Notes of Reservation of Sir Francis Hill and Mr R. C. Wallis envisage different possibilities (both from the main report and from each other).

The Teesside situation is also of some significance. In this instance a newly created Teesside County Borough was set up during an early phase of the team's work programme, and its boundaries were derived from the various deliberations which had taken place previously. The reform of local government structure precedes the overall appreciation of urban growth policies.

The point of these observations is that planning for urban development and change, and the reform of government structure or boundaries to achieve this change, still proceed along their separate paths to distinct ends. It would seem more logical that a strategy for a region or sub-region should be recommended, together with the administrative structure to achieve these developments, as one overall integrated exercise. This tremendous if not unique precedent has in fact been established in the Norfolk–Haldimand Study by the Ontario Provincial Government. In this instance, as the responsible Minister has stated, 'a regional government proposal, based on the findings of this plan, will be made'.[1] The details are that a major new industrial complex is to be erected on the Lake Erie shore, and on the border between two counties and astride two regional units. The first phase of the study programme is a planning phase, and the second a local government review. 'The value of the planning study phase can be readily appreciated. Once the basic future development patterns are determined from a careful study of development trends and the characteristics of the area, the municipal government structure can be examined with future needs in mind and the recommendations can reflect these needs.'[2] In Britain, these two interrelated components remain exercises which are completely distinct one from the other, even though at the time of the Studies there was one government department for the effective co-ordination of planning and government machinery – the Ministry of Housing *and* Local Government.

[1] The Honourable W. Darcy McKeogh, Minister of Municipal Affairs, *Municipalities: Where the Action Is*, Ontario Provincial Government (Toronto), 1969, p. 6.

[2] W. H. Palmer, Deputy Minister of Municipal Affairs, *The Progress of the Regional Government Program in Ontario*, Ontario Provincial Government (Toronto), 1970.

REGIONAL IDENTITY

A final point is to ask whether the total of physical, social and economic traits identified in the Region or Sub-region suggests a distinct identity? Regretfully, little or no evidence is presented about distinctive regional traits or characteristics, and there is no discernment of those unique and special qualities which might identify the personality, the individuality and the regional consciousness of a locality. This is quite at variance with the historical evolution of the regional idea,[1] the philosophical and geographical basis for regional studies and the earlier regional planning studies which were concerned with describing the region as an entity (e.g. the post-war contributions by the West Midland Group).[2]

The special characteristics of regional identity could have been identified and discussed. Strategies may then be able to retain, or foster, some particular regional attribute. If these aspects are not considered, then some distinctive trait may unwittingly be lost in the formulation of policy. As Cherry (1969) has written, 'one of the important objectives of regional planning is ... to build on and enhance a sense of regional distinctiveness and so contribute to a rich kaleidoscopic pattern for the country as a whole, namely a texture of inter-regional varieties. Such a policy is really part of the overall planning goal to present alternatives, to extend opportunity and choice, and to offer variety and so overcome a deadening normality.'[3]

SUMMARY

Industrial location and the provision of land for housing provide two significant determinants of urban growth. Each provides a central theme in the Studies. Some localities are self-supporting for industrial development, others require external assistance. There may be the internal direction of industry to localities deemed suitable for expansion, in which case the distance of willing transfer can become a critical factor. Service employment, though increasing at a greater rate than manufacturing employment, perhaps receives less attention than it deserves in the Studies. The land needs for housing are considerable, and several different procedures of allocation are used.

[1] E. W. Gilbert, 'The Idea of the Region', *Geography*, Vol. 45, 1960, pp. 157–75.

[2] Especially those concerned with the Black Country and Herefordshire in *Conurbation* and *English County*, respectively.

[3] G. Cherry, *The West Midlands Region and its Environment*, Conference of the West Midlands Provincial Council for Local Authorities, March 1, 1969.

The suggestion is made that a 'reserve land capacity' should be provided to offset the rather rigid nature of planning procedures and to provide a greater degree of freedom in development.

Shopping centres receive varying treatment, from exclusion to an important element in the design of strategic proposals, and existing town centres are preferred rather than the North-American style out-of-town shopping centre. Recreational provision is rather less than might be expected given the burgeoning demands and the rural scene, as a social economy, receives less attention than it deserves. Some Studies prefer containment of the large city to its continued growth. Administrative boundaries as a factor in urban growth are rarely considered, and a need exists for closer integration between the processes of land use change and the means of achieving that change through local government reform. The concept of regional identity is not covered in the Studies.

Chapter 8
Movement and Accessibility between Land Use Activities

The concern in the Studies is with the whole job of city building and city planning, in which no one function can be justified, financed or operated in isolation. The content has many inputs, of which transportation and the traffic network is but one very important ingredient. Has sufficient co-ordination been achieved in practice, when organization is vertical in functional departments whereas the problems are horizontal requiring the integration of functions affecting transportation and urban development? Have land use planners recognized the full contribution of movement and accessibility in achieving urban forms, and have transportation planners appreciated the full effects of land use developments on their networks? Whether the two-way mutually interacting processes have been fully appreciated for their total and related impact on the regional environment provides the subject matter for discussion in this Chapter.

THE TRANSPORTATION FACTOR

Transportation has certainly been regarded as an important component in all the Studies. Motorway access points and principal traffic routes have influenced the location of new developments and patterns of traffic flow, points of congestion, journeys to work (but not journeys to leisure), the shopping trip and the use of public transport facilities have each been considered. Alternative land use strategies have been combined with different transportation systems. Thus in the North-Glos Study, 'as the strategies were significantly different in terms of the disposition of major land uses and hence in the location and scale of activities, each implied different patterns and volumes of travel between all parts of the sub-region. Therefore each strategy required a basic transportation network specific to itself in order to meet its particular pattern of travel demands. The evaluation of the five strategies was based on the operational implications and the estimated costs of providing and using each network.'[1] For Notts–Derby, 'the model made possible an evaluation of the transportation costs likely to result from the patterns

[1] *North-Glos Study*, p. 72.

of development put forward in the six strategies, together with an assessment of the suitability of their associated road networks. In particular, it permitted the identification of the maximum quantities of development which could be accommodated in different parts of the sub-region without incurring expensive new road works.'[1] Or, from the Leicestershire Study, 'the strategy exploits the opportunities provided by the M1 motorway and other existing and proposed major roads by relating areas of new growth to areas of high accessibility. . . . Our strategy has thus integrated proposals for major land use changes with principal road proposals at the sub-regional scale.'[2]

A basic tenet of belief in all Studies is that the regional road programme must be co-ordinated closely with land use developments if the preferred strategies are to be achieved. Indeed, their major recommendations would not be feasible without this co-ordinated approach. The Notts–Derby Study does however note that the present priority given to road works on grounds of traffic congestion is at variance with the above needs. One critical statement is that 'it is also necessary for the programme of road works in the sub-region to be closely co-ordinated with that for development, as without such co-ordination it will be extremely difficult to obtain sufficient employment and population growth in some of the places indicated in the recommended strategy. The present practices in determining road works priorities will not necessarily secure this co-ordination . . . long-term as well as short-term considerations should be taken into account in determining priorities.'[3] Subsequently, in September 1970, these two responsibilities at the national level have been placed under the aegis of a single Department of the Environment whereas, over all postwar years, road construction has been the responsibility of the Ministry of Transport and land development that of the Ministry of Housing and Local Government. These changes in administrative structure should make the essential plea for harmony between road planning and land planning more acceptable. If not, then the recommended strategies in the Notts–Derby Study and elsewhere cannot be consummated and will not be achieved in practice.

As a result of their respective analyses, and in conjunction with their forecasts and land use demands, all Studies make extensive provision for new highways and improvements to the existing system. Comparisons have not proved possible in terms of either cost or the amount of provision per capita, but commitment to the private vehicle for the majority of all trips will continue to place increasing

[1] *Notts–Derby Study*, p. lxxiv.   [2] *Leicestershire Study*, p. 86.
[3] *Notts–Derby Study*, p. 81.

costs on society. The Teesside Study, which provides the most detail, recommends a primary and secondary road system at an additional cost of £109 million between 1961 and 1991;[1] 'the number of cars is likely to rise by four times and the total number of weekday person-trips to double. . . . It would be difficult to provide for the efficient movement of more than about 20 per cent of person-trips by public transport.'[2] In the Notts–Derby Study, 'the major road works needed to meet requirements (excluding national motorways) will cost about £14½ million a year between now and 1986. For comparison, the Ministry of Transport advise only £11 million a year is likely to be available up until 1980 and £13½ million a year thereafter, which is about 16 per cent less than the estimated minimum need.'[3] As car ownership is expected to double by 1982 and as 27 per cent of existing principal roads are overloaded it is clear that these amounts 'will be inadequate to meet the needs of the existing population if present growth rates continue, and even without any population increase there will be severe congestion in the central part of the Sub-region.'[4] In the Warwickshire Study, transport investment on principal roads outside the conurbation is at about £90 million in the period 1966–1991 plus £130 million on motorways; 'this investment would be slower than the local authorities have felt necessary to meet their demands'.[5] It is again based on estimates provided by the Ministry of Transport.

Against these pleas for additional expenditures, the North-Glos and Leicestershire Studies present their required road construction programmes by describing the improvements which are deemed necessary to accord with the recommended strategy. A good summary of the overall position is made in the Hampshire Study. 'We do visualize one item which in the long run is likely to cost a good deal more than has been the case in most urban development since the war. This item is the provision for movement. This is not because we are proposing any elaborate methods of movement, but because we think the problems of movement have not yet been properly confronted in any urban areas in Britain, and that solutions are bound to cost more than most people have contemplated so far. We see no escape from this.'[6]

The Studies have therefore advocated greater needs, increasing expenditures and more public investments to accord with the expected increases in vehicular traffic and the environmental issues which result from higher rates of personal mobility. By contrast with these very

---

[1] *Teesside Study*, p. 104. [2] *Ibid*. See Summary, para. 16.
[3] *Notts–Derby Study*, p. 78. [4] *Ibid.*, p. 21.
[5] *Warwickshire Study*, p. 15. See also p. 89. [6] *Hampshire Study*, p. 149.

necessary planning requirements, the Chancellor of the Exchequer in October 1970 announced that expenditure on roads and transport would be £13 million lower than planned for 1971 and 1972, and £43 million below plans for 1974 and 1975.[1] This decision should be criticized severely because most economic studies tend to show a high rate of return on road investments, the cost of building roads will increase as the emphasis shifts from rural to urban roads, and there is also the factor of higher environmental standards and its significance for costs. If the necessary resources are not made available then the planning strategies are foredoomed to failure. Within this budgetary context, it should be noted that the elaboration of alternatives to achieve growth and the provision of the associated transport network have been undertaken outside budgetary ranges, whereas much of urban transportation planning is subject to budgetary control and limitations on the quality of service which may be provided.

TRAFFIC MODELS

All Studies except Hampshire make extensive use of traffic models to simulate the flow of traffic in each of their proposed strategies. This approach is indeed referred to as 'the accepted practice' in the North-Glos Study, where use is made of the EGTAC computer programme.[2] Notts–Derby use the SCOTCH model derived from the West Midlands and the London Transportation Surveys,[3] and Leicestershire use the SYNTH model which had been developed for the Teesside Study.[4] The basic philosophy is that traffic results from spatial interaction between separate land use zones, so that alternative strategies can be tested provided the land use characteristics are known. The number of trips generated from each zone depends on the number and composition of households within this zone. Trip generation is estimated for each category of household, car-owning and non-car-owning, by purpose which includes work trips and non-work trips, and by mode such as by car driver, car passenger or public transit. To these details are then added commercial trip generation by each employment group. Trips are then distributed to the highway network from the centre of each traffic zone, on the assumption that all traffic between two points uses the most convenient route, and to the public transport system.[5]

[1] *The Times*, October 28, 1970.   [2] *North-Glos Study*, p. 72.
[3] *Notts–Derby Study*, Record Report 37, p. 1.
[4] *Leicestershire Study*, Vol. II, pp. 105–23.
[5] For a general discussion see, for example, M. J. Bruton, *Introduction to Transportation Planning*, Hutchinson Educational (London), 1970.

There are many statistical difficulties at each stage of this procedure, including the definition of traffic zones, inadequate knowledge about car ownership, varying relationships between car ownership and car usage, whether one or more routes should be followed between two points, in the details of trip distribution, and above all in the nature of the modal split between the usage of a private vehicle and public transit and how this might vary as a function of the relative cost and capacity of alternative transportation systems. These problems can be clarified by further research, and by the introduction of refinements in data collection and analysis. It is however important to note that, for the existing land use situation, the outcome of traffic assigned to the road network because of existing conditions can be checked and verified against the actual circumstances of traffic movement, as determined from traffic counts at selected points on the road network. These assignment checks can be used to amend the formula where discrepancies are found, and thus assist towards a better match between the two sets of data – the one derived from population, employment and land use conditions, and the other from the observed conditions of traffic flow. For example, three such calibration cycles were carried out in the Notts–Derby Study. The imbalance which remains between the synthetic and counted flows varied by location. It was incorrect by 2 per cent in the traffic flow across the Trent Bridge and for the cordons around Nottingham and Derby, higher for the cordons around the smaller towns (Chesterfield, −10 per cent and Worksop −15 per cent), and least reliable where a motorway (M1, +21 per cent) and major road (A61, −30 per cent) ran parallel. A mathematical model as a replacement for reality does not produce precision, but the extent of the present divergence can be known. To facilitate useful future comparisons an allowance can be made for such discrepancies if so required in the future simulations of traffic flow derived from the model, and alternative future assumptions can be introduced.

Proceeding into the future, alternative patterns of land use can now be tested for their transportation implications. The future road network is composed of existing highways, plus proposals now included in the Ministry of Transport programme, plus new highways required in association with the specific pattern of land use proposals. Traffic flows are estimated from the presumed pattern of land use, which reflects the distribution of households and of employment and, on certain assumptions, the trip generation characteristics. Trips are assigned to the network, to show the flow on each link in relation to the capacity of that link. The costs of new routes,

211

and the cost of remedial measures to relieve points of congestion, can then be calculated and compared for each alternative land use scheme.

Thus, in the testing procedures of the Notts–Derby Study, 'these journeys were then allocated to particular roads, making use in all cases of the shortest route between origin and destination. The resultant traffic flows were compared with the capacity of existing and proposed roads and it was then possible to determine how expensive new development would prove in terms of travel time, congestion, and road construction costs. In this way, the model made possible an evaluation of the transportation costs likely to result from the patterns of development put forward in the six strategies.'[1] It is important to emphasize that the journey origins and destinations are calculated from and depend upon the envisaged population and employment characteristics, and that the model then relies upon several critical transportation assumptions about the future. The model cannot be better than its input of land use data. It has provided a conditional prediction in that it depends on certain variables which have been fixed in advance.

Models are not used only in the Hampshire Study where the preference of the team is for motivation studies. 'We are by no means convinced that a conventional full-scale "transportation study" would be required as a basis of quantification of the ideas expressed. . . . In the early stages we think the emphasis would need to be on questions of "motivation" – that is to say, one would seek to learn what the factors are that determine a person's desire to travel, his choice of destination and his method of travel. This suggests intensive small-scale motivation studies.'[2]

In the traffic allocation procedures to a transportation network, certain difficulties arise under this broad heading of motivation. How far are different routes followed between the same origin–destination by trips for different purposes or, as a route gets overcrowded, can traffic be transferred to an alternative which, though not working to capacity, involves a longer journey? Are there alternative destinations given varying degrees of traffic congestion along the preferred route, i.e. instead of improving the route should a change be made in destination when this might be feasible as in the instance of shopping and recreational trips? How do price variations between retail stores and different urban centres influence shopping trips? Are tolls assumed on major new projects, such as the Humber Bridge? How does the fare structure influence travel by public transport, and

---

[1] *Notts–Derby Study*, p. lxxiv.   [2] *Hampshire Study*, p. 151.

capital and operating costs the use of the private car? If a surcharge is placed on the use of congested road routes at peak hours, and public transport is both given priority in traffic movement and has its fares reduced, how would these related changes then influence travel habits? The point is that the analysis considers travel habits, rather than the causes or the decision factors that govern the motivation for travel. The relative importance of time, cost and convenience, and the weight of preference for different modes given different circumstances, are not fully known today and must be assumed for tomorrow. Assumptions must also be made to indicate at what stage an existing facility becomes overloaded, and the standards to be attained upon replacement.

Each sequential phase of the traffic analysis thus occasions difficulties in interpretation. These phases are (1) the generation of trips from each land use area, (2) their distribution between zones within and beyond the Region, (3) their assignment to the existing or an assumed network and (4) their division between different modes of transport. Even if all the facts are known, there are different possible procedures at each stage (e.g. the division of total figures between longer and shorter routes, or variations by cost to attract or repel the use of a particular facility). There is further the limitation of the computer, its handling capacity and memory storage abilities. As with land use *per se*, an infinite variety of different systems by location, capacity, speed, cost, level of service, convenience and modes of transport can be envisaged.

THE TESTING OF ALTERNATIVE STRATEGIES BY TRANSPORTATION CRITERIA

Assumptions are made in the Studies for each of the above items, and their sum significance is then presented in terms of travel time, user and construction costs for each envisaged strategy. The outcome from these complex procedures results in one somewhat unexpected conclusion. This is that, of the strategies tested by transportation criteria in each Study, very little difference could be discerned in the transportation costs of each alternative strategy. All are broadly comparable by transportation criteria, even though substantial differences exist in the locations and forms of the hypothesized urban development. This conclusion may perhaps be explained by the extent of the similarities (existing plus committed developments) between each strategy, the generalized nature of the assumptions and costing analyses, the limited extent to which really radical changes

213

in the sub-regional environment are considered, and the built-in relationships at the stage of strategy formulation between population and employment distribution and between home and shopping.

Teesside provides the exception, and preferences emerge from the analysis in this Study, with the compact strategy being the cheapest in capital and operating costs. The additional costs to the consumer, by diminishing the use of private transport and increasing the use of public transport, outweigh the savings from providing a cheaper road system. The form and direction of new development has virtually no effect on this modal split. Strategies envisaging dispersal have greater capital and operating costs than the compact groupings of population.[1] The overall conclusion, as with all the Studies, is that 'the predicted rise in car ownership requires ... a transportation system capable of accommodating a high level of travel by private car.... The major item of capital expenditure should be for the construction of a primary road system much of which will consist of urban motorways and expressways, that is, grade separated roads on new alignments with full or partial control of access.'[2]

Warwickshire has as one objective, 'to locate new principal roads to serve the new population and employment so that there is the greatest possible benefit to all road users'.[3] The performance criterion is by a measure of congestion, rather than by cost evaluations. It refers to 'the degree of congested road space for each alternative strategy, quantified by the amount of traffic on congested roads expressed as a percentage of the total traffic on the road network in each strategy'.[4]

Leicestershire test their strategies against vehicle miles, vehicle hours and average speeds. 'From a traffic movement and demand point of view, there was no clear advantage for any of the strategies at 1981.'[5] As between the alternative strategies, divergence between total vehicle trips was less than 2 per cent, in daily total of distance travelled about 1·6 per cent, and less than 1 per cent in the number of persons making trips. Such proportions must be less than the statistical limits of error. 'Differences of the magnitude we have described are obviously not sufficient to enable a choice to be made with any degree of confidence.... From the aspect of travel demand alone there was no clear advantage to be gained by adopting any one of the six strategies.'[6] The same argument could be advanced for the four strategies tested at 1981. The traffic model had been useful in

[1] *Teesside Study*, p. 81.   [2] *Ibid.*, p. 92.
[3] *Warwickshire Study*, p. 69.   [4] *Ibid.*, p. 166.
[5] *Leicestershire Study*, Vol. II, p. 117.   [6] *Ibid.*, p. 118.

measuring the amount of travel and its reasoned distribution to achieve a suitable network, but not in distinguishing between networks.

The conclusions are very similar for the Notts–Derby situation, where a framework of roads is considered, rather than optimum route locations and the detailed design of each proposal. The overall conclusion is that the road proposals are necessary anyway, but the sequence depends upon the strategy selected. 'With practically no exception the road improvements would be required in any event, but the development strategy would be instrumental in determining a revised schedule of priorities.'[1] Priorities only are involved as between the alternative strategies, rather than need *per se*. It then becomes possible to examine in detail the proposed alignments for any one road proposal, and to suggest the preferred alternative.

For North-Glos, where both construction and user costs are calculated, 'the estimates of capital costs required by each of the strategies were all of the order of £45 million at current prices. . . . . Two-thirds of such costs would have to be incurred on schemes which were common to all strategies.'[2] Such costs are however once-and-for-all expenditures from the public purse and, if comparable, then the recurring annual expenditures become important by this cost measure of relative performance. From this point of view of the annual user costs, then all strategies are 'of the order of £120 million at current prices'.[3] Only a small margin, 4 per cent, prevailed between the lowest and the highest estimate, and four strategies were within £·9 million of an estimated annual cost of £121 million.

Minimal differences which are probably statistically insignificant also result from the Humberside and South East strategic appraisals. In the Humberside Study, capital costs are $1\frac{1}{2}$ per cent higher for a combination of the most expensive schemes on the north and south bank and, for daily operating costs, the dispersed developments 'would be rather more expensive than concentrated schemes'.[4] If these two conclusions are amalgamated into a total assessment, then 'when the capital costs and operating costs were brought together, the difference in per capita costs of the alternative schemes appeared remarkably small'.[5] Two Major Cities (the cheapest) costs 3 per cent less than the linear form (the most expensive) but 'these differences are so small that, having regard to the limitations in the techniques used, they are probably not statistically significant'.[6] Or again, and referring to the South East Study, after the two possibilities for 1991

---

[1] *Notts–Derby Study*, Sub-Regional Road Network, 1970, p. 1.
[2] *North-Glos Study*, p. 75.   [3] *Ibid.*, p. 75.
[4] *Humberside Study*, p. 125.   [5] *Ibid.*, p. 125.   [6] *Ibid.*, p. 125.

are evaluated, the comment is that 'several different criteria were used to evaluate the alternative traffic predictions and all showed that, taking the region as a whole, there was little to choose between the strategies. . . . A comparison of the operation performance of the road and rail networks demonstrated that the margin between the strategies was too narrow for either to be preferred and this was confirmed by analysis of the total costs (both time and money) consumed by travel in each strategy.'[1]

Thus the Studies use traffic models, and rely upon an evaluation of the transportation network in the testing procedures. User costs and capital construction costs are assessed in the Teesside, Notts–Derby, North-Glos, Humberside and South East Studies.[2] The total amount of travel is considered in the Teesside, Leicester, Notts–Derby and South East Studies; average trip level in Teesside, and work trips to each main centre in the Leicestershire Study.

Certain points arise from this type of appreciation for comment:

1. Economic appraisals do not provide the total answer. Environmental attributes should always be taken into account when routing a new highway or providing some transportation feature in an existing landscape. There must be a qualitative assessment of each proposal. Road schemes may require special landscape treatment, and the quality of an established scene can be jeopardized when routes are scheduled primarily on engineering and other technical estimates of need and cost. Aware of such issues the Notts–Derby Study records that 'we took a consensus of team opinion on the effect of each proposal on landscape as one of the tests of each strategy'.[3]

2. What difference is required between the calculations in order to reflect genuine and acceptable differences in performance as a basis for preference? Several of the Studies have stated that there are no clear advantages, that the differences are nominal or statistically uncertain. Despite the numerical similarity of results, they are then incorporated in the testing procedures and strategies are ranked on this basis! Differences may simply reflect the efficiency with which the planning team have succeeded in fitting road networks to activity distributions.

3. The whole concept of a 'rate of return' calculation on road

[1] *South East Study*, p. 71.

[2] The phrases used are 'a comparison of the operational performance of the road and rail networks' and 'analysis attempted to compare the net changes in benefit'. These appraisals are in addition to 'estimates of numbers of peak and off-peak trips between traffic zones'. *South East Study*, pp. 70–1.

[3] *Notts–Derby Study*, Record Report 36, p. 3.

improvement schemes can be regarded as spurious, because of the limited range of costs which are taken into account. Capital and user costs exclude land use and community costs, whereas the need is for the total appraisal of *all* costs and *all* benefits as in the development balance sheet to be discussed in Chapter 9. More important than the rate of return might be a measure of efficiency with which the network is used to minimize spare capacity and overloading. Warwickshire's congestion index has relevance in this respect.

4. Rates of return are usually only expressed for the horizon year, and hence the importance of annual user costs and their cumulative reflection over time of the differences which exist between strategies.

5. An interesting ethical point is whether different values should be ascribed where national and local goals are in conflict. For example, motorways have been constructed ostensibly for the free flow of fast-moving long-distance through traffic. In each Study they have however been used for local community, shopping journeys and other sub-regional travel purposes. They have, inevitably, attracted new sub-regional developments in the formulation of strategies. These local developments may in the long term prejudice the original purpose of the motorway.

6. A point made frequently in discussion with Study Directors and colleagues is that traffic models enjoy a gargantuan appetite for data.[1] A high proportion of a Study's resources in terms of time, staff and finance are frequently directed towards feeding this greedy model, to the neglect of thought about fundamental alternative possibilities. The traffic tests may have cost more than all the other evaluation procedures put together. Is this necessarily the best procedure given both the somewhat slender differences which have resulted in both the British Studies and the American metropolitan transportation–land use studies, and the relative starvation of resources available for urban and regional research?

THE SIGNIFICANCE OF MAJOR NEW ROAD ROUTES

New major road routes transform the pre-existing factors of accessibility, time-distance and inter-urban relationships. They promote new land values, provide new opportunities for the location of homes and workplaces, and create new markets for recreational outlets. The population within stated time-distance catchment areas is

[1] A contributor to the South East Study has stated that 'feeding the transport model had been the major area of work (unforeseen at the setting up of the team).' Branch reports, *Journal of the Town Planning Institute*, 1971, Vol. 57, p. 40.

aggrandized for each urban function to encourage new patterns of social mobility, provide new economic opportunities and hence, for all these reasons, to influence considerably the potentials of land for new urban developments. Motorways and radical change have become inseparable companions, and the Studies cover a thirty-year span of time for the dynamic expression of these new forces on spatial distributions. Four examples are noted of where a greater impact on development than envisaged in the Studies may occur.

1. *The North-Glos Study.* At the *inter*-regional level the completion of the Severn Bridge in 1966 changes centuries of traditional urban history. Gloucester no longer enjoys its former privileged nodal situation at the lowest crossing point of the River Severn, and time–distance relationships are transformed between South Wales and Southern England. The completion of M4 will further emphasize an already favourable axis for urban development westwards from London towards Bristol and the Severn crossing and, taken in combination with the M5 route which changes accessibility into and from the West Midlands conurbation, most parts of the Sub-region will soon be located within one-and-a-half hours by road and rail from *both* Greater London and Greater Birmingham. The London–Birmingham and the Birmingham–Bristol motorways form the open end of an inverted 'V' along major development axes, and these will eventually be closed by the addition of an east–west London–Bristol link to the system. North Gloucestershire lies at the western apex of this vital national triangle for movement and urban interaction. In such circumstances, an accelerated or an induced in-migration of people and of basic job opportunities could have been considered as a reasonable possibility, in addition to the analysis of internal forces of growth and the present trends of in-migration.

At the *intra*-regional level, such motorways *must* change radically the relationships which have evolved between historic market towns and their established hinterlands, and disturb the established hierarchy of urban structures. All American evidence is to the effect that, quite apart from the reduction in traffic along existing routes, traditional markets and loyalties are changed when there is the ease and convenience of rapid movement along new road facilities. The space relationships between centres become quite different in the new situation, and the larger or more accessible service centres can be expected to grow at the expense of certain smaller towns. Large-scale new regional shopping centres are often developed at one or the other of the principal intersection points, with their huge potential

218

catchment areas and because of the relief which they will provide to the traffic situation of hard-pressed existing centres. All these factors exert their impact on existing towns and achieve pronounced changes in accessibility during a period of increasing personal mobility.

Following the same vein of argument that transportation and land use change are inseparably interwoven, the Study notes the socio-economic and physical problems which have been associated with industrial decline in the Forest of Dean. An important contributory factor is the relative isolation of the area from the main routes of communication. Access from Monmouth and South Wales over the river Wye is prejudiced by the narrow one-way streets of Chepstow, and by the height, weight and width restrictions through the town gate and over the river bridge. Further, existing access points along the M52 have not been located with the needs of the Forest in mind. Within this related context of economic conditions and poor accessibility, the preferred strategy indicates a new principal traffic route (or motorway feeder) from the southwest and Lydney is promoted in its service status. At this point in the argument some examination of the consequences of this new major highway on land development, and an examination of the desirability of a new motorway access into the Sub-region (towards Mitcheldean?) from the M50, might reasonably be expected. How might either route change the existing situation? If the incidence of relative isolation is removed from the Forest of Dean, a likely consequence is pressure for *more* development and change than anticipated in the North-Glos Study.

2. *The Notts–Derby Study.* In the Notts–Derby situation the existing M1 motorway passes between Nottingham and Derby, lies closer to Nottingham and, although it provides improved access to both cities, it may be expected to exert a greater impact on service activity in Nottingham to which it functions as a tangential feeder. The recommended strategy indicates two further motorways, the proposed Stoke–Derby motorway to the south of Derby and a motorway from Nottingham to Birmingham to the east of Derby, to create a triangle of motorways between Nottingham and Derby. The only major development recommended in the Study in association with this new fast highway system is the southern expansion of Derby up to the Stoke motorway. The triangle and its immediate vicinity do not receive any special discussion, nor does the Report discuss those pulls which might be exercised by the new extra-regional routes, the role which they might play in encouraging development, or their possible effects on the Nottingham–Derby urban complex. The pattern of

219

constraints is high and the Study prefers to take advantage of the accessibility provided by the existing motorway to meet its internal planning objectives. As a consequence the only cautious comment about the possible new external circumstances is that 'the improvement of road communications may make the [Swadlincote] area attractive for sponsored major growth, such as a West Midlands overspill scheme, or for more rapid expansion without such assistance.'[1] The prospects of major additional growth because of motorway developments are not considered.

The preferred strategy advocates development in a more northerly growth zone astride M1, rather than the encouragement of growth forces in the Nottingham–Derby complex. The argument is

> that there would be considerable economic advantages in promoting an axis of development between Nottingham and Derby. However, this would have the effect of depriving areas further north . . . of adequate employment growth to provide for their existing population and would lead to a large-scale southward migration contrary to many of the objectives for the strategy. In addition, the open land between Nottingham and Derby is less suitable for development than many other parts of the sub-region, the area would be difficult to provide with adequate roads at a reasonable cost, and there would be very little room for expansion in the longer term. The economic advantages are not sufficient to out-weigh these objections.[2]

This may be true in order to fulfil the stated objectives, but all planning objectives are not necessarily equal. To this assessment should have been added a discussion of the improved and extended motorway system, its possible impact on development, and whether or not such economic pressures outweigh other considerations in a period of technological change and increasing mobility. As the motorway improves travel and changes all established patterns of accessibility in its vicinity, it may be presumed that it would heighten the already strong existing forces of economic attraction. There should in such circumstances be a more critical judgement on whether or not to encourage policies for the relocation of development elsewhere.

3. *The Humberside Study.* A point not sufficiently made in this exercise is the essential need for east–west *and* north–south routes in

[1] *Notts–Derby Study*, p. 43. It should also be noted that many industrialists regard the availability of labour as of greater importance than immediate access to a motorway.
[2] *Ibid.*, p. 104.

association with the Humber Bridge, not as separately conceived components but in terms of their total related impact. Only by such co-ordinated efforts can the problems of present isolation, the revival of declining industry and an influx of new business be achieved. These related events would offset the psychological disadvantages to which the Study refers, and create a new climate of economic and social opportunity. It must also be assumed that no tolls are included when traffic flows and the impact of the bridge are considered; these would represent a tax on regional development required for national purposes and, if other than a low nominal charge, it would defer potential users and frustate the very purposes of construction.

Nor are the prospects of urban development and the new road network always considered as an integrated operation in land management. For example, each of the four hypothetical development schemes are quite different in terms of location and their internal expression, but they are accommodated on the same main road network plus some intuitive road networks interlinking home and workplace produced for each scheme. Would not these additional road networks also attract development? As the concern in the Study is with accommodating almost a million extra persons, this approach would seem to deny the now well-established fact that major routes of communication structure the possibilities for urban development and that urban development structures communications. That different patterns of development would create different demands on the transportation network, and vice versa, has been ignored. Reference may again be made to the critical quotation from the Hampshire Study which *must* be accepted as the basis for all planning exercises: 'we have in mind the manipulation of land uses, densities, etc. in order to encourage economical movement systems; and, vice versa, the design and phasing of transport systems in order to foster desirable patterns and phases of growth'.[1] It is not one before the other, but both together and in harmony.

4. *The Warwickshire Study.* In this instance the possibilities of underestimation are discussed in the Report. The impact of motorways is not assessed but is regarded with caution for its significance on the recommended strategy.

The emergent motorway box around the Conurbation and the inter-regional motorways connecting to it may appreciably alter the economic geography of both the region and this sub-region. . . .

[1] *Hampshire Study*, p. 104.

We have not put undue reliance on the economic benefit of these roads, but given them a significance equal to their capacity relative to that of the existing roads in the sub-region. One of the main Studies in the monitoring of sub-regional change must be of the extent to which industrial and commercial interests put a higher emphasis on the new roads and of their impact on the locational pattern of regional activities.[1]

Or, in terms of the impact on service centres, 'the emergence of an urban motorway between Nuneaton and Warwick will increase accessibility in the corridor of towns between, and may encourage further specialization in the six town centres it links.'[2] Full significance is given neither to the strength of the London to Birmingham transportation axis, nor to the exceptionally favoured situation of the Rugby area in relation to the London, Birmingham, West Riding and East Lancashire Conurbations with the completion of a motorway link between the M1 and the M5/M6 systems.

PUBLIC TRANSPORTATION

The only certain thing about future modes of transportation is that neither of the extremes – full motorization for individual movement or all movements by public transport – is feasible. Controversy exists over the extensive intermediate area, as to either the saturation point of car ownership or the extent to which the present car owner can be persuaded to transfer to a public form of locomotion for certain journeys. The dilemma is compounded when to these uncertainties are added such prevailing beliefs as relating access to environmental capacity, or the complex of relationships between transportation and urban form.

Every Study therefore considers the role of public transportation. The overall conclusion is that it should be encouraged, but not to the detriment of the advantages to personal mobility which accrue through the individual ownership of a private motor vehicle. Substantial expenditures on new road construction are always required and are advocated, even with some encouragement being given for public transportation. An argument in all Studies is that we cannot live in an era of increasing private mobility, without investing substantially in a greater freedom of personal movement.

The North-Glos Study states that 'it is likely that it will become increasingly costly, in the urban centres of Gloucester and Cheltenham, to cater fully for the space demands for the private car in terms

[1] *Warwickshire Study*, p. 183.   [2] *Ibid.*, p. 87.

222

of highway capacity and parking areas by the end of the century, and . . . there will continue to be a section of the community which will always need to use public transport facilities.'[1] The alternative strategies are therefore evaluated for their respective advantages to the provision of public transport facilities, and especially to the future role of bus services operating on public roads. It is also mentioned, under the heading of 'Further Studies', that 'work is proceeding on a quantitative assessment of the role that could be played by public transport in the future'.[2]

In the Notts–Derby Study, it is argued that '60 per cent of those working in the centre of Nottingham and at least 50 per cent of those working in the centre of Derby will continue to travel by bus. In order to maintain this level of bus usage it will be necessary to introduce controls and inducements favourable to buses, including lengths of reserved route and express bus systems. The smaller towns will also be helped by stimulating bus traffic.'[3] The extent, possibility and desirability of such developments require considerable examination, but it is also imperative that the impact of different solutions on the total urban structure be evaluated as an essential part of such studies. The transportation component is not something which can be examined in isolation as if it were detached from the urban milieu. These assessments, as with North-Glos above, are *both* urban exercises *and* transportation studies.

The Warwickshire Study is blunt about a deteriorating situation, and considers that planning has little scope for remedial action. 'The future for public transport looks poor, and there is little that any strategy for the sub-region can do except to avoid adding to the difficulties.'[4] This pessimism is based on declining bus services and fewer passengers from larger populations. The public transport potential of each strategy is assessed in relation to the accessibility, frequency and quality of services, and the range of destinations served. One recommendation is 'that the possibility should be examined of giving buses priority on the north–south road axis into the centre of Coventry'.[5]

The Leicestershire Study also considers 'that there is likely to be a continuing decline in the demand for public transport services.'[6] In such circumstances, 'the strategy of concentration we recommend – within Greater Leicester and along the growth corridors – gives the best possible basis for the development of high-quality services.

[1] *North-Glos Study*, p. 75. [2] *Ibid.*, p. 103.
[3] *Notts–Derby Study*, p. 78. [4] *Warwickshire Study*, p. 166.
[5] *Ibid.*, p. 90. [6] *Leicestershire Study*, p. 98.

Indeed, such services could of themselves help to implement the strategy; this is especially true of express and limited stop services along routes within the growth corridors.'[1]

The closest attention to public transportation is given in the Teesside Study, where different modal splits are considered. Three alternative public transport systems are compared. These are:

1. an extended and modified form of the present system, i.e. bus services are provided for areas of new development;

2. the present system plus an improved system for rapid public transport, i.e. improved rail passenger services, express bus services and feeder bus services to the rapid transit stations;

3. a system which deliberately attempts to direct traffic to the rapid public transport services.[2]

The conclusion is that 'the general dispersion of activity leads to a demand for a more flexible and dispersed type of public transport system such as a bus service',[3] and the two rapid public transport systems (with the exception of one route) are not acceptable. Notts–Derby reach a similar conclusion; 'traffic volumes would be insufficient to support a high-frequency mass transit system, and anything less than a high-frequency system would not be sufficiently convenient for users to reduce road traffic appreciably.'[4]

AREAS OF RESEARCH INTEREST IN PUBLIC TRANSPORTATION

The Studies frequently refer to the need for further examination of the transportation situation. The North-Glos Study suggests that more detailed investigations of the transportation implications of the preferred strategy are required,[5] and in Cheltenham the Teesside consultants are considering such issues. The Notts–Derby Study states that 'it will be necessary to manage traffic by physical and financial means in order to achieve a proper balance between public and private transport having due regard to all interests'.[6]

Although these issues will be critical in later planning investigations, the Studies have not considered the effects of variations in the fare structure on the demand for travel, and hence in its impact on future urban forms. Thus the effects of *free* public transport along main routes and feeder services, plus considerable restraints on the private motorist by providing only limited and expensive parking

[1] *Ibid.*, p. 98.
[2] *Teesside Study*, pp. 89–90.
[3] *Ibid.*, p. 90.
[4] *Notts–Derby Study*, p. 78.
[5] *North-Glos Study*, p. 103.
[6] *Notts–Derby Study*, p. 79.

space in central areas and abundant *free* space at outlying stations, could have been examined.[1] The fare structure, taxation policies and subsidies in relation to public transport are not assessed to determine the possible effect of variations on the urban environment. Nor are the behavioural implications of varying convenience, speed, cost, frequency and capacity considered. Public transport possibilities, assuming this to be a *social service*, are not examined. The point is that, in many urban areas, the cost of one person travelling by public transport is now higher than the marginal cost of using a car for the same journey. In addition there is usually more convenience and higher speeds in most personal door-to-door travel. The reversal of these relationships may be necessary if movement is to be attracted away from the private vehicle.

The possibilities of providing *new* modes of public transport in relation to development, such as monorail loop schemes or dial-a-bus possibilities, could also have received more critical examination. In the Leicestershire Study such considerations were, indeed, expressly excluded: 'it is not within our competence to suggest particular forms of public transport, such as monorails'.[2] Also, if there is the possibility of increased personal mobility by the use of small electrically-driven vehicles, then an even greater travel demand than as envisaged may be anticipated because of the time-saving, convenience and comfort of personal travel (with cost not being the decisive factor in each journey). Further, no Study examines the impact on its major city centres of fast inter-urban train services by British Rail as speed and frequency increases with advanced passenger trains, or the implications of such possibilities as guided motorway travel for traffic volumes and movement.

There remains the danger that suggestions about transport will be treated as if the costs of public transport, and the costs of extending and up-grading the road system, and the significance of either on travel habits and locational decisions and hence upon the form of urban development, are separate and unrelated things. Advances in terms of the interrelationship between transportation and land use have been made in the Studies under review, but this does not extend to truly imaginative consideration of new possibilities and their significance for urban form over extended periods of time.

[1] E.g. as in Greater London Council, *The Future of London Transport: A Paper for Discussion*, 1970. See also the discussion in Lichfield and Associates, *Stevenage Public Transport: Cost Benefit Analysis*, Stevenage Development Corporation (Stevenage), 1969; and P. M. Williams, 'Low Fares and the Urban Transport Problem', *Urban Studies*, Vol. 6, 1969, pp. 83–91.
[2] *Leicestershire Study*, p. 98.

Part of the difficulty is that, in the official approach to transportation problems, the dominant theme is often still concerned with the movement of passenger traffic and goods, the resolution of traffic problems in congested localities, the free flow of vehicles along major roads, and the relationships of different forms of transport to each other, *rather than with these important considerations within their total urban context and in terms of the consequential changes upon the urban environment.* For example, the 1966 White Paper on Transport policy states that 'the overall transport plan should reflect the needs of the individual regions. . . . Decisions about road, rail and airport investment need to be taken in the light of comprehensive studies of the *transport needs* of each region. . . . These studies in turn are *dependent* on, and must be related to, the overall planning objectives for the region, and must take into account not only existing transport requirements, but also future population growth, changes in the structure of industry and employment standards.'[1] There is no comment in the reverse direction of how transport policy might be used to structure desirable regional patterns of settlement, to encourage industrial location in preferred localities or to promote new developments such as regional shopping centres. Yet the effects of transport policy on regional development patterns and the distribution of income have long enticed regional analysts, and transportation costs have played a classic role in the theory of firm and household location. Tariffs are known to alter the pattern of regional advantage. The *achievement* as well as the service of such objectives is a necessary aim of a transport plan or policy.

In terms of the Studies under review an important point not covered is the impact of subsidized city-centre oriented transportation systems on urban form. Such a policy might lead to a reinforcement of existing urban forms with a dominant centre or centres, and with dormitory residential areas along corridors of movement. In addition to assessing the contribution of such a policy, it would have to be examined in terms of the decentralization which might be encouraged if such city-centre oriented services are not provided or if road pricing schemes in congested inner areas are introduced. For example, the Ministry of Transport state that the 'deliberate restraint of traffic could be expected to affect the pattern of social and economic activity, and, in the long run, the location of land uses in urban areas. In general, journeys cannot be suppressed without interfering with the other activities of which they are part. In addition a price-

[1] Minister of Transport, *Transport Policy*, HMSO (London), 1966 (Cmnd. 3057), p. 17. Author's emphasis.

based system would affect the distribution of income.'[1] The suggested effects are then identified – slight for journey to work in a town centre by car, not great on the supply and demand for labour in central areas and 'limitations on shopping traffic could lead to an increased use of and pressures for development of out-of-town shopping centres on the North American pattern'.[2] Transportation change is seen, correctly, in its wider land use implications, but such generalities must then be assessed for their *specific* impact in given urban environments. The need is for something akin to the Buchanan Report (concerned with issues within towns) to provide the necessary bridge of understanding between transportation planning and land use planning at the *inter-urban* and *sub-regional* levels of appreciation. As the approach in the Studies involves the preparation of integrated land use and transportation plans, its supporting research must not overemphasize the significance of transportation variables; the concern must always extend to an assessment of change and implications within and over the whole urban environment.

ACCESSIBILITY AND MODEL BUILDING

It has been demonstrated that the purpose of traffic models is both to understand the present position and to forecast future possibilities. Previously reference has been made to the extensive use of shopping models, land use models relating population distribution to the distribution of employment in the Teesside, Leicestershire and Notts–Derby Studies, and a model to indicate the potential of different areas for economic growth in the Notts–Derby Study. Thus the Studies generally take advantage of new mathematical techniques to simulate conditions. An important point is that such models have generally graduated into planning practice via highway and transportation studies, and with American antecedents in which transportation flows are related to land use patterns on the then assumption that land use data summarized the economic and social complexity of an urban environment. The future pattern of trips was thought to depend upon the allocation of future activity to the various segments of a metropolitan area, and the resultant traffic flows were then calculated on this basis.

[1] Ministry of Transport, *Better Use of Town Roads: The Report of a Study of the Means of Restraint of Traffic on Urban Roads*, HMSO (London), 1967, p. 7. See also Ministry of Transport, *Road Pricing: The Economic and Technical Possibilities*, HMSO (London), 1964.
[2] Ministry of Transport, *Better Use of Town Roads*, op. cit., p. 7.

Descriptive models were devised which, like the Lowry model,[1] established relationships between selected facts which could be culled from census and land use data. Predictive models followed, and these tested the degree of change between past events such as two census periods, and then used this model to predict events over the same time period into the future. The complexity which arose was the slow yet gradual realization of the two points which have been emphasized above, namely (1) that transportation is not just a simple derivative from land use but itself assists in the creation of that environment, and (2) the forces of urban creation are more extensive than can be explained only through the land use environment. Economic incentives, social pressures, institutional control, land ownership patterns, the incidence of taxation must each, inter alia, be included in the traffic models.

The whole subject matter of model building for planning purposes has thus become more complex, involved and extensive than originally envisaged when traffic and transportation models were first conceived in the early 1960s. Sub-models are now developed to deal with different aspects of the urban scene, and no one all-embracing urban model covering all aspects of urban life can reasonably be expected. However, in most of the models referred to in this text, the central notion remains that of accessibility. Accessibility to shops and accessibility between home and place of work are important ingredients but, as Stegman (1969) notes, 'it is essential to break away from this confining notion that accessibility rules the location decision-making process'.[2] Neighbourhood quality in residential choice, social preference for prestige areas, the quality of schools nearby, perhaps a nearby golf course or airport for the convenience of travel, a love of the countryside and price differentials are operative factors other than accessibility. The significance of such factors in determining residential locations requires empirical study so that hypotheses about accessibility can be tested for their validity. More behavioural studies are required, and then a feedback into planning practice so that models can be modified to improve upon their now over-simplified assumptions about accessibility. Further, the accessibility quality of alternative locations is described in models in terms of travel time or distance. These measures are insensitive to changes in the *ability* to move in the real world. In particular they do not reflect changes

[1] I. S. Lowry, *A Model of Metropolis*, Rand Corporation, RM 4035–RC 20 (Santa Monica, California), 1964.

[2] M. A. Stegman, 'Accessibility Models and Residential Location', *Journal of the American Institute of Planners*, Vol. 35, 1969, pp. 22–9.

in cost as a result of congestion, the price of parking, the level of public transport fares or the possible application of road pricing policies. The accessibility quality of a point will vary with levels of congestion, and this factor does not seem to be an input to allocation models.

The Garin–Lowry model may be used to illustrate this problem of over-reliance on accessibility and how the element of accessibility interweaves with other considerations. If most people locate quite close to their workplaces, as the zones around the major employment centres fill up, the model then allocates excess capacity to the zones immediately beyond the suburban ring. Jobs are therefore allocated at an increasing distance from work, so that more people will have to accept the additional costs, time and inconvenience of travel. Alternatively, some of the basic jobs may be moved outwards to more distant locations, which is a traditional aspect of the urban growth process. Also, the transportation network is not fixed, and new *distances* of travel are introduced by high-speed motorway or fast rapid-transit routes. In this example neither the location of the jobs nor the location of homes nor the transportation situation are fixed. Each must be regarded as a planning variable with a changing set of relationships over the period of the planning strategy.

The Garin–Lowry model used in the Notts–Derby Study was in fact adapted in a series of stages from the model designed by I. S. Lowry for the Pittsburgh urban region and its transportation study. Professional advice was received from M. Batty who states (1970) that, 'in interpreting any projection from a model, the output must always be considered in the light of the assumptions on which the projection is based. Quite frequently people criticize the results produced by a model without realizing that it is the structure of the model – its limitations as reflected in its assumptions – that they should be criticizing, not the results.'[1] As the Studies are weighted heavily towards the use of traffic models, this cautionary note sounds an important warning in their interpretation. It is important always that assumptions about transportation are made, considered and incorporated into strategies in relation to the total urban complex of relationships.

SUMMARY

Transportation is recognized as a critical and an important aspect

[1] M. Batty, 'Models and Projections of the Space Economy,' *Town Planning Review*, Vol. 41, 1970, p. 129.

of all Studies. Considerable relationships exist and have been established between land use and transportation aspects of the urban dimension, the interactions between movement and land use activity have been considered with care, accessibility plays an important role in many land use allocations, and much effort has been used to forecast traffic movements between zones at future dates, to allocate these flows to the network, to note deficiencies and to provide for new facilities. Testing procedures generally consider both the construction and annual user costs of the proposed network, but only slender differences are revealed. An index of congestion might be used with greater effect.

It is suggested that the full strength of the continuing interaction between transportation and land use has not been fully appreciated, and examples are noted where future events could be different from those enunciated in the Studies because the motor vehicle, with its ease and convenience of personal mobility, transforms *all* individual and group relationships. The attitudes towards public transport are noted, as is the dependence of traffic and land use models on American antecedents with their undue emphasis on accessibility as the prime force in urban growth to the neglect of other contributory factors. The outcome, in all Studies, is the urgent need for considerable expansion and improvement to the existing road network in association with the recommended strategy. The costs involved may be high, but then movement is a very necessary ingredient of a prosperous and expanding society. Government cuts in the road budget are likely to result in considerable problems as the volumes of car ownership increase.

Part 3

THE TECHNIQUES OF INVESTIGATION

'The locational planning task is to find that spatial arrangement that will optimize human interactions and the conduct of human activities, while simultaneously allocating mineral, land, and other resources in some optimal fashion for the production processes. This becomes so complex a job as to defy my efforts as to comprehend what it means, much less to discuss it effectively.'

L. Wingo (ed.), *Cities and Space: The Future Use of Urban Land*, Resources for the Future, Johns Hopkins (Baltimore), 1963, p. 239

Chapter 9

Cost–Benefit Analysis and the Planning Balance Sheet

Cost–benefit analysis provides an established but debatable procedure for assessing the desirability of alternative projects by enumerat-
ing and evaluating all the relevant benefits and costs of a given
decision. The aim is to maximize the benefits and/or to minimize the
economic costs of a given scheme. The approach grew in prominence
during the 1930s, both through the work of A. C. Pigou[1] and in its
application by the United States Government to evaluate public
works projects and river basin schemes.[2] Its practices were embodied
in the 'Green Book' of 1950.[3] Its application in Britain is more recent,
with landmarks being the use of this methodology in two pioneer
traffic studies, the London to Birmingham motorway[4] and the
Victoria Line extension to the London underground network.[5] It
graduated into land use planning through the works of Wibberley
(1959) and Stone (1963) in connection with the conservation of land
for agricultural purposes,[6] and in the Buchanan Report (1963) where
the technique was used to compare three alternative schemes for the
development of Newbury.[7] The greatest single contribution is however through Lichfield's (1956) concept of a 'planning balance sheet'

[1] A. C. Pigou, *The Economics of Welfare*, Macmillan (London), 1913. An
earlier contribution is by J. Dupuit, 'On the Measurement of the Utility of
Public Works', *Annales des Ponts et Chaussées*, 1844.

[2] E.g. J. V. Krutilla, *Multiple Purpose River Development*, Johns Hopkins
University Press (Baltimore), 1958.

[3] Report to the Inter-Agency River Basin Committee Prepared by the Sub-
committee on Benefits and Costs, *Proposed Practices for Economic Analysis of
River Basin Projects* (Washington, D.C.), 1950.

[4] T. M. Coburn, M. E. Beesley and D. J. Reynolds, *The London–Birmingham
Motorway: Traffic and Economics*, Road Research Laboratory, Technical Paper
46, HMSO (London), 1960. See also C. D. Foster, *The Transport Problem*, Blackie
(London), 1963.

[5] C. D. Foster and M. E. Beesley, 'Estimating the Social Benefit of Constructing an Underground Railway in London', *Journal of the Royal Statistical Society*,
Vol. 126, Part I, 1963.

[6] G. B. Wibberley, *Agriculture and Urban Growth*, Joseph (London), 1959 and
P. A. Stone, *Housing, Town Development, Land and Costs*, Estates Gazette
(London), 1963.

[7] Ministry of Transport, *Traffic in Towns*, HMSO (London), 1963. See Appendix
2 for method.

233

and his continuing advocacy of this need within the planning process since the mid-1950s.[1]

COSTING AND COST–BENEFIT PROCEDURES IN THE STUDIES

Some interesting variations exist in the approach of the various Studies to costing and cost–benefit procedures. In the North-Glos Study costing is used to assist in the evaluation of alternative plans, and includes road construction costs for the inter-urban network, the annual user costs of the transportation system and the alternative schemes necessary to provide for surface water drainage. Costs such as the provision of public utility mains and services, the development of social and welfare facilities, and the incidence of house construction are excluded because of their expected similarity between one strategy and another. The authors, ideally, would have preferred a complete accounting of the social costs and the social benefits of each strategy. 'Clearly the most comprehensive basis would have been to assess the total social costs against the total social benefits of each alternative strategy in financial terms. However, for a number of reasons it was found impossible to undertake such a complex analysis.'[2] These reasons are stated to be the lack of sufficiently advanced techniques, the difficulties in amassing all the information required, the impossibility of attributing monetary costs and benefits to certain qualitative factors, and the restricted availability of staff to undertake this exercise.

In the Notts–Derby Study one objective is 'to keep down construction and operation costs, particularly of roads and services',[3] but a total cost–benefit analysis is not undertaken by the team. Their view is that 'as many of the construction and operation costs of development will be the same whatever strategy is adopted, and others are quite unpredictable until detailed planning is completed, no attempt has been made to estimate the total costs of alternative strategies. Instead, attention has been concentrated on the costs which may show significant differences dependent on the location, form, or organization of development. These are the costs arising from the provision of public facilities and utilities, precautions against subsidence, the choice of density and form of development, and the method of co-ordinating investment.'[4] With regard to the true cost to

[1] N. Lichfield, *Economics of Planned Development*, Estates Gazette (London), 1956.
[2] *North-Glos Study*, p. 71.   [3] *Notts–Derby Study*, p. 29.
[4] *Ibid.*, p. 89.

the community of using land for a new purpose, 'it has been concluded that its measurement in financial terms is meaningless. Much of the cost arises from loss of natural resources, such as agricultural land, timber, minerals and landscape, whose long term value is incalculable and depends on public opinion. This cost has therefore been discussed in non-financial terms.'[1]

On matters concerned with the quality of the environment, much of the argument in the Notts–Derby Study is for a *social* perspective as a necessary supplement to the economic and financial evaluation of alternative possible locational strategies. This social attitude is implicit in the preference for the Mansfield–Alfreton growth zone, rather than for further urban concentration in the Nottingham–Derby areas. It occurs when discussing derelict land; 'the cost of clearing up this dereliction will be high, and there will be little return from the subsequent use of the land except where its location makes it suitable for development. Occasionally, it may be possible to deliberately locate new development on derelict land and to thus assist reclamation, but this will not normally be in the economic interests of either the developer or the community.'[2] It occurs again when discussing bulk water supplies; 'it must be emphasized that the problem of selecting sources for extraction and storage is not purely an economic and engineering one, and the effects on environment and recreation potential must be taken into account.'[3] It is likewise with river pollution where 'it may well be that purely economic criteria do not justify the cleaning of these rivers, but there is a very strong case on amenity and recreation grounds for doing so, and proper account should be taken of this in the River Authorities' investigations, particularly in the cost/benefit sections of the . . . economic model'.[4] Again, the social arguments against blight are its discouraging effects and the defeatist attitude which it engenders towards environment; given clean air, and a hopeful outlook towards the future, then civic, community and individual action can be more effectively harnessed than at present. The overall Notts–Derby attitude is therefore that not everything can be accounted for in monetary costs; social considerations are extremely significant in the formulation of long-term strategies for development. The purposes and objectives of planning are different from those of a cost–benefit analysis.

Costs are not assessed in the Hampshire Study. Thus, 'we were not asked to provide absolute estimates of the cost of any scheme for expansion we might put forward. This would have been an impossible

[1] *Ibid.*, p. 90.　　[2] *Ibid.*, p. 17.　　[3] *Ibid.*, p. liii.　　[4] *Ibid.*, p. xli.

235

exercise in any case in view of the vastness of the project, the long term scale, and the "decide-as-you-go" philosophy which we have been discussing . . . As to the cost of the "built environment" we have not made any detailed design studies that could be costed.'[1] The viewpoint is also that, 'when it comes to implementing our approach, it would be an almost continuous process of assessing and deciding between alternative courses of action on the basis of cost–benefit studies'.[2] The argument precludes a total cost–benefit appraisal of the regional strategy, but suggests that the details within this broader compass should be subject to the discipline of precise cost–benefit procedures.

The Humberside Study, like North-Glos above, costs sewerage and drainage costs, and the capital, operating and total costs per head of transportation for each hypothetical development form. Special attention is paid to the cost–benefit aspects of the Humber Bridge. 'As far as cost–benefit assessment in the narrower sense is concerned, any proposed road or bridge is expected to show a reasonable rate of return in relation to the capital cost involved.'[3] It is expected that a threshold rate of 15 per cent will be required during the 1970s, and this rate of return would first be obtained at some period between 1976 and 1986. Other arguments are then used to urge that the construction of a bridge should precede major urban developments and it is argued that a bridge, anyway, is desirable in its own right.

When assessing the total costs of development account is taken of the differential costs of adopting Humberside for major national developments in preference to other localities. As other possible locations are unknown, 'we have therefore chosen the concept of comparison with a theoretical "minimum cost" site by which we mean a notional area where each of the possible elements of cost is as low as anywhere in Britain. In practice, of course, no one area would have minimum costs in respect of all the factors involved in development.'[4] The costs identified include the loss of better quality agricultural land calculated on the basis of a 25-year purchase at 8 per cent, additional water supply costs, the costs of inducements to industrialists and a second crossing of the estuary.

The Warwickshire Study considers, but rejects, the possibilities of cost–benefit appraisal.

We did consider using a planning balance sheet or cost–benefit

---

[1] *Hampshire Study*, p. 149.   [2] *Ibid.*, p. 148.
[3] *Humberside Study*, p. 30.   [4] *Ibid.*, p. 41.

technique to evaluate the alternative strategies. A full cost–benefit assessment would have involved putting monetary values on accessibility, the value of the landscape and so on, avoiding the need to judge the 'weight' of one objective relative to another. . . . We could see no conceptual advantage in putting a price on the intangible to compare with the tangible, rather than weighting the tangible to compare it with the intangible. The technical difficulties in cost–benefit analysis would have been as great as in objective – achievement evaluation.[1]

A budget ceiling is placed on transportation but not on housing, and the costs of sewers and sewage disposal facilities is compared between strategies.[2]

The Leicestershire Study, by implication, would have preferred to undertake a cost–benefit analysis. The six alternative solutions 'represented credible situations, but they were not all necessarily equally economic. . . . The results which are most easily compared are those which are expressed in monetary terms, as they have a common basis.'[3] In their evaluations, the costs of the transportation systems and the costs of land development are compared, with the non-costed items including accessibility in terms of time and convenience, aesthetic considerations, living qualities, environmental conditions and the flexibility of each strategy.

The Teesside Study, in their evaluation procedures, are concerned with cost factors of the future sewage and sewerage system, and more especially with transportation costs. Annual operating costs and the capital cost of primary roads are each calculated. The capital costs of different road systems and of three different transportation systems are also assessed for the preferred strategy. A range of estimates are calculated, including:

1. The net savings were calculated in the form of savings in operating costs achieved by additional investment in capital cost. . . . Alternative discount rates of 6 per cent and 8 per cent were used to establish the total additional capital cost over twenty-five years and the total savings in operating costs over thirty-five years.

2. The rate of return was calculated which would make the discounted savings in operating costs over the thirty-five years equal to the discounted cost of additional investment in roads over a period of twenty-five years.[4]

Estimates are also made of the total costs of implementing an

[1] *Warwickshire Study*, p. 61. [2] *Ibid.*, pp. 63–4.
[3] *Leicestershire Study*, p. 59. [4] *Teesside Study*, pp. 91–2.

urban structure policy. The results include the costs of land acquisition and 'must be treated with great caution. Forecasts of construction and land acquisition costs of development over a twenty-five year period can only give a most general indication of the scale of investment.'[1] The headings include the capital costs of industry and employment, housing, central areas and other commercial and retailing uses, civic and institutional uses, open spaces and recreation, utilities and services, and the transport system. Such details are not attempted in the other Studies.

The South East Study undertakes a cost evaluation of various aspects of their two schemes for 1991. The full costs and benefits of concentration could not be measured, so the emphasis here is on the size and growth prospects of major employment centres, factors of accessibility between jobs and population and of jobs to population, and the degree of self-containment expressed as the proportion of residents in a district who also work there.[2] Transportation aspects are costed, as elsewhere, and it is determined that 'neither the 1991A nor the 1991B strategy would make unreasonable demands on the scale of public investment in the light of the expected population increase'.[3] In approaching these individual cost estimates, it is stated that 'such analytical techniques as are available and relevant pose problems when attempts are made to apply them to a regional strategy. Various adaptations of cost–benefit techniques have been devised to deal with the multiplicity of projects involved in town and country planning. These are difficult to apply on a regional scale because of the very large number of variable factors and because of difficulties over quantification.'[4]

The impression from these accounts is that economic assessments are used only as a *partial* means for evaluating between alternative possibilities, but with the emphasis then being on the costs of the transportation network and public utility provision. All developments have been costed only by Teesside, and a comprehensive financial analysis has not been undertaken in any Study. By contrast, reference may be made to the Yorkshire EPC analysis. Their Halifax area study uses varying levels of investment as criteria for the determination of policy,[5] and the Doncaster Study notes the varying incidence of cost for energy, water and certain minerals.[6] The effects of alternative patterns of development on the rateable values and the tax income of different local government units is not assessed in any Study, yet this

[1] *Ibid.*, p. 107.   [2] *South East Study*, p. 70.   [3] *Ibid.*, p. 71.
[4] *Ibid.*, pp. 65–6.   [5] *Yorkshire EPC* (Halifax), pp. 107–9.
[6] *Yorkshire EPC* (Doncaster), pp. 28–36.

might assist with the selection of the preferred sites as in the study of the Metropolitan Minneapolis–St Paul area; here, 'the size and number of commercial centres was a key feature of the alternatives, and the allocation of these centres to the local municipalities was an important basis for determining the political acceptability of the alternatives'.[1]

A legitimate field of analysis would also have been to assess the per capita cost of at present living in towns of varying size in the region under review. What are the costs per head of providing all the various local government services and public utility undertakings? Are there any particular financial arguments for achieving urban units of a particular size? Would additional populations in certain areas lead to a lower, or greater, efficiency in public services? Cost revenue analysis concerned with the financial costs and returns of proposals could also be extended from public agencies to the producers of services in the private sector. Another possibility, suggested by Lean and Goodall (1966), is that changes in aggregate land values should be used to measure how efficiently urban planning affects the use of resources.[2]

The Studies are thus chary of financial and cost–benefit analyses, yet also rely on certain of the methods and principles of economic investigation for some of their arguments. They also often imply that a fuller approach along these lines might be desirable, if only the techniques were more advanced and more data of an adequate conceptual character were available. The planning balance sheet, a methodology applied elsewhere for the purpose of plan evaluation, has *not* been used in the Studies. The preference has been to specify certain objectives which the plan sets out to achieve. Alternative policy proposals are then evaluated according to how effectively the objectives are met and, where possible, at what expense by isolating the factor under review – transportation, water or drainage, in particular. In these circumstances the potential role of cost–benefit analysis and its planning expression through the planning balance sheet require a much greater appreciation of its potential value at the regional and sub-regional levels of planning analysis. These possibilities, and the associated difficulties, will now be suggested.

THE CONCEPT OF THE PLANNING BALANCE SHEET

In the words of its principal advocate, 'the planning balance sheet

[1] D. E. Boyce and N. D. Day, *Metropolitan Plan Methodology*, Institute for Environmental Studies, University of Pennsylvania (Philadelphia), 1969, p. 39.

[2] W. Lean and B. Goodall, *Aspects of Land Economics*, Estates Gazette (London), 1966, Chapter 14.

groups the community into homogeneous sectors distinguished by the kind of operations they wish to perform. It then evaluates the alternatives from the point of view of the advantages (benefits) and disadvantages (costs) accruing to every sector from each alternative, to see which provide the maximum net advantages.'[1] The essential argument is that

. . . . any planning solution has to resolve a complex series of current and future problems which arise because towns are intricate organisms catering for the operational demands of their inhabitants and visitors. Proposals for their alteration or development will have advantages and disadvantages for every individual or group within them. While it is impossible to plan for optimum conditions for every current and future inhabitant or user, the plan proposals should aim to provide the best solution for as many requirements as possible, *or the greatest aggregate net benefit for all concerned*; and an evaluation of alternative plans should be able to demonstrate how the relevant operational demands of each individual or group have been taken into account.[2]

By such criteria, cost–benefit analysis may be used to assist in the choice between alternative decisions, on the basis of selecting that scheme which will yield the greatest margin of benefit over costs in relation to the resources invested. It was applied at Swanley to evaluate two alternative plans for the central area of a small town.[3] More extensive and recent applications have been undertaken for urban expansion schemes at Peterborough[4] and at Ipswich.[5] In the latter instance, a proposal to locate the bulk of the additional population to the west and southwest of the town gave rise to considerable controversy, as rural interests thought that this expansion should take place on poorer land to the east. Eight alternative forms of urban growth are examined with certain conditions, such as the

[1] N. Lichfield and H. Chapman, 'Cost–Benefit Analysis in Urban Expansion: A Case Study, Ipswich', *Urban Studies*, Vol. 7, 1970, p. 158.

[2] *Ibid.*, pp. 157–8. Author's emphasis.

[3] N. Lichfield, 'Cost–Benefit Analysis in Town Planning, A Case Study: Swanley', *Urban Studies*, Vol. 3, 1966, pp. 215–49.

[4] N. Lichfield, 'Cost–Benefit Analysis in Urban Expansion, A Case Study: Peterborough', *Regional Studies*, Vol. 3, 1969, pp. 123–55. In this instance five hypotheses are examined. These are linear growth to the northwest of the existing city, peripheral development to the north and west, limited peripheral growth and major expansion in a new settlement, limited peripheral growth and expansion in a linear series of small townships and villages, and peripheral expansion plus growth in a series of villages.

[5] Lichfield and Chapman, *op. cit.*

amount of new construction and facilities within the expansion areas, remaining the same in each instance.

In this instance as in all procedures using the development balance sheet, the community is divided into its main homogeneous groups. These are 'defined in broad terms only and in wider groupings than in some previous studies, to concentrate on the main principles of the repercussions of cost and benefit from the alternatives'.[1] The prime distinction is between those who create and operate services, and the consumers who would use these services. The different sectors of the community are then grouped within these two categories. 'The various sectors of the community were defined in relation to the major operation they would be making in using the resulting town – for instance, travelling, shopping, working – and then grouped with reference to the major land use – for instance communications system, town and district centres, industrial areas.'[2]

The next stage is to define the 'instrumental objectives' for each sector of the community (Table 9.1). These are 'the requirements in respect of operations they wish to perform against which people within the sectors would judge the quality of the expanded town and therefore forming the basis for comparing the alternative proposals. . . . They were framed in general terms consistent with the broadness of the plans. . . . The formulation of these objectives should ideally be based on consumer research to ascertain specific needs but since research into such objectives is scanty and nowhere very concrete, the majority were based on our own judgements.'[3]

Costs and benefits are then calculated for each item separately and indicate, for every item, the scheme deemed to offer the net advantage for that item. Some measurements are in the directly comparable terms of money, time or some other physical expression; others are intangible and have been deduced. Value judgements are used, but the approach is rigorous and open for public inspection.

It remains to emphasize that simply because the analysis must by definition concern itself with costs and benefits which cannot be measured, it must therefore involve a great deal of value judgement – for example, in selecting instrumental objectives (is proximity of a dwelling to a traffic road undesirable and therefore a cost to be minimized?); in comparing the amount of intangibles in different projects to arrive at conclusions; in weighting entries in the reduction process; in drawing conclusions from the summation.[4]

[1] *Ibid.*, p. 160.   [2] *Ibid.*, p. 160.   [3] *Ibid.*, pp. 161–2.
[4] Lichfield, *op. cit.* (Swanley, 1966), p. 224.

241

Table 9.1. *Assumed Instrumental Planning Objectives in Relation to Sectors of the Community at Ipswich*

Sectors of the Community	Instrumental Objectives
A. *The Producers and Operators of Services* Development agency.	Lowest net financial cost of opening up and developing the land for the various uses required. Early development of the land. Allowance for future growth of the town.
Current landowners displaced in urban and village areas.	Compensation for their property at market value.
Displaced agricultural land-owners and farmers.	Compensation for their property at market value. Minimum annual loss in agricultural output.
Current landowners not displaced in urban and village areas.	A choice of accessible centres for work, recreation and services. A pleasant environment in relation to the attractive quality of buildings and/or landscape, and the provision of ancillary services.
Current agricultural land-owners and farmers not displaced.	Minimize possible loss of agricultural output from interference by urban intruders.
Local authorities and rate-payers.	Minimum municipal cost commensurate with the standard of service to be achieved.
B. *The Consumers of Services* Occupiers and users of public and private buildings in the town and district centres.	A wide choice of different types of facilities and of different facets of the same facility. A suitable location in relation to the expanded town. A suitable location in relation to the surrounding catchment area. A pleasant environment in relation to the attractive quality of the buildings and/or landscape and the provision of ancillary facilities.

Table 9.1 (*contd*)

Sectors of the Community	Instrumental Objectives
Occupiers and users in the principal residential areas	Minimum severance of residential areas by main roads. Minimum interference from aircraft noise. A pleasant environment in relation to the attractive quality of the buildings, and/or landscape, and the shelter afforded by the topography from prevailing winds.
Occupiers and users in the principal industrial areas.	Occupational qualities of buildings for efficient and pleasant production. Provision of space for potential expansion.
Occupiers and users of open space, recreational areas and the countryside.	A wide choice of different facilities and different facets of the same facility. A pleasant environment in relation to the attractive quality of the landscape and ancillary facilities.
Vehicle users on the principal communication system. (a) Internal traffic (b) External traffic (c) Through traffic	Freedom from accidents. Low direct journey costs such as journey time, vehicle operating costs and nervous strain. Ease of movement to and from destination. Pleasantness of route for drivers.
Public transport users. (a) Railway station (b) Airport (c) Port	Accessibility to the remainder of the town.
Pedestrians.	The safety and amenity of surroundings. Accessibility to various destinations.
Current occupiers.	As for landowners.

Derived from N. Lichfield and H. Chapman, 'Cost Benefit Analysis in Urban Expansion: A Case Study, Ipswich', *Urban Studies*, Vol. 7, 1970, pp. 161–74.

Lichfield then remarks that by definition, decisions which are made without such analysis involve mighty value judgements. The decision can be improved, it is submitted, if the analysis breaks down the points of decision into the smallest possible sections.[1]

[1] Lichfield, *op. cit.* (Swanley, 1966), p. 224.

This type of argument is accepted for its essential validity. The resultant decision emerges from a clear line by line analysis of the problem to be resolved.

THE DEVELOPMENT BALANCE SHEET IN REGIONAL STUDIES

The technique of the planning balance sheet has been applied at the Sub-regional level for the Limerick Region of Western Ireland, but for the evaluation only of certain alternative possibilities rather than for the comprehensive testing of alternative strategies.[1] Three alternatives are considered for the location of new growth including its dispersal to all centres of population, its concentration or a midway course. The approach is qualitative and subjective, with the alternatives being ranked in order of importance against broad sectors of the community such as industrialists, work-force and residents in established communities. Nine different possibilities are examined for crossing the Rivers Shannon and Fergus, varying by location and whether the crossing would be by hovercraft, bridge or causeway. The third consideration is the growth of the town at Shannon.

The first full-scale application of comprehensive social cost–benefit analysis to issues in urban and regional planning is in the West Midlands Regional Study.[2] In this instance the community is divided into identifiable sectors on the basis of producing or consuming goods or services, instrumental objectives are postulated for these functional groupings, the gains and losses to affected sectors are measured and the results are presented in a planning balance sheet. The context, as described by the Director (John Stevenson, 1971), is for an extensive region centred on the Birmingham Conurbation.

The initial stage involved the use of professional judgement to comprehend the problems of the region and to reduce them to manageable proportions. The central part of this stage was the production of about one hundred different strategies which gave early indications of the total range of possible solutions. These intuitively developed strategies were not evaluated in great detail, for the important part of the exercise was not 'the plan' as the end product, but rather the development of an approach leading to the

[1] N. Lichfield and Associates, *Report and Advisory Outline Plan for the Limerick Region*, Vol. II, Stationery Office (Dublin), 1967.

[2] West Midlands Regional Study, *An Evaluation of the Fine Options*, Nathaniel Lichfield and Associates (London), 1971. This report has been received from the Director of the Study and from the Consultants for an examination of its method of inquiry. The West Midland Regional Study (*A Developing Strategy for the West Midlands*) was published in September 1971.

isolation of strategies based on contrasting principles. More explicit use of evaluation techniques began at the second stage, which was the production and testing of 'coarse options'. These were eight relatively undetailed strategies . . .[1]

which had emerged from both the first stages and the work on topic studies such as physical constraints or economic prospects. These coarse options are tested by communications criteria and result in four 'fine options'. It is at this stage that two tests are undertaken, for communications and by the development balance sheet.

The four options for final testing include peripheral growth of the Conurbation, expanded towns and sectors of growth in two different directions. The cost–benefit appraisal 'is only likely to be at best indicative rather than conclusive of the differences in the cost and benefit comparison between the development strategies. This fact does not obviate the necessity of undertaking the analysis: it simply conditions the conclusions to be drawn from it.'[2] Against this cautionary introduction, the following points on method may be noted from the testing process:

1. The evaluation compares the differences between strategies. It includes costs other than incurred by the direct expenditure of money (e.g. journey times), but for most items a money measure of the benefit or cost is attempted.

2. A rate of return is not necessary in a comparative evaluation, benefits are treated as negative costs and results are expressed in terms of least cost.

3. Cut-off points are where 'the analysts had to impose limits upon themselves in the search for differences of cost or benefit between strategies'.[3]

4. It had been the intention to trace through the impact of proposals to the ratepayer and taxpayer sectors, but this proved impossible because of the many secondary effects and 'the sheer weight of analysis involved'.[4]

5. Transfer payments from one sector of the community to another are assumed to be self-cancelling, 'unless the distribution consequences are serious'.[5]

6. The analysis is in terms of the region at the one date of 2001, a linear build-up of costs and benefits is assumed and, after 2001, the

[1] J. Stevenson, 'Evaluation of Structure Plans: Lessons from the West Midland Regional Study', *TPI/CES Conference*, University of Birmingham, 1971, p. 1.
[2] West Midlands Regional Study, *op. cit.*, pp. 7–8. [3] *Ibid.*, p. 12.
[4] *Ibid.*, p. 14. [5] *Ibid.*, p. 14.

costs and benefit differences are assumed to remain at the 2001 level.

7. A discount rate of 10 per cent per annum is used, to an end date at 2006. Comparisons are also made with a discount rate of 5 per cent over an extended time period from 1971 to 2021, and at 15 per cent per annum to an end date of 2006. 'There is no simple answer' to what discount rate should be used;[1] 'the actual rate used in this analysis could affect the outcome of the comparison if one Test has heavy capital outlays but low annual cost flows compared with another. Perhaps more obviously, the findings of the analysis in terms of present value money differences between Tests will be less clear if a high discount rate is used.'[2]

8. After reaching a first broad conclusion, sensitivity tests are used to 'help on the assessment of general significance of the findings'.[3] Changed assumptions are made about job accessibility benefits, local facilities, the transportation cost differences to industrial occupiers, journeys to the Conurbation and disbenefits to existing occupiers through loss of their proximity to open countryside. The first conclusion is that a particular option 'is preferred in the analysis. This arises despite the fact that it is not preferred for any one item.'[4] After the sensitivity tests a second option is pushed 'marginally into the preferred position. But the difference between the tests is sufficiently small for the general conclusion to be drawn that it is unlikely that [the new option] would be preferred, all things considered. It should be remembered that it only just becomes preferred in this sensitivity analysis when all possible assumptions are in its favour to the fullest extent possible.'[5]

9. The assumption of a linear build-up in costs and benefits (item no. 6 above) presents the difficulty that 'new town' solutions are at a disadvantage compared to those 'attached' to existing developments, because initial benefits in terms of accessibility and local facilities are low in contrast with a peripheral location, and the greater benefits occur later on. As the phasing of development is not included in the regional strategy, allowances for this factor (though difficult) are made in the final assessment.

The sectors of the community used for the analysis are broadly as identified in Table 9.1 for Ipswich, but with amendments because of the different nature of the problem. For example, included under the producers and operators of services are the differential redevelopment costs to the urban fabric including land costs and construction

[1] *Ibid.*, p. 16.   [2] *Ibid.*, p. 16.   [3] *Ibid.*, p. 73.
[4] *Ibid.*, p. 70.   [5] *Ibid.*, p. 78.

costs, regional infrastructure costs of providing water, sewerage and drainage facilities and power supply to the option areas, and the extension of local authorities and ratepayers to include government and taxpayers.

The objectives used are most important. They include for new residential occupiers general accessibility to jobs and urban facilities, availability of local urban facilities, local environmental amenities, nearness to open countryside and access to rural recreational facilities. For new industrial occupiers objectives refer to labour costs, transport costs for supplies and movement of products to customers. These objectives should be compared with the Warwickshire objectives in Table 10.2, and later discussion will focus on the significance of similarities and differences. After defining objectives, assumptions are made about the relative performance of each alternative strategy and the differences are expressed item by item in comparable monetary terms, and are then totalled to yield information which permits a recommendation about the preferred strategy against these various approaches. It is emphasized that judgements have to be made at several stages in the analysis. The results are not 'correct'. They indicate the 'best' solution against stated assumptions.

THE LIMITATIONS OF COST–BENEFIT PROCEDURES

The discussion will note some of the difficulties involved in using costing procedures, cost–benefit analysis and the planning balance sheet as a methodology to evaluate between the merit of alternative possible strategies. The comments are made within the context of a most useful procedure which requires further encouragement and understanding; a considerable degree of caution must also be exercised over the necessary assumptions and limitations of the technique. As a method it has both its adherents and its doubters. Hall (1964) has argued in support that 'we can actually add up the social costs and benefits, in money terms, by asking what value people would themselves put on them. We can then express them as a rate of return on capital, as an ordinary capitalist would, and so determine our investment rationally, from the point of view of the community as a whole.'[1] A contrary view is quoted from Peters (1968); the art of cost–benefit analysis is likened to 'the problem of appraising the quality of a horse and rabbit stew, the rabbit being those consequences that could be measured and evaluated numerically, and the horse "the amalgam of external effects, social, emotional

[1] P. Hall, *Labour's New Frontiers*, Deutsch (London), 1964, p. 173.

247

and psychological impacts and historic and aesthetic considerations that can be judged only roughly and subjectively". Since the horse was bound to dominate the flavour of the stew meticulous evaluation of the rabbit would hardly seem worthwhile.'[1]

Some of the problems involved include:

1. *The extent of spillover effects.* The difficulty is when and where do the ripples in a pool stop from a new investment decision, and at what stage is there a recognizable claim for detriment or a benefit from a distant service? What items should be measured? Is noise a cost, and if so, over what distance, and how precisely should the scale of damage be assessed? Can decibels be translated into monetary value? If all road construction and user costs can be calculated (as they are in most Studies), there may be some transfer to the new route by those formerly using public transport. As motoring becomes easier, should the cost of subsidizing public transport now be included? A motorway also creates new opportunities for industrial location, housing and commercial developments. Are these aspects included and, if so, what about their further feedback on the road system in terms of additional traffic? Where should the line be drawn?

A typical answer to this type of conundrum is to confine the cost-benefit analysis to the particular system under investigation. As already noted, the externalities and the wider planning implications are thus excluded deliberately. For example, in the London–Birmingham motorway study,[2] assessment did not extend to the effect of the motorway construction on land values, pressures for development and the economics of nearby towns; the changed possibilities for expansion schemes in relation to overspill from London to Birmingham; or the effects of this interconnecting link upon the expanding conurbation areas at either end. And likewise with the study of the Victoria Line, where the authors did not attempt a full social accounting;[3] thus it is government policy to divert the movement of office accommodation away from Central London, whereas the construction of this line eases movement and contributes toward making London more attractive to firms and office workers. In each instance the new opportunities for urban growth and change have not formed part of the analysis.

[1] G. H. Peters, *Cost–Benefit Analysis and Public Expenditure* (Eaton Paper 8), Institute of Economic Affairs (London), second edition, 1968, p. 43. See also E. J. Misham, *The Costs of Economic Growth*, Staples Press (London), 1967.
[2] T. M. Coburn *et al., op. cit.*   [3] Foster and Beesley, *op. cit.*

The standard paper on the economic assessment of road improvement schemes considers *only* the traffic aspects of the situation. 'In assessing the economic return from a road improvement the only benefits considered are those accruing directly to traffic. Increases in land value should not be considered; these are mainly caused by changes in accessibility which are reflected in the gain to traffic and to include them would involve double counting.'[1] Excluded from consideration by this type of argument are all those community and individual benefits and losses which result from new industrial opportunities, new possibilities for residential location, new patterns of recreational activity, changes in inter-urban accessibility and the behavioural response to new potentials for mobility. Amenity costs are also excluded, but this omission is admitted; 'amenity costs, such as the effect of noise and fumes, arise from increased traffic flow. Moreover, it is difficult to assess, particularly when considering individual schemes, the effect that extensive road improvements may have on the character and development of an area.'[2]

An example from the Studies is that the 15 per cent criterion for the First Humber Crossing is related only to anticipated construction and road user costs. The Humberside Study takes a wider perspective. The effects of a new bridge on inter-communication within the region, its impact on inter-urban accessibility, on the changing relationships between settlements, in encouraging industrial development and removing the existing deprivations of isolation are each considered. Narrow economic assessments are therefore not used in isolation to determine its important contribution to the regional scene.

Within this connection a comment by Reynolds (1966) may be noted. 'It is almost impossible to justify an investment by cost–benefit analysis because, for example, one would have to show that the resources allocated nationally to roads would yield a higher rate of return than if used on other things, that investment in London–Birmingham routes was the best road alternative open, and that the final form of the motorway was the best of a range of alternatives. For these reasons cost–benefit analysis is best at choosing between a limited range of alternatives and can only produce answers if based on many preliminary assumptions.'[3]

[1] R. F. F. Dawson, *The Economic Assessment of Road Improvement Schemes*, Road Research Laboratory Technical Paper No. 75, HMSO (London), 1968, p. 3.

[2] *Ibid.*, p. 7. See also K. M. Gwilliam, 'The Indirect Effects of Highway Investment', *Regional Studies*, Vol. 4, 1970, pp. 167–75, which also concentrates on benefits to the users of the highway system.

[3] D. J. Reynolds, *Economics, Town Planning and Traffic*, Institute of Economic Affairs, 1966, p. 14.

The planning balance sheet covers a wider dimension. It is concerned with land use and transportation impacts in their urban context but, even so, it must necessarily remain incomplete and cut-off points are included. For example, how does one measure the quality of life in two different locations, or the changes which result to amenity, privacy, quietness and clean air? What are the effects of different urban forms on the crime rate, the quality of education, social welfare or the health of the population? How will business efficiency, regional income, industrial productivity and the inflow and outflow of goods be changed? Has mobility between regions been encouraged or new inter-regional links fostered to offset difficulties of spatial separation and if so, with what total impact on the regional economy? Complete regional accountancy procedures have yet to be devised to assess such phenomena in their changing importance through time, so that the full contribution of different sets of planning proposals can be measured.

2. *The sectors of the community for consideration.* Benefits have been ascribed to various groups in the planning balance sheet. The consumers include the occupiers of new buildings, motor vehicle users, the shopping public and so on as demonstrated. This breakdown is of considerable interest. Discussion should now focus on its relevance, and on whether alternative possible groupings are either feasible or desirable. For example, would it be relevant to classify householders by their place of residence, grouped into owner-occupiers, private and local authority tenants, with further sub-groups by either rateable value or the amount of space occupied? An important factor in the selection between alternative strategies may be to understand the impact of each proposal by the 'class' of the people which are affected, with as much detail as is possible so that there can be an accurate impression of where satisfaction and distress will occur by cultural and socio-economic groups. The point is that the same benefit does not necessarily give the same value to each recipient. Public policies have ends in view other than the best economic return, in that they seek to invest money to offset the various levels of deficiency and deprivation, or to redress an existing imbalance between favoured and less fortunate localities. Should all members of a society be regarded as equal, or should benefits be weighted if the gains are to the low income, the under-privileged, the unemployed, the aged or the unhealthy sub-groups of the population? Do policies which affect ethnic minorities deserve some special consideration on other than economic criteria?

The danger is that cost–benefit analysis would appear to answer such complex social questions, whereas, in reality, it presents answers against the implicit assumption that every pound's worth of benefit (or cost) is equivalent to every other pound. There is no recognition of 'favourable' or 'more desirable' monetary effects for the same value, though these differentials could perhaps be introduced. Identical rates of benefit which accrue to different localities for the same cost should not necessarily be regarded as equal, even though the monetary values are the same in each instance.

3. *Rates of return.* A rate of return need not be calculated in the comparative evaluation of the development balance sheet where the results are expressed in terms of lowest cost but, normally, the final stage in cost–benefit procedures is to compare net benefits with the capital cost of the project. A figure results, as for the Humber Bridge, which is expressed as a percentage rate of return on investment. Such investment rates can be compared for different projects, but there are difficulties. Rates of interest should vary according to the financial security of the project, and hence certain low-cost long-life projects could receive more favourable rates in a presumed open market. Also low rates of return (e.g. from land reclamation) may yield immediate short-term benefits, but also continuous long-term advantages and thus strengthen in this latter aspect the framework of future society. In the words of Peters (1968), 'difficulties of this nature are common in cost–benefit studies. . . . Indeed it is now widely held that the choice of an appropriate rate is purely a value-judgement and that it is impossible to lay down any clear-cut rules of procedure. But if this is so does it not reduce the whole procedure from an exact science to an art dependent on personal judgement, preferences and perhaps prejudice ?'[1] There are considerable difficulties in appraising the correct rate for public development schemes, whether it should vary between projects, and whether it should be the same as earned by private commercial enterprises or at some lower rate because of social considerations.

The consideration of differential regional multiplier effects for a given expenditure may also be significant, because the consequences of a given expenditure are known to vary considerably by the type of input, and different rates of employment may result from the same initial investment. 'If money is injected into an economic system, the income of that system increases not by the value of that injection but by some multiple of it. . . . The income of one group by

[1] Peters, *op. cit.*, p. 19.

its expenditure adds to the income of another group. As the initial injection goes round it generates further income. The multiplier is the relationship of final income to the initial injection.'[1] This concept of differential subsequent incomes would seem to be highly relevant for the measurement of costs and benefits at the urban and regional scale. If it could be applied, it would make an important contribution to planning analysis.

4. *The measurement of costs.* Quite apart from these items which are difficult to measure in comparable monetary terms, the actual costs are difficult to ascertain with precision. The construction costs of proposed installations, public works and buildings must generally rely on some form of existing average or unit costs, whereas every accountant and auditor can provide examples of where 'estimated' costs and 'achieved' costs are at substantial variance. The reason can be some unexpected technical difficulty, or a trade dispute, or some problem of supplies, or an unforeseen physical obstacle to actual achievement. But, in each instance, the costs are higher than envisaged. Most Studies have costed, for example, the specific costs of drainage work or road proposals, but these figures must be suspect. The best available present information has been used, but this may not be the same as actual future costs. The farther into the future a particular development, the less likely that its assumed costs will be valid because technological innovation can change relative prices. Further, many costs are not the actual cost, but include a variable tax element. Travel provides an important case in point, with high fuel costs being included in the costs of movement by road. Changes in the level of tolls, different tariffs on road haulage, and encouraging the use of mass transit by reducing fares, are items for possible consideration in assessing the relative costs and benefits of alternative propositions.

A related point is whether the measurement of costs should include the amount of external government control or new legislation necessary to achieve a particular object. Does it matter whether a project is to be undertaken by private enterprise, the local authority or by direct government action (e.g. housing development, an industrial estate or a new town)? Does one or other means have a positive value, and if so by how much, or is the concern only with the financial

---

[1] K. J. Allen, 'The Regional Multiplier: Some Problems in Estimation', in S. C. Orr and J. B. Cullingworth (eds.), *Regional and Urban Studies*, George Allen and Unwin (London), 1969, p. 81.

cost of commitment to the final product irrespective of this means of achievement?

5. *The time factor in measurement.* Problems are involved in the relationship between present costs and future benefits. Assume, for example, two sites with 'A' being on better agricultural land and having higher productivity than 'B', but with 'A' costing less in terms of site preparation. Both factors are known. The difficulty arises over the appropriate rate of discount, the higher the discount rate, the less important the life of a project. But what is this life? Should it be presumed for a particular period of time, or to the end of the plan period? Should some form of credit be allowed for developments which survive into perpetuity? Thus the costs of site preparation and of buildings are a one-time commitment (though buildings have varying lives), versus a time-stream of agricultural incomes. Different arguments are possible about the respective merits of this agricultural land, and how this continuing asset should be capitalized. This issue is aggravated further when the comparison is between agricultural land and a mineral deposit, because the mineral resource can be worked only once whereas the agricultural yield is in perpetuity. Further, technological advance may reduce the demand for minerals, and increase the productive yield of agricultural products. To what extent should rates of discount involve assumptions about future benefits, present satisfactions and social preferences in time?

Another aspect is that costs and benefits will accrue at different points in time and will change during the life span of a scheme, both in absolute terms and in their relative incidence. Buildings become obsolete and have to be replaced, or a mode of travel may be replaced by a more competitive substitute. Changes in social conscience and group attitudes introduce new values, e.g. the present demands for clean air, pure water, and more recreational space for camping, day visits and weekend solitude. Thus, if agricultural land is acquired for recreational use, the costs of conversion may be known, but the benefits may be expected to increase incrementally in time with increasing use of this asset. Costs or gains which occur in different time periods are not of equal value.

The outcome in several of the Studies and from cost—benefit exercises is sometimes that the costliest scheme provides the greatest benefit with the lower cost scheme offering fewer advantages, but in such circumstances the choice between alternatives for the community remains unresolved. The normal dilemma in making any purchase remains – quality versus cost in relation to need and the resources available. A graphical curve may indicate the benefit–cost ratios, and perhaps indicate where further advantages are minimal relative to the additional costs involved, but the political–social choice between alternatives has not been resolved. Take, for example, the delicate problem posed in the Humberside Study about the first Humber Bridge. Should the initial suspension bridge be built with excess capacity for nearly a quarter of a century, or should there be a second bridge at a later date?[1] In other words, what amount should be paid *now* for *future* benefit, bearing in mind that many existing assets have been provided by past generations. Also, if standards and incomes are rising, should investments be made now in order to meet the standards expected in twenty years' time? If the answer is 'Yes', how does one strike a balance between making adequate provision for future needs and the limitations of present day resources? If the answer is 'No', may not the result be the construction of an environment which is sub-standard or obsolescent by the standards of tomorrow?

This type of question is of particular relevance when considering, for example, the degree of motorization and the reliance on public transportation. It may occur when considering the provision of public open space for recreation, or whether to permit development which sterilizes underlying mineral deposits. A key question in planning must be the extent to which costs should be incurred for the advantage of future generations. When does foresight and a prudent purchase become a waste of public funds? What degree of obsolescence and replacement can or should be built into an urban environment to meet the challenge of unforeseen changes?

6. *The treatment of intangibles.* Some benefits are also so intangible that no market-determined price is possible. The approach in the development balance sheet (or in Warwickshire's development potential technique), is to subject these elements to a variety of quantitative measures and qualitative judgements. The results may be reasonably clear and suggest one or other of the alternative schemes. When doubt intrudes, then the various items may be weighted in order to achieve a definite outcome. A cynical comment is to state that this is the analyst coming to a pre-determined conclusion by weighting his own prejudices in the required direction; alternatively it may be emphasized that the value assumptions have been made clear, item by item, and have been exposed for full public scrutiny. The truth

---

[1] *Humberside Study*, p. 30.

would seem to lie somewhere in between these two attitudes. The end-results are simple to interpret, but each line of the final tabulation masks the fact that the basic components of the analysis are each exceedingly complex. It must be assumed that the analyst has come to an honest decision, but all weighting procedures involve an element of professional discretion.

The input into cost–benefit analysis is highly varied. Some items are costed on the planning balance sheet; others are less tangible and expressed in a preferred order against various criteria. As different objects and means are involved, and as benefits are so diverse and dissimilar, it would therefore seem reasonable to argue that comparisons *can* be made line by line to assist interpretation and as an aid to decision-making. However, the *total* would seem to have far less value than this line by line appraisal.

Consider the following net balance of three alternative strategies:

Input	*Alternative I*	*Alternative II*	*Alternative III*
Capital costs	£x + £1m.	£x.	£x − £1m.
Intangible A	Worst	Best	Average
Intangible B	Best	Average	Worst
Intangible C	Average	Worst	Best

Is it not rather too easy to assume that Alternative III is preferred? It costs the least and, if the three intangibles are thought to be self-cancelling, there is the *apparent* saving of £1m. It would be preferable however to state that Alternative I is best for Intangible B. Alternative II for Intangible A, and Alternative III by its estimated financial cost for Intangible C. Pursuing the usual process of addition, Alternative III would be the preferred strategy, because it is best on two counts against one for Alternatives I and II. But this again can be incorrect, because it makes the implicit assumption that each line is of comparable merit. If Intangible B is for some reason regarded as the most important and significant of the four inputs, then Alternative I could be the favoured strategy despite its higher costs.

There are also considerable difficulties over the number of sub-headings and the items to be included when totalling by the number of items. For example, if the line for Intangible C is replaced by three distant interpretations of this characteristic, if each still favours Alternative III, then Alternative III now appears to be even more satisfactory both in monetary terms and because it is supported by three different intangible criteria. In reality, the situation is

255

unchanged from the above tabulation and the argument of the previous paragraph remains as relevant.

The point for emphasis is that non-comparables can only be totalled when they are reduced to a similar and acceptable basis. This for many items is some form of monetary cost, but society also has other values. As soon as the analyst seeks to quantify these other factors algebraically on a balance sheet, there is a serious danger of misinterpretation for the very reason that monetary values often cannot be ascribed. Quantifiable items are likely to be given the greater weight, because recognizable comparisons are possible. The rationale for cost–benefit analysis is thus more as an analytical exercise which defines a range of recognizable costs and benefits, rather than as a medium for adjudicating between the different values which are presented. As such the technique provides an important contribution towards understanding, but it must not be accepted uncritically as providing *the* answer because of difficulties in defining and measuring those social, intangible and non-monetary aspects of the urban condition. Also calculating the benefits side poses more problems than the costs side of the balance sheet. The critical point is the weight that must be given to intangibles in order to offset an otherwise favourable alternative by measurable financial criteria.

Indicative of these difficulties is the public response to the Roskill Commission's report where cost–benefit analyses are used extensively. In the words of a *Sunday Times* review, the investigation is

... uniquely sophisticated. The economic indices have been exhaustively marshalled and the projections into the next century most painstakingly attempted. No aspect of the third London airport, it would seem, has escaped the eye of the computer. Surely such a monument to pure reason cannot be instantly dismissed? ... In fact, as was inevitable, the Roskill judgement derives from subjective opinions about the proper relative importance of such varied factors as air travel, accessibility to airports, historic buildings, regional planning, disturbance of communities, noise and so forth. It is open to any interested citizen to hold a different opinion about these factors. ... The Commission gave too much weight to short-term cost and too little to long-term benefit.[1]

These are among the harsh difficulties which face cost–benefit analysis as it seeks to extend economic evaluation over social intangibles and to make valid comparisons between tangibles and intangibles.

[1] Leader, *The Sunday Times*, December 20, 1970.

7. *A conceptual difficulty.* Cost–benefit analysis is concerned with *objects*, such as the return from a new road. The planning balance sheet identifies an end-product, and evaluates the respective advantages of alternative propositions. Yet planning is now avowedly a *process* concerned with urbanization in continuous evolution, rather than with achieving a specific land allocation by a set date. The Studies are concerned with broad distributions of people and employment rather than with allocations to specific sites, and with the preferred bundle of interrelated policies rather than with particular projects. Also to be noted are the recommendations in each Study for flexibility to accommodate unexpected events such as social change or technological innovation, and their recommendations for monitoring procedures, review and modification in the light of new circumstances, changes in government policy and changes in the regional situation.

Against this process for the strategic formulation of policies, cost–benefit procedures measure a presumed achievement and a reality which is fixed in space and time so that its direct impact can be recorded. Because of this difference in outlook certain Studies indeed comment to the effect that cost–benefit analysis is most relevant at the stage of detailed design. It is thought to have more to contribute towards the preparation of local plans than at the strategic level. The use of a planning balance sheet in the West Midlands exercise does however indicate that these two points of view can to some extent be brought together and suggests that, despite difficulties, the planning balance sheet can contribute towards the evaluation process in selecting strategies at the regional and sub-regional levels of appreciation. The West Midlands approach is thus different from that pursued in the Studies under review, where criteria related to planning objectives are used to evaluate alternative possible strategies.

THE ROLE OF COST–BENEFIT PROCEDURES

Cost–benefit analysis implies that all benefits can be measured, and that they should exceed costs for a project to be justified. The higher the ratio of benefits to costs, the more favourable the scheme in the eyes of government. Cost–benefit analysis may therefore be used to help in the choice between alternative policies to reach desired ends. Its particular advantage, according to Prest and Turvey (1965),

... is that it forces those responsible to quantify costs and benefits as far as possible rather than rest content with vague qualitative judgements or personal hunches. This is obviously a good thing in itself; some information is always better than none. . . . Even if cost–benefit analysis cannot give the right answer, it can sometimes play the purely negative role of screening projects and rejecting those answers which are obviously less promising. This role is akin to that of a University or College entrance examination. . . . The case for using cost–benefit analysis is strengthened, not weakened, if its limitations are openly recognised and indeed emphasised.[1]

The great strength of the planning balance sheet lies in its full explicit tabulation of all the significant costs and benefits, against the groups to which they relate. This may or may not indicate a preferred strategy, but it does provide an economic base against a series of assumptions for each item upon which value judgements can be made. It therefore provides a useful tool, but one which diminishes in value as the operations increase in scale, magnitude and complexity.

Historically, cost–benefit procedures have proved most effective in practice where the need is to appraise investment projects which are variants on the same theme, such as whether it is best to use a bridge or a tunnel, and at which location, to cross an estuary. Or given a congested shopping centre, is it preferable to remove the shops or to divert the traffic, and what are the respective costs and benefits of the various possible solutions under each major heading? But regional planning is much more complex, diverse and all-embracing in terms of the range of factors which are involved, the many possibilities which exist for each factor, the diverse attitudes of varying social groups, the enormous magnitudes of development, the many different physical terrains which are involved and, indeed, because of all the numerous issues which are under discussion in this book. The subject matter is concerned with the interweaving of many different economic, social and physical considerations and, as soon as one policy is initiated, there are repercussions across the board. Even the Roskill Commission, with its extensive use of cost–benefit procedures, had the simple task (relatively) of deciding between four possible airport sites. In regional planning, a new airport or motorway represents but one ingredient in a complex urban pattern with an abundance of interrelationships.

For these reasons, the Studies generally prefer to take advantage of costing procedures where the details are reasonably limited and circumscribed as with transportation facilities, drainage costs and

[1] A. R. Prest and R. Turvey, 'Cost–Benefit Analysis: A Survey', *The Economic Journal*, Vol. LXXV, 1965, pp. 730–1.

COST–BENEFIT ANALYSIS

water supply schemes. These details are then used to supplement the specification of the objectives which the plan seeks to achieve, some of which will be concerned with financial and cost criteria but others will include the achievement of social, welfare and environmental considerations. The alternative possibilities are then tested, and the measure of success in a strategy is the measure of its performance against these objectives. How effectively have the objectives been met and, where possible, what is the cost for the achievement of these objectives?

At this point the wheel has turned almost full circle because, *provided* the instrumental objectives identified for each sector of the community in the development balance sheet are precisely the same as the objectives and the interpretations used in the planning generation and testing of alternative strategies, then the outcome *must* be the same. In either instance, alternative strategies are *judged* by a comparison of the degree to which stated objectives are achieved. When differences result, then these are differences in judgement, objectives or their interpretation between the two methodologies. For example, in the West Midlands Study, the instrumental objectives for residential occupiers' include accessibility to job opportunities and to shopping and other urban facilities, the availability of local urban facilities, local environmental amenities and nearness to open countryside. These features have each been discussed over previous pages, but what precisely is the value attached to each factor? As the Provost of King's College, Cambridge, has remarked, 'with hindsight it is easy to see what has not been done in any particular case, but when we look forward what principles should we apply? In whose interests do we plan? How far ahead? With what end in view? If we are concerned with innovation, how do we relate social costs to economic costs? If we are concerned with conservation how do we relate the products of culture to the products of nature?... I want to drive home repeatedly the fact that the decisions are moral–aesthetic decisions, they are not rational decisions.'[1] The decision remains a value judgement, dependent upon assumptions and interpretation, even when presented through the neat and apparently accurate formulation of a planning balance sheet. The opportunities for social choice are obscured only by the complexity of the analytical process.

SUMMARY

The Studies examine only selected aspects of their proposed future

[1] E. Leach, 'Planning and Evolution', *Journal of the Town Planning Institute*, 1969, Vol. 55, p. 7.

environment by financial and cost–benefit procedures. The essential emphasis is on highway and public utility projects, but with suggestions that more extensive cost–benefit analysis might be desirable. The specific application of such procedures is via the planning balance sheet, which has been used to indicate the advantages and disadvantages accruing to sectors of the community for specific proposals. The first full-scale application of these techniques in regional planning analysis is in the West Midlands Study. This process, though very desirable within planning, includes several problems of measurement such as where to draw the line and how to evaluate spillover effects, whether some sectors of the community require some special consideration, the appropriate rate of return, the period of investment, and the allocation of comparable monetary or other symbols to different intangibles. Finally, it may be noted that the planning balance sheet depends on instrumental objectives and the suggestion is made that, when there is accord between these and the planning objectives, then comparable conclusions should emerge.

Chapter 10
Goals and Objectives

If all was perfect in urban affairs, the one planning objective would be to retain the status quo. Given dissatisfaction with existing conditions, a cynical objective might be to obtain the maximum grants-in-aid from the central government for the locality under review! Another single purpose objective might be to achieve the lowest cost solution, or the highest return from capital investment, or to provide the greatest increase in per capita income. Unfortunately, planning is not quite so simple because an urban system has multiple objectives, which are often incommensurable and perhaps contradictory so that there is often a need for some form of trade-off between the varying possibilities. This is done subjectively by planners at various stages of the technical process, but no general consensus or agreement exists either about the objectives which should be pursued or about the amount of trade-off when conflicts occur. There is not yet available one Study in which the objectives are stated clearly, in which development is located logically against stated objectives, in which conflicts between objectives are revealed with clarity, and where the Report states how and why all differences have been resolved. Objectives are stated and a preferred strategy emerges, but in between there is often a somewhat murky area where further clarification is desirable. This chapter trespasses into this realm of uncertainty because 'public goals in a democratic society are seldom set through a methodical procedure, but, since they provide the direction and purposes of plans, planners must find a way to determine and establish unequivocal goals'.[1]

OBJECTIVES IN THE STUDIES

The approach which should be followed is to specify in advance the objectives and values to be achieved through the planning process, and then to devise strategies against these criteria in order best to achieve in terms of land use and transportation the long-term objectives which have been envisaged. Likewise, there should then follow the systematic analysis of the performance of each alternative

[1] R. C. Young, 'Goals and Goal Setting', *Journal of the American Institute of Planners*, Vol. 32, 1966, p. 76.

strategy against the stated objectives. 'Crucial to the process of successful regional planning is a clear understanding of regional goals. ... The role of this process of scanning the region for issues and goals is not only to provide a point of entry into the planning continuum but also to provide a basis for testing the acceptability of proposed plans.'[1] Against this background, in which goals and objectives have been identified as a central feature in the planning process, varying approaches have been adopted in the Studies. The discussion will first refer to the earlier Studies and an examination of the procedures; Warwickshire, where the use of objectives attains its fullest expression, then follows in a subsequent section.

The Teesside Study obtains its objectives in a sequence of stages. There is first the derivation of objectives from the study of physical, social and economic conditions; this 'was concerned with the objectives which should govern the future distribution of activities and the direction and form of development'.[2] The second stage is comparable, and emerges from additional survey data and planning studies of key areas for future development. To these are then added transportation objectives to provide a 'full list of specific objectives for urban structure policy'.[3] Alternative land use strategies are then explored, and their examination yields further objectives. Thus 'the specific planning objectives for guiding the future growth of Teesside ... are formulated within the context of the broad aims and basic assumptions about regional policy ... are based on a thorough appraisal of the problems and opportunities latent in the present situation ... and on an exploration of alternative forms for land use and transport policy. As such, these objectives are of fundamental importance, defining the sort of place which Teesside should become.'[4]

These specific objectives are then described under the five headings of employment structure, conservation of natural resources, urban form, transportation system, and environmental quality and standards of living. The details are fairly precise and exact. Thus 'the employment structure should be diversified by the attraction of about 53,000 more jobs in light manufacturing industry'; 'the better quality agricultural land should not be used for urban development'; 'future residential development should be located relatively close to the existing built-up area, rather than in a satellite or new town'; 'the

[1] W. A. Steger and T. R. Lakshmanan, 'Plan Evaluation Methodologies: Some Aspects of Decision Requirements and Analytical Response', in Highway Research Board, *Urban Development Models*, National Academy of Sciences (Washington), 1968, pp. 53 and 56.

[2] *Teesside Study*, p. 77.   [3] *Ibid.*, p. 78.   [4] *Ibid.*, p. 93.

build up of employment in a single dominant centre should be avoided'; or 'the regional centre at Middlesbrough should become the centre for more specialized activities on Teesside'.[1]

The Notts–Derby Study likewise places considerable emphasis on objectives. The first stage of the technical process 'comprised the survey and technical analysis, and the formulation of objectives for the strategy. This stage lasted six months. . . . The objectives and factual information derived from this first stage were then used as a basis for the strategy formulation and testing process.'[2] The source for these objectives is varied. 'A number of objectives for the strategy arose from the need to stimulate the economy and assist in meeting social needs. . . . Further objectives are necessary to conserve and improve the environment and allow its development in a satisfactory manner. Where there are conflicts between these objectives a compromise will be necessary. . . . Two further objectives arise from the general need for economy.'[3] The twenty-two objectives which resulted (Table 10.1) are phrased in more general terms than for Teesside.

Objectives, though still central to the development of the planning argument, are less pervasive in the Leicestershire and the North-Glos Studies. Leicestershire states that 'our terms of reference broadly defined our objectives for the physical planning of the sub-region. Identifying the relevant issues from these objectives was approached through studying the sub-region's specific problems.'[4] In the North-Glos Study objectives, though not explicitly stated as such, provide the basis for the selection of options and hence for the selection of alternative strategies. Criteria such as the lowest cost for the construction of transportation facilities or drainage works, or the least amount of travel for the shopping trip, are used to evaluate the performance of alternative strategies.

At the Regional level of consideration, objectives are most used in the South East Study. The method of procedure is that 'the team's recommendations must take the form of regional objectives and measures to achieve these and an indication, in broad outline, of the pattern of development which might result from their adoption and which would facilitate their achievement'.[5] The objectives are grouped under economic, social, countryside, transport and feasibility headings. They are stated in general terms such as, 'to enable the best use to be made of the region's labour resources and to provide for an efficient distribution of employment within the region'; 'to match as far as possible population and employment growth'; 'to provide more

---

[1] *Ibid.*, pp. 94–7.   [2] *Notts–Derby Study*, p. lxvii.   [3] *Ibid.*, p. 29.
[4] *Leicestershire Study*, p. 29.   [5] *South East Study*, p. 65.

scope for open air recreation requiring extensive areas of land'; 'to identify those areas where conditions are particularly suitable for the further promotion of agricultural productivity and to provide for the

Table 10.1. *Objectives for the Strategy in the Notts–Derby Study*

1. To encourage a location of population which will provide a labour market in which a choice of jobs is ensured.
2. To provide attractive sites for offices, research establishments, warehouses and institutions in proper relationship with the environment, labour supply and the communications network.
3. To provide ample attractive and substantial industrial sites conveniently located for the supplies of labour.
4. To promote policies which have the effect of encouraging the growth of firms.
5. To provide ample and attractive sites for housing for all socio-economic groups.
6. To provide good transport facilities.
7. To encourage the efficient and convenient distribution of shopping, social, cultural and recreational facilities.
8. To improve the appearance of the sub-region.
9. To provide an environment which is adaptable in character so that it can accommodate changes in the requirements of society.
10. To promote policies likely to encourage the conservation, improvement or renewal as appropriate, of the existing urban environment.
11. To promote policies likely to ensure that new urban areas are attractive, convenient, safe and healthy.
12. To conserve good agricultural land and encourage full utilization of its potential.
13. To conserve land used for growing timber.
14. To avoid sterilization of mineral resources.
15. To conserve land of high landscape value.
16. To reduce air pollution.
17. To avoid siting development in foggy locations.
18. To conserve water resources and eliminate water pollution.
19. To reclaim or tidy up derelict land.
20. To conserve areas of high natural history interest.
21. To prevent wasteful use of land.
22. To keep down construction and operation costs, particularly of roads and services.

After *Notts–Derby Study*, pp. 9 and 29.

protection of these areas from encroachment by inappropriate land uses'; 'to stimulate, as appropriate, the mobility of employment within the region and to encourage, in particular the further dispersal from London of employment, in both the manufacturing and service industries.'[1] The alternative strategies are then tested against these objectives. Stage I is in the terms of groups of objectives over the region; 'no attempt was made, at this stage, to consider the inter-action of the objectives or to deal with any conflicts'.[2] Stage II is within each sub-district to identify the main areas of opportunities for growth, and the main areas of difficulty in the light of objectives and their conflict or feasibility problems. Stage III involves further consideration of these areas of difficulty.

In the Humberside and Hampshire Studies the prime given objective is the feasibility or otherwise of expansion, and further objectives have been identified which might impose limits or restrictions on the location, scale, form or phasing of this expansion. Thus Hampshire idealized three urban structures, and examined these against five criteria, which are maximum freedom of choice, efficient functioning at each phase of growth, the possibility of change and renewal in the elements, versatility and growth without distortion or deformation. The four Humberside strategies are evaluated against six 'planning considerations', each of which imply objectives. These are physical factors, the urban hierarchy, the need for industrial sites, sewerage schemes, transportation and the staging of development.

The formulation of goals and objectives is thus a key element in these Studies. It plays an explicit and especially important role in the procedural approach of the Notts–Derby, Leicestershire, Teesside, and South East Studies, and in the planning balance sheet discussed in the previous chapter. It is more implicit in the other studies. In the words of McLoughlin (1969), 'public planning must identify the goals which it seeks. This is a logical progression from the first stage of adopting planning since that in itself needs justification by a set of aims. The goal-formulation stage is thus . . . a sharpening-up of the notion of purpose. Goals are typically somewhat vague and general, though this is not inevitable. Usually, progress towards a goal will require the attainment of certain objectives which are more precise and clear. . . . The formulation of goals is of great importance since much of the planning process depends upon them.'[3] Those goals and objectives which underlie the planning process should be stated clearly in every Report. If at a later stage in the analysis, general objectives are refined to the requisite performance levels, then these too should be summarized and presented in published documents.

[1] *Ibid.*, pp. 67–9.   [2] *Ibid.*, p. 69.
[3] J. B. McLoughlin, *Urban and Regional Planning: A Systems Approach*, Faber and Faber (London), 1969, p. 97.

265

Otherwise the procedures followed in the Study, and the nature of the underlying assumptions, will not be apparent for public examination and an awareness of how strategies are devised and selected as a basis for action.

OBJECTIVES IN RECENT AMERICAN PRACTICE AND THE WARWICKSHIRE STUDY

Methodology in planning relies heavily on the mistakes and successes of earlier exercises, as techniques are refined and improved. In particular, statements about objectives, their interpretation and specific use in the preparation and testing of strategies have become more definite and explicit. The full transition from an abstract statement to a computable content, which is accepted as 'correct' and recognized to be 'exact', will not be easy. It requires that precise performance measures be defined for each objective, so that each alternative strategy can be tested for its effectiveness against each ranking measure. This process, however, still leaves unresolved the method of summation, the weighting to be attached to each measure, and whether each line is equal, or whether variations in importance should be reflected (and if so to what degree) in the analysis.

Two recent American approaches to these problems may be noted. In the Boston metropolitan programme,

> for each of the twelve objectives, one or more performance measures having a distinct and logical relationship to that objective were developed. . . . A total of twenty-one such measures was chosen. Once the objectives and performance measures were defined, and the measures computed for each alternative, each of the four alternative plans was ranked on each performance measure in order of increasing performance ability. Thus, in principle, for each measure the best alternative was assigned a score of four and the worst a score of one. A score for each alternative on each objective was obtained by summing the ranks achieved on that objective's performance measures, and dividing by the number of measures for that objective. Then, these scores were summed over the twelve objectives to obtain an overall score for each plan. In this summation, four of the twelve objectives were given double weight – that is, their scores were counted twice – in order to reflect their greater importance. The alternative with the highest overall weighted score was the preferred alternative.[1]

[1] D. E. Boyce and N. D. Day, *Metropolitan Plan Making*, Institute for Environmental Studies, University of Pennsylvania (Philadelphia), 1969, p. 44.

Three important queries are whether the relative weighting should be applied to the number of objectives or to the number of measures, what the basis for the selection of the four more important objectives was, and why the 2:1 ratio was chosen as a measure of their greater importance?

In the Milwaukee exercise, the procedure was broadly comparable, but with the objectives being grouped into three major categories. 'For each alternative the scores on each category of objectives were weighted or multiplied by the rank order of the objective itself. These weighted scores were summed for each alternative achieving an overall score for each plan. Finally, this score was weighted by a "probability of implementation" subjectively reflecting the difficulty of implementing the plan. The alternative with the highest weighted score was considered to be the preferred alternative.'[1] A prime difficulty in such procedures must again be the nature of the objectives, their translation into performance measures, their respective weighting, and the extent to which objectives are applicable to all sections of the community or exert a selective impact. The outcome may be correct, arbitrary or misleading depending, to a considerable extent, on the subjective views of the recipient and his interpretation of the proposals.

In British practice the Warwickshire Study makes a substantial advance in systematic terms over previous procedures as demonstrated in the Notts–Derby or the South East Studies. The approach, known as Goals-Achievement Matrix Evaluation when applied to transportation planning,[2] is that 'we evaluated the alternatives by measuring the promise of each one against each of the objectives for the strategy. Performance scores were calculated to show the degree to which each objective was likely to be achieved by each strategy, and the scores for individual objectives were weighted to reflect their relative importance. The weighted scores were then summed so that the overall performances of the alternatives could be compared.'[3] An example will clarify this procedure:[4]

Objective 4

To locate new development so that the loss of workable mineral resources is kept to a minimum.

[1] *Ibid.*, p. 45.
[2] A. M. Hill, 'Goals Achievement Matrix for Evaluating Alternative Plans', *Journal of the American Institute of Planners*, Vol. 34, 1968, pp. 19–29.
[3] *Warwickshire Study*, p. 61.   [4] *Ibid.*, p. 66.

THE URBAN FUTURE

Performance Criterion

The area of each mineral deposit sterilized by new development in each strategy expressed as a percentage of the total area of that mineral within the sub-region, summed for all minerals.

Performance Assumptions

1. The depth of any mineral deposit is uniform.
2. All surface deposits are workable.
3. No deposits under overburden are workable.
4. The greatest variety of deposits should be maintained at any one time.
5. New development would in all cases sterilize the mineral deposit; i.e. no deposit would be worked prior to development.

Performance Results

Strategy	Score	Rank	Performance level
902	35	2	95
903	25	1	96
904	36	3	94
906	42	4	93

The objectives are derived from several sources including the local knowledge of policy issues which led to the establishment of the Study, a scrutiny of Council minutes, discussions with officers, items of local news and the editorial opinions of local newspapers, and professional consensus. They are refined during the analytical process into 'essential' objectives and 'discriminatory' objectives. The essential objectives do not vary between the alternative strategies and include the quantity inputs that have been discussed, i.e. the land requirements to accommodate the population and employment forecasts at appropriate space standards and with all supporting services; the clearance, rehabilitation and conservation of the housing stock; the conservation of sites of architectural, historical or ecological significance; and the greatest opportunity for the recreational use of land, inter alia. The attainment of discriminatory objectives, 'would vary between alternative strategies. The *quality* of each alternative tested was established by the extent to which it met each objective.'[1]

[1] *Ibid.*, p. 28.

The twenty discriminatory objectives are listed in Table 10.2. The wording and emphasis on the objectives express the purpose of planning and may be compared with the Notts–Derby formulation (Table 10.1) and the instrumental objectives of the Development Balance Sheet (Table 9.1). The procedures used to generate industrial and residential patterns have been discussed on pages 166–7 and, in greater detail, on pages 180–81. An important aspect is that a variety of weights are used at the stage of generating alternative strategies and again when evaluating between their respective qualities. Different degrees of importance are therefore attached to varying combinations of objectives. For example, a part of the weightings used to select between the final strategies is:[1]

	Weighting Set Nos.				
Objectives	2	3	4	5	6
1 Landscape	2	1	2	6	6
2 Farmland	6	1	6	1	6
3 Land servicing constraints	2	2	2	2	6
4 Residential environment	1	6	6	1	6

The purpose of the Study has been exemplified by these means. There is a logical and orderly progression from terms of reference, the establishment of objectives, the statement of performance standards through to the generation and testing of alternative strategies. The especial importance of this systematic method, as with the development balance sheet previously, is the undisguised presentation and testing of alternatives against given and stated assumptions. There remain four very important and critical questions for those who wish to consider the conclusions from this type of document. (1) Are each of the objectives valid? (2) Are the performance criteria for each objective acceptable? (3) Are these performance criteria interpreted correctly? (4) Are the weights used a valid index of relative importance between different objectives?

Against this background of the practice and procedures which have been used both in the Studies and in preparing the development balance sheet, a series of thoughts are offered for further consideration of these issues. They relate back to the comprehensive nature of the planning process, to its continuing nature, to the fact that plans and proposals must be feasible, and that they are prepared on a rational basis in the best interests of the community. A discussion of goals and objectives suggests some of the dilemmas which are

[1] *Ibid.*, p. 44.

Table 10.2. *Discrimatory Objectives in the Warwickshire Study*

---

1. To locate new development so as to conserve areas of high landscape value (R) (I).
2. To locate new development so that the loss of good quality farmland is kept to the minimum (R).
3. To locate new development so that the costs of new utility services and land development generally are kept to a minimum (R) (I).
4. To locate new developments so that the loss of workable mineral resources is kept to a minimum.
5. To locate residential development in areas of high environmental potential (R).
6. To locate new development so that there is the greatest possible choice of housing sites available to residents seeking new homes.
7. To locate new development so that physical disturbance to existing development is kept to a minimum.
8. To locate new development in areas which will not be adversely affected by atmospheric and noise pollution (R).
9. To locate new population and employment so that there is the greatest possible choice of jobs available to all workers (R).
10. To locate new population and employment and new investment so as to give particular assistance to those areas where existing industries are declining and where job growth potential generally is low.
11. To locate new population and employment so that there is the greatest possible choice of labour supply for all firms (R) (I).
12. To locate new population and employment so that there is the greatest possible opportunity for all residents to go out to work.
13. To increase the potential range of shopping facilities available and to provide the greatest possible accessibility to them for all residents (R).
14. To locate new principal roads to serve the new population and employment so that there is the greatest possible benefit to all road users (R) (I).
15. To locate new population and employment where there is the greatest possible potential for public transport services (R).
16. To locate new population and employment where there is the greatest possible choice of transport route and mode available.
17. To be able to adapt to changes within a possible range of departures from 'most likely' forecasts (F).
18. To be able to cope with sudden and unexpected events (F).
19. To be able to respond to changes in social values (F).
20. To retain as far as possible the option of switching from any preferred strategy to one of any other strategies examined once implementation has begun (F).

Notes: (R) Used to generate residential developmental potential.
       (I) Used to generate industrial development potential.
      (F) Used to test for flexibility.

After *Warwickshire Study*, p. 29.

involved when attempting this planning acumen, because 'the case for efforts at genuinely comprehensive planning has generally rested heavily on the thought that planners can resolve conflicts among goals in expert fashion. If they cannot, if they can only articulate specialist goals, then elected officials would seem required to act as the comprehensive arbiters of conflict.'[1]

The discussion is general; it does not refer specifically to the Warwickshire approach, but rather to certain problems posed when using goals and objectives as an integral part of the planning process. As such the comments are complementary to those made when discussing cost–benefit procedures.

THE ESTABLISHMENT OF OBJECTIVES

Three possibilities exist for the establishment of objectives. They can (1) be given through outside decree by society or by government when commissioning a planning study. In this the values are not primarily the concern of the planner, but are received by him. His function is to prepare the lowest-cost or the best-welfare or some other clearly defined strategy. They can (2) be determined by the planning unit, through estimating the preferences of the public for certain objectives by attitude surveys, community studies, interviews and questionnaires. They can (3) be formulated as a research task on behalf of the community, through surveys and analysis of the existing situation and on the basis of their professional skills, experience and understanding of the situation.

Method No. 1 exists in all the Studies, and has been discussed when considering the terms of reference in Chapter 3. It provides at least the introductory framework and some indication of the necessary minimum commitment. Afterwards, Method No. 3 tends to prevail. Objectives are determined by the planners arising out of *their* appraisal of conditions within the study area. Advice and assistance is also available, or is obtained from, technical officers with a specialist knowledge of the locality. The formulation of objectives, the values for attainment and the criteria to be applied remain the prime concern and responsibility of the planning unit.

Method No. 3, an in-depth citizen involvement in the formulation of goals and objectives, has not been pursued in any of the Studies though, in Warwickshire, 'to assist the professional judgement of the planners, a sample cross section of people in Coventry, Solihull and

[1] A. Altshuler, 'The Goals of Comprehensive Planning,' *Journal of the American Institute of Planners*, Vol. 31, 1965, pp. 190–1.

Warwickshire was interviewed on the relative importance of the objectives, and the response helped in the final stages of selecting the recommended strategy'.[1] In most instances reliance is placed on 'team consensus', perhaps supplemented by discussions with technical officers, and some planners would express doubts about the validity of citizen involvement at either this early stage of the planning process or for an area so complex and diverse as a sub-region. The argument (as expressed by Altshuler, 1965) might be that

> there is an enormous range in the amount of time, and in the degree of immediacy of a threat or opportunity, that it takes to move different groups of people with potential interest in a proposal to the threshold of organizational expression. Government never moves slowly enough or poses issues clearly enough to give everyone his say (and when it does, there are so many divergent views that a consensus of opinion is difficult if not impossible). It is fair to say that only when government moves at a snail's pace and deals with issues of rather direct and immediate impact can a significant proportion of the great multitude of interests express themselves. Therefore, democratic planning of a highly general nature is virtually impossible.'[2]

In contrast with this type of statement, an ambitious project to encourage active citizen participation in the formulation of Subregional objectives is being undertaken for the South Hampshire Plan. A questionnaire, distributed to a random sample of 3,000 electors *prior* to the selection of the preferred strategy, invites the public to indicate the degree of importance which they attach to each of eight aims (Table 10.3) which are thought to be the most important for the future of South Hampshire. The wording is, 'please give a score of between 0 and 5 to EACH of these aims – putting a circle around a high number if you attach a high degree of importance to the aim, or around a lower number if you think that the aim is relatively less important'. The public are then asked, 'if there are any broad aims which should be included, please state them below and give a score which reflects their importance in relation to the one above'.[1] This direct involvement of the public in the mainstream of the planning process provides an extremely important innovation in the technical process of plan evaluation, and is to be warmly commended.

[1] *Warwickshire Study*, p. 14.   [2] A. Altshuler, *op. cit.*, p. 190.
[3] South Hampshire Plan Advisory Committee, *South Hampshire Plan: Four Possibilities for the Future*. The questionnaire was distributed in September 1970.

Of the sample questionnaires 62 per cent were returned, and 55 per cent could be analysed. The response was higher from the county areas than the cities, from men than women and from white-collar

Table 10.3. *Objectives in the South Hampshire Plan for Public Appraisal by Questionnaire*

AIMS	SUMMARY OF AIMS	SCORE
To be adaptable so that the plan can cope with circumstances which are at present unforeseen.	Flexibility	0 1 2 3 4 5
To ensure that the plan can be put into operation and carried out efficiently.	Implementation	0 1 2 3 4 5
To ensure that people can travel easily about the area.	Mobility	0 1 2 3 4 5
To create a clear framework for all development in the area, whether existing or new, and so help to give identity to the various parts of the area.	Image	0 1 2 3 4 5
To provide people with a wide freedom of choice for housing, working, shopping and recreation, and, for the private developer, of industrial and commercial sites.	Freedom of choice	0 1 2 3 4 5
To conserve the important natural resources and man-made features of the area, with the least disturbance to the existing urban and rural areas.	Conservation	0 1 2 3 4 5
To see that financial resources and investment are used wisely and efficiently, especially where these are the responsibility of public and local authorities.	Economy	0 1 2 3 4 5
To create high quality surroundings for living, working, shopping and recreation.	Local environment	0 1 2 3 4 5

After South Hampshire Plan Advisory Committee, *South Hampshire Plan: Four Alternatives For the Future.*

than blue-collar workers. The results 'suggest that the public's preference for particular aims are not very strong. Economy achieves the highest score, followed closely by conservation, environment,

273

mobility and freedom of choice. Flexibility and implementation received below average scores, while image was significantly different from the other aims with a lower score.'[1] This type of information should be most important when conflicts between objectives have to be resolved in the land allocation process.

With regard to additional possible aims, '43 per cent of sample respondents suggested at least one additional aim. The majority of these were found to be either re-statements in new wording or else emphasis of specific objectives relating to aims already given. . . . Some of the additional aims had not been previously defined. Some were concerned with proposals (i.e. specific developments, particularly on the coast); others related to assumptions common to all strategies (e.g. housing density or improvement of existing facilities).'[2] The important point is that citizens *had* been consulted in the course of preparing strategies for *their* Sub-region. A Report gains tremendously in value if it can be demonstrated that it relies on a proven volume of substantial public support in the pursuit of its basic objectives, and is the more likely to receive approval by government in such circumstances. Objectives have professional and operational ingredients; they must at the same time be acceptable and appear reasonable to the public.

THE WEIGHTING OF OBJECTIVES

Objectives in several Studies are not weighted and are thus apparently of equal importance, whereas in the Warwickshire Study, the South Hampshire Plan and in certain cost–benefit exercises[3] considerable attention is paid to the differences in importance between objectives. Weighting between objectives is considered necessary because it is highly improbable that twenty or more objectives are each of equal significance and importance for the urban future. There is certain to be a conflict between two or more objectives in the allocation of land, so that priorities between competing objectives will have to be determined by the planning team at various stages in the selection and evaluation process. Thus an objective to provide attractive industrial sites close to supplies of labour may be at variance with the objective of conserving high quality agricultural land.

---

[1] South Hampshire Plan Advisory Committee, *Comments on the Four Possibilities for the Future*, 1970, p. 2.

[2] *Ibid.*, p. 5.

[3] For example in the evaluation of a shopping centre at Edgware, *Journal of Transport Economics and Policy*, Vol. 2, 1968, pp. 280–320.

The challenge posed by stating objectives does not remove the element of conflict in reaching a planning decision, but it does provide both a rational means for testing such decisions and a vital opportunity for public comment at an early stage in the planning process. In the South Hampshire Plan, there is both a professional weighting for each of the planning aims *and* the important complementary information about the nature of the public ranking of objectives from the above questionnaire. It would, if necessary, be possible to prepare different strategies on the basis of these different convictions. Also, when evaluating between strategies and when there is a conflict between objectives, the planning team are in a stronger position to decide between competing aims, when public attitudes are known explicitly rather than assumed.

THE MULTI-STAGE FORMULATON OF OBJECTIVES

The selection of problems at an early stage of the planning procedures itself implies value structures and goals. The planner has some conception of the public interest and of preferred policies or conditions as soon as something can be described as an issue or as a problem for resolution. Values or assumptions are being included by the very fact that some alternative situation is deemed to be preferable. At least two and generally three stages in goal formulation may therefore be identified. The first stage introduces or precedes the survey and analysis of existing conditions. The second stage involves a critical examination of the region under review by the team for its strengths and deficiencies against these primary goals, and this should lead through to the listing of regional goals for resolution in the formulation of strategies as in the Notts–Derby, Warwickshire and South East Studies. The third stage, as in the Teesside Study, is the derivation of further goals after testing the respective achievements of the various strategies.

In illustration of this sequence in goal formulation, in the Ontario Regional development programme, Stage 1 in the approach to development planning in each region is to 'identify provincial goals'. These are based on a White Paper (1966) which sets out basic government policy[1] and subsequent cabinet announcements which detail certain fundamental regional development policies. It is only subsequently, *after* reviewing growth trends, conducting social and economic base studies and after examining the present and potential land use, the impact of technology and considering possible urban

[1] *Design for Development*, Ontario Provincial Government (Toronto), 1966.

centres of opportunity, that *regional* goals are identified. Thus, in the words of the Report for the Niagara Region, 'this report *began* with the discussion of broad provincial goals for attaining the full social, economic and physical development potential of Ontario's ten development regions. . . . What does differ from region to region is the nature and severity of the local problems which must be overcome if each region is to attain these goals.'[1] It may be suggested that there are important lessons from this sequential approach for British practice. The Warwickshire Study for example recommends that 'before concluding Structure Plans the planning authorities should obtain from the Government a statement of long term national land use, social and economic planning policy'.[2] In logic, the formulation of regional objectives should depend on and follow on from national objectives. Otherwise vital assumptions have to be made at the discretion of each Regional and Sub-regional planning Study.

THE GENERALITY OF OBJECTIVES

The objectives which have been outlined are generalized statements. They yield almost as many problems of exact and meaningful definition as they resolve. What, in precise and exact terms, is meant by 'high quality agricultural land', 'the diversification of employment opportunities', a location 'relatively close to', or 'the greatest possible choice of jobs', and so on. These are the topics, with varying possible interpretations, which have been discussed over the previous pages.

It is certainly helpful and desirable to list objectives, but the greater problem lies in the gulf between these broad expressions and their ultimate translation into terms of land use and land development. The danger is that individually and in sum total, they tend to say little more than that we want the best, imperfections must be removed, difficulties resolved and a better society must be created. Presumably, most people would agree that 'good transport facilities' must be provided, or that 'the appearance of the sub-region' must be improved. The problems arise in the means of achievement, where, by what means, at what cost and with what adverse side effects. It is the means and the consequences of achievement, rather than stating the objectives, which provide the real difficulties to be overcome. An

[1] Regional Development Branch, *Design for Development: Niagara (South Ontario) Region – Phase I: Analysis*, Department of Treasury and Economics (Toronto), 1970, p. 95.

[2] *Warwickshire Study*, p. 30.

276

important gap has to be bridged via performance criteria and performance assumptions in order that strategies and policy recommendations may emerge from generalized statements of objectives.

It follows that, whenever possible, objectives should be stated in specific terms of plan achievement. Perhaps they can refer to targets which should be achieved, so that progress towards these targets can be measured and recorded on a regular basis. For example, a transportation objective might be to achieve certain average speeds on different parts of the network or not to exceed a certain degree of congestion. Housing objectives might be concerned with the clearance of so many units a year. A public open space objective might be related to the achievement of 'x' acres per 1,000 population, with additional refinements about its accessibility and its location relative to existing population depending upon their income and the densities which are involved.

Planning requires creative workable propositions which can be presented to the public and through political leadership gain their support. If the goal is to attain transportation speeds of 'x' m.p.h., it can be demonstrated that this would cost so much to achieve. However, transportation speeds of '$x+10$ per cent' m.p.h. would require an additional expenditure of y per cent. It would be easier allocating expenditure against this type of planning basis than trying to compare the performance of various strategies against several different and incompatible objectives.

Closely associated with the statement of objectives are therefore the 'tests of preference' or the 'criteria of performance' by which the relative attributes of different strategies can be measured systematically and consistently. One step is to examine the consequence of different actions and to infer the resultant sets of relationships by the use of models, which themselves rely upon the inclusion of objectives for their successful performance and interpretation. Thus shopping models are developed on the objective of accessibility, and the Garin–Lowry model on stated relationships between employment and residential development. In each instance, only *some* of the consequences can be identified, measured, and evaluated. Complete prediction of every aspect of urban affairs over a lengthy period of time is impossible and hence the closely related problem arises of *which* consequences are significant over what time period and for which groups of the population. Tests are not definitive, but selective. This task would not be easy if only one objective, e.g. lowest cost, was to prevail, but invariably several objectives are involved in the analysis of alternative regional strategies for development.

An example of this close relationship between objectives and models is stated in the Notts–Derby Study. 'The Potential Surface is a technique devised within the Unit for systematizing and quantifying the potential for development of different areas of the Sub-region. This involved the identification and measurement of the various elements making up potential, these being ultimately derived from the Objectives using principles developed by Alexander.'[1] Or, in the Leicestershire Study, 'the simulation process of itself could not be operated without clearly stated policy assumptions, themselves related to sub-regional planning objectives; we had to define these in collaboration with the local authorities'.[2]

THE RESOLUTION OF CONFLICT BETWEEN OBJECTIVES

Multiple objectives are recognized in each Study. The headings have typically included economic growth, social criteria, transportation objectives, land use arrangements, flexibility and the quality of the environment. Objectives may be directly related to performance characteristics of the system under study (e.g. of transportation, recreation or housing obsolescence), or may be contextual and arise because of the way in which performance has to be realized (the use of high quality scenery for a motorway route, new development on high quality agricultural land, noise or pollution from a new traffic route).

The trade-off between conflicting objectives poses many difficult issues. How much high quality agricultural land should be 'sacrificed' in order to conserve a mineral resource or vice versa, and how are the equally strong claims from the different interests and pressure groups measured? Despite the difficulties, the comparison here is relatively easy, because it is between two physical objectives in terms of location. More complex is the barter between an economic or social objective and physical considerations, such as whether an amenity resource should be developed to reduce the length of the journey to work. Difficult again is the distinction between long-term and short-term objectives, in terms of the allocation of limited fiscal resources. How are objectives of critical importance to one section of the community (e.g. the reclamation of derelict land or atmospheric pollution which are of limited occurrence by their areal extent) reconciled with objectives which permeate all localities of the region

[1] *Notts–Derby Study*, p. lxxi. The reference is to C. Alexander, *Notes on the Synthesis of Form* (Cambridge, Mass), 1964.
[2] *Leicestershire Study*, Vol. 2, p. 79.

but which may be of less importance (e.g. the accessibility of residential areas to durable shopping facilities)?

The objectives themselves are quite different in *purpose* (economic, social, aesthetic). When a cleavage occurs, should economic or social intentions take precedence? For example, the diversion of industry to a depressed district may relieve personal and family hardships of unemployment and provide new job opportunities for school-leavers and hence reduce emigration, but it will not contribute to the national objective of increased productivity if transport costs are high or if the locality is unsuitable for industrial growth. The depressed district can also be highly congested (e.g. Liverpool or Glasgow) so that the achievement of one objective (new industrial development) conflicts with the pursuit of another (such as the dispersal of population to an outlying centre).

Further, there may be conflicts within the pursuit of any one objective, because most refer to a hierarchy of possibilities and the separate elements can be perceived in a different manner. For instance, the attitude to amenity objectives of the city dweller who wishes to enjoy rural amenities is quite different from that of the marginal farmer who may live in such an area and seek a ploughing subsidy to convert downland from grass to arable. An objective of a reduced tax rate can be taken to mean either higher incomes or lower municipal expenditures, and the latter can imply either less development and poorer maintenance and servicing of existing structures, or greater efficiency for the same capital commitment. Yet almost everyone, in theory, must support 'a higher level of amenities' or 'reduced taxation' as generalities. There are conflicts not just between objectives, but within objectives when they are broken down and examined in terms of their several detailed implications.

Also at what level should conflicts between objectives be resolved? In the South East Study objectives are formulated at the regional level, but are evaluated in relation to each other when in conflict at the district level. This means that conflicts which occur at the regional level, or between regional objectives and local circumstances, are not resolved. Each issue is resolved separately and in physical or spatial isolation, rather than as part of an interconnected series of events which is the supposed approach to the formulation of strategies. It would seem that, in the preparation of a *regional* strategy, the repercussions of changes in policy or of alterations to the strategy at the local level have to be re-assessed because of their further possible repercussions at the regional level.

Another factor is that decision-makers may prefer to focus on

279

short-term issues and the resolution of obvious conflicts for their immediate advantage in political and election terms, rather than long-term commitments. Social pressures may also be concerned with immediate objectives for the amelioration of existing problems which provide a public irritant. Thus traffic congestion or pollution may be seen as more immediate and important issues than the reservation of some distant site for recreation or a strategic policy to extend a city in a particular direction or some abstruse argument about needs thirty years ahead which may turn out to be a mirage on the horizon.

All the objectives in the Studies are fixed in terms of time, and do not change over different periods of strategy formulation. It is conceivable, for example, that objectives concerned with recreation, amenity, conservation and landscape values will increase in importance with larger populations, higher rates of income, larger disposable incomes and the loss of some existing physical assets. In such circumstances an additional weighting might be applied to offset the pressures of short-term demands. Another example is that, as incomes rise and car ownership becomes more prevalent, then the length of the journey to shops or entertainment becomes less important and the customer is more able to select between a range of competing alternatives; the objective of choice becomes more important than objectives concerned with spatial separation such as the time, cost or distance of travel. Planning for sub-regional strategies must somehow encompass both immediate detail *and* long-term vision. Short-term and long-term prospects should not be in conflict because the progression towards the future, as demonstrated in Chapter 3, is by a series of 5-year or 10-year steps.

When objectives are in conflict, the costs and the advantages may relate to different segments of society. The decision must often therefore lie in the realm of deciding between who gains and who loses. Is there such a thing as a 'general interest', a 'common concern' or an 'agreed policy'? This dilemma is for example brought out in every discussion between the respective roles of public transport and the private vehicle. Thus the Teesside Study notes that the capital cost of providing a transport system 'falls almost entirely on the public sector whereas operating costs, expressed as an annual cost, are met by the private individual. A major factor affecting the capital cost of a transport system is the modal split, that is the proportion of person-trips made by public and private transport respectively.'[1] The distinction is between community objectives and individual objectives

[1] *Teesside Study*, p. 80.

which may be mutually antagonistic, and political controversy has always existed on this point of where to draw the fine dividing line between public and private responsibility. The real problem is not to want something, but how to get it – and it is this which causes political divisions and social conflict. In the words of Miller (1962) writing as a political scientist,

> the common concern will sometimes be found in the society at large, and sometimes not. More often it will not be there. That is to say, societies of a developed character, which contain a wide variety of competing and differential interests, will only now and then show sufficient agreement to enable us to say that a common concern exists throughout the society. It would be unreasonable to ask that every single person in the society should agree at the same time; this would be humanly impossible. . . . The normal condition of opinion in any free country is that of division.[1]

Another example is that of a road improvement scheme. When two or more proposals are in conflict, should the prime objective be to minimize accidents to pedestrians, to provide the greatest time saving for commercial and/or private vehicle users, to effect the lowest capital cost for the works or to minimize the impact of the scheme upon the environment? Quite different conclusions can arise, according to the importance attached to one or more of these objectives by different segments of society.

Some members of the public may have little or no interest in certain objectives. Thus the residents of urban inner areas may have explicit demands for rehabilitation and environmental improvement, and transportation systems to resolve commuting problems from outlying suburban estates will be of little concern. Several environmental and conservation issues have been labelled middle-class, and certainly policies such as the provision of green belts, the pressure from some nearby rural counties for conurbations to use higher densities, and animosity to public schemes for the overspill of population and industry into 'select' areas contain elements in their presentation of 'I'm all right, Jack. Some other locality, please, but not to these pleasant rural acres.' In the words of a report on the pros and cons of the Greater London Plan there is 'the old division between the central boroughs, which have the greatest problems of decay, congestion, and human suffering, and the suburbs, where life is pretty good and green and gracious and not to be spoilt by the arrival

[1] J. D. Miller, *The Nature of Politics*, Penguin Books (Harmondsworth, Middlesex) 1969, pp. 54–5 (first published 1962).

281

of those they class as idle ill-deserving slum dwellers who will vandalize their tranquillity, and may be black, to boot.'[1] Regional strategies must adjudicate between these quite different and conflicting demands and claims. In the allocation of growth pressures, preference has to be given to one set of demands over another; the reasons for the priorities which are awarded are rarely clear in the Studies.

Objectives might also vary over space, whereas in each Study objectives are deemed to be the same over each sub-area of the region under study. In reality, they might vary considerably between an expanding city, a declining coal-mining district, a market town and a rural locality of predominantly agricultural pursuits. Certainly the priorities, the demands of the local councils, public pressures, civic attitudes and the citizen response to planning objectives may be expected to vary when classified by location because of socio-economic differences. Should these political differences which exist between areas be reflected when strategies are being formulated?

Under the present approach, a danger exists that aggregate objectives conceal important local differences which should be taken into account when considering strategic development proposals. For example, the objective of preventing development on high grade agricultural land might be relaxed next to major centres of population, whereas a minor scenic asset next to a concentration of population takes on an additional significance in such circumstances. The Notts–Derby Study implies this spatial variation of objectives with the statement that 'the extent to which the Sub-region is attractive or suitable for urban growth (i.e. has potential) depends upon the weight attached to a number of considerations. . . . The importance of these will vary from place to place and is being considered in preparing the strategy, although it is complicated by the lack of a commonly agreed scale of weighting.'[2]

FLEXIBILITY IN OBJECTIVES

Planners are concerned with resolving conflicts in a complex urban system. The system as it exists today with its many interlocking perspectives is imperfectly understood, and yet objectives are established so that the form of development can be given some meaningful direction and purpose. Further, the system itself is not fixed, determined and static. It will vary into the future with social and technological change, and is also influenced to a substantial extent by the

[1] J. Hillman, 'A long look at London's Plan', *The Guardian*, October 5, 1970.
[2] *Notts–Derby Study*, p. 23.

input which results from the injection of planning strategies. It is a difficult if not impossible task to devise objectives which are at once realistic, meaningful for all segments of the public, and sufficiently precise for direct translation into terms of land development.

Despite these problems, objectives in the Studies are fixed. The alternative strategies have been developed against a common set of objectives in each instance. Instead, alternative sets of objectives or different degrees of emphasis on particular objectives could have been hypothesized. Thus, different objectives towards space standards could have been adopted, or various assumptions made about the role of industrial mobility or the extent of the connection between home and place of work. Reasonable parameters need to be developed, so that a range of feasible opportunities for each characteristic or feature can be considered in the strategies. For example in the Notts–Derby Study, where the first consideration of alternative strategies is concerned with welfare, trend, economic potential and other basic possibilities, these interpretations of the planning function could have been examined in detail as they represent different objective assumptions about the nature of the plan-making process.

OBJECTIVES NOT CONSIDERED

Objectives not considered in the Studies include, for example, the objective of encouraging emigration from declining and sub-standard areas. In the words of Wilson (1965),

> when labour is fully employed in the rest of the country, migration affords an escape from structural unemployment: it may often be more appropriate to assist the migrants by removal grants, assistance with housing, re-training facilities and the like rather than to foster industrial growth in their native areas.... Migration has really done more to relieve structural employment than has the opening of new factories under official schemes for regional development. If this fact is not much emphasized in public statements, the reason may be that it is likely to provoke political resentment in the areas that have lost population.[1]

Illustrative of other possibilities than those offered in the Studies are the objectives which underlie the formulation of the Ontario Regional Development Program. These are of some considerable

[1] T. Wilson, *Planning and Growth*, Macmillan (London), 1965, p. 125.

interest, because the phrasing and content are quite different from their British counterparts. Their relevance for British circumstances might therefore receive some very careful attention. The objectives are:

1. That the vital role of the private sector be recognized, that its contribution to the provincial economy be continuously assessed in view of provincial needs and resources, and that provincial policies be formed to encourage a rational expansion of the private sector.

2. That individuals be encouraged to develop their full capabilities through provision of a climate of expanding social and economic opportunities for each region.

3. That regional and resource policies encourage adequate development of the natural environment while conserving the aesthetic qualities of that environment.

4. That the timing and impact of Ontario's large and expanding public expenditures be effectively planned and co-ordinated to fulfil, in an orderly way, the needs of the regions in the Province as well as of the Province itself.

5. That this be a Program for Regional Development which must necessarily involve a working partnership between all of the people of Ontario and Government.[1]

The vital role of the private sector, the importance of the individual and the significance of citizen participation (items 1, 2 and 5) receive less attention in the British planning Studies, because the prime emphasis has focussed on urban growth, its location and *government* policies to secure their co-ordination, rather than upon government as *one* of several important inputs into the evolving urban situation in its regional dimensions.

OBJECTIVES AS A CONCEPTUAL TOOL

Objectives such as the city-beautiful, the city-efficient, green belts, new towns and improvement to the quality of environment represent long-established planning objectives which have become almost creeds to certain members of the profession. Almost every planning report champions some particular planning philosophy or utopian

[1] Regional Development Branch, Niagara Region, *op. cit.*, pp. 10–11. For a discussion of Canadian experience in participation see N. H. Richardson, 'Participatory democracy and planning', *Journal of the Town Planning Institute*, Vol. 56, 1970, pp. 52–5.

dream to secure its ideal of a better future; optimism is a planning trait. The more recent trend is to conceptualize the planning approach in order to assist with the problem-solving process, so that economic, social, transportation and other objectives are now added to previous 'idealistic' statements about the possibilities of urban achievement. The establishment of objectives, firstly in broad and general terms and then in more precise measured quantities which can be assessed, the design of alternative strategies which meet these requirements, and the selection of that option which performs best against the stated objectives have become central themes in the new planning methodology. Many difficulties still exist, but these do not deny the logic which insists on a more systematic approach to the urban environment than previously. 'Viewed in this manner, planning goals are not merely a list of platitudes to be appended to a plan as a means to justify conclusions of specialists. They are the vital force that determines not only the action proposals but the entire course of inquiry and study. . . . The problem before us is to provide a methodology that will facilitate the establishment of meaningful goals concise enough to act as directives to the rest of the planning process.'[1]

SUMMARY

Goals and objectives are important in the planning process. They have always existed implicitly, but the new technique is their explicit statement and the preparation and testing of alternative strategies against these objectives. Objectives help to define the purpose of planning, but they do not provide the planning solution. They may provide guidance, but do not in themselves indicate the specific action which can be followed. The challenge posed by the need to state objectives neither removes the elements of conflict nor reduces the necessity for planning judgement in reaching a planning decision; it does however provide both a rational means for testing such decisions and an opportunity for public comment at an early stage of the planning process. Difficulties involved in the use of objectives include the need for greater precision and exactness, and the probability that objectives are not all of equal value. The multi-stage formulation of goals and objectives may be desirable but, in their application to different circumstances, conflicts must be resolved. Short- and

[1] R. C. Young, *op. cit.*, p. 79. For a general discussion see N. Lichfield, 'Goals in Planning', *Town and Country Planning Summer School 1968*, Town Planning Institute (London), 1968, pp. 21–7.

long-term issues may be in opposition and, in the trade-off between different objectives established for different purposes, the incidence of the gains and the losses might be critical. It is suggested that objectives might change over space and time, that strategies could be prepared against different sets of objectives, and that other possible objectives could have been considered in the Studies.

Chapter 11
Private Enterprise and Citizen Participation

Certain formative ideas have crossed the Atlantic for inclusion in the British planning process. These include transportation models, mathematical techniques and their expansion into land use models, the powerful impact of Rachel Carson's *Silent Spring*, thought about the impact of the motor car on urbanization including the achievement of regional shopping centres and the pressures for low density suburban living, and some cost–benefit procedures. Other aspects with strong American connotations are that private enterprise and citizen participation each have important roles to play in the planning process. Citizens as members of a community exercise a dual role. They are at the same time both co-operators in a common enterprise, and yet rivals for the material and intangible rewards of successful competition with each other. This chapter is concerned primarily with the former aspect; it will default if it does not refer briefly to the latter consideration.

THE ROLE OF PRIVATE ENTERPRISE

The citizen is both a resident and a voter. He may also be involved in business, trade or commerce and have a substantial role to play in this professional or entrepreneurial capacity. The role of private enterprise in creating a future regional pattern has received little comment in the Studies under review, except implicitly in connecton with the provision of recreational facilities, private housing, industrial and retailing facilities. The emphasis has been very much on the role of public sector investment, and how this may best be expended. But 'of course, not all the goods and services required by society are publicly provided. Indeed, one important question in relation to goals is the extent to which goods and services can be or should be provided through private market mechanisms, and to what extent through public planning.'[1]

Presumably the planning argument would be that the preferred or recommended strategy provides an abundance of opportunity for

[1] A. G. Wilson, *Forecasting Planning*, Centre for Environmental Studies (London), 1969 (CES WP 38), p. 28.

industrial, commercial and other managerial enterprise. Favourable conditions will be created for all aspects of private investment, and the sum total of these innumerable individual and group decisions will then create the emerging urban environment in its Regional or Sub-regional context. Most types of development require some type of joint approach between government and the private sectors of the economy for their successful outcome. One planning objective, as mentioned in Ontario's regional programme for development, could well be 'to encourage private investment' in the Sub-region or Region under review.'

The Teesside study is the exception which comments upon the role of the private sector. The argument is that 'the precise calculation of future capital investment is much less important than the demonstration that a substantial amount of future development will depend upon investment in the private sector. This stresses the need to see the urban structure policy document itself as an incentive and guide for future investment in the private as well as the public sector.... The policy should be a powerful force to influence the size, location and timing of private investment.'[1]

It is sterile to argue whether public finance is more or less beneficial in assisting a regional economy to develop. Neither public projects nor private capital can meet all demands, and both are essential. Indeed, private investment may have greater residual effects, in that it represents entrepreneurial vision, confidence in the locality of investment and the introduction of new managerial and technical skills to the environment; and a new element of social leadership might be involved. Using an analogy from international development, the Lester Pearson Commission has stated 'there can be no doubt about the contribution which private capital can render to economic development. Indeed, dollar for dollar, it may be more effective than official aid both because it is more closely linked to the management and technology which industrial ventures require, and because those who risk their own money may be expected to be particularly interested in its efficient use.'[2] Growth prospects are not just a public responsibility. The role of private enterprise in achieving planning objectives should, like citizen participation, be clearly identified in each Study. Its special contribution is in providing initiative, personal responsibility, management and leadership in the provision of capital for investment purposes.

[1] *Teesside Study*, p. 108.
[2] Commission on International Development (Chairman: Right Honourable L. B. Pearson), *Partners in Development*, 1969.

CITIZEN PARTICIPATION IN THE STUDIES

Not one Study discusses either the role of citizen participation or its contribution in achieving the recommended strategy. It is almost as if planning is regarded purely as a technical and professional subject in which detailed studies and recommendations are produced, rather than an exercise aimed at being the forerunner to the achievement of development strategies. Taking a broader viewpoint, concern may be expressed at the failure of most Studies (a) to involve the public in their preparation and (b) to explain their critical role in the achievement of planning policies. Objectives, as noted in the previous chapter, do not include anything about the role of the individual citizen and the terms of reference also exclude this very necessary ingredient of the planning process. It is essential to devise some form of systematic, consistent and practical procedure whereby planners do not have to make their own judgements on problems, priorities and the relative importance of different criteria, but can find out what society as individuals and collectively wants. The task is certainly not easy, but advances towards the initiation of this process are not made in the Studies.

The purpose of preparing a planning strategy is to achieve action. It is concerned with implementation in the preferred or some other form; otherwise, the problems under review are inconsequential and unworthy of action. This necessity for implementation involves the administrative process with its conflicts, its political realities, its delegated responsibilities and the public reaction to policy issues concerned with their urban future. People and organizations thought to be injured by the proposals will resist, exert their powers, lobby elected representatives, provoke critical comment in the mass media, present alternative possibilities and arguments, and will generally be prepared to press for a change of the strategic policies which are proposed in the Studies. Other groups may offer their support and backing, but public conflict on the pros and cons of each proposal is inevitable – and hence the importance of identifying in a planning balance sheet those sectors of the community likely to gain and lose by each project. The point for emphasis is that it cannot be assumed either that the strategies are perfect, or that ensuing action may be taken for granted. Reports are not self-executing.

Within this context the Teesside Study notes in its final observation on the discussion of planning objectives that 'in the last resort, however, the outward appearance of the Teesside environment will depend on the wish of its citizens to set higher standards of design and

K

289

cleanliness than in the past and on the quality of the professional advice available to them'.[1] In the Notts–Derby Study the recommended strategy is 'put forward for discussion . . . because the opinions and value judgements which have influenced the proposals are matters requiring a consensus of view from society as a whole, over and above the advice of professionals'.[2] The North-Glos Study will 'enable a broad section of the public to consider the issues raised. . . . It is considered that the next stage should combine a full public discussion of the policies embodied in the preferred strategy.'[3] The other Studies do not comment. Also, as far as is known, not one Study included on its policy advisory committee any direct citizen participation, and citizen advisory committees have not been referred to in the Reports.

THE OFFICIAL MECHANISM FOR CITIZEN PARTICIPATION

The official mechanism for public participation is provided by the Town and Country Planning Act 1968, which requires that 'persons who may be expected to desire an opportunity of making representations to the authority about structure or local plans in preparation are given an adequate opportunity of doing so. It is intended in this way that individual members of the public, and local and national bodies with an interest in planning should be able to participate far more in the process of planning than hitherto.'[4] This statutory responsibility has thus been awarded to local planning authorities and not to the wider grouping of joint planning teams which prepared the Studies, and strategic or policy plans are not referred to in this legal enactment. Citizen participation is not required in law at the subregional level of planning procedures.

The prime report concerned with public participation in planning is the Skeffington Committee which reported *after* the Planning Act of 1968, and was again concerned to a large extent with citizen participation in the official machinery of structure plans and local plans. The essential argument is however that planning

affects everyone. People should be able to say what kind of community they want and how it should develop: and should be able to do so in a way that is positive and first hand. It matters to us all

[1] *Teesside Study*, p. 97. [2] *Ibid.*, p. 31.
[3] *North-Glos Study*, Preface and p. 103.
[4] Ministry of Housing and Local Government, *Development Plans: A Manual on Form and Content*, HMSO (London), 1970, p. 9.

that we should know that we can influence the shape of our community so that the towns and villages in which we live, work, learn and relax may reflect our best aspirations. This becomes all the more vital where the demands of a complex society occasion massive changes; changes which in some areas may completely alter the character of a town, a neighbourhood or a rural area. The pace, intensity and scale of change will inevitably bring bewilderment and frustration if people affected think it is to be imposed without respect for their views.[1]

These comments are general, but may be taken to imply all levels of the planning process including that of strategy formulation. Strategic plans, which are necessarily concerned with the achievement of 'massive changes' in the environment, are particularly important. The danger is that, if the public is excluded until the preparation of structure plans then, as Skeffington argues, 'the public will inevitably receive the impression that proposals are almost cut and dried . . . those who have prepared the plan are deeply committed to it. There is a strong disinclination to alter proposals which have been taken so far.'[2] This type of comment is most valid for the Studies under review, with their inter-weaving of many different considerations at the initial stages of projection and forecasting and throughout all subsequent stages of analysis until a recommended strategy has been chosen. At the final stage of a selected option, it is too late to amend a detail or to change a development proposal without changing the whole sequence and purport of the planning analysis. Thus, in the words of the Notts–Derby commitment, 'the individual proposals in the strategy are closely interrelated, particularly with regard to the location of employment, population and investment in roads and services and any decision (by government or the local planning authorities) to modify one would have implications on *some* of the others. Both in the immediate future *and* in the longer term, it will be necessary to consider the *strategy as a whole* if individual proposals are not acceptable or not implemented.'[3] This statement very much implies a *fait accompli* situation.

It may be too late to remedy this feeling of cut and dried proposals after alternative possibilities have been considered, with some rejected and a recommended strategy put forward for public reaction. This recommended strategy is itself in a sophisticated form, with a

[1] Ministry of Housing and Local Government, *People and Planning: Report of the Committee on Public Participation in Planning* (Chairman: A. M. Skeffington), HMSO (London), 1969, p. 3.
[2] *Ibid.*, p. 3.   [3] *Notts–Derby Study*, p. 32. Author's emphasis.

close degree of integration and inner cohesion between its several parts. It cannot easily be amended, without again going through the whole planning sequence of testing procedures. Citizens may well feel frustrated when such a complete and apparently unalterable study is presented for consideration, unless they have been involved intimately at all stages of its preparation. The recommended strategy gains considerable credence if the authorities concerned with its preparation can demonstrate conclusively that the conclusions rest on a public consensus of opinion. There are also likely to be fewer delays between the formulation of strategies and the preparation of structure plans (and indeed their then approval by Central Government) if public support can be demonstrated.

Planning strategies have been presented in the form of large packages of interrelated commodities. Everyone would agree that the package is subject to public scrutiny but it would also be both more efficient in time and cost, and wiser as an object lesson in participation, if the underlying assumptions are disclosed and examined for their degree of public acceptance and reliability. In the words of the American Regional Plan Association, 'the function of public participation in regional planning is to uncover the assumptions lying behind the planning recommendations in order to (1) weigh the values in conflict and (2) identify forgotten factors. The process is to inform the participants as fully as possible about the issues, identifying the conflicts in values as clearly as possible.'[1]

This discussion has referred to the Studies, but the same approach should be followed if the use of the planning balance sheet is to become more prevalent. Extensive consumer research could be undertaken, to ascertain both the instrumental objectives and the relative attachment to each by the various sectors of the community. Thus land-owners, farmers, industrialists, the occupants of commercial premises, residents, vehicle users, etc. would be surveyed for their attitudes *before* the balance sheet is prepared. Reliance would then not be on 'personal judgement', 'qualitative assumptions', 'readily available information' and the 'opinion of the team'. Direct information from the various sectors would provide additional confidence to the balance sheet, and reduce the assumptions on which it is based.

THE SCOPE FOR CITIZEN PARTICIPATION

The most critical areas where citizen involvement should have been

[1] W. B. Shore and J. P. Keith, *Public Participation in Regional Planning*, Regional Plan Association (New York), 1967, p. 15.

included are in connection with the establishment of objectives, in the study of behavioural patterns and attitudes, when assessing quality, in applying relative weights to alternative possibilities, and throughout the survey and analysis stages generally of the planning process. For instance, the important role of objectives and how these have been derived from the surveys of existing conditions by the planners has been noted. The approach in the South Hampshire Plan has established that objectives *can* be tested for the public response (a) to their validity and (b) to establish their relative weighting and importance. When the planning decision has to be made between competing objectives, this knowledge of consumer reaction is imperative. Otherwise, planners can all too easily impose their own preselected and predetermined ideas on the community.

The Skeffington Committee would not agree with this point. They state that,

> we have been urged to recommend that the public should be involved from the start in the establishment of the broad aims or goals that the community wish to see achieved. We doubt the necessity for that in this country. . . . There shall be an examination of the needs of the community, such as housing, employment, recreation and the means of communication, and a proper provision worked out for them. . . . In the context of British planning these aims are implicit and accepted; it is the attainable objectives specific to the plan itself, the policies and alternative ways of achieving them that need to be debated.[1]

Strong disagreement can be voiced at this distinction; the broad aims and goals that the community wish to achieve are *not* implicit and accepted. As Lomas notes in his prize paper at the 1970 Town and Country Planning School,

> if it were the case that all the goals are implicit and accepted there would be little gain in encouraging public intervention in a planning process which aims to satisfy these aspirations. The political theorist Isaiah Berlin makes this point when he says: 'where ends are agreed, the only questions left are those of means, and these are not political but technical, that is to say, capable of being settled by experts or machines like arguments between engineers or doctors.' This is no mere academic disputation. Goals are only out of reach of argument

[1] Skeffington Report, *op. cit.*, p. 24. See also para. 36 where it is again stated that 'once the general strategy has been determined', the views of the public may be sought.

when cloaked in the euphemisms of planning reports. In the context of scarce resources and competing ends, there is surely scope for debate.[1]

It is necessary to emphasize firmly that citizens should never be excluded from this, the most fundamental and introductory section of the planning thought processes.

Value judgements have been referred to on many occasions throughout the previous chapters, for example in relation to such quite disparate objects as the quality of the physical environment or the relevance of distance in the shopping journey or in determining the modal split for each type of journey between public transport and the private vehicle. Such topics are quite amenable to public discussion, and public attitudes and preferences can be determined. Planners now spend so much time putting information into models, and in reaching their own evaluative judgements that the tendency is to forget that every underlying assumption can (and should) be examined by field studies, including social surveys. The point is not new;[2] it was made continually by Patrick Geddes[3] and is reiterated in standard planning texts. Lomas may, however, again be quoted. 'It should be in the surveying process that a planner comes to understand the goals and values of the people in the area he is concerned with. Skeffington argues that public mistrust of planning arises because development proposals are only made known when it is too late to criticize them. But if planning surveys had been on the right wavelength there would be much less cause for criticism. . . . It is a matter of pounding the pavements, armed with appropriate survey questionnaires, and backed by adequate training.'[4] A simple but necessary point is that expenditure on shoe leather provides the essential preliminary to computer analysis. Study of the existing environment, its problems and its opportunities, provides the foundation stone for every planning exercise. It is immaterial whether it is strategic, structure or detailed planning; the public *must* be involved in those subjects where they can contribute to the technical process of planning.

[1] G. M. Lomas, 'The contribution of the Skeffington Report to the discussion on citizen participation in planning', *Town and Country Planning Summer School 1970*, The Town Planning Institute (London), 1970, p. 19. The quotation is I. Berlin, *Two Concepts of Liberty* (Oxford), 1968, An Inaugural Lecture for the Chichele Chair of Social and Political Theory.

[2] For example, a chapter on social surveys is included in J. N. Jackson, *Surveys for Town and Country Planning*, Hutchinson University Library (London), 1961.

[3] P. Geddes, *Cities in Evolution*, Norgate and Norgate (London), 1915.

[4] G. M. Lomas, *op. cit.*, p. 20.

It may be argued in opposition to these arguments for constructive citizen involvement that strategic plans are complex, on the far distant horizon and lack the immediacy of popular appeal. The public will only wish to be involved when the issues are limited to familiar objects and when they can appreciate the results in real terms and the consequences in terms of their own immediate understanding. This type of comment may be true at the level of detailed design, but it also infers that only measurable objects can be assessed by public opinion. Surely the basic fundamental attitudes to life, and the preferences of the public for different types of environment, and the willingness or otherwise to forego certain advantages for other pleasures, should be ascertained. The planning alternatives are not just whether site 'A' or site 'B' should be developed and the respective advantages and disadvantages, but also with the prior issue of whether that development is required anyway by the public generally and/or by the public which are specifically involved.

A preferable form of argument is that the sheer complexity of planning analysis makes *continuing* citizen participation an imperative ingredient of *every* planning study at three stages. These are (1) throughout the exercise, (2) at the date of publication and (3) subsequently as an integral part of the implementation procedures. Given the increasing degree of sophistication in analysis to which reference has been made on several occasions over the previous pages, the ubiquitous use of the computer, the development of models to facilitate an understanding of meaningful relationships between phenomena and mathematical techniques of forecasting, it becomes critical that the increasing wisdom, experience and familiarity of planners with new techniques be translated into comprehensible terms for public discussion. The danger, otherwise, is that professional expertise, technology and know-how will separate the planner and the planned. If planning becomes some remote statistical exercise, a mutual dialogue will become more difficult, if not tenuous and impossible. It is certain that the underlying assumptions must always be clearly stated in every Study, as one vital contribution towards resolving this dilemma of the essential need for public understanding. Mathematical formulae may not be understood by the public, but this need not interfere with public appreciation of their content, provided the nature of the input and the sequence of argument is stated clearly in technical appendices for public examination of the findings. Planning techniques for *understanding* complex issues must not advance beyond the profession's ability of public communication.

The tenor of much preceding comment and discussion is that an

295

undercurrent of assumption and intuition must underly the formulation of a long-term strategy for development. Various degrees of uncertainty permeate the apparently sophisticated techniques of analysis. Many such assumptions have been referred to over the previous pages, including such items as where the line should be drawn in safeguarding agricultural land, a cherished scenic resource or superficial deposits of sand and gravel. Population, employment, housing and traffic patterns are studied in terms of their past trends and projected possibilities, and suggestions have been made as to which elements of the natural backcloth are of greater importance than others. Assumptions have necessarily had to be made, and a choice determined between alternative possibilities.

The point for continual emphasis is that many of the judgements in each Report must depend upon the professional discretion of the planners involved. This may be clear from the text and is inevitable, given the complexity of man's urban and regional environments. There can be no overall agreed scale of evaluation between the relative importance of differing elements, because of the very fact that many different social groups exist in society. Qualitative judgements cannot be avoided, and it is this recognized degree of uncertainty in the planning process that provides one compelling justification for citizen participation. The Studies have indeed been published for this very purpose. Their concern is with providing a basis for public discussion, and a basis for action by elected representatives. But how this delicate task is to be achieved, given both the technical complexity of the analytical arguments on which each Study depends for its competence and the great degree of interdependence of the several proposals, is not explained in any Report. A statement about the role of citizen participation and how this might be encouraged is an important aspect of strategy implementation, which always deserves specific consideration. The issue is so important and public acceptance so critical for the achievement of policy, that this matter *cannot* be left to elected members and officials. These views are the opposite to those expressed in one Study where the Director has stated, 'it was not possible to recruit to a temporary study team sufficient planners of a type who, by wide experience, could divine what the consensus of public opinion would be on any major issue. The chief planning officers (of the four authorities sponsoring our work), therefore, provided an invaluable first test of political and public acceptability.'[1]

[1] A. Thorburn, 'Preparing a regional plan: how we set about the task in Nottinghamshire/Derbyshire', *Journal of the Town Planning Institute*, Vol. 57, 1971, p. 216.

This consensus of public opinion can only be obtained, and even then with considerable doubts and difficulties, from detailed studies. It is very much doubted that this information is known to chief officers, because their concern is with the technical feasibility and practicality of proposals.

In making these several arguments it is appreciated that, in one sense, the Studies have already contributed to the delicate task of citizen participation by the fact of publication. By implication planning is not a secret process; it is open for public inspection and, at worst, public information is desirable. Commendable efforts have also been made to write and present complex material so that it may be appreciated and understood by a wide section of the public. Particularly welcome is the North-Glos statement that their Report 'is intentionally written in general terms so as to enable a broad section of the public to *consider* the issues raised, and to *take part in* the processes which will eventually establish the basis for planning the future development of North Gloucestershire.'[1] In addition, the public should take part in *all* the previous processes, including the establishment of the basic objectives with which planning is concerned.

The above comments dissent from the statutory attitudes and would *encourage* citizen participation at the strategic levels of planning. It is maintained that this preferred approach would have strengthened the value of those conclusions which arise from the Studies. It would strengthen materially the planning demands for action and the need to allocate increasing resources to the resolution of urban, environmental and regional problems. It would provide a valuable check on underlying planning objectives and would have contributed towards measuring the acceptability or otherwise of value judgements which have been made on behalf of the public. Weightings associated with intangible aspects of life such as the quality of environment, its aesthetic attributes, its convenience, its accessibility and its degree of public acceptance would have gained from full public involvement. An ever-present danger in the planning process is that most planners have been trained in Universities and have professional ideals. They tend to express middle-class attitudes through either their education, home background or office experience. Social goals are critical because the total time stream of costs and benefits must be summed up in some fashion and the abandonment of conflicting goals appraised, if the concept of 'a better place to live' is to have any substance. 'The critical policy question is not only how

[1] *North-Glos Study*, Preface. Author's emphasis.

much the community is prepared to give up to realize the goals implicit in the master plan, but *who* gives up *how* much so that the fruits of the plan can be realized – quite frequently by others.'[1]

Planning seeks to replace speculation and the market forces of society with some form of conscious and rational determination of the community's welfare, i.e. 'the custodial view of the community's future that dominates the current perspective of city planning'[2] and which has been demonstrated clearly over the previous pages. The attempt is to replace or supplement one series of forces, with a different series of motivations. Public participation would seem to be the means whereby these new values can be tested for their worth, against the 'evil' monetary forces of private gain, speculation and laissez-faire.

The studies have also been concerned with many forceful expressions of discontent with the urban situation – obsolescence, traffic congestion, overcrowding, squalor, the decline of inner areas, the shortage of land, limited recreational space. But now there arises an important dichotomy from the standpoint of citizen reactions. A striking disparity exists between the abundant literature of protest and criticism, and the lethargy of many citizens because they can move away from the worst areas, purchase more pleasant living space, pay for transportation and enjoy leisure pursuits in different environments. As incomes rise, the dissatisfactions with urban life decrease and its satisfactions in terms of its possibilities increase. There are different degrees of stress, different opportunities and different needs arising from the variety of urban groups. In the words of Duhl (1963)

the ecological world of some human beings cannot be contained within a physically or geographically defined community: they use the physical environment as a resource in contrast with the lower socio-economic groups who incorporate the environment into the self. . . . Communication and transportation have become very important for the group whose ecological world has become so broad. For others the world is quite small, and most often it is a world of slums. . . . My concern is with the needs of the individual, the family, and various significant groups and institutions within this large ecological system. . . . The impact of the planners' manipulations of space falls most heavily on the lower socio-economic

[1] L. Wingo, 'Urban Space in a Policy Perspective: An Introduction', in L. Wingo (ed.), *Cities and Space: The Future Use of Urban Land Resources for the Future*, Johns Hopkins (Baltimore), 1963, p. 5.
[2] *Ibid.*, p. 6.

groups. Their rights to their aspirations and the satisfaction of their needs require a new dimension of physical planning.[1]

Have the Studies attained this new dimension? Do the proposals reflect the needs of *all* groups in society, or is there a bias in one or other direction? Are the sectors of the community and their objectives as described on a development balance sheet indicative of *all* the costs and benefits of a given scheme? Should there be a weighting in favour of schemes which contribute more benefits to particular groups? Such questions, in the present inadequate state of our urban knowledge, can only be put to the public for their response.

SOME DIFFICULTIES OVER CITIZEN PARTICIPATION[2]

There is a three-cornered tussle (at least of personal conscience) in any public participation exercise. The contestants are the councillors as elected representatives of the public, the officials as experts knowledgeable in the topics under examination, and the public who are affected by the decisions which are made. In the words of Hampton (1971), 'there is a great deal of scepticism: councillors find it difficult to envisage institutions with influence rather than power; and officers resist incursions into their professional sphere. . . . Those who participate as councillors, officers, social workers, or general public (and as business men or members of interest groups) often pursue separate and incompatible objectives: some are bound to be disappointed.'[3] In the meantime the need for mutual understanding becomes greater as the units which establish policy grow larger, the techniques of planning survey more complex and divorced from public understanding, and the decisions more pervading and emphatic on people's lives. The difficulties of citizen participation are great, but the dangers of technocratic dominance are even greater. The root issue is that a planning strategy is not just a physical statement of possibilities, but a highly-charged political document which may critically affect people's lives.

It must be admitted that there are certain instances where citizen participation will prove to be an impossible ideal. Very few people

[1] L. J. Duhl, 'The Human Measure: Man and Family in Megalopolis', in *ibid.*, pp. 137–8.

[2] For a useful discussion see J. B. Cullingworth, *Town and Country Planning in England and Wales*, George Allen and Unwin (London), 1970, third edition, Chapter XIII and 'Public Participation', *Journal of the Town Planning Institute*, Vol. 57, 1971, pp. 167–82.

[3] W. Hampton, 'Little Men in Big Societies', *Journal of the Town Planning Institute*, 1971, Vol. 57, p. 168.

want a motorway through their front garden or wish to have their house value diminished by a noise nuisance from a nearby airport. There is always the problem, e.g. in feasibility studies for large-scale growth, that the priorities of a resident population will be quite different from the priorities of immigrant groups to be attracted to the growth locality and that certain 'sacrifices' may be necessary in relation to what these priorities might be. The designation of New Town and overspill sites for urban expansion have often been contested strongly by the existing community, and the endemic conflict between conflicting rural and urban interests is bound to occur on many future occasions. A veil of secrecy may also be necessary in the preparation of planning studies, so that advance knowledge will not be used to vitiate the planning proposals. It would be both naive and misleading to even think that all planning issues can be resolved by the mechanism of citizen participation. People likely to be adversely affected are unlikely to participate in the decision, but they may be encouraged to influence its form or detail after the basic decision has been taken.

One important question is whether people, generally, can be expected to appreciate a total regional strategy, or whether the only concern is with the parts thereof and the personal disadvantages which might result. This is a serious dilemma which is posed at many public enquiries. The local planning authority are concerned with strategy and policy; the objectors with the detailed incidence of the proposals. Prior public discussion and involvement will not remove the irksome nature of planning controls to the aggrieved applicant, or the distaste for the public acquistion of a cherished property, or the presumption of diminished land values if an overspill scheme is approved. In the words of Walker and Rigby (1971) based on experience in the Rhondda Valleys, 'meaningful participation may be difficult to achieve at structure plan level, as most people have a limited interest in general issues. There will always be a tendency to particularize the discussion because people are most concerned about the local impact of planning policies.'[1] Or, as the General Manager of Peterborough Development Corporation has stated, 'nor have our efforts evoked much response by way of constructive comment on draft proposals. My personal conclusion is that public participation in plan-making in this sense and in our kind of context is a costly and largely fruitless exercise. It is far more important in my view, for us to be accessible and approachable, to give whenever it is sought, and in

[1] G. Walker and A. G. Rigby, 'Public Participation in the Rhondda Valleys', *Journal of the Town Planning Institute*, Vol. 57, 1971, pp. 159–60.

anticipation of it being sought, the fullest and best information we can.'[1]

There are difficult questions about the role of pressure or interest groups, and whether any special importance should be attached to their presentations. The point here is that the motives for private development are financial, whereas the determination of a change in use is a public decision. To be specific, should the strategy proposals for new shopping centres and changes to the existing situation be discussed with retailing interests? Should the extent of mineral-bearing land be discussed with mining and quarrying interests? In each instance, an extensive array of background information is required and numerous assumptions are necessary to permit the formulation of policy. It is therefore reasonable to argue that the evidence and the reasons for reaching a decision should be discussed with representatives from the groups concerned, provided that the final discretion for the policy decision (which should anyway be explained in the Final Report for public examination) remains with the Planning Team. It would seem that the more effectively public and private interest groups can be involved in the stage of formulating alternative strategies, the more likely is this to be reflected in both increasing accuracy and acceptability of the Study. The evaluation between alternative possibilities will take on a wider perspective.

A difficulty now is that of mediocrity, and the dismissal of all ideas and possibilities which are innovatory, enlightened or otherwise distinctive and unconventional. Compromise may become inevitable, so that only the most innocuous of proposals receive full consideration. This danger, however, also exists without consultation, because not all planners have either visionary insight or knowledge about unusual technical possibilities, and a typical accusation against planners is their lack of imagination when formulating future proposals. Innovation can be impeded by involvement, but involvement may also yield imaginative new concepts and new opportunities. The general need is for the planning team always to retain control of the situation, and for ideas to be received rather than to allow every forceful expression of opinion to sway the decision-making process. More important again is the need to appoint planning teams where the senior personnel have creative and fertile powers of visual and objective imagination. This requirement of gifted and capable appointments may in its turn depend on the quality and the degree of vigour in the commissioning authorities. A further safeguard is the

[1] Wyndham Thomas, 'New Town Management', *Town and Country Planning Association Conference* (New Towns in the Present and Future), 1970.

need to consult with a variety of different interest groups, and thus to ensure that several different and conflicting suggestions are received. It remains a prime planning task to interpret and elucidate between all information and advice that is acquired.

Citizen participation to be effective must be organized, and how to ensure a 'representative' cross-section or range of opinion poses several difficult problems. A strong, and large, citizens' advisory committee would seem a useful adjunct in many regional planning exercises. This would meet only occasionally, but if it has members nominated from an extensive range of industrial, business and social groups, the committee should provide the opportunity (a) for the receipt of ideas from various interest groups in the region under surveillance and (b) for full explanations of progress to be given by the planning team for feedback through members to their own organizations. A two-way process involving the exchange of information and ideas is thus initiated, but caution is also necessary against the simple fact that council members are elected into office by members of the public.

A citizens' advisory committee is not representative of public opinion, nor is it elected publicly, nor are its members responsible to the electorate. Elected officers and officials have the responsibility of interpreting the common good, of acting as guardians of the public interest and of providing political leadership for the community. In the words of Ash (1970) reviewing an extensive participation exercise in Los Angeles,

as the goals council report did not have any muscle, its conclusions did not cause dissension. But the earlier campaign revealed the conflict between the city council, elected by the public, and public participation, which excluded the council. . . . The committee had to withdraw its publication, which criticized the structure of municipal government in Los Angeles and complained of the undisclosed pressures of powerful special interests. As a result the planners determined to work more closely with the elected representatives, and bring them into all public discussions on planning.[1]

In this instance, to illustrate the point that citizen participation can be over-played, four alternative structural plans were prepared and 'the goals programme sought to elicit goals from the public. . . . [It] was intended to select the concept which would most nearly

[1] Joan Ash, 'Participation in Los Angeles: planning with people', *Official Architecture and Planning*, 1970, p. 1070.

fulfil the agreed goals.'[1] There were specialist committees, including an inter-religious committee which set up a series of centres for discussion manned by a volunteer corps who were trained, given filmstrips, display panels and discussion pamphlets. A goals council was set up representing the major municipal authorities, and short questionnaires were sent out to 1 in 4 telephone subscribers. 'The Banner Day celebration in June 1967 kicked-off this goals programme with a banner parade, bands and bagpipes; the director of planning delivered a pantomimed speech accompanied by clowns carrying placards containing the gist of the speech.'[2] Although the vision of certain English chief officers in this role is enticing (and is certain to secure the full attention of the public media), a spectacle of this type can hardly be envisaged in the British context. Even so, five conclusions presented in this paper are of direct relevance to the preparation of regional and sub-regional strategies in Britain. These are that:[3]

1. public participation cannot be a substitute for good planning, but good planning must take the needs of the public into account;
2. goals can be agreed, even though citizens and organized interests may differ profoundly about the means by which they should be implemented;
3. public participation in metropolitan planning should consult organized interests and independent citizens' groups about the draft plan and the decisions which concern them;
4. democracy can be strengthened by carefully considered public participation, but its ultimate test is whether its representative institutions are capable of taking effective action to serve the interests of the people;
5. public participation in planning is worth while if it enables planners to gain insights into the needs and the demands of the various sections of the public, and if it enables members of the public to appreciate the issues in planning and take a more active part in civic life.

As with all methodological procedures, citizen participation in the process both of strategy formulation and selection between alternative options raises difficult and contentious issues. It is costly and time consuming, but it is not an aspect to be lightly discarded in favour of full professional interpretation. In the words of Cullingworth (1970), 'an approach to planning which welcomes and encourages citizen participation is a good thing in itself. . . . If

[1] *Ibid.*, p. 1067. [2] *Ibid.*, p. 1068. [3] *Ibid.*, p. 1070.

democratic planning is to cope with the mounting problems of a complex industrial and land-hungry society, it is essential that the public image of the planners should be improved. There is, of course, a definite limit to which "government by participation" can replace "government by consent", but an authority which can take the public into its confidence and enlist its support will thereby become a more effective planning agency.'[1]

SUMMARY

The Studies do not demonstrate clearly how either private enterprise or citizen participation might contribute to the achievement of recommended strategies, yet each are vital to success. Public sector and private sector investment both have substantial roles to play in assisting a regional economy to develop along preferred lines, and neither can proceed far without the other. Citizen participation, though not required statutorily in the Regional and Sub-regional Studies, is nevertheless essential because their underlying purpose is to achieve action. The strategies are prepared on behalf of the public and the people who are affected, favourably and unfavourably, are members of the public. The planning process is complex, but need not be remote from public appreciation. Its methods, its arguments, its assumptions, its value judgements and its basic objectives should be subject to public scrutiny. Otherwise a considerable danger exists that planning strategies will be regarded as unalterable. An all-or-nothing approach is not conducive to public support. Finally there is always the danger that the attitudes, beliefs and assumptions of the planners are different from those of the society for which he is planning. The advocacy is for citizen participation as an essential ingredient of all planning studies. Certain difficulties are admitted, but their resolution is necessary. Citizen participation will strengthen greatly the planning conclusions and assist materially towards implementation.

[1] Cullingworth, *op. cit.*, p. 327.

Part 4

CONCLUSIONS

'We have as yet no authoritative example of a Regional Plan, Mark 1965. . . . We have yet to formulate the model for contemporary regional plans in this country.'

N. Lichfield, Inaugural Conference on Regional Studies, *Regional Studies*, Vol. 1, 1967, pp. 12 and 14.

Chapter 12

The Urban Future: A Choice Between Alternatives

The previous chapters have dissected and interpreted the approach and planning ideas of the Studies under review in terms of their forecasts, their provision for particular land using activities and their use of certain methodological procedures such as the formulation of objectives. These elements are now recombined to provide both conclusions and summary for this text. The relevance of Regional and Sub-regional Studies is first re-examined, and the processes involved in the preparation and testing of alternative strategies are then discussed in general terms. The various stages in this dual process are presented more in the form of ideas and opinions than as a definitive statement. The attempt is at a synthesis of advice and opinion derived from the Studies and the previous commentary. The purpose is neither to persuade nor to convince the reader, but to open up thoughts for further discussion and examination.

THE PURPOSE AND CONTRIBUTION OF THE STUDIES

Sub-regional and regional planning exist as new ventures in British planning. The approach in the Studies must be to urban and rural localities as equal partners in the development process. Problems and issues can no longer be isolated and confined to distinct administrative localities. Co-operation and collaboration between different units and levels of government have become essential prerequisites for action. Comprehensive studies are necessary to review in an integrated manner a whole range of physical, economic and social factors, which together create the urban and regional environments of present concern. Their purpose is to provide a guiding strategic policy as a basis for public and private actions in conditions of future uncertainty.

The basic underlying expectation in all Studies is that of 'sustained growth'. In the words of the Warwickshire Study, 'the sub-region's economic and social well-being depends upon it very considerably; it is a consequence of the country's choice to increase its population and its economic growth'.[1] It is also, in a wider perspective, part of that worldwide aggrandizement of the urban environment which is

[1] *Warwickshire Study*, p. 7.

307

causing concern to most if not all nations – but neither argument means that growth always and everywhere should be encouraged. Also where growth takes place, its form and its condition, is the responsibility of society. With L. Reissman, 'I would emphasize only that the city must be considered as a human invention; one very much like society itself, that man has evolved to organize his existence. . . . The city is still an imperfect product physically and socially. . . . But there is little chance for a perfect solution; the economics of avarice, the politics of ignorance, make the perfect city only a utopia.'[1] The Studies attempt an approach to this 'perfect' future on the basis of rational and logical argument.

In terms of their methodological contribution, there has been continuing improvement in the skills of planning and a steady learning process from the experience of previous exercises as a contribution towards urban improvement. The Town and Country Planning Act 1947 ushered in the concept of development plans, and the pressures of traffic movement and congestion brought in transportation–land use studies for the conurbations. Whether for land use planning or for transportation planning, each type of study requires the forecasting of land use, an estimation of future traffic flows and the appraisal of a broadening array of socio-economic data to provide the necessary foundation for realistic future proposals. Intervention in the affairs of the environment has relied increasingly on systematic procedures, rather than hunch or premonition. Hypotheses have been established, tested and accepted, amended or discarded as a process of gradual improvement to the planning method.

This cumulative accretion of knowledge and the improved techniques of analysis are brought together in the planning Studies under review, which express the climax of the technical skills and expertise at their date of preparation. As the Studies have themselves explored new possibilities, they each contribute towards further advances in methodology. Each has improved, in its versatility and professional competence, on the foundations which have been laid previously. This progressive increase in accomplishment, and the attainment of new standards, is the hall-mark of professional progress and is recognized as follows in the Warwickshire Study. 'The Teesside Survey and Plan crystallized several new planning techniques and consolidated many others which had emerged since the 1950s to deal with specific planning problems. . . . The Leicester–Leicestershire Study was concerned with broader principles than the Teesside

[1] L. Reissman, *The Urban Process: Cities in Industrial Societies*, Macmillan Free Press (New York), 1970 (first published 1964), pp. 9 and 10.

Plan, but developed further many of its techniques, and in particular introduced a more intensive analysis of the alternatives open for the growth of the sub-region. . . . The Notts–Derby Study introduced a systematic analysis of potential for development . . . and developed a strategy after a progressive refinement of the strategic possibilities.'[1] Warwickshire's conceptual advance, in their own words, is to 'concentrate on system and logic to ensure that the sum of the parts of the Study was as sound as the parts might be separately'.[2]

It is opportune, therefore, for this text to consider these recent advances in planning skills and their ability to understand and project the characteristics and condition of the urban environment. This justification is increased by the fact that local planning authorities are required to prepare structure or policy plans under the new legislation of the Town and Country Planning Act 1968, and that joint presentations by two or more adjacent authorities are also encouraged by this legislation. The Studies under review may therefore be expected to provide the curtain-raiser for planning procedures and methodology during the 1970s. Their essential feature is ideas. In particular a continuing and long ranging debate may be expected on a critical aspect of these Studies, namely the means whereby alternative strategies are conceived, the validity of these procedures and the testing process whereby the 'best' strategy is presented as a reliable basis for public action.

THE RANGE OF ALTERNATIVES

Decisions made during the preparation of alternative schemes will affect the range of difference between the alternatives. For example, physical constraints are deemed to prevent the use of certain types of land for major development projects, but the range of such factors, the definitions which are used and the extent to which a constraint can be lifted vary from Study to Study. Projections are developed in the form of a consistent series, so the strategies do *not* consider variations in the amount of population movement extending from a large-scale influx to substantial emigration, or even a range of possibilities within the context of substantial growth. Sometimes the range of variables for initial consideration are restricted to one factor such as basic employment, or they may include a variety of industrial policies or public transportation systems. Thus preferences between alternatives begin to emerge before the formal stages of evaluation, based on the value judgements and the professional interpretations of the

[1] *Warwickshire Study*, p. 23.   [2] *Ibid.*, p. 23.

planners involved. It could also be that the administrative arrange-ments for the conduct of the study have influenced the consideration of alternatives, and even apparently precise and objective statements will frequently include a subjective element. A feature so apparently free from subjective treatment as floodland or high quality agricul-tural land will vary both in definition and in the interpretation of its significance, so that its impact on development does not receive the same objective and consistent treatment in all localities.

It is certain that a wider spectrum of alternatives should be con-sidered, with the elements as numerous and as different in value as can be handled by the processing techniques. The city of the future may be envisaged in a variety of concentrated forms, and expanding in various directions and at various densities, and in part relying upon dispersal to new towns, new localities and the creation of new independent centres. It may be desirable to visualize both the city-region assuming complete motorization, and various forms of development in close relationship with rapid transport systems. There are many distinct and different possibilities for industrial and commercial location, for recreational developments and housing provision, and these should be explored for the advantages and the opportunities which they offer. The technological prospects of change are considerable, socio-economic change might be radical, and the political and organizational possibilities are numerous. To use Denis Gabor's phrase, the future must be *invented*, not against one variable but in terms of situations in which several interrelated components interlock and function together as a series of mutual responses and counter-responses.

The selection of a range of alternatives may be based, initially, on a wide variety of opinions obtained from a great diversity of sources. Ideas must be listed and their potentials recognized, but each must then be quantified and elaborated in detail so that the alternatives can be evaluated systematically against chosen criteria. A broad ranging kaleidoscope of imaginative ideas should be received and studied for their possible relevance, and citizen participation should here be encouraged. The public media should be used to invite thoughts, ideas and expressions of opinion from a broad range of the population. A fruitful approach might also be to receive informed judgements from 'brainstorming' sessions with professional organ-izations, business groups, social clubs, extra-mural classes, trade unions and university audiences. Many ideas should be received, tested and examined for their relevance.

When reliance is placed on objectives to underpin the whole

planning process, one difficulty is the tacit assumption that those formulated in the social and technological circumstances of today will remain representative of the future. 'The particular danger in the area of social technology is the conscious or unconscious selection of goals which are representative for the present and not for the future – the problem of the "perpetual present" or of "timeless time"... The problem is to break out of the extended present, the "logical future", and to select the best feasible anticipation in order to make it a "willed future".'[1] The concern must be with the future as an interpretation from the present, rather than as its mirrored extension. It must be an *envisaged*, rather than a projected future. Otherwise the danger exists that the planning exercise becomes a self-fulfilling prophecy. Forecasts suggest a particular magnitude of development, the strategies indicate a preferred location, public and private investment decisions are related to these proposals, and other possibilities are excluded by local planning policy with government, ministerial and professional support. The trigger of approval can set off a volley of decisions in the same direction, but is the aim necessarily at the right target? The clear formulation of an objective can be advantageous or inhibitive of other possibilities, but in either instance, it is not something which should be fixed and unalterable.

The danger in anticipating the future is that an excessive reliance will be placed on existing trends and that there will be an overdependence on linear projections. The need is more to *design* an urban future in its regional setting. The alternatives presented in the Studies are almost too similar, too close to each other and too close to existing conditions. They tend to express the timelessness referred to above, i.e. a little more but with the same mix and the same ingredients as today. Masser (1970) makes the point that 'wherever uncertainty is involved, the existing distribution of population and employment is *more* credible than any of the other possibilities. Consequently, it may be necessary to assess the extent to which the winning plan ... was the one which departed *least* from existing distributions of population and employment.'[2] Within this context, a longer time span for broad and generalized planning appreciation should assist towards developing new possibilities, and favour a more discerning approach to those many subtle changes which are possible in future urban environments. Plans which retain a strong physical

[1] E. Jantsch, *Technological Forecasting in Perspective*, Organisation for Economic Cooperation and Development (Paris), 1967, p. 93.
[2] I. Masser, 'Methods of Sub-regional Analysis,' *Town Planning Review*, 1970, Vol. 41, p. 159. Author's emphasis.

emphasis on land use and transportation can be extended still further into the future to include more social and economic variants, and more possibilities of change can be visualized.

THE DETAILING OF ALTERNATIVES

The number of alternatives which can be formulated and tested depends upon the funds which are available, the access to and cost of computer facilities, staff resources of trained talent in this new and expanding field, the time schedule for the work and the extent of external assistance from government and the commissioning authorities. The data input for models is substantial, and may have to be collected as a special exercise by the Study team or be re-organized from existing sources of information; in either instance, a time-consuming commitment occurs and many American studies have not completed even their assigned tasks because of these difficulties.

Important and often neglected aspects of improved statistical handling and the application of complex models are the associated doubts and mistrust, both within and beyond the boundaries of the planning profession. The point made by Boyce and Day (1969) is important. 'The experience of the past few years also indicates that the growing understanding of metropolitan processes on the part of professional planners outstrips their ability to communicate this understanding effectively to public officials or to the general public. This situation has clear implications for evaluation methods and public participation. The decision process too often appears to have been a matter of sophisticated analysis versus blunt political or subjective reaction.'[1] A critical aspect of model construction and handling statistics is the ability to convince people (including decision-makers) that the work undertaken is sound and constructive. This requires summary presentations in a language that can be understood.

Although certain detail in the Studies may be criticized, and although inadequacies have been noted under each of the following headings, the alternatives which have been developed are generally:

1. realistic, i.e. capable of achievement;

2. comprehensive, i.e. interrelate transportation and land use, and physical, economic and social planning;

3. extensive, i.e. cover the whole region or sub-region in their proposals at one or other level of generalization;

[1] D. E. Boyce and N. D. Day, *Metropolitan Plan Making*, Institute for Environmental Studies, University of Pennsylvania (Philadelphia), 1969, p. 14.

4. authenticated, i.e. backed by a sufficient degree of statistics, policies, standards and objective statements to permit some broad appreciation of their salient characteristics;

5. policy oriented, i.e. different from the forms of growth which would occur without planning supervision and direction;

6. varied, i.e. sufficiently different from each other to permit some forms of selection; and

7. successful, i.e. they present a wider range of choices to the public and the decision-makers than previous planning exercises.

These alternative strategies for the urban future have been generated by a variety of means, including the distinction between cyclic and non-cyclic processes and varying degrees of emphasis on plan form and locational alternatives. Some differences in key structural characteristics, such as concentration versus dispersal, have also been introduced. The emphasis has been on the interacting process of urban growth and change, i.e. on the geographical appreciation of the fact that as one element is modified in one urban sub-system so too are there repercussions elsewhere. The most notable example is the interacting response between land use and transportation. As buildings generate traffic, variations in the distribution and intensity of land uses will exert differential consequences on the associated traffic movements, so that each alternative also has its own distinctive transportation system, patterns of journey to work, incidence of the shopping trip, and so on. It is also possible, within the agreed land use plan and transportation network, to devise transportation alternatives with greater or less reliance on public transport and with varying degrees of efficiency and cost–benefit.

Other methods for the generation of alternative strategies which were *not* employed, include the possibility of exaggerating certain existing urban tendencies in order to envisage the extreme response of the sub-region in such circumstances. The statutory and legalistic framework could have been varied, for example, by assuming that national policy for the location of industry would be diminished whereas, more typically, the underlying value judgement is that such a policy would be extended to meet regional needs. Another example might include a substantial relaxation of development control procedures in order to provide for more incentive and initiative in the processes of land development. Fiscal and taxation measures and grants-in-aid of development could have been varied to change both the priority and the likelihood of investment programmes by the public and private sectors of the economy. Objectives could have been changed and different groups of interrelated objectives could

313

have been considered, whereas in the Studies all strategies satisfy the same objectives and are but variants on similar themes. Nor should possible future changes necessarily be examined in a light which is always favourable to the locality under review; it is quite feasible that national policy towards housing or industrial location or investment allowances can be detrimental to the wishes, aspirations and preferences of certain localities. Pessimism and planning for the future are not comfortable bed-fellows, but healthy fears may be more realistic than the optimism which ordinarily prevails in a planning report.

Having selected the range of alternative prospects, each Study must then elaborate on these possibilities in greater detail. Models and mathematical procedures can here play an important role, and have been used wholly or partly in order to forecast regional totals of population, employment, travel and shopping expenditures; to allocate regional growth to particular localities; and to simulate certain aspects of human behaviour from observed conditions. Conditions have been reproduced spatially either for a certain end-date, or for a succession of evolutionary tendencies at stated intervals against the background of the existing regional environments. These conditions both accept existing urban commitments *and* introduce innovations in accordance with the hypothetical approaches to development, but are always swayed strongly by the pressures from existing urban resources. It is also thought that a ten- to fifteen-year time lag exists before new policies can exert any effective or substantial impact on the existing physical environment.

Hand manipulation of data in the allocation procedures has the advantage of being more responsible to subtle local differences, but relies more on subjective judgement than the more formalized procedures of a model. The latter is more consistent, but requires a significant and predetermined data input, and is less susceptible to modification in the special circumstances of a particular locality. Further it is also most important that the limitations and provisos both of models and their contribution to planning thought be abundantly clear. Batty (1970) refers to the Garin–Lowry model used in the Notts–Derby Study as follows.

The model treats both land-use activities and interactions between these activities in the spatial system. The theory identifies population and service employment as the critical activity variables and movements between workplace and residential areas, and between residential areas and service centres as the critical interaction

314

variables. . . . The model does not involve the processes of change characteristic of such systems, and the model only simulates an average behaviour at one point in time. This does not mean that such a model is irrelevant to the problems of spatial planning; it does mean, however, that the model can only be used for conditional projection and impact analysis which involves interpreting the equilibrium state of the system resulting from given changes in activity.[1]

Both the usefulness and the limitations of models in the formulation of alternative possibilities are clear from this type of statement. The model helps to systematize and to quantify thought about possibilities, but it is a 'compromise' between theoretical ideas which are either incomplete or uncertain, the rigours of precise computation for unknown future circumstances, the need to produce a convincing report as a basis for the achievement of action, inadequate existing statistics and incomplete understanding even of the present situation. The proposals which result in the Studies have examined the relative effects of alternative assumptions; they remain 'subjective' rather than 'scientific', and 'imprecise' rather than 'exact', because they depend on important value judgements, assumptions and varying degrees of professional discretion about an unknown future. Political decisions have been assisted, but they still have to be made on deficient, uncertain and speculative evidence.

CRITERIA OF PERFORMANCE

The stage has been reached where there are a number of interrelated policies and prospects for examination. Just as subjective judgement can prejudice the number, range and competence of the alternatives available for inspection, so too is it possible to be biased or influenced at the equally crucial stage of plan testing. Thus, not one Study tested at the bar of public opinion the procedures to be used in the selection between options and the relative weight (if any) to be ascribed to different factors. Each Study developed its own methodological techniques to appreciate the performance characteristics required of its strategies, and called forth its own best response. The techniques are not perfect but, in the words of Steger and Lakshmanan (1968),

metropolitan plan alternatives must be evaluated in terms of the

[1] M. Batty, 'An Activity Allocation Model for the Nottinghamshire–Derbyshire Subregion,' *Regional Studies*, Vol. 4, 1970, p. 308.

human ends (or benefits) they will serve, the other ends forgone (opportunity costs) and the differing means (or costs) required to achieve these ends. Each of the alternatives of an urban area is a bundle of goods with an associated set of values and life styles and a specific price tag. But ... it is a hypothetical package and in the present state-of-the-art evaluation, it is very difficult to know exactly what the goods are or what the cost may be. The objectives or ends can be compared in proximate goal statements such as housing choice, job accessibility, income or racial distribution. But the deeper indirect socio-economic benefits are not easy to identify or assess: individual opportunity, productive efficiency, family welfare, privacy, security, cosmopolitan character and stimulus, flexibility to further change.[1]

Having designed a range of feasible and possible strategies which distribute in a spatial context the expected demands on land and safeguard important sites for resource uses such as agriculture, recreation, mining and forestry activities, the next stage is to devise systematic procedures in order to select the single best solution from among the range of practical yet competing alternatives. Table 12.1 summarizes the methods used in these deliberations in the Studies. The methods include, either singly or in combination and in approximate order of importance:

1. the performance, costs and amount of travel on the transportation network;

2. the testing of possible strategies against objectives derived from the analysis of existing conditions;

3. the significance of accessibility between home and employment, and to shops;

4. the partial use of costing and cost–benefit procedures, especially of public utilities, services and housing;

5. the testing for flexibility in achievement;

6. the degree to which physical constraints and/or opportunities are respected;

7. the location of industrial estates;

8. the development of a predetermined regional service pattern;

9. the theoretical evaluations of urban structure.

The tax, financial and land value implications are not assessed in any Study. Nor are the relative effects of different alternatives on

[1] W. A. Steger and T. R. Lakshmanan, 'Plan Evaluation Methodologies: Some Aspects of Decision Requirements and Analytical Response', in Highway Research Board, *Urban Development Models*, National Academy of Sciences (Washington), 1968, p. 35.

Table 12.1. *Factors Used in the Testing of Alternative Strategies in the Studies*

Factors	Teesside	Leicestershire	Notts–Derby	North–Glos	Hampshire	Humberside	South East	Warwickshire
Physical constraints/Opportunities	*	*	*	*			*	*
Accessibility:								
To shops			*				*	
To employment			*				*	*
Transportation network:								
Amount of travel	*		*	*		*	*	*
User costs	*		*	*		*	*	*
Construction costs	*		*				*	*
Congestion			*				*	
Flexibility		*					*	*
Selected cost factors			*	*		*	*	
Theoretical appraisal (B)					(B)	*		
Development of regional services			*				*	
Location of industrial estates			*				*	*
Other factors (A)			(A)				(A)	(A)
Explicit statement of objectives			*	*			*	*
Mathematical simulation of the urban system:								
Traffic and/or shopping models			*				*	*
Extensive further reliance on models			*					*

(A) The degree of self-containment, dependence on mobile employment and doubts about the success of small growth centres in the South East Study. See also the tabulation of objectives for the Notts–Derby and Warwickshire Studies.

(B) Many of the previous factors are integrated in the theoretical model of the Hampshire Study.

317

industrial productivity, private initiative and enterprise, the regional flow of goods, or the extra-regional impact on the national economy. Social aspects such as the degree of public preference, the effects on social institutions and the ease of implementation are not considered, and social objectives do not occur in the above listing. Nor is there any attempt to apportion costs and benefits between the various public and private sectors of the community, as undertaken in the planning balance sheet.

The Studies generally combine several computations, arguments and analyses in order to achieve their assessment of which alternative makes the best and most effective contribution to the future. This question has to be answered, but against the difficulty of not having any fixed parameters – the budget available is not known, the incidence of physical constraints and physical opportunity is determined by the team, and the objectives are not obtained from a national strategy for development but depend upon the internal analysis of sub-regional problems. In the words of one commentary, Wilson (1969) has stated that 'it has been shown that the planner *professionally* has a developing and increasing capability; he can analyse and predict increasingly effectively, and he is becoming a more self-conscious and effective designer. He has improved tools for policy-making. However, all this stops short of more effective policy-making! If urban planning is about *society achieving its goals*, then the main issue about planning is whether the professional planner can link with society sufficiently effectively to ensure that it is society's goals which are being achieved, and not his own.'[1] This criticism may not be so much about planning, but of the sociological input into planning. As this is meagre, planners have to rely on their own best assumptions of the present and future situations.

As multiple objectives exist, some relative weighting between objectives must occur to permit their trade-off one against the other when goals are in conflict. These details are not necessarily stated in the Studies, and the weight of attachment to each objective is not always made explicit. The details may be lost in the sequence of the analytical processes. The reader cannot generally refer to a particular Study, and find out when and why a particular idea, location or feature was discarded. The resolution of conflict between objectives is resolved by internal and subjective judgement; it is important that such decisions should always be made explicit.

As the objectives (except in the Warwickshire Study) are not

[1] A. G. Wilson, *Forecasting Planning*, Centre for Environmental Studies (London), 1969, (CES WP 38), p. 26.

defined in measurable terms, it is difficult for the Studies to be rigorous, consistent and systematic in their evaluation. It is not clear what constitutes a 'significant difference' between alternative strategies, or when a particular strategy or a part thereof should be excluded from further consideration. The selection of the preferred or recommended strategy generally depends upon a line by line ranking for each factor considered to be of relevance, and the strategy receiving the highest number of commendations receives the stamp of approval. By this procedure, there are no reasonable doubts about the preference in any of the Studies. Accepting both the range of alternatives and the validity of the tests, the winner has received a clear cut majority over its competing possibilities. Presumably some form of weighting procedure would have been designed had the outcome been less certain. The preferred strategy therefore generally results from a combination of objective and subjective criteria, with each factor of analysis being awarded an equal importance in the final assessment.

The Warwickshire Study is more systematic. It defines objectives in precise, measurable terms, so that definite and explicit comparisons can be made between alternative strategies. But, even so, the difficulty remains that 'unless all the factors involved are reduced to a common measure, comparison between them is difficult. With different factors being evaluated in different terms, different persons are likely to give them different relative weighting in the analyses and as a consequence a degree of arbitrariness is introduced. . . . It is necessary for the planner to make a very large number of value judgements. . . . This reduces the objectivity of the analysis, for the essence of value judgements is that they are subjective to the persons concerned, and are likely to vary according to the person's psychological make-up and his political and moral views.'[1] The problem here is that, as frequently noted over the previous pages, planning is not an exact science. There are many different ways of measuring even existing variables, and every planning argument must rely upon a professional interpretation of the available source material. There can be no alternative to this, but it is important to appreciate that all planning decisions depend (ultimately) on professional judgement, however precise and systematic the methodology.

At present it would seem to be that plan evaluation is either by plan effectiveness in relation to objectives, or by economic efficiency in relation to the costs incurred and the benefits received.

[1] W. Lean, *Economics of Land Use Planning: Urban and Regional*, Estates Gazette (London), 1969, p. 82.

Considerable scope exists for harmonizing and blending these two approaches, because each attitude is important. Effectiveness and efficiency are each desirable traits for measurement. As the two procedures each rely both on performance against objectives and on a sequence of value judgements in order to determine the relative advantage of alternative strategies, then accord between the two approaches, would seem to be a reasonable proposition. The processes must also be seen in perspective. Their purpose is to identify a significant variation or a number of variations between strategic alternatives in order to achieve responsible action by political decision-makers. The problem(s) should have been identified, and various solutions considered. But there is little merit in developing more complex and refined evaluation procedures if the alternative strategies have little merit, or if they are inadequate or deficient in some vital respect.

The alternative strategies which have been generated and tested represent a peculiar blend of assumption and knowledge about existing conditions, and subjective thought and objective interpretation about future possibilities. The important questions may not always be about the methods of evaluation, but the prior inquiry about the merit, quality and relevance of the alternatives under review. A good strategy cannot emerge from a set of poor alternatives. In the words of the Warwickshire Study, 'evaluation effectively began when the scope of surveys and forecasts was settled early in the Study, and the testing of the final short-list of alternatives concluded a long process in which, with an increasingly intensive evaluation, diminishing returns were obtained in the sense of refinements to the evolving strategy'.[1] The present writer, with respect, would go back to the previous stage and to the team appointed to execute the Study. Had this been of different composition, or under different leadership, then the results would have been different in some vital respect. Different professional judgements would have been made somewhere along the line of reasoning. Planning is not an exact science, where any group of professionals would reproduce the same inevitable conclusion.

A SUGGESTED RANGE OF CRITERIA

Boyce and Day (1969) present 'a partial list of plan characteristics for evaluation'.[2] The Local Government Operational Research Unit (1970) has 'identified the important planning factors in urban scale

[1] *Warwickshire Study*, p. 30.   [2] Boyce and Day, *op. cit.*, p. 90.

planning and considered the possible mathematic representations of them'.[1] Table 12.1 has summarized the approaches adopted in the Studies under review. The tests of effective achievement in the Warwickshire Study combine sixteen tests for objectives concerned with landscape, farming, land servicing constraints and so on with four tests for flexibility.[2] An amalgam of these sources, plus comments made in this text, is attempted below.

The details have not been tested in practice for their comprehensiveness, the accounting may be incomplete and the elements are not necessarily mutually exclusive. They suggest criteria against which alternative regional strategies *could* be evaluated, possibly locality by locality and possibly at different time periods. The input requirements against each heading have not been ascertained but may be expected to prove quite considerable. The suggestions are not presented in any order of significance and include:

1. flexibility, i.e. the ability to adapt to change;

2. feasibility, i.e. within an acceptable technological and fiscal range;

3. cost and performance appraisal of new and existing public works, including sewerage, water power and drainage facilities;

4. transportation costs including congestion, construction and user costs, suitability for public transportation, and the degree of encouragement or control over private movement;

5. the ecological impact on land, air and water resources including wild-life habitats, vegetation and marine resources, and changes to the existing incidence of pollution;

6. the effects on community living patterns of different social groups, including the gains and the losses to each group and the net balance;

7. the element of choice in the availability of jobs, shops, transport, homes and leisure;

8. the effects on education, health, housing, welfare, unemployment, environmental improvement, social services and other indices of community well-being;

9. the effects on industrial and service location, performance, productive output and marketing efficiency, the flow and movement of goods, and the availability of employment opportunities;

10. the organizational and administrative requirements, including

---

[1] B. Pilgrim and R. Carter, *Systems Design Project: A Computer Program To Evaluate Urban Land Use Plans*, Local Government Operational Research Unit (Reading), 1970 (Report No. C.70), pp. 8–9.

[2] *Warwickshire Study*, pp. 65–9 and 75–6.

the extent to which implementation can be achieved by the existing structure of government and institutions;

11. the use of existing resources, including the loss of land and its productive capacity in terms of agricultural, horticultural, mineral, fishing, forestry, scenic, green belt, recreational, landscape, architectural and historical values;

12. construction and demolition costs for buildings, structures and other works to be demolished or replaced;

13. the degree of disturbance to existing residential development, other than obsolescent buildings to be replaced, and the contribution to the quality of residential living including the elements of variety and location in disturbance-free, attractive and accessible localities;

14. the relative responsibilities of the public and private sectors of the economy in achieving the new development, and the scope for encouraging new investment opportunities;

15. the effects on land values for existing uses, including changes in site, locational and accessibility benefits, and upon the rate-payer and tax-payer.

16. practicability, i.e. the likelihood of achievement as determined through community attitude surveys, political leadership and the ability to achieve the desired development without disruption of established interests and values;

17. the effects on the rural economy including village life, employment, population movement, services and facilities.

18. effects outside the sub-region on the regional and national economies.

19. the equity issue of the special benefits to declining, depressed, stagnant and physically unattractive areas, and to deprived social groups.

Having identified the possible tests for the effective or best achievement of a strategy, it is then necessary to establish indicators which represent the level of achievement for each strategy against the above tests. These have been demonstrated in the cost–benefit, the Sub-regional and the Regional Studies, but occasion concern because of their many necessary assumptions about the value judgements and preferences of society. Choice of travel, accessibility, cost of achievement, the loss of agricultural land, annoyance, congestion and other criteria of performance do not provide either easy or generally acceptable measurements. Those 'indicators of performance' which are used to select between alternative strategies should however be agreed in advance *before* the preparation of strategies in order to

322

avoid the possible complaint of bias by the planning team, and the relative degree of importance to be attached to each should likewise be determined. Both aspects provide fields where citizen participation should prove of considerable assistance as an active ingredient.

The final choice between alternative strategies depends on the weight that is attached to the performance of each strategy against the criteria selected for evaluation. They may be regarded as equal, in which case the final selection results from adding the results of each performance test as if they are a column of equivalent and comparable figures. Alternatively, a differential weighting can be applied according to the respective value which is attributed to each criteria. The criteria can be grouped in grades of importance and be given this weighting as in the Boston and Milwaukee exercises. They may be given a variety of different weighting schemes, as in the Warwickshire Study where different sets are used. The differences between the Team's appreciation and that of the public in this instance is that 'there was substantial agreement on the importance of landscape, residential environment, choice of home sites, no disturbance and private transport, and on the lesser importance of land servicing constraints, mineral resources, and opportunity to work. The major areas of disagreement are where the Public place greater emphasis than the Study Team on farmland, help to areas with declining industries, choice of shops and public transport, and less emphasis than the Study Team on choice of jobs, choice of labour, and choice of transport.'[1] But who is right?

The whole planning process has therefore become more systematic and refined in its detail, but in the final analysis, there *must* be considerable reliance on value judgements and intuitive decisions. Incompatibles cannot be summed, there is no common denominator of firm public or community agreement on all issues, and planning is for a diversified and complex society. However precise and scientific the analysis, these differences will remain. The recommended strategy should therefore be presented in terms of this professional judgement. A succinct argument should draw the necessary deductions from the available evidence stating which factors, features and characteristics are deemed to be the most important, and how and why this leads through to the final planning decision as a realistic basis for the necessary action and commitment of resources. By such means the approach to the future of the urban and regional environment is shown to involve both systematic procedures *and*

[1] *Ibid.*, p. 71.

judgement, with each assisting the other throughout the whole process.

THE URBAN FUTURE

The outcome from deliberations about generating, detailing and evaluating alternative possible strategies is the preferred or recommended set of policies which, if implemented, then achieve the urban future. In the words of the Warwickshire Study, 'the recommended strategy is designed to safeguard farmland, provide good residential environment and a balance between public and private transport, and proposes that urban growth in the next twenty years be focussed on five areas. . . . Urban growth in the next twenty years should be less fragmented than in the recent past and rural building should be further restricted by the County Council's policy of selective restraint on village expansion. But the strategy is not simply to focus major urban development on these localities and retain open land between the towns. It necessarily involves a positive role for the countryside, agriculture and the rural economy.'[1] A whole train of events and policies are set in motion as a result of the Study, *if* the recommendations are accepted by the agencies concerned with the decision-making process. The environment of the future is under active achievement based on the best available assessment of the situation by the planning team.

The form of this future as envisaged by responsible planning teams has been presented and discussed over the previous chapters. These interpretations and the commentary may now be reviewed against two other informed judgements:

1. White (1969) is concerned with the city in the year 2000. It is noted that 'the non-city is disappearing so completely that it is impossible to talk about the direction of change of the city without talking about the direction of the society as a whole'.[2] As an increasing proportion of the population is resident in urban areas, the future of mankind lies in urbanized areas of growing magnitude. Two very important consequences result from this assessment. The first is that the form, quality and significance of this emerging urban environment is of great if not of extreme importance to most nations. The second is that the city, though dominant, must never be allowed to predominate. Society depends on agriculture, forestry, recreation and

[1] *Ibid.*, p. 4.
[2] O. White, *Societal Determinants of Urban Form – some thoughts on the city in the year 2000*, Centre for Environmental Studies (London), 1969, p. 9.

the lakes, the seas and the countryside as the physical antithesis of urbanization and for its very existence. Planning for the future must not be for the city as the prime or the sole environment of man, but for the environment of society as a whole. This, in its turn, implies rural *and* urban environments with their close interlocking and mutual inter-associating *and* the dependence of the one upon the other. Studies at the regional or sub-regional level will fail, absolutely and irretrievably, unless this dual response to environmental dignity is (a) recognized and (b) developed for the mutual advantage of both.

Another point is that 'as transportation and communication improve, the number of choices open to the individual will increase'.[1] One revealing example about this anticipation of change is the situation in Los Angeles. It has been fashionable for planners since the late 1930s to revile this caricature of man's environment and to criticize its dependency on an auto-dominated culture. By contrast 'a lot of people have noticed the advantages of living in Los Angeles. Between 1950 and 1960, the population . . . increased by 2·5 million people, from 4·0 to 6·5 million. This makes it the second largest urban area in the country (USA) exceeding the Chicago–North-western Indiana urban area by more than $\frac{1}{2}$ million. The 10-year growth alone was more than the total population of all but four of the other urban areas in the US. This does not sound like an ailing community . . . and I think it is because of, not in spite of, the automobiles there. There are 3·3 million automobiles in the Los Angeles urban area, and more than 200 miles of freeways.'[2] The phrase automobile-oriented is suggestive for the future, yet the Studies have been reluctant to accept the *full* implications of this attribute of personal mobility for increasing proportions of the future population. Decry the Los Angeles situation at the will of each reader, but a continuing and greater emphasis on the motor vehicle is the probable future of all urban environments in Britain.

One consequence of an automobile-oriented culture is that 'a wide variety of "non-place" communities will develop based on mutual interests rather than on propinquity, occupation, or social class. . . . This will bring diversity back to the city and make it a more interesting and stimulating environment.'[3] Have the Studies provided for this

[1] *Ibid.*, p. 11.
[2] K. Moskowitz, 'Living and Travel Patterns in Automobile-oriented Cities', in G. M. Smerk, ed., *Readings in Urban Transportation*, Indiana University Press (Bloomington, Illinois), 1968, p. 161.
[3] White, *op. cit.*, p. 11.

possibility, or are they so stereotyped in time, confrontation with the future and by existing urban traditions that they over-emphasize the present triumvirate of propinquity, occupation and social class? Have they been sufficiently venturesome into the future to envisage the lives of a new generation and *their* attitudes and responses to an urban environment because 'whether this speculation becomes a reality . . . depends upon the priority assigned to policy decisions which emphasize the goal of maximizing choice for the individual.'[1]

Another thought is that two major trends are operative in cities and each is significant for the city of the future. Suburbanization and decentralization have their roles to play, together with those of concentration and an increasing emphasis on the urban core. 'The continued dispersion of both residences and industries to the suburbs, and the concomitant tendency for both to opt for lower densities have been well documented. At the same time there has been an opposite polarization of certain kinds of businesses, particularly offices . . . in the central core. . . . There is also a strong trend towards regional specialization and self-sufficiency.'[2] Are those Studies which provide only for dispersal, and which resist an increasing tendency to centralize and to concentrate, correct?

An even more critical question is how planning might order its priorities for the urban future. Technology has, within its power, the ability to overcome any *one* of the annoyances to urban living which detract from the quality of living in urban environments. Traffic congestion, slums, air and water pollution, waste and inefficiency, can each be eliminated within a time span of thirty years, if man so desires. 'However, it seems highly unlikely that the capital resources for solving all of these problems simultaneously will be forthcoming by the year 2000. . . . We can, however, expect to make considerable strides in mitigating all these problems.'[3] Have the Studies taken these strides forward, or have they opted for a more leisurely progression?

Another thoughtful comment is that 'the emphasis we place on the physical problems of the city (for which we can at least see concrete, albeit expensive, solutions) may mask more important city problems. . . . We are likely to perpetuate social evils and to produce an urban environment which by its nature perpetuates life styles and distributions of income and opportunity which are out of line with what the community as a whole desires.'[4] The safeguard here is for the planner always to remember that almost every 'fact' about the future depends on some form of subjective assessment. There is a

[1] *Ibid.*, p. 12. [2] *Ibid.*, pp. 13–14.
[3] *Ibid.*, p. 14. [4] *Ibid.*, p. 15.

326

topic here for major investigation – not by planners, but by philosophers, sociologists, moralists and (to use that much misused phrase) the community. The Studies have not answered the question, 'why and for whom do we plan?' because 'our training in most cases has taught us to look for the technically correct solution. . . . Belatedly, we realize that even with considerably more knowledge of the social and economic environment in which we work, we *cannot* depend upon the idea that the standards which we use for making decisions are compatible with those of the public which we serve. . . . To do this requires an understanding not only of the goals and objectives, but of the impact of policies on the whole fabric of public and private interests.'[1]

2. A second set of interpretations about the urban future results from a working group established by the Centre for Environmental Studies to consider developing patterns of urbanization in Britain.[2] The conclusions of Cowan (1970) refer to the expectation that 'future society in Britain, as in other developed nations, will be more mobile, both socially and geographically'.[3] This could mean a movement towards home-centredness, a growing dispersal of social networks, the filtering downwards and diffusion of certain urban and middle-class life styles, an increasing burden on a limited set of resources for leisure and recreation, and a continuing demand to spread, both geographically and socially. 'The continuing and continual raising of standards must be a major factor in calculations of future demands for urban services. There will undoubtedly be large increases in demands for space, both inside the home and away from home, for leisure and for learning.'[4]

The major constraints on the urban future are considered to be more the massive investment in pre-existing structures, rather than a shortage in the supplies of land and water resources. Hence the thought is that 'most changes can only occur to the extent that the past can be destroyed, so that there is unlikely to be much physical change in patterns of urbanization in Britain during the next thirty years.'[5] Social and functional change will take place largely in the existing framework. There will also be the problems of planning for the contraction of certain centres, which must be considered through changes in the location of jobs. The overall picture is therefore

[1] *Ibid.*, p. 20.
[2] P. Cowan (ed.), *Developing Patterns of Urbanisation*, Oliver and Boyd (Edinburgh), 1970.
[3] P. Cowan and D. Diamond in *ibid.*, p. 202. [4] *Ibid.*, p. 202.
[5] *Ibid.*, p. 203.

expected to remain that of an increasing concentration of the population on national and regional scales, coupled with a deconcentration of population on a metropolitan scale. In terms of form, 'the expansion of city regions is thought most likely to take the form of radial or corridor extensions of development, along which a variety of urban centres are strung out at varying distances along lines of high speed communication'.[1] The currently projected motorway network will become the High Street of metropolitanization.

THE STUDIES AS A PLATFORM FOR RESEARCH

Emphasis has been placed not only on the range of determinants which influence the present urban condition, but also on the selection of certain key variables in estimating and moving towards the unknown urban future. The difficulty is that the form and the directions of urban growth are influenced by a whole range of public and private decisions, which are undertaken for the most part without regard to the form of urban development but for reasons in relation to that activity. The location of a new university, improvements in the speed and frequency of inter-urban railway travel, entry or rejection of the European Common Market, and the national motorway network provide case examples of where the justification is *not* primarily from the urban standpoint – yet the pressures for change are on urban environments, either in sympathy with their internal processes of growth or at variance with these trends. Many such public decisions are subject to control but others, such as most private, commercial, business and industrial decisions, involve greater degrees of freedom. It would indeed be impossible for the planner to consider the effect of every locational decision which, either separately or in combination, exerts some impact on the pattern of land development because this requirement would include virtually all individual and group actions. His procedures, both of understanding and of control, *must* be selective.

This argument leads to the proposition that the key items are identifiable for each community, that rational decisions can be made and that prediction and/or control become feasible. The distinction is, therefore, important between those actions which initiate locational behaviour, and those which result as a consequence from the initiating action. The access points along a new major highway, like the stations and the depôts along a mass transit route, are initiating factors. The resultant effects in attracting industry, housing or

[1] *Ibid.*, p. 206.

shopping centres to the favoured point of initiation are triggered off by the first primary action. Successful planning must, therefore, first expose these forces, so that the secondary impact can be detected and understood in its relationships to the primary force or forces.

But is the statement in the previous paragraph over-simplistic? Is it the tram, the suburban railway, new bridges and tunnels which made possible the concentration of business activity in the central area of towns, or is it the earlier presence of these centres and the voice of their influential representatives which demanded and secured the arteries essential for their growth? Does one development so create another in a self-reinforcing cycle that it becomes futile to isolate a chain sequence of cause and effect? Perhaps there are so many seeds for growth, decay and change that isolation of but a few significant variables becomes meaningless, and only an explanation of the *interrelatedness* between all factors takes on any specific significance for the future.

The Studies have each presented their precise interpretation of this development process, based on measurements of the urban and regional pattern as it now exists. Statistical tests have interrelated the selected factors to indicate the likely future patterns. A groundwork for research has been laid, because the state of knowledge about even existing urban processes is incomplete and changes in the future must by definition be unknown. The sequence of change in urban growth processes, the nature of physical constraints, the social value systems and the technological possibilities which underlie human actions and behaviour patterns, and indeed the nature of the control processes necessary to achieve some desired strategy, each require continual study at the level of meticulous enquiry oriented towards the practical purposes of securing the best forms of urban development. This understanding is likely to occupy a central place in social research over the next few decades. Much of this research task lies ahead, but the Studies have demonstrated a commendable first stage of inquiry and commitment.

There should also be a major focus of research attention on the question, by what criteria should urban development strategies be (a) generated and (b) evaluated? This responsibility could logically be sponsored by the Department of the Environment. As the Government Department which makes daily decisions about development, it presumably already uses certain regular and consistent criteria for measuring the effectiveness and the viability of proposals which are submitted to it. The listing and the study of such criteria would also be a salutary exercise for the Royal Town Planning Institute as

329

the professional body concerned primarily with planning methodology, but the question could also be elucidated as an inter-professional exercise in association with other professional bodies and in relation to public response, attitudes and anticipations. This would be a demanding research task for any University team.

Having listed the range of criteria, attention should then focus on the relative importance of each characteristic. Weights may have to be assigned if an overall ranking is required. The Studies generally apply a weighting of one, with each item being assumed to be of equal importance, but with transportation and/or measurable costs sometimes receiving the greater weight. There are also examples of where differential weights are assigned, but this approach can also be as arbitrary, biased or deceiving as the unitary assignment. Social science research is required to elucidate upon the best techniques for resolving dilemmas between conflicting objectives.

From a research and methodological standpoint, the overall conclusion is a growing *strength* of the Studies in terms of logic, factual content and the scientific development of an argument from present conditions into an unknown future. Population, employment and transportation features are distributed rationally within the physical environment against certain precise relationships, and these distributions are then assessed. But this very rationality and logical succession of events conceals a *weakness* in terms of ideas, intuition and inspiration. The physical backcloth, ecological, rural and recreational aspects tend to receive insufficient attention, as do innovatory ideas within the context of long-term progressive continuity in the evolution of the urban environment. The Studies evaluate between valid but limited land use and transportation alternatives, goals could have been varied and the preoccupation with physical form could have been extended into more concern with social and economic phenomena. The systems approach to planning is extremely valuable, but it must take more account of political determinants to the spatial system, and future planning exercises must combine the two elements of creative art and scientific technology on a scale far greater than ever before envisaged. At the moment technology and analysis are to the fore, on foundations which are inadequate in depth and incomplete in dimension. By these improved means urban society may, on a grand scale, advance into the future with confidence.

Index

331

Public transport, 149, 153, 222–7, 254, 280, 323
Qualitative Studies – *see* Environmental quality
Recreation, 62–3, 95–7, 102, 104–5, 114, 120–1, 132, 149, 190–4, 280, 287, 316
Regional identity, 205
Relief, 90, 102–3
Report of the Studies, 65–7, 76–7, 296–7
Residental – *see* Housing provision and residential demand
Retailing – *see* Service centres
Royal Town Planning Institute, 130, 329
Rural planning and development, 40–1, 48, 83–108, 120–1, 132, 190–5, 321–2, 324–5
Rural–urban conflict, 40–1, 105–7
Schools – *see* Education
Scenic resources – *see* Environmental quality
Service centres, 36, 39, 50, 61–3, 110, 114–15, 122–3, 128–9, 132, 135, 149–50, 154, 156–8, 173–5, 185–90, 194, 212, 240, 258, 263, 287, 316–17, 326
Shopping activities – *see* Service centres
Slope, 90, 98, 102–3
Social and behavioural patterns, 37–8, 52, 56–8, 101, 110, 114–16, 121, 123–8, 130, 136–42, 180, 250–1, 298, 308, 321, 326–7
Staffing the Studies, 73–8
Structure plans, 25–6, 43, 300, 309
Study leader, 68–9, 74–8
Sub-regional and regional planning, 25–31, 39–49, 61–79, 307–24
Sub-units of the Study area, 94, 114–15, 117–18
Technological change, 52, 56, 139–40, 253, 326
Terms of reference for the Studies, 61–4
Time period of the forecasts, 52, 111–12, 130–6, 253–4, 311–12
Town and Country Planning Acts, 1947 and 1968, 25–6, 39, 41–3, 46, 130, 290
Town centres – *see* Service centres
Traffic and transportation, 37, 43–5, 47, 49–50, 55, 61–3, 110–11, 113–15,

124, 128, 139, 150–3, 157–61, 192, 196–8, 207–30, 234, 236–8, 248–9, 262, 277, 280–1, 313, 316–17, 325
University of Manchester, 50–1
Urbanization, Its nature and characteristics, 32–9, 111–12, 119–20, 139, 175–6
Utilities, 49–50, 55, 86–7, 91, 131, 135, 234, 236–7, 252, 316, 321
Urban forms – *see* Forms of urban growth
Vacancy rate in land provision, 183
Villages, 91, 100–3
Weighting, 95, 166, 181, 184, 274–5, 315, 318, 323, 330

3. *Authors and References Cited*

P. Abercrombie, 45, 46; *et al*, 46
K. J. Allen, 252
W. Alonso, 126, 129
A. Altshuler, 271–2
F. J. Amos, 44
J. Ardill, 202
R. V. Arnfield, 111
J. Ash, 302–3
W. Ashworth, 40
Barlow Report, 41, 199
J. Barrow, South Hampshire Plan
M. Batty, 179–229, 315
S. Beer, 47, 60
M. E. Beesley *et al*, 233, 248
I. Berlin, 294
B. J. L. Berry *et al*, 36, 47
R. H. Best *et al*, 109
H. Blumenfeld, 35
C. M. Bowra, 7
D. E. Boyce *et al*, 49, 50, 52, 72, 146, 152, 239, 266, 312, 230
H. E. Bracey, 41, 83, 106
G Breese, 32
P. Brenikov, 43
M. J. Bruton, 210
C. Buchanan, 43; Hampshire Study
Buchanan Report, 44, 233
T. L. Burton, 194; *et al*, 97
R. Carson, 104
Central Office of Information, 156
Central Unit for Environmental planning, 62; Humberside Study
Centre for Environmental Studies, 66, 324–8

333